Joe Remiro at fourteen, in his first year at Sacred Heart High School, San Francisco. "An undistinguished forwarding station into such safe and traditional Irish-Catholic careers as the police and fire departments, civil service, hacking for the Hearst press, running a neighborhood saloon, and, for a saintly few, the glory of the priesthood."

JOSEPH REMIRO
12C
Rally Committee 4; Service
Club 4; Cheerleader 4.

Graduation photo from the *Shamrock* yearbook, Sacred Heart High School, 1964.

CHEERLEADERS

(*Top*) Joe Remiro, second from left, cheering the basketball team on in the Sacred Heart gym and (*bottom*), at right, in posed stop-action, cheering the fighting "Irish."

Vietnam duty for Remiro

Army Private Joseph M. Remiro, 19, son of Mr. and Mrs. Charles Remiro, 1476 Seventh Ave. was assigned as a wireman to the 54th Signal Battalion's Company A in Vietnam.

Remiro entered the Army in January 1966, and was last stationed at Fort Benning, Ga.

He is a 1964 graduate of Sacred Heart High School and attended San Francisco City College. He is a member of Alpha Kappa Rho fraternity.

————o————

Joe Remiro as a grunt in a Long Range Reconnaissance Platoon, Vietnam, 1966. "The infantry was black, man. It was black and Mexican. . . . Only the leadership was white. I was trained to be a switchboard operator but I was put in the infantry because I had a Mexican name. . . ."

You Have Just Been Dealt
With by

"THE DEALERS"

A Fighting Arm of the
Strike Force Widowmakers

(*Top*) Search and Destroy mementos and (*bottom*) Search and Destroy
waiting. ". . . two weeks later here comes the American Army. They get in a
line. They go through the area and they kill everything living—dogs, cats,
women, children, anything. When they're through, there's not supposed to
be anything alive behind them. . . ."

(*Top*) R & R—Rest and Recreation. "This ain't no war, it's a whorehouse."
(*Bottom*) A threesome spared(?) from Search and Destroy.

AMERICAN - SERVICEMEN

The Johnson Government had told you that : your coming to South Vietnam is aimed at « Helping on request of the South Vietnamese Government to fight Communism ». This is nothing but a deceptive contention.

U.S. Government with this psychologica warfare trick is forcing you into the ag gressive war in South Vietnam with an a tempt to turn South Vietnam into U.S. m litary base. The South Vietnamese peo are taking up arms against U.S. aggresso and the U.S. set up — trained — equipe paid — puppet Administration. Figh against « Viet Cong » means against e whole Vietnamese people.

They said that : Americans are de fri ends of the Vietnamese people give

A Viet Cong flyer.

'If you will stop the bombing of
North Vietnam,
we will promise never to
bomb New York.'"

ĐÂY LÀ KẾT - QUẢ

CỦA VIỆT CỘNG

NHỮNG NGƯỜI ĐÃ TẠO CHO VỢ HỌ THÀNH
QUẢ PHỤ

COMPLIMENTS OF
THE STRIKE FORCE
WIDOW MAKERS

SAFE-CONDUCT PASS TO BE HONORED BY ALL VIETNAMESE GOVERNMENT AGENCIES AND ALLIED FOR

MANG TÂM GIẤY THÔNG HÀNH
nầy về cộng tác với Chánh Phủ
Quốc Gia các bạn sẽ được :
  ● Đón tiếp tử tế
  ● Bảo đảm an ninh
  ● Đải ngộ tương xứng

Nguyễn Cao Kỳ

The San Francisco Phoenix

TẤM GIẤY THÔNG HÀNH NẦY CÓ GIÁ TRỊ VỚI TẤT CẢ CƠ - QUAN
QUÂN CHÍNH VIỆT-NAM CỘNG-HÒA VÀ LỰC-LƯỢNG ĐỒNG-MINH.

(*Top*) Another Viet Cong plea and (*middle*) the inevitable "scorched
earth" flyer reply. (*Bottom*) Safe-conduct pass to be honored by all Vietnamese government agencies and Allied forces.

Thanksgiving Day

VIETNAM
1966

Thanksgiving Day Dinner

~~Shrimp Cocktail~~
~~With Cocktail Sauce and Crackers~~

Roast Tom Turkey   ~~Giblet Gravy~~

~~Poultry Dressing~~

Snow Flaked Potatoes — *THAT MEANS DEHYDRATED*

~~Glazed Sweet Potatoes~~   ~~Cranberry Sauce~~

~~Buttered~~
Peas ~~and Corn~~

~~Crisp Relish Tray~~

~~Parkerhouse Rolls~~   ~~Butter~~

Pumpkin Pie
~~With Whipped Cream~~

~~Mincemeat Pie~~   ~~Old Fashion Fruit Cake~~

~~Fresh Chilled Fruit~~

~~Mixed~~ Nuts

~~Assorted Candy~~

Tea   Coffee   ~~Milk~~
FREE BEER

PRAYER

Father of mercies and giver of all good, by whose power we were created, by whose bounty we are sustained, and by whose spirit we are transformed, accept, we beseech Thee, our prayer of thanks.

For those who love us and of whose love we would be more worthy; for those who believe in us and whose hopes we cannot disappoint; for every good gift of healing and happiness and renewal, we bless Thy name. We thank Thee for all that is just and true, noble and right, wise and courageous in our history. We praise Thee for our place in the community of nations and we invoke Thy blessings on men of goodwill wherever they may be and who labor for a world of justice, freedom, and fraternity.

Most of all, Eternal Father, we thank Thee for Thyself, the nearness of Thy presence and the warmth of Thy love, whereby our minds and hearts find joy and peace. Freely we have received, O God; freely let us give ourselves to Thy gracious purposes. For Thy love's sake. Amen.

COMMANDER'S MESSAGE

This Thanksgiving Day we find ourselves in a foreign land assisting in the defense of the rights of free men. On this day we should offer our grateful thanks for the abundant life which we and our loved ones have been provided. May we each pray for continued blessings and guidance upon our endeavors to assist the Vietnamese people in their struggle to attain an everlasting peace within a free society.

W. C. Westmoreland

W. C. WESTMORELAND
General, United States Army
Commanding

Thanksgiving Day, Vietnam, 1966. "Pilgrims' Progress" as the latest American "turkey."

Dear Abby

'Finds' His

ABBY

DEAR ABBY: I am in the United States Navy. I love the service, but most of all, I love my parents. Before I came into the service I felt I knew just about everything. I was sure my parents no longer needed me, and all I could think of was the day I would be "on my own."

The first time I realized how much my parents cared was the day they took me to the train depot to see me off. When my father said goodby to me, he broke down and cried. I had never seen my father cry before, and I won't forget it as long as I live. I have had a lot of time to think. I never told my father I loved him, and I gave both my parents a hard time when they tried to guide me for my own good.

Now I write home every chance I get, and I am trying to make up for all the heartaches I must have caused them, and for my failure to be a better son. When my next leave comes up I am going home and get acquainted with my wonderful parents. I have written this letter in hopes that other thoughtless teen-agers will wake up before it's too late. Thanks, Abby, for letting me get this off my chest.

D.D.H.: SAN DIEGO

money
know thi
Very
children,
still war
How can
bing it?
school si

DEA
children
must ma
bill in ;
you knov
mother
don't tr

DEA
cently a
sion [sh
tique clo
clocks a
mother v
it looked
I hat
have an
have ha
collector
have tol
collectio
family h
should t

A "Dear Abby" clipping from Joe Remiro's scrapbook around the time he completed his first combat tour, August, 1967.

THIS SOLDIER
STILL AT WAR

THIS SOLDIER STILL AT WAR

John Bryan

HARCOURT
BRACE
JOVANOVICH
New York and London

Copyright © 1975 by John Bryan

Printed in the United States of America

Library of Congress Cataloging in Publication Data

Bryan, John, 1934-
    This soldier still at war.

    Includes texts of S. L. A. documents.
    Includes index.
    1. Symbionese Liberation Army.   2. Remiro,
Joseph Michael, 1946-   I. Symbionese Liberation
Army. II. Title.
F866.2.B74   322.4′2′0924 [B]   75-5528
ISBN 0-15-190060-4

First edition

B C D E

To Joan Barr,
who got me into this mess

Contents

THIS SOLDIER STILL AT WAR

1

"They call it terror / if you are few / and have no B-52's . . ."
—A Weatherpoem to the S.L.A.

"IF YOU'RE NOT PART OF THE SOLUTION, man, you're the problem, and that's the way you'll be dealt with," says Joe Remiro, carefully misquoting his favorite black author as he sits locked inside an eternally sunless concrete prison set high above Oakland, California. Enormous energy and confidence radiate from this little man in his late twenties with the Zapata mustache, generally smiling brown eyes, the large ears loosely concealed by a bush of coarse, black hair, and a streamlined adaptation of a big Sicilian nose. He wears a white prison jumpsuit, unzippered halfway down his hairy chest.

Joe is talking to a reporter. It is the fifth time they have met in this thoroughly bugged and minutely observed fish tank of a visiting cell, and it's a very special trip. For Joe (facing both murder and shoot-out charges and in jail for four months now) seems finally ready to open himself up.

It is the first chance the two have had to talk since six of Joe's comrades were barbecued in the best-recorded auto-da-fé of the century. Joe had to sit in his cage for two hours *listening* (but not seeing, since the TV is several cells down the row) as his six friends and lovers died quite literally with their combat boots on after a tiny frame cottage deep in the black ghetto of Los Angeles was set on fire, allowed to burn to its foundations, and they (members of a small but funkily futuristic band of urban guerrillas called the Symbionese Liberation Army) were scooped into plastic bags and carted out many cooler hours later as no more than little piles of charcoal and bone—martyrs to some, object lessons to others. But most certainly blown away, wiped out, utterly removed from all fleshly reality. And Joe sat four hundred television-transcended miles away sweating, exulting, frying, and dying with them. He was careful to shed no visible tears.

Remiro had lasted out two combat tours in Vietnam that way (1966–68)—keeping it all inside, saying nothing for a long and dangerous time.

Joe talks about the prevailing aftershocks of the S.L.A. massacre and most especially about an absurd mass media wail of disbelief and misapprehension when it was determined that all but one of the six shoot-out victims had been middle-class young whites. Their inability to understand how an escaped black prisoner could lead a small band of children of the odorless middle class into a stinking ghetto deathtrap was both comic and tragic. It is to these members of the Media Mod Squad that Joe refers as he describes the kind of people he considers the problem today in America (while Mixmastering Eldridge Cleaver's language in his own extravagant way).

The reporter (who is himself a refugee from the bad, gray dailies) doesn't entirely agree, but he lets it slide since Joe is really wailing now and this is a crucial time in their relationship—the point from which they must either go forward into mutual revelation (while locked inside the Belly of the Beast) or go nowhere. Today a lot's been accomplished.

"Would you have rather died in that fire with them?" asks the reporter while they talk out the first shock of what's happened in L.A. "Would you have rather been there than in your cell that night?"

"What are you talking about, man?" says Joe in a sudden flare-up of that impatient moral superiority which he feels he's paid well for the right to flaunt. "Of course I'd rather have been there. Hell, man, jail ain't no place for a revolutionary!"

"Some of the strongest revolutionaries are in jail," says the reporter.

"Ya, certainly," says Joe. "Look at Malcolm X, man. Look at how many years ahead of his time he was. You know, I mean, it's inevitable. The first stage of revolutionary warfare is what we're in now. We're in the beginning stage and it's the most dangerous stage 'cause revolutionaries are going to make a lot of mistakes. A lot of us are going to get killed like on May 17 in Los Angeles. You can't learn out of books. You've got to put theory into practice. If it fucks up, then the next people have learned something, you know. But it is a very necessary period so that we can get rid of this dogmatic bullshit and formulate our own strategy and tactics for a revolution in this country. We expected to get our asses kicked, and they may get kicked worse than we thought, but if the entire S.L.A. and everybody who relates to the S.L.A. would be killed tomorrow, the next day they'd have to kill a lot more because there's no way of going back and telling people to forget what happened, forget what they saw, forget what the S.L.A. did. We accomplished more than we had expected. We were more successful than we had ever imagined. . . ."

"So what the S.L.A. has done," answers the reporter, "is they sacrificed six lives now because a future revolution requires it."

"No way," says Joe impatiently. He's really a man of action and the word game is too long-winded and obscure for him. He's wiry and energetic, small in stature but big on hand-waving, arm-swinging body language in that very Latin and emotionally satisfying kind of way that speaks with boyish candor and directly to the heart. (It is not until much later that you discover how very manipulative this can be.)

"No, those six lives weren't sacrificed," he says with a vast, right-hand wave. "That wasn't a sacrifice, man. They didn't commit suicide or anything. They were fuckin' engaged in revolutionary warfare, man. I can't call it sacrifice."

And the reporter remembers that when it comes to talking about warfare, Joe Remiro has got to be listened to. He's been through the worst of it and it was this young San Francisco street kid who brought true military knowledge to a group of campus word-warriors and turned them into fighters. It was Remiro who trained them in shooting, in breaking down and cleaning their M-1s and M-16s, their shotguns and revolvers and automatic pistols. It could have been Joe who taught them how to modify semiautomatic weapons into "full" machine guns (which almost made up in psychological effectiveness what they lacked in accuracy).

Remiro has been a soldier ever since 1966 and he regards the Los Angeles confrontation as just one more battle in that long war which began in Vietnam, a fight he was initially forced to wage against the *wrong* side as he machine-gunned men, women, and children, cats and dogs, anything that moved in pathetic little thatch villages in central Nam. It is a war he is now determined to fight against the very people who urged him to do his first killing, the American Establishment who taught him that deadly black-and-white logic of the Good Guys versus the Bad Guys, the fight of the Righteous against the Heretics. Joe was taught to wage war in a very absolutist way and he hasn't really changed the methods he learned in Nam—he's just changed sides. There's blood in his eye and revenge in his heart and he long ago got used to the idea of being a killer.

Remiro is not the only one who came back from Nam this way. That protracted and immoral war left a heavy imprint on the consciousness of more than three million Americans who were sent there. Remiro was not the only one to instantly compare the Los Angeles shoot-out with what he'd seen in Southeast Asia. Dozens of Namvet newscasters watched a small army of Namvet-trained cops use typical anti-VC fire-fight tactics against a holed-up band of guerrilla fighters in an epochal two-hour battle and immolation.

"It's just like Vietnam," they said almost in chorus. "The war has come home."

But, unlike thousands of other veterans who remember the war but long ago gave up fighting it, Remiro has signed no peace treaties. He regards every circumstance and person he encounters as just one more facet of the long war he will fight until he dies. You are either with him or against him. And if you're not FOR him—and all the way— then you're clearly the *enemy,* and they taught Joe long ago how to handle those motherfuckers.

The reporter gets the message loud and clear and shifts conversational gears.

"All I'm saying, man," he continues cautiously, "is that a lot of people are crying now over what happened May 17. A lot more tears are going to be shed if you're right about the way the future is going to go down. And that kind of revolution is horrible to look forward to—years and years of urban guerrilla civil war in America—horrible to so clearly see it coming and know how many fine people will be killed. . . ."

"Yes, it's horrible," says Joe with his dander still up and his fine fighting spirit rising to the occasion. He reminds you of some battered, undersized fighting cock dumped into the killing ring as a last-bout afterthought—the one all the regulars will routinely bet against, but a savage winner in the end, a tough, stringy little fucker who crows victory with his sharp spurs buried deep in the throat of a dying opponent, the sand rapidly reddening with thin, red blood.

"But at the same time," says Joe, "there's the other side of it. . . . What would happen if the revolution didn't happen? How horrible will things be in America after the government declares a state of emergency and throws all you fuckin' liberals into concentration camps? How horrible was it in Germany when the Jews were marched off peacefully into the gas chambers? They were pacifists, too. What's the most horrible, man—people dying passively or people dying fighting?

[6]

"So many people in this country—yourself included—just won't see that if we're gonna have power, it's only gonna come because we're gonna organize ourselves and take it . . . it's gotta be taken!"

"That means you believe in immediate armed uprising," says the reporter. "You believe it must be accomplished by a guerrilla army run pretty much like the Man's Army—the Army you went through in Vietnam."

"The revolution don't have nothin' unless they have an organized military," says Joe with great emphasis. It is obviously central to his belief. "Unless you have military tactics and strategy and trained theoreticians. Military theoreticians. Discipline is a necessary evil, man. I mean, most of these anarcho-American hippies say they want a revolution, you know, but they don't want to be manipulated. They don't want to be controlled. They want absolute artistic, individualistic freedom, and sometimes that has to be squelched in favor of a collective value. The military teaches you that. The military indoctrinates and ingrains the importance of discipline into anybody who serves with them. Sure the Army taught me a lot. But it wasn't just killing.

"Americans are scared shitless by the idea that all the veterans from Vietnam are mad killers and someday they will turn that killing loose on this country. But they're dangerous in more important ways—in terms of the *real* revolution. Mao will be proven right when he said that this country has sowed the seeds of its own destruction.

"It did it in Vietnam. Through its racism, America trained an army made up mostly of nonwhites and it created a *revolutionary* army—the best-trained revolutionary army in the world. We ain't got to learn nothin'. We ain't got to learn *nothin'*, man, from artillery down to forty-fives. . . . And we've been indoctrinated in discipline and organization and that's just as threatening as any aspect of our military skills.

"There's an underground growing in America, man—a truly *military* underground. What happened in L.A. was only a battle. The war has just begun."

2

"It may upset your idealistic view of the world, man, but when the roar of tanks replaces the familiar sound of the N-Judah, you're going to have to pick up a gun. . . ."
—Joe Remiro

WHILE IT IS TRUE that it was the 101st Airborne Division which first taught Joe Remiro how to kill, the military does not deserve all the credit. America had made a fighter of him long before that.

("Eldridge Cleaver said it, man. . . . By the time a white male gets to draft age, they don't have to teach him how to kill or why to kill . . . all they gotta show him is who. . . .")

Joe first became a fighter at the age of eight out on the windswept playgrounds of St. Anne's Parish, that enormous Catholic fiefdom whose hulking twin towers lord it above the miles of paved-over sand dunes San Franciscans call the Sunset District.

("From the first day, you know, I fought everybody in my class, man. I was the nigger of this Irish-Catholic grammar school, man. I'm lighter than my mother and she's pretty dark, you know. . . . I've always been dark-complexioned and I never really considered myself white although culturally I'm as white as anybody, man, and I used to say I'm white. . . . I always used to want to try to be white, you know. . . .")

St. Anne's is the largest parish in the City, with about five thousand families on its rolls. The church is physically impressive, with its strangely mutated Romanesque-Byzantine-Mission-style basilica and its square block of neatly stuccoed (and institutionally deadly) outbuildings, which include a rectory, convent, and grammar school. There are some 750 students registered these days and boys and girls now go into the same classrooms. In Joe's time, there was strict sexual segregation.

But St. Anne's means considerably more to its neighborhood than

[9]

a collection of expensive old buildings and a staff of rosary-mumbling nuns and priests. As even the most casual observer will tell you, in a parish like St. Anne's—where the great majority of houses for many blocks are occupied by pious Catholics—the church becomes a kind of enormous cultural and moral transmitter which radiates an antique and strongly opinionated life style at least as far as one can see its square, 164-foot twin towers.

You can *feel* St. Anne's a long way away. You first feel it when you clank out onto Irving Street aboard the old N-Judah streetcar, and that's more than a half mile away. You almost immediately experience the first vibrations of St. Anne's and you know you have crossed a cultural frontier and are locked in a very sticky time-warp.

There is a certain oldness, a certain resignation, a certain *orthodoxy* in the air the moment your little green streetcar charges out of the long tunnel which cuts through the twin-peaked mountain and major windbreak that divides San Francisco into two distinct moral and meteorological zones. To the east of Twin Peaks there is "the City" itself, which grew up like some drunken gold miner's hedonistic hallucination around San Francisco Bay, close to the ships and the whorehouses and the saloons on every corner . . . a compact, mostly mountainous little resort of thieves and sailors, boomers and pleasure seekers, artists and bland tourists, rubes and con men of every description—a once-swarming international seaport open to a hundred tongues and attitudes, a never-quite-tamed Bonanzaland where the password has always been a lewd wink.

If there is any sun to be had at all in San Francisco (a very chancy thing in the summer), you'll generally find it on the "City" side of the tit-topped mountain. Once your N-Judah car clickety-clacks out of the west end of the tunnel and into "the Avenues" (everything west of the Peaks), the chances are you'll be met by that brooding, gloomy overcast which is so often driven in from the sea. When the mists hang low, the area is wrapped in a timeless fog that lingers on for days, removing all sense of time and place.

The Avenues have always been for the "decent" folk of the town, the relatively stable craftsmen and shopkeepers, the mildly successful office help. Tight rows of two-story frame houses slapped over with a uniform camouflage of bland stucco fill nearly every inch of available real estate from the western slopes of Twin Peaks down to the sea. Architectural innovation is frowned upon here.

If you're feeling high and irreverent when you board the N-Judah on the sunny side of the mountain, you quickly change your tune as you pop out into the fog belt. The Avenues lay a cold hand on such silliness and you begin to watch yourself out here. You keep in place. You avoid any loud or sudden actions that might bring unwelcome attention. You are being watched. You are being judged. You cannot yet see St. Anne's square and uncompromising towers but you know they are there.

It has been this way in the "Inner Sunset" since the original St. Anne's was erected atop a sand dune in the year 1905 to serve that first "flight to the suburbs" by land-hungry Irish Catholics who removed across Twin Peaks toward the sea in their first determined effort to put Sodom and Gomorrah behind them and raise their children in the Way of their Fathers—which means a heavy hand in the woodshed, a lot of fish and self-congratulation on Fridays, a loud and angry drinking bout each Saturday night, and a hung-over Sunday morning devoted to repentance at St. Anne's.

San Francisco's Irish population has always been clannish, and newcomers from other ethnic groups long found it difficult to settle in St. Anne's Parish. Racism is not worse here than in the rest of San Francisco, just more accepted.

Joseph Michael Remiro was born to an inner-city (North Beach) family on September 11, 1946. His father, Charles, was a World War II veteran who emigrated to this country as a Mexican farm worker. He now drives a laundry truck. His mother (nee Antoinette Balistreri) was the daughter of a very outgoing and emotional family of Sicilian fishermen. She is distantly related to San Francisco's present mayor, Joseph Alioto, whose ancestors also brought their catches into Fisherman's Wharf in those uncluttered years before it became a plastic tourist trap. Joe Remiro was named after Antoinette's brother, a soldier who was killed overseas in the last "great war."

When their son was six, the Remiros moved from North Beach out to their present neighborhood on Seventh Avenue near Judah. They live in a square little frame "cottage" with a "modernized" tan front. It fits inconspicuously into a long, unbroken line of row houses that parade down Seventh to Irving, where there is a funky old shopping center. The N-Judah streetcar clanks up to within a block and a half of the family home.

Charles Remiro saw very quickly which way the cold, wet wind was blowing out in the Avenues. He found it expedient to call himself "Spanish" rather than Mexican-American. He was eager to erase all traces of his true culture and made no attempt to teach his son and daughter (Christine, who is two years younger than Joe) either his native language or the rich Chicano culture. Joe felt that his father was ashamed of his heritage.

("As far as he's concerned, the only reason a Mexican is not where he's at is that they're lazy and all that racist shit. And he won't even admit he's Mexican. . . . He never taught me Spanish. . . . I feel cheated. . . . . . I had to study Spanish as a second language and it was hard. . . . I was always embarrassed that my father was a Chicano until I went to Vietnam, but the fact was that I wasn't white and I was cheated of the Mexican culture I could have learned. . . . So I still can't really say I'm a Chicano. . . .")

Joe may have been confused about what he was, but the tough little Irish kids who ran St. Anne's to suit themselves had no doubt about it. (The presidents of Joe's graduating class were Gerald Courtney and Ellen Gintey. The Right Reverend Patrick G. Moriarty ran the parish, may all the saints be praised.) The kids beat shit out of Remiro and another little Chicano kid from the day they entered the parochial school. Joe tried to blend in—the only route to survival.

("I was a traffic boy, an altar boy. In high school I was a cheerleader. . . .")

His terrific drive to appear "normal" may not have fooled the kids, but his teachers were apparently indifferent. "Normal" is, in fact, the only word they seem able to marshal up these days when trying to remember this one of thirty-kids-to-a-class who got into notorious trouble.

Sister Mary Bernard, a member of the Presentation Sisters, was principal of St. Anne's for a good part of the time Joe attended. She was his eighth-grade teacher. She obviously did not see him too clearly— or maybe it's just her advanced age and long retirement from life behind a black and forbidding habit.

"Oh, he was very regular, very obedient. But you can say that about *all* my boys," Sister Mary Bernard sort of recalls in the dimness of a convent reception room as she tries to find Joe's portrait in a crowded class graduation picture. She squints into the pale, fogged-over afternoon light, which seems to die without a murmur in an atmosphere of wax and plastic flowers, agonized plaster crucifixions and ancient, bloody-hearted saints.

"He was *normal* . . . oh, yes, very *normal*." Sister Mary Bernard finally finds Joe's picture. She recognizes it because the name is printed underneath. "How did Joe get along with his classmates?" we ask, wondering if she even noticed the daily bloody confrontations on the playground.

"Oh, he was very cooperative, very sociable with his companions. He got along with his companions very well," says Sister Mary Bernard distantly. "Oh, he never had any difficulties with them. Oh, no, he was very cooperative in the classroom and very sociable with the boys in the yard. . . ."

We wonder if Joe had any special skills—was he especially good at anything?

"Oh, he was an *average* student," says Sister Mary Bernard, and you realize that she would say exactly the same thing about any of the four or five thousand kids she has so routinely processed over the years.

"Now that's a good way to express it. He was what I call a real *average* student—otherwise he would never have made Sacred Heart High School, oh, no. . . . I prefer when a child is *average*. I never was for brilliant people. Brilliant people never attracted me. I was always for good students, that's all . . . *obedient* students. . . ."

We get up to leave.

"Now you be sure to mention Monsignor Moriarty," she says, ushering us out into the dull, chilly summer afternoon. A layer of gray sea fog has already settled over the Avenues. Ribbons of low cloud have wrapped themselves around the low-lying flanks of Twin Peaks. Foghorns have begun to sound on the Bay. "Monsignor was the pastor. He's dead now. He was very deeply interested in the boys. He's dead a year now. He was for the boys. . . ."

Joe puts the matter of his Catholic education a bit more succinctly:

"Those priests and nuns . . . they really fucked with my head. They really turned me around," he says. "By the time they got through, I was a stone reactionary. They trained me right, boy. They taught me to hate commies . . . you know, 'Kill a Commie for Christ,' man. When it was time to go to Vietnam, I just couldn't wait to get over there."

Although the Church had its way politically with the young Joe Remiro, it failed to make any lasting inroads theologically. By the time he was twelve, Joe stopped going to confession. He also managed to avoid Sunday mass most of the time.

One of Joe's first girlfriends, Mary Slattery, recalls that "by the time he was fourteen, he wanted nothing to do with religion. I had the scruples of a nun in those days and I thought it was shocking that he didn't want to go to church. He said his mother would try to get him up to go. 'Joe, come on, get out of bed and go to church.' 'Oh, I'm too tired,' he'd say."

Joe himself describes the moral dilemma his twelve-year-old mind was getting into as he began to see clearly that life's realities just did not match up to Sister Mary Bernard's vision of "normality."

"I couldn't believe that a just God or whatever existed after what I had seen in my small capacity as a child," says he. "There's no way a just God could possibly allow this to go on for so many hundreds of years. . . . The Romans grabbed this dude and tortured him and nailed him on a cross and they used mysticism to say that was the greatest thing that ever happened, you know. Well, if they ever nail me on a cross, man, don't let anybody say that's the greatest thing that ever happened, 'cause I ain't no mystic and I haven't seen God liberate *anybody* lately."

Certainly the stolid, most unspiritual image of the Church itself did little to convince young Joe Remiro that any kind of selfless dedication lay beneath its comfortable façade.

As Warren Hinckle, raised a Catholic in San Francisco and sent to the same kind of "reform schools," recently described the Church during those good, gray Eisenhower years:

"The Church I knew was not the Church of Savonarola, nor of James Joyce—it was too settled and comfortable to summon the fire and brimstone for Stephen Dedalus type retreats. The priests who weren't stuck in the confessional box on Saturdays put on Pendleton sports shirts and went off to play golf at the Irish-Catholic Olympic Club. Our confessors did scare us a little by warning that we could lose our minds and maybe even our hair if we touched ourselves, but suggested that if we pulled hard on an ear, it would dispel temptation. Naturally, we tugged our ears but otherwise the operating principle was to accept everything the Church taught while paying as little attention to it as possible. Thus we went to mass on Sundays and sinned on Mondays and went to confession on Saturdays so we could receive communion on Sunday and be in a state of grace to sin again on Monday.

"I came to accept the Church for the tinsel, lazy, corrupt and at the same time appealing thing it was. During the gray and quiet years, the Church was like some pervasive, closed system dominating an endless science-fiction novel. . . ."

Despite its overwhelmingly repressive effect on his life, the Catholic Church was most certainly not the main influence on this little Chicano-and-Italian kid. Joe's parents were, of course, the center of his universe.

His mother was (and is) warm and devoted to him. But his relation with his father (the crucial one for a boy) was distorted and painful from the first.

Charles Remiro and his son were completely out of touch by the time Joe was arrested as an S.L.A. soldier and charged with the murder of Marcus Foster. If you ask Joe what communication exists today, he'll say something like, "I communicate with him with a left hook."

He describes his father as "still patriotic" and "still telling World War II hero stories." He's one of those people, says Joe, "who believes that whether the President's right or wrong, you know, that *nobody* has the right to criticize him 'cause, after all, he *is* the President and shit like that. . . .

"The only time I can remember him hugging me when I was above the age of . . . you know, some mystical age when you stop hugging young boys . . . was when he'd get drunk, you know. He wasn't a drunk or anything, but when he'd get drunk after a party or something, he'd hug me and tell me he loved me. . . . That's the way I'd know he was drunk, you know. I left my parents' house when I was seventeen, a couple of months before I graduated from high school. . . . I didn't realize until I was in South Vietnam that I had lived my whole life up till then trying to live a life my father wished he'd been able to live.

"He's had a very hard time. He lived a very repressed life, you know. He had to quit school at a really young age and work, you know, and never knowing his father and being raised by his sickly grandmother and alcoholic grandfather, you know. He was raised with Mexicans as a migrant worker. . . .

"And it was my father who told me how to be a man and . . . I don't know . . . he's a sad story. It's really a sad story, one of the great American tragedies. . . ."

Charles Remiro obviously tried as well as he knew how to instill that "manly image" he wanted his son to grow into. The macho legend of guns and violence obviously had a lot to do with it.

Joe remembers his father taking him to all those movies where the cowboys proved themselves right with instant hot lead and the good Indians were dead ones.

"I used to go to all the John Wayne movies," he recalls, "and I used to dig all the movies where they shot the Indians and shit . . . I didn't have to be taught any violence in Vietnam. . . . Hell, when I was a little kid, I wouldn't get out of bed and walk around the house until I had my toy guns on . . . till I had my little guns on . . . I'm serious. . . ."

In Vietnam a decade later, nineteen-year-old Joe Remiro began to have serious doubts about that kind of upbringing and his furiously frustrated attempts to live a life his father would approve of.

"I've seen my friends die and it's not a lot of John Wayne movies," he says morosely. "It's a terrifying thing. . . . War is a very real thing with me 'cause I've really seen it and when I think of war now I don't relate to John Wayne movies."

He began to straighten out the problem of identifying with his father:

"You know, somebody asked me a long time ago when I was just beginning to understand things," he says, " 'Who do you relate to the most, your mother or your father?' And I said right off, 'My father,' you know, 'I'm a man.' Then I thought about it. And I thought, 'No, that ain't true at all.' You know I never thought about it before at all. It's my mother, you know. . . . All my life I lied about my father being the one who did the most when, in fact, it's never been the case and even he realizes it now, you know. . . .

"My mother is a very strong woman. . . . My father has just realized that, contrary to his beliefs and boasts, that she's the one who's been sustaining the family as long as it's been together, you know. . . . And through his own sex and ego he's oppressed her and not realized he's oppressed himself and now he's come to the point where he's getting old and realizes he can't shit without her. . . . She was sick a while ago and had to stay in bed a couple of weeks and so what he had to do was come home from work and cook her dinner, wash the dishes, do the laundry, you know, and then go to work again. You know, the same things she's been doing all the time I can remember. She's always taken care of the family and had a job, too. Two or three days of that, man, and he blew it. He was having a nervous breakdown, you know. . . . And now he's getting older and less secure and he's realizing the realities of where the strength is and everything, you know. . . ."

Mary Slattery, who first met Joe at a Catholic high-school dance when both were fourteen, says that he seldom spoke about his father but that "I had the feeling there was a lot of hate. . . . He talked a lot about his mother. . . . He really counted on his mother. . . . He'd tell me how his mother did this or that for him or how his mother fixed a special dinner for him. . . . He didn't get along too well with his sister. . . . I talked with him on the phone once for six hours when my mother wasn't home and his parents weren't home and he was fighting with his sister the whole time because she wanted the phone. . . .

"I remember when I first saw Joe at that dance and I immediately fell in love. . . . He and his friends, Dan Sheehy and Bill Sheehy and Denny Weston, they sort of breezed in and sort of took over the whole place and they were really *smooth* and all the girls were asking, 'Who are *they,* anyway?' And I just met him and he took my phone number and he phoned me every single day. . . . And he didn't have a car then, you know, or any transportation. So at any dance we could go to or any party, we'd always meet each other over there.

"He was just marvelous. . . . He just seemed to handle everything really cool. He didn't seem to be a terribly deep thinker but he was such a *normal* guy. . . . It was puppy love . . . *super* puppy love. I thought Joe was the greatest guy that ever walked the earth . . . really, he was so fun-loving. . . . I loved to listen to his stories, about all his little exploits, like going down with his friends and drinking on the beach and going in the water and getting all their clothes wet and I thought that was *too much!*

"Joe wasn't ambitious at all. He just wanted a good time and fun and he had a good time everywhere he went. I mean, it was genuine . . . it wasn't phony. It's hard to imagine he would have gotten serious about anything. . . . He never wanted to read. He really didn't seem to be academic at all. I think he was in THE dumbest class in high school and he was perfectly content to stay there. . . . He was always doing something. He was always going somewhere. His friends meant a lot to him. . . . He was very loyal. . . .

"So when Joe Remiro was arrested as a revolutionary, I just couldn't believe it. Joe was so *normal.* I was just sick. . . . What struck me was, here's a man who is, for all intents and purposes, just like me. I mean, he's not some crazy person out to destroy the world. What I'm saying is that I knew him when he was young and I couldn't believe it. . . .

"The friends who kept in contact with Joe after he went to Vietnam —the ones who saw him just after he came back—they didn't want to talk about what he was like. He went a little crazy, they say. They say he came back a different person. . . .

"I guess the war will do that . . . even to someone as normal as Joe."

3

"The all-male student body was frequently warned about the physical dangers of public high schools, not the least of which was reported to be the hazard of bloody kotex which shameless Protestant and Jewish girls were said to drop carelessly on the dark stairways. Although we were constantly admonished about sex, most direct questions about the subject were put off with some embarrassment by my religion teacher, a florid faced Brother whom I always presumed was a homosexual because when proximity allowed, he habitually stroked the pants legs of the boys. When the chapter on sex came due he appeared disinterested in it, and simply told the class to read the religion text and be prepared to explain, in an examination, the basic workings of the mysterious rhythm system and the strict circumstances under which married couples were allowed to use even that abstential method of birth control. . . .

"The text from which we studied European history was titled 'A History of Western Christianity' in which St. Augustine loomed larger than Caesar and Constantine weighed in heavier than Mohammed.

"Our knowledge of current events was limited to mandatory special pleading with the Lord to free Cardinal Mindszenty from an atheistic holding cell in Hungary. We also read the 'Junior Catholic Messenger,' a publication of crossword puzzles and contemporary affairs which I remembered featured a front page picture of the eminent Catholic junior senator from Wisconsin, Joseph McCarthy, riding on the Senate subway on his way to expose Communism. . . ."

—Warren Hinckle, describing a typical San Francisco Catholic high-school education in the late '50s and early '60s. From *If You Have a Lemon, Make Lemonade*

AROCHIAL GRAMMAR SCHOOLS in San Francisco end with eighth grade and the Catholic high schools begin with the ninth. That makes Joe Remiro fourteen years old as he begins his first year at Sacred Heart, an undistinguished forwarding station into such safe and traditional Irish-Catholic careers as the police and fire departments, civil service, hacking for the Hearst press, running a neighborhood saloon and, for a saintly few, the glory of the priesthood.

Sacred Heart (whose football team is still called "the Irish" and whose yearbook goes under the proud title of *The Shamrock*) is a relatively small secondary school for boys only, set inconspicuously off a few blocks from one of the town's two major arteries, Van Ness Avenue, and just beneath the City's vast new and very modern Catholic cathedral, whose winglike roof sections project lifelike shadow-play images of ample and well-formed breasts upon each other as the sun swings lazily overhead. It is on the eastern side of Twin Peaks, and Joe had to ride to school each day through the tunnel on the N-Judah streetcar, transferring at the foot of Van Ness to an electric trolley bus whose imitation-leather seats were generally in shreds by the time the switchblade-wielding school-year traffic was a month or two old.

Like parochial grammar schools, the secondary prisons of this archdiocese are famed for their "discipline," and Sacred Heart's beefy "Christian Brothers" (who also own a number of wineries and make the best brandy in California) are especially notorious for the "firm hand" policy . . . at times of the clenched-fist variety. Here, too, we find that Joe Remiro is remembered as no more than a "normal" boy, except for a few drinking incidents that marred his senior year. (Did he dare to appear anything else but *normal?*)*

"I never read a book the whole way through. I never read a book until I was in Vietnam," he readily admits in summing up the intellectual climate of his high-school years. "You know, if you got the money, you get through Catholic school, you know . . . if you want to pay the tuition. . . ."

His grades reflected his general lack of interest, with abysmal records in U.S. history (D), Spanish (D), and trigonometry (D), and a C in algebra. He did better in literature and religion (B in both).

Brother Arnold, chief disciplinarian at Sacred Heart when Joe went there and now its principal, is just as given over as Sister Mary Bernard to the word "normal." He says, in fact, that Joe was "VERY normal" while he was under the brother's watchful eye and firm fist.

---

* Joe himself has little to say about his high-school years except to admit that he kept himself busy on the side as a cheerleader and occasional auto thief. He ran with a tough gang of kids who liked to beat up on "weirdos" . . . like beatnik poets and homosexuals.

. . . "Everyone who knew him found it hard to believe he was arrested for murder," says the brother.

Joe tested out at 105 on the IQ forms. His yearbook entry shows that he partly made up for his academic indifference with a lot of time spent at extracurricular activities. He was not only a cheerleader but also on the Rally Committee and in the Service Club.

The four-color center spread of the 1964 *Shamrock* yearbook (the year Joe graduated) shows him in a very carefully contrived "jump" pose, cheering on the fighting "Irish" from an airborne position several feet above their heads. He is also seen in the gymnasium (monochromatic), cheering on the basketball team.

Joe found quite early that these nonplaying associations with athletics were just as valuable for impressing the girls as being a team member. He had given up a fairly promising hobby as a sandlot baseball player at about fourteen because "it was a choice of sports or girls and I didn't have time for both." He very early found that, despite his short stature (five foot eight), he had a way with women, a certain intensity and charm that quickly won them over. Everyone who knew Joe from the age of fourteen on until his arrest remembers him as being a virile and successful "ladies' man."

After Brother Arnold had used up a week's supply of the word "normal," he did recollect that Joe was indeed "very outgoing in school . . . and more interested in social life than studies," as the good brother found out at a senior-year dance when Joe snuck in a bottle of booze and proceeded to get loudly crocked.

His career as a bare-fisted boxer did not end when he left St. Anne's bloody playgrounds. Joe says he remained a "real rowdy," and Mary Slattery (who stayed in close touch with Joe all through high school although they ceased dating after the age of fourteen) can attest to the fact. Now the battlefields were parties where the young parochial studs contended for timorous female favors.

"He was always at every dance, at every party," says Mary, "not making a fool of himself or anything . . . but, I mean, you really knew he was there. . . . Mostly everybody liked him. He was hotheaded, though. He did have a temper. As a matter of fact, he got into a fist fight with my friend Lou once. . . ." "I won," says Lou. "He's much shorter than me and I guess I threw the first punch. . . . I remember that everybody was drinking . . . that's when we were really into drinking as a macho thing. . . . I think it was in sophomore year in high school. . . . It was really no big thing but I just remember it. He was little but he was scrappy. . . ."

"And the girls really liked him, too," Mary fondly interjects Lou and Joe finally made up some years after the fight.

"He was around. . . . I remember just especially when I started getting around more myself," says Lou. "Junior and senior year in high school. He never showed up at anything political, though. We used to have these clubs that debated political issues, and it didn't interest Joe at all. I just remember seeing him at all the dances, parties, and football games . . . he was the cheerleader, for instance. He was just around a lot and I noticed him all the time. For a while I had a kind of grudge against him because of that stupid fight but it wasn't really a big thing and we finally made it up. . . ."

Mary recalls that "he was always doing something. He was always going somewhere. His friends meant a lot to him . . . he was very loyal. I mean, a friend could be an idiot and could do a lot of wrong things like pop off at somebody or whatever and Joe would stick by him . . . and I liked that. . . . He was very warmblooded, very Latin, very impulsive. . . ."

She also remembers that Joe was in the habit of "running with the crowd." (Protective coloration after all those years of being "class nigger" at St. Anne's?) "He was never a loner, always into the group spirit. He didn't really have a sports career, though," she says, "I just remember when he was a freshman he did play football. But he played football not for the sake of the game but because all the other guys did it and it was really fun to do it with all the other guys. . . . But that sense of lightness and fun . . . that carried with him throughout high school. . . ."

Like every other teen-ager in the early '60s who was hot after the girls, Joe soon realized that he had to have a car. His home situation continued to deteriorate until he finally had to move out a few months before his high-school graduation. To earn the car and a measure of independence, he went to work as a part-time fry-cook in a drive-in restaurant a few blocks down Van Ness Avenue from his high school.

Another buddy who knew Joe briefly in his teens recalls that he very much impressed his peer group.

"Like I said, he had his own car and he had his own job which at the time we didn't," says Charlie Garner, today a San Francisco electrician. "So that would make him one up already, I guess, being able to do what you want to do . . . drive where you want to drive. . . . He seemed a little more carefree than most of us . . . maybe a little more macho. He had a way with the girls. I remember we had a party once and everyone was supposed to bring a date with the shortest skirt and whoever had the girl with the shortest skirt, he'd win . . . and that was even before miniskirts became so popular. . . . Anyway, Joe won. . . ."

So far we have a picture of a guy heavily into cars, girls, and being one of the gang. Up to this point, Joe Remiro could be a character out of *American Graffiti*. No books, no politics, no thoughts of his own. Just a "normal" kid. Frighteningly normal.

But there are a few chinks in this bland armor. Things are not going well at home. They never have. The feud with his father worsens as Joe begins to assert his newly won adolescent independence:

"My father wanted me to be in the Sea Scouts even when I was in high school," he recalls. "When I was about fourteen, they went on a summer cruise and I just went AWOL from the Sea Scouts. . . . I went home, you know. I said, 'This is bullshit,' and so I split and when I got home my father was flipped out. . . . Shit, you'd have thought I'd deserted ship during wartime. You know, he really took it seriously. . . ."

His relationship with his mother continued to be loving and helped to sustain him as he grew away from his childhood. . . .

"She and I . . . we don't have this 'Being a Man' thing between us and we got really honest with each other. You know, man, I used to sit and talk with her for hours and we'd start laughin'. . . . I'd laugh so hard my sides would hurt . . . and my father would come walkin' in and I'd leave, you know. . . ."

Things were pretty sedate in San Francisco between the late '50s, when the North Beach "beat" literary and artistic movement came and went, and the late '60s, when the spiritual children of that period streamed into the Haight-Ashbury District in the thousands to become known as "hippies." "Youth Culture," with its own independent life style and ethics, had yet to come into being. The aura of '50s conformity and institutionalized anticommunism was still heavy upon the nation's consciousness. Joe Remiro, a "normal" product of a parochial Catholic education, the son of a "patriotic" World War II veteran who boasted of his military machismo and talked a lot like a Chicano Archie Bunker, showed almost no true signs of rebellion against this kind of conformity.

But there were a few slight hints that Joe would not always be this way. In the late '50s, Remiro would pass up and down Upper Grant

Avenue, principal bohemian walkway through North Beach, to visit his grandmother, who owned property down by its northern end. A spunky little kid being raised like a lot of other North Beach Italians, he watched wide-eyed as the "beats" began to crowd up and down Grant singing, drinking, declaiming poetry, pissing openly on the streets and on all authority, loudly proclaiming a new cult of total individual liberty. It was the first demonstration of this kind seen in America since the rebellious days of the '30s and it impressed little Joe Remiro.

"When I was a kid—no more than eleven or twelve," he recalls, "I decided I wanted to grow up to be a beatnik . . . but the Catholics soon got that out of my head."

In his later high-school years, several coffeehouses modeled after the early beat hangouts began to again flourish in North Beach. One of them, a stopping-off place for an extremely young crowd of bohemians, was located at the east end of Broadway, the main North Beach nightclub drag. It was called the Last Exit.*

Joe spent a fair amount of time casing the action around Last Exit, and he was aware of some aspects of the pacifist, antisegregation ideas that by 1964–65 were current among the City's young nonconformists. It was a year of civil-rights sit-ins and lie-ins, arrests and trials. Great demonstrations were held in a major downtown hotel and out on Van Ness Avenue's "Auto Row," just a few blocks from Sacred Heart, where Joe was then in school. (Some of the demonstrations were staged at drive-in restaurants near the one where Joe worked part-time.)

Things got busy in 1964–65, and a cultural renaissance began in North Beach as a number of the famous beats—like Allen Ginsberg and Neal Cassady—returned to live in town to help revive the flagging literary scene.

Over in Berkeley, a new generation of civil-rights-trained campus activists was about to turn that once-staid diploma factory into the launching pad for an entire era of student uprising. It began late in 1964 (the year Joe got out of Sacred Heart) as the Free Speech Movement.

But Joe was not yet ready to rebel against what his parents and pious educators had drilled into him.

"If those civil-rights demonstrators had come out to the drive-in where I worked, man, I'd have kicked ass," he says in amused retrospect. "I'd have thought they were nothing but a bunch of commie weirdos."

* A block farther east, Broadway becomes a four-lane freeway. You turn off here or you end up in San Jose.

The impression made upon him by the Last Exit crowd was equally lightweight.

"I didn't really talk to those creeps in there," he says. "I was just there for the good times and the women. I really didn't have anything in common with them. . . . I was just a rowdy in those days . . . just a rowdy after all the girls I could get."

The hassles with his father and his general anger and frustration led to heavy drinking in his last year of high school and to the two incidents that almost prevented his graduation.

As Mary Slattery recalls it:

"Joe and two of his friends were involved in this drinking thing and Joe and this other friend had been in trouble before and they were going to be kicked out of school if they hadn't pinned it on the other guy. . . . So that's what they did and they felt bad for doing that. I remember that Joe couldn't even talk to me afterwards . . . he just felt terrible. It's just, like, he and the other guy felt, 'Well, what can we do?' It was an understandable thing to do . . . they didn't want to get kicked out of high school just before graduation. . . . But, still . . ."

Brother Arnold and his Christian associates must have breathed a collective sigh of relief in June of 1964 when "rowdy" Joe Remiro graduated from Sacred Heart.

Joe was now on his own—but not for long.

The Vietnam war was tooling up. It was no longer a bush-league action requiring only a few so-called American advisers. Recruitment of thousands of young studs out to prove their newly tumescent manhood in battle was well under way and Joe Remiro was more than a likely candidate.

Joe's cousin, Barbara Lockwood (who likes to remember that she could out-arm-wrestle him when they were kids), says Joe went around singing the "Green Beret Song." He tried to enlist in the Berets but wasn't tall enough. His father encouraged enlistment but his mother was horror-stricken. Joe had been named after her brother, who had been killed in World War II, and Antoinette Remiro wanted no part of the Vietnam war. But "she was afraid to open her mouth about it in front of my father," Joe recalls. "He would have blown it, man."

With a poor high-school record and little interest in college, Joe knew he stood no chance of avoiding the rapidly expanding draft. He checked into San Francisco City College in 1965, figuring it was only a stopover on the way to Nam. (As he says repeatedly, "I was gung-ho, man. I wanted to kill a commie for Christ in those days. . . .")

Few City College students take their time at that two-year institution very seriously, anyway. It's a free, city-supported extension of high school devoted mostly to wet-nursing kids with lousy academic records so they stand some chance of entering a true college, or to convincing them once and for all that they don't have what it takes.

"I just played there," says Joe. "I wasn't really into any intellectual thing, you know. . . . I never seriously read a book until I got to Vietnam. . . . As soon as I heard about the war, I couldn't wait to run and enlist. . . . I never really went to college."

His situation was not unique. Charlie Garner recalls that everybody at City College was just "waiting around to go in the service."

"At that time," he says, "how many were they drafting a month—forty thousand? It was inevitable . . . unless you were blind and crippled you had to go." Garner went in the Air Force himself and helped keep the bombers flying from Okinawa to Nam.

Remiro and Garner shared only one major experience—their period of pledging as "baby brothers" in City College's Alpha Kappa Rho fraternity. (Mary Slattery, who also briefly attended the college, found it strange that Joe should join a fraternity there, since "almost no one who lived in the City joined those fraternities," she says. "Only the out-of-town kids who didn't know anybody joined. . . .")

Garner's strongest recollection of the pre-Vietnam Remiro was a "Hell Week" initiation trip the two made into Marin County, where they were released alone in deserted hill country in the dead of night.

"They kidnapped me and him and they blindfolded us here in the City and then they brought us across the Golden Gate Bridge blindfolded," says Garner. "Then they dropped us in the hills of Marin somewhere, and I had no idea where we were.

"There weren't any houses, but Joe knew right away which way to walk. He got us out of there. Without him, I probably would have gone the wrong way. . . . I'm poor at directions."

Garner and Remiro were also part of a crowd of pledges taken out into the San Bruno Mountains a bit later, stripped naked, and covered with molasses, feathers, and Tabasco sauce. He remembers that Joe's resourcefulness again served them well. Before the "ceremony," Joe had stashed a car not far away—he immediately led Garner to it and they drove away.

"All I can remember about him now is that he was strong . . . very strong, very self-reliant . . . and very gung-ho about going into the military," says Garner. "He really wanted to go into the Army or into the Marines. That's all he talked about. . . ."

On January 31, 1966, the Army obliged and accepted Joe Remiro's three-year enlistment. He was sent to Fort Ord, California, and then to Fort Benning, Georgia, for training as a member of the 101st Airborne Division.

By August 1, 1966, he was in Vietnam.

4

He's five foot two and he's six foot four
He fights with missiles, and with spears.
He's all of thirty-one and he's only seventeen,
He's been a soldier for a thousand years. . . .
And he knows he shouldn't kill and he knows he always will. . . .
And without him all this killing can't go on. . . .
      —Buffy Sainte-Marie, *"The Universal Soldier"* *

LET'S SUPPOSE THAT JOE REMIRO had been born a generation earlier . . . in 1926 rather than in 1946. He would have been eighteen in time to be drafted (or, more likely, to enlist) into World War II. He would have "done his duty" against the Nazis or the Nips, and, if a bullet hadn't caught up with him first, he'd have come home as just one more "GI Joe" (a term the contemporary Remiro abhors) and he'd have felt he most certainly had earned the victory parades and near orgies of V-J Day, the general sense of honor and respect, the job preferment and educational benefits freely provided to World War II vets. He would soon have married a nice, quiet Catholic girl and continued to go through the formalities of his religion. There would have been five or six kids (or more . . . he likes to screw a lot) and a steady job driving a truck or something equally uninteresting. He'd have sat around as his kids grew up, telling them proud (and mostly bullshit) war stories about how we were the "good guys." He'd have joined the American Legion and voted for whichever politician was the most energetic flag-waver. He would, in other words, have lived up to all of his father's expectations and shortcomings.

There is nothing in the actual history of Joe Remiro up to August 6, 1966, that would contradict such a set of conclusions. Nothing until that date, upon which he was assigned to his first active-duty Nam unit, that would indicate Joe was ever likely to do *anything* more (or less) than could be expected of an average-intelligence, party-timing, quick-

* © 1963 by Caleb Music

conning, girl-chasing, run-with-the-gang kind of young punk from a San Francisco working-class family.

Joe was a TV baby. Reading did not interest him, nor did radical causes. He simply ignored politics except for a very violent antagonism toward anything unconventional. He had gone through all of the usual hassles of growing up and becoming independent and his machismo had run head-on into that of his father, but he had never really questioned the basic perimeters his parents and teachers had set around his life. True, he'd quickly seen through the workaday hypocrisy of the Church . . . but that is nothing unusual among male Catholics, especially Latins, who traditionally drop the wife off for mass each Sunday and then amble across the plaza for a drink or two. Piousness is for women. Macho men in Mexico and France and Italy do not get down on their knees for some mumbling, black-robed castrato. Anticlericalism is a father-to-son inheritance in these lands.

So we can reach only one possible conclusion. The war changed Joe Remiro. He is almost too quick to admit it, although he is not subtle enough to see just how deeply it worked its sadistic and decadent tentacles into his naive consciousness. He still suffers a kind of war-induced, black-and-white tunnel vision which divides all humanity into "Our Side" and "Their Side." He still urgently wants to be a hero of the revolution in an era when even the noblest soldiers have come home defeated and full of guilt.

One wonders why the Vietnam experience was such a total mindbender for Remiro. What was so different about that part of the war which they dropped him into—the period from August 6, 1966, to March 2, 1968, when he was on combat duty? Why should its effects be so much at variance with those of previous American wars? Why couldn't Joe have come home as his father did—patriotic, proud, and more than ready to fall back into all the old patterns of familiar civilian life? Why was this slightly screwed-up kid so quick to become a freaked-out doper and then a superviolent revolutionary?

Perhaps it is time to take a considerably longer look at the Vietnam war and what it did to the soldiers who fought it.

There was a lot more to it than the fighting, the massacres, the atrocities. (There was more than one My Lai. Joe claims he saw a dozen actions very much like it: "My Lai wasn't no isolated incident," he says. "I saw a lot of that kind of thing.")

It wasn't just murder and it wasn't just racism that fucked with his young head. (American soldiers saw no real distinction between civilians and combatants. They were all "gooks." They were all "dinks." Everyone with yellow skin and slant eyes was the enemy.)

It was a war whose progress was measured in barbaric "body counts"—success depended upon the size of the pile of corpses you killed. Chopping off ears and hands and genitals as souvenirs was common—it also proved how effective a soldier you were.

Anyone dead was automatically a "VC," automatically the enemy. As one Namvet summed it up: "Nothing was there to stop us. The policy was 'Anything you want to kill, any time you want to kill it—just don't get caught.' "

Murdering innocent civilians was not just fun—it staved off the utter boredom and inertia that was the main emotion recalled by the majority of Namvets. "You know, if Vietnam was not violently painful, it was such a crashing bore you couldn't stand it," says one survivor.

Remiro—like most of his buddies—knew very little about the people he killed. The few pro-Saigon Vietnamese the American GIs met, they detested—and with good reason.

Fifty years of French colonial rule had produced a class of landlords and politicians who served as middlemen between their own people (who regarded them as traitors) and the colonial Europeans. With their complicity (and to their immense profit) the French-speaking major cities and market towns of South Vietnam quickly became great supply depots providing the latest conquerors with every kind of prostitute—choose your favorite sex—with every kind of dope known to man—opium, grass, scag, you name it. With the best in ripped-off and bootleg merchandise. (No real problem to transfer tons of stuff from overstocked PX shelves onto the black market—the obliging military brought in everything such a market might need.)

Says Paul Halverson, a once-evangelistic, anticommunist Christian who was transformed into a revolutionary, atheistic Marxist by his Nam experience, "We just turned the whole fucking country into a den of prostitutes. They would sell their own bodies and sell their daughters and their sons, sell their wives. And they would take a chance and grow dope and sell dope and heroin and anything else they could get their hands on."

Says Bob Hood, a former Army sergeant who was later Joe's comrade in Vietnam Veterans Against the War—Winter Soldier Organization, "I'd been to Tijuana, which is the whore capital of Mexico, and I swear to God, the first day in Vietnam, I thought, 'Wow! It's just like Mexico!' The garbage, the people . . . it even smelled like Mexico."

"This ain't no war," said an amazed trooper on his arrival at the garrison town of An Khe. "It's a whorehouse."

And so it was into this friendly little abattoir and bordello that they dropped naive Joe Remiro at the age of nineteen.

And if the war itself, the racism of his comrades, the corruption of one part of the population and the lethal hostility of the rest were not enough to contend with, Joe found yet another booby prize awaiting him—the murderous incompetence of the Army itself, the Army that quickly made the one decision from which Joe has never recovered. They made a full-time combat soldier of him.

Joe was quickly funneled into that small and little-heard-of minority of fifty thousand American soldiers in Nam (about one-tenth of the half-million men committed there at the high point of U.S. intervention), the guys who actually did the fighting. For every real combat grunt in Nam, the Army's enormous, top-heavy Green Machine had nine men assigned to "support" roles. They ran things. The war seemed to be mostly for their benefit. As one combat soldier summed it up, "Grunts don't exist. We're just meat."

When they slapped an M-16 into Remiro's hands and told him to go out and kill Charlie, it came as something of a surprise, for the Army had led him to believe he'd be just one more support trooper.

"They sent me out to fight because my name was Remiro, man," he says angrily. "The infantry was black, man. It was black and Mexican, you know. Only the leadership was white. I was trained to be a switchboard operator but I was put in the infantry because I had a Mexican name. . . ."

"All veterans are marked by the war experience," comments Bob Hood, "and that mark remains. But I think that each mark is a representation of each man's experience, and Joe's experience came out of being in this place where history found him. If you think in terms of a sort of gradation, in terms of combat involvement, that might be interesting, because Joe was an LRRP and that's the heaviest combat job there is.

"In the minds of many, being in a Long Range Reconnaissance Platoon is *the* worst, is *the* heaviest kind of situation to be in. That's point-of-production killing, so to speak. These were the people who produced down on the one-to-one level, not on the mile-high, B-52 kind of route. That LRRP trip was a heavy one, man. . . ."

Remiro's initial training at Fort Ord, California (February 1 to April 22, 1966), had gotten Joe ready to be a "wireman," that is, a telephone specialist. His stint at Fort Benning, Georgia (June 16 to July 16, 1966), had provided paratrooper training. (Mostly getting in and out of helicopters for this war.)

All of this proved to be a waste of time, and any idea that Joe may have developed about serving through his Nam tour as a kind of telephonic trainee was short-lived. His initial assignment to the 54th Signal Battalion lasted only three months. By November 10, 1966, Joe was just one more grunt serving with the 5th Regiment of the 27th Artillery. Four months later (March 28, 1967) he was assigned back to his own outfit (the 101st Airborne, 1st Brigade) and, from then until the end of his Nam duty, it was one-to-one killing on hazardous LRRP patrols for Remiro.

Not that this kind of misassignment was particularly unusual. As former Army Lt. Col. Anthony Herbert reports: "Men had been assigned to jobs far removed from their skills. Radio technicians as machine-gunners, machine-gunners as wiremen, wiremen as riflemen, riflemen as radio technicians. . . . Promotion orders were running at least eight weeks behind schedule, a failing that often required men who had been promoted in the field to give up those same promotions after rotating out of the country and to return 'overpayments.' Sometimes they were court-martialed for 'impersonation.' Other men never received medals and decorations they had earned. . . ." *

For all intents and purposes, Remiro was just one more foot soldier to be chewed up in the gigantic humbug hamburger grinder that was the Indochina war.

There was, however, *one* distinction that being an LRRP brought to Remiro. The name "Long Range Reconnaissance Platoon" is pretty much self-defining. LRRP's were sent long distances from their base camps on extended reconnaissance missions deep inside "enemy territory."

Once they were discovered, the LRRP's felt free to mow down everything in sight. They liked to use the grunt's favorite method of murdering the opposition without taking any real chances with your own precious ass—that is, "recon by fire," a procedure in which American troops approached inhabited areas and would then "reconnoiter" simply by firing at everything in sight.

"Whenever we stepped into a village we would fire upon houses,

---

* Joe finally got a few of his—the Combat Infantryman's Badge, the Parachutist Badge, the Vietnam Service Medal, the National Defense Medal, the Vietnam Campaign Medal, and three overseas service bars.

bushes, anything to our discretion that looked like there might be something hiding behind or in or under. What we did was we'd carry our rifles about hip-high and we'd line up on lines parallel to the village and start walking, firing from the hip. That's how we would uselessly kill so many civilians without giving them a chance. . . ." (Testimony from the Winter Soldier Investigation.)

Such tactics were also common during those "Search and Destroy" missions Joe participated in. (The My Lai massacre, which occurred in the same "central" portion of Vietnam where Remiro served out most of his time, was an S & D trip.)

Explains Joe: "A Search and Destroy mission is . . . you drop in leaflets—the Air Force or somebody drops in leaflets about two weeks before the Army gets there. And the leaflets say—first of all, you take it for granted that the peasants can read—you drop in leaflets saying that the American Army's gonna be here in two weeks. If you're the Viet Cong, stay. If you're not, leave. These people are starving, just barely surviving. They're supposed to leave their homes and what little material they have, whatever livestock and chickens they have, and split, right?

"Well, two weeks later here comes the American Army. They get in a line. They go through the area and they kill everything living—dogs, cats, women, children, anything. When they're through, there's not supposed to be anything alive behind them. . . ."

(As another Namvet summed it up: "Nothing was to be left walking, growing, or crawling. . . .")

It was this kind of merciless "combat" that made the LRRP's famous as bad-ass killers.

Paul Halverson, one of the 90 percent of the troopers in Nam who were on "support duty," vividly remembers meeting an LRRP. The contact was nearly fatal.

"The Army was completely loose with them," says Halverson. "The LRRPs could carry any kind of weapon they wanted to, even a Viet Cong AK-47. . . . They had their own special rations so they could travel light. The LRRPs were the ones who were doing all the fighting while I was there. . . . The LRRPs were the killers, they were all trained killers. . . . They did a lot of Search and Destroy and, if they ran into a small enough unit, their mission was to immediately kill them.

"One day when I was stationed in Saigon—I was still shacked up with this chick and we were living in a kind of a whorehouse, you know—but I was standing up on the roof one night waiting for her to come home from work and ran into this LRRP up on the roof. And we started talking and he asked me where I was stationed and I told him in Saigon. And we talked about it and I told him how easy it was—living in an air-conditioned hotel room and working in an air-conditioned office and everything—and he said, 'Well, that's pretty chickenshit, isn't it?' He said, 'I'm out there fighting the war and you're in here living the life of Riley, shacked up with a chick all the time and working in an air-conditioned office. You don't even carry a gun,' he said, and he was getting *really* angry.

" 'You're a motherfucking coward,' he said, 'and I ought to blow you away right here.' And he was going to kill me and he was standing there with an M-16 and I said, 'Hey! Wait a minute, man! We're supposed to be on the SAME SIDE!' "

Like this fellow LRRP who had to be reminded that the Saigon office help was *not* the enemy, Joe Remiro lived in a world of jungles, rice paddies and wooded, high mountain plateaus. He spent most of his eighteen months in the open countryside of Nam, which remained the primary battlefield until January of 1968 when Charlie outgrew his stereotyped role of rural guerrilla and opened a full-scale Tet Offensive on the cities.

From the time Joe rejoined the 101st Airborne in March of '67 until he finally went home almost exactly a year later, units of the "Screaming Eagles" worked out of camps located along the coast in the first range of mountainous provinces ninety to two hundred miles north of Saigon. Such major staging areas as Phan Thiet and Phan Rang provided good strategic positions from which to send out their HUEY and Chinook helicopters, which were the Airborne's main transport in Nam.

Phan Rang sits on the South China Sea about 180 miles north of Saigon and it straddles Route 1 at a crucial point between the prosperous and corrupt capital city and the estranged and bloody far northern provinces just below the border of North Vietnam.

Control of the highway is imperative since it remains Saigon's main land link with many of the constantly fought-over rural areas which stand between the seat of the so-called Second Republic and its revolutionary enemies to the north.

Accomplishing this prime objective of U.S. headquarters proved an exhausting task. For Remiro it meant participation in a number of "pacification" missions against the thousands of disaffected little villages along the asphalt control corridors. Between May 27 and December 20 of 1967, Joe was part of the 101st Airborne's 1st Brigade, which conducted S & D missions in Quang Nghai Province. This is the very area where the My Lai massacre would take place on March 16, 1968.

A typical 101st Airborne mission of this period was described by former Pfc. Charles Stephans during the Winter Soldier Investigation.* Stephans was a medic in the 101st Airborne's 1st Brigade in '66–'67 and he was stationed at Tuy Hoa. Shortly after arriving there, he was sent out to "attack the enemy" in a nearby village.

Stephans says his group went into this village near Tuy Hoa and "we reconned by fire. We wounded women and kids going into the village. . . . We let 'em die. Then we went up on a hill right above this same village and we fired down on this village the next day while the people were trying to bury their dead. . . . We went down that same day to get some water and there were there two little boys playing on a dike and one sergeant just took his M-16 and shot one boy at the dike. The other boy tried to run. He was almost out of sight when this other guy, a Spec. 4, shot this other little boy off the dike. The little boy was, like, lying on the ground kicking, so he shot him again to make sure he was dead. . . ."

Later, soldiers of the 1st Brigade (to which Joe belonged from May to December of '67) were ordered to "cut off the right ear of everybody we killed to prove our body count. . . . Guys would cut off heads, put them on a stake and stick a guy's penis in his mouth. . . ."

(Other Winter Soldier Investigation testimony runs the gauntlet of every war crime known to human history. One witness opened his statement by saying he would discuss "the burning of villages with civilians in them, the cutting off of ears, cutting off heads, torturing of prisoners, calling in artillery on villages for games, corpsmen killing wounded prisoners, napalm dropped on villages, women being raped, women and children being massacred, CS gas used on people, animals slaughtered . . . bodies shoved out of helicopters, tear-gassing people for fun, and running civilians off the road." All very matter-of-fact—just a day in the life of an average trooper.)

In My Lai some five hundred innocent civilians were massacred by an infantry company led by a freaked-out five-foot-three lieutenant from Florida and his madly ambitious Chicano captain. It happened because during those years when Remiro served in the same geographic area every restraint of civilization had been deliberately broken down.

* On January 31, 1971, the VVAW held its own "war crimes tribunal" in Detroit, Michigan. Seventy-five Namvets gave full public testimony about the atrocities they had seen and participated in.

It started simply enough. Ron Grzesik, a member of Lt. William Calley's company, puts in in Grunt Language:

"First," says Grzesik, "you stop people, question them, and then let them go. Second, you stop the people, beat up an old man, and then let him go. Third, you stop the people, beat up an old man, and then shoot him. Fourth, you go in and wipe out a village."

This kind of thing permeated all ranks. War correspondent Richard Boyle is one of those who simply does not believe that a handful of grunts and one lonely lieutenant cooked up My Lai all by themselves. "My Lai was not the act of one man. It was not the act of one platoon or one company," writes Boyle. "It was the result of an ordered, planned-out and well-conducted campaign conceived at high command levels. . . ."

The state of mind that created My Lai is described by Joe Remiro in terms of what he personally saw and felt in Nam:

"You know it was a goddamn game for a bunch of goddamn young kids set loose with more power than a young kid should have," he says. "No one even talked politics. Nobody knew anything about politics. All we knew was the United States was the good guys all the time. We were fighting the dirty commies. . . ."

Remiro says it was made clear to him from the beginning that he could kill just about any "gook" he wanted to.

In August of '67 Remiro completed his first combat tour. He still had a year and four months to finish before discharge and the Army offered its standard choice—rotate home from Nam and then serve out your entire three-year enlistment, or volunteer for a second combat tour (this one for six months) and then get out of the service five months early. Joe re-upped, although it was becoming apparent by this point that the war was not going well with him.

In the fall, he got the usual "R & R" (Rest and Recreation) leave and chose to go home to San Francisco rather than spending the time in some whorehouse in Hong Kong or Thailand as so many GIs were doing in those days.

When he got home there was no sense in telling his father what was bothering him. The problem of trying to please his dad still troubled Joe. In his scrapbook from this period we find a "Dear Abby" clip, a letter from a young sailor away from home for the first time, and his concern is obviously one that Joe identifies with. The sailor writes that "when my father said goodbye to me, he broke down and cried. I had never seen my father cry before, and I won't forget it as long as I live.

I have had a lot of time to think. I never told my father I loved him, and I gave both my parents a bad time. . . ."

And Joe sees no sense in further troubling his mother, who is already worried to death about him. He does tell his cousin Barbara that he did "a lot of praying" as the bullets zinged in close. He admits later that he's scared a lot of the time in Nam: "I can be as chicken as they come," he says. "In one of my first actions, I nearly tore off my leg in some barbed wire, I was running so fast from the enemy's bullets, man. . . ."

But Joe has learned to live with his war experience—at least for a while. Dope helped a lot—everybody in Nam is smoking grass by the middle of '65. The black troopers always have the best stuff, so Joe quickly gets in tight with them. "Whenever I went anyplace," says Joe, "you know, I changed outfits a lot, the first thing I did was I hit up the black dudes, man, because I knew that if there was any dope they had to have it. . . .

"Everybody turned on, man," he says. "If you look at the war in the sense of how many cases of shell shock, battle fatigue, things like that, there were almost none—it's almost nonexistent in Vietnam and I think the reason is marijuana. There was a time when I'm sure I was about to have a fuckin' mental breakdown. I couldn't deal with it any longer, you know, and I'd been smokin' dope before that, but I got into it heavily, man. I was smokin' twenty-four hours a day, and I couldn't smoke cigarettes because I was coughin' too bad—had to just smoke dope, you know."

Vietnamese weed is strong shit and, like a great many Namvets home on leave, Joe wanted to bring a little back to share, but his luck didn't hold out and Customs grabbed him on September 11, 1967, when he hit Frisco. They charged him with smuggling marijuana, but the case was referred to the Army's Criminal Investigation Division for routine handling. Too many GIs were into smoking grass to screw around with the matter as a "crime."

So when he got home to the little row house on Seventh Avenue he said nothing about the grass, about the atrocities he'd seen, nothing about his own fear and gradually dissolving belief in what he was doing. All that would come later—when he came home for good.

There was a big sign over the garage saying "Welcome Home, Joe," and a large, square cake especially baked and designed for a conquering-hero party. Color photos in Joe's scrapbooks show the whole event. Joe is in civvies, still crew-cut, one arm draped around the nearest girl or fixed protectively around his mother, the other arm hoisting a drink. He has changed. There is a certain intensity now; he seems to be listening and watching for something that is just beyond sight and hearing. But he puts a good face on it all. Only a few of his friends sense that this is not the old Joe.

While he's in town, Remiro ambles over to the Haight-Ashbury district, less than a mile from the family homestead. His motives are pretty much the same as those that took him into the bohemian Last Exit coffeehouse a few years before when the hippies were only *beginning* to get it together and Haight-Ashbury was still a rather isolated Golden Gate parkside community of European and Latin-American families blending successfully but rather self-consciously with a slowly rising black tide of newcomers moving over from the nearby Fillmore ghetto.

What Joe found along Haight Street in the fall of '67 (the name was then equated with love, but within a year it was to be logically respelled HATE) was a gross overamplification of those same energies and styles that were then popping up in Nam with his young buddies. He'd heard about the Haight during the preceding eight or nine months, as it had been sensationalized in the national magazines as *the* place to freak out.

The visit must have made a profound impression on the young soldier. By 1969, Remiro would be calling himself a "hippie" as he began a two-year odyssey of hanging out around the Haight, over on "Tele" (Telegraph Avenue in Berkeley), and in rock palaces like the Fillmore West Ballroom. He would be smoking so much dope and dropping so much acid that hallucination would become a "normal" state of mind.

A few weeks after it had begun, Joe's brief leave was over, and on December 20 he was transferred to the 3rd Battalion of the Airborne's 506th Infantry, headquartered first at Phan Rang and then in Phan Thiet. This was to be Joe's last transfer before he came home for good the following March.

When he first joined the 506th, the group was engaged in Search and Destroy missions in the mountainous areas north of Saigon. On January 29 they were back in Phan Thiet when the entire character of the war changed and the Viet Cong went on the offensive during the Tet Lunar New Year cease-fire.

Charlie came charging out of the dark rain forests and up from the rice paddies and jungles to move on the cities. Fighting erupted within Saigon itself. Provincial capitals fell all across the country. The attacks erupted everywhere and the American Army found that it was no longer fighting an "Indian war where we've got the Sharpe rifles and all they have is bows and arrows." Suddenly the grunts were fighting for their lives, staging a desperate holding action. Nearly ten thousand people died in ten days.

In the Phan Thiet area, the 506th Infantry was attacked by a full battalion of Cong, and the Americans found themselves hard pressed to hold on to the vital Route 1 sector which they controlled to Phan Rang. Heavy fighting continued until February 23 (just about a week before Joe went home). The 506th claimed a "body count" of over five hundred by the time it was all over, and Charlie once again withdrew to the jungles and mountains.

Nothing was the same after Tet.

"After the first Tet Offensive, the whole war changed," explains Joe. "People I talked to who were there after that were into smack and downers, you know, and all sorts of shit got there. The whole war changed, the whole fighting, the whole method of fighting, everything changed. . . ."

It was, in fact, a very short road from Tet to the fall of 1969, when American soldiers began to mutiny all across Nam. The best-known incident was the September, '69, refusal of Alpha Company, Americal Division, to go into battle at Queson. The troopers of the 101st Airborne also made it clear that they would no longer die quietly after the disastrous battle of Hamburger Hill. Members of Joe's old division posted a ten-thousand-dollar reward for the assassination of the officer who had given the insane order to attack.

Such revolts do not happen overnight, and, as Remiro or any grunt who fought there in '66–68 can tell you, the enlisted combat trooper was in a totally different time and cultural zone from that of ambitious career officers and "lifer" NCOs.

The grunts knew they were fighting a hopeless, meaningless, and immoral war.

As more and more Namvets pop up in the headlines, as more Joe Remiros very violently prove that *they* have not forgotten the war and that they are determined to bring a hunk of it home to share with the rest of us, we begin to ask, just what happened to their heads?

Three million men went to Nam. Hundreds of thousands came home with a completely new vision of the world and themselves, with a different cultural fix, with a new political stand—antiwar, anti-Establishment, identifying more with the Viet Cong communists than with their own capitalist system.

("The main thing that Vietnam taught me," says Paul Halverson, "was that I was on the *wrong* side. I came home an atheist communist who had not yet read Marx.")

While the grunts were stuck with the vicious reality of fighting this war, they developed what psychologists call a "survivor" mentality. They lived it out a day at a time until the nightmare would be over and they could finally go home and try to become civilized human beings again.

You watched the calendar. You counted off the days. Remiro kept most of his shit inside until a few days before he left Nam for good.

"I became a pacifist the *day before* I left Vietnam," says Joe. "I thought about it a lot since then and when I became a pacifist all of a sudden I realized—all these events that had happened the previous months—the question always would come to my mind and I would block it out, and two seconds later I wouldn't remember that I had asked myself the question. About whether this was right, you know. And all of a sudden, the day before I left, I got hit in the head with all this shit—and it was a really heavy experience—and I remembered all these things that I had really forgotten I'd ever thought. And after thinking about it a real long time I realized that if I had become a pacifist before that I never would have gotten home. . . . You see, subconsciously I'd seen enough people killed trying to be nice guys to realize that I had to be a terrible motherfucker if I was going to get home. . . . The nice guys, they got killed, the guys who thought twice, you know, they all got killed."

So the tougher troopers who were determined to get out alive held on to their badly cracked marbles until the end. But there were a million little—and not so little—signs to be found everywhere in the American camps that the grunts had long ago mentally mutinied against the war and everything it stood for.

Not too many people in the peace movement (which was generally suspicious of Namvets) were aware of it while the war was going on but, as a number of stiff-backed officers could disgustedly tell you, the cultural revolution that hit Haight-Ashbury and the East Village, the beaches and the hamburger stands and the rock concerts, anywhere the young gathered in America, had also hit Vietnam.

The word "hippie" got thrown around a lot, but what was under way was a general youth revolt all through American society, and the kids who fought in Nam were mostly eighteen and nineteen and twenty and they were far from immune. (Square dudes with crew cuts just couldn't get laid back home any more.)

The Army would not let them wear their hair long nor could they grow beards and mustaches. But thousands of young troopers had long been into the same styles and attitudes espoused by the peace movement and by the sisters and brothers back in the Haight.

One of the great ironies of Nam was that while 500,000 men were supposedly there to "protect the American Way," they were actually engaged in a cram course in dope and alienation, and the values of the youth movement. (There was one essential difference. At home in '66–'67 the favorite philosophy was nonviolence, but that made no sense to a bunch of soldiers who were in the habit of blowing the opposition away with a magazine or two of .30-caliber bullets.)

The common link of good dope had a lot to do with it. American officers had never dealt with an entire army that stayed stoned every moment it could. They also had a bit of trouble getting used to combat soldiers who universally greeted each other with the peace sign and painted peace symbols on tanks, planes, and field guns.

As Lt. Col. Anthony Herbert noted at An Khe in 1968:

"The troops were slovenly, disrespectful and sluggish . . . they preferred pot two to one. . . . At An Khe the troops wore what they damn well wanted to wear, including beads and bracelets. They capped their teeth with different colors—red, blue and gold—and they called the hierarchy 'motherfuckers' and printed 'Fuck the Green Machine' on their jackets and hats. Some of them wore earrings, a few sported nose-rings. . . ."

Fragging—throwing fragmentation grenades at those you dislike—was well under way.

(It was said that the grunt's "favorite calling card" on his superior officers was a grenade. By 1969 there were 126 *reported* fraggings in Nam. In 1970 there were 271. By July of 1971 there were 210 being investigated by CID.)

A disproportionately large number of the fraggings involved black enlisted men attacking white officers. As in America, the spirit of rebellion burned strongest among blacks who found themselves in Asia fighting for whites against Orientals while back home their own people were burning down ghettos and violently attacking the Man on all fronts.

More and more black troopers became convinced they were fighting the wrong enemy. A lifer sergeant was a lot more obviously the enemy than some poor Nam peasant whose main crime was the color of his skin.

(A study done in 1970 by Wallace Terry II showed that 45 percent of the black troopers interviewed in a cross-section survey said they would join riots and take up arms if necessary when they returned home.)

None of this escaped Joe Remiro's notice:

"I never had any black friends until I went in the Army and got put in the infantry," he recalls. "I never had any Mexican friends until then either . . . I mean, just a few here and there, you know. But nothing that I could say, 'Well I've got *friends,*' you know. In the Army I realized that I had nothing to be ashamed of about being Mexican. In the Army I realized that trying to be white wasn't getting it, you know. I finally realized that not being white wasn't something to be embarrassed about. . . ."

The black troopers hated the Army more than the Viet Cong, and while they sat around smoking dynamite Nam shit the concept of becoming a revolutionary first entered the fringes of Remiro's consciousness. He began to look toward blacks for ideas and leadership.

"Dope provided us with our first point of unity," says Joe about this first period of reaching out to black and Chicano Americans. "And after that it just went on from there, you know. On the streets this kind of unity wasn't possible, but in Nam I found I loved the hell out of these people, man. And now I'm thrown in prison and who do you think I find here, man—you know, the same kind of brothers. . . ."

That word "brother" comes up a lot in Joe's conversation. So does the word "comrade." An almost blind loyalty to his friends and political associates has had a lot to do with Joe's history.

It doesn't take any deep psychological investigation to understand how this sense of intense loyalty, this very righteous kind of comradeship, grew to its present, somewhat exaggerated, place in Joe's head.

Ask any Namvet who went through tough combat assignments in a country where the vast majority of the population is considered the "enemy." He'll tell you that a war of this kind produces at least *one* positive result: you learn to completely trust and count on your buddies. (The word "comrade" was used by armies long before the Russian Revolution.) The degree to which Namvets built up that degree of brotherhood is almost scary.

When you talk to them about the war and other vets, you quickly get an unspoken message: "What do *you* know about it? You were a civilian. You weren't there."

Namvets feel a large degree of responsibility and guilt toward those buddies they saw die in battle. "Why wasn't it *me?*" they wonder. And then they swear that "I'm going to make sure they died for *something*." Many Namvets feel they must take positive actions against what created the war simply because they *survived*.

You get a strong feeling about the depth of Joe Remiro's intense sense of responsibility and comradeship as you flip through the hundreds of snapshots he sent home from Nam. Very few are of Joe himself, and only a handful show the countryside or the Vietnamese. The natives appear only occasionally.

Most of the pictures are of Joe's buddies. He shows them clustered around a recently opened grave, posing sweating and bare-chested with a gleaming white skull. Close-ups reveal the leg bones of the long-decayed corpse—little bits of flesh and rag cling loosely, and a trooper wrinkles his face and holds his nose in disgust.

There are photos of soldiers chugging down big bottles of whiskey. There's a fantastic series of an American stripper plying her tantalizing trade out under the hot Vietnamese sun while a mob of horny troops crowds around her. (An immense Buddha stares vacantly down upon this awkward bacchanal from the top of an adjoining hill.) There are shots of the whorehouses and tired, cynical little women perched precariously on some dirty khaki GI knee. There are portraits of evil-insect helicopters hanging over bombed-out jungles and of guns, guns, and more guns.

But mostly we see the buddies, the friends, the comrades who shared this fucking nightmare with Joe Remiro. He has them enshrined in fat, well-cared-for photo albums, and they are not just his past—you know they are alive in his mind.

The strongest emotional overtone you get from a careful examination of these pictures is that Vietnam soldiers developed group empathy that was considerably greater than anything you might see on the streets of America. Fighting and suffering through the war unified kids from different races and economic backgrounds as nothing else possibly could have.

They've got something important going between them, and they have created a kind of collective personality that is very strong shit.

The photos get fewer toward the end of the Tet Offensive. Joe has survived, but he's gone through hell and he's beginning to get angry.

He spends more and more time with his black buddies. When things get especially tough (he's a short-timer now and it would be stupid to get killed just before his tour is up) he sneaks in a quiet prayer or two to a God he no longer believes in. He makes an abortive attempt to assauge his growing sense of guilt in the traditional Catholic manner. For the first time since he was twelve years old, Remiro goes in to make a confession to the company chaplain:

"So I went to him and I said, 'It's the first one I've made in eight and a half years, man. That's how important it is to me.' And I started telling him about all those atrocities and all the shit that's goin' on and all the shit that's goin' through my head. After I finished, he said, 'Do you smoke marijuana?' And I says, 'Ya.' And he started givin' me a lecture about smoking marijuana and he said nothin' about all the killing and I walked out."

A few days later, they shipped Remiro home. He took his guilt with him.

5

"The New Left said, 'I protest!'
The Hippies said, 'I am!' "
—Jerry Rubin

ALTHOUGH JOE REMIRO would not be formally discharged from the Army until January 21, 1969, the remaining nine months of his three-year enlistment would be served at Fort Ord, California, in an experimental battalion. A lot of this time between April 22, 1968, when he showed up for duty at Ord, and the following January 21 would be spent on leave in nearby San Francisco, where the twenty-one-year-old GI would switch into civvies and—like any other young man his age—would head for where the action and the girls were. In San Francisco during 1967–68, this was still pretty much the Haight-Ashbury, which was both a geographic designation covering some thirty to forty square blocks and a neighborhood of the mind, the capital of an international youth culture which quickly began to transform the entire city. Two of its important outposts were the tastefully hallucinogenic Avalon Ballroom, at Van Ness and Sutter Street, and the somewhat grittier and more profit-oriented Fillmore West Ballroom (the old Carousel), a mile south down Van Ness at Market. Like thousands of other young men and women who got into the habit of calling *themselves* "hippies" simply because it seemed to fit if you were young and turned on, not because you had any idea of what it meant, Joe would soon be making a continual pilgrimage back and forth from those very special eight blocks of Haight Street where you found the heaviest action and the two outlying rock palaces. In the three and a half years following his return from Nam (he still calls them his "hippie years"), he would take a whack at every generational experience and experiment his peers were into, dropping acid at the Fillmore, becoming a Janis Joplin camp follower, hitchhiking up and down the Pacific coast, and crashing in any pad or commune where visiting strangers were welcome. He would sell underground newspapers on street corners for an extra buck or two, jump and jive to the heaviest rock of the time, and repeatedly stand up for peace (both as a member of the biggest marches ever seen in America and as an individual so concerned about the sacredness of life that he would neither kill a fly nor eat any form of meat). He would study a wide range of Eastern metaphysics, everything from the rather monotonous drone of the Hare Krishna cult to the somewhat more speculative suppositions of Paramhansa Yogananda.

Joe Remiro was searching. A young man searching and wandering, trying to find a new identity, trying to become something entirely different from all that he had originally been molded into by his parents, the Church, and the Army—something that he could honorably support and believe in, something to utterly submerge and replace the "American Way" whose total immorality he had decided to reject in Vietnam.

It is not so unusual a story. In fact, Remiro's odyssey could well be that of any of a million or so other kids who dropped out of the system in the late '60s to seek a more meaningful life, to recondition their heads, to learn the reality of fantasy and the fantasy of reality, to use pot and acid and sex and rock and an endless weekend of drifting, partying, reading, and thinking, to start their lives all over again. But crucial differences separated Remiro from the Flower Children. He was a trained killer. This would prove to be a bit of conditioning that could not be undone. And, unlike all too many of the late-arriving mob of young hedonists who were only on the scene for the immediate kicks, Remiro was dead serious about beginning again. He came back from Nam considerably older than his twenty-one years. He came back with strong feelings of brotherhood for the blacks and Chicanos he had fought beside and he did not ever get so stoned he forgot them. He came back with firsthand knowledge that political power *does* grow out of the barrel of a gun.

Like a lot of the hippies, Remiro tried for a while to retreat from the all too painful outside world by staying as stoned as possible. It was too ugly, too uncontrollable, too corrupt out there.

"You want to know what happened to the political awareness I had when I got back? It was submerged through dope," says Remiro.

What had happened to him in Nam had strongly altered a once very outgoing and carefree personality. His mother was appalled. "Her son went to war and a stranger came back," Joe recalls. He says that when he first got back he couldn't "talk to people that I knew or didn't know. I couldn't go out and meet new people. . . . I could not go outside my house without being completely drugged out of my head and talk to somebody. . . ."

What made communication the hardest for Remiro was the heavy load of memory and guilt he'd brought back with him from Nam. He'd killed a lot of innocent people in some horrible ways. Those Americans back home who believed that the atrocities were actually going on (mostly those who were active in the peace movement) were so antagonistic to the returned "trained killers" who had perpetrated the massacres that they wanted nothing to do with them. The great majority—like Joe's relatives—either did not believe such barbarism was possible or, if they suspected that it might be so, did everything they could to avoid talking about it.

Yet Remiro *had* to discuss it. He *had* to confess. He had to clear his conscience at least a little, work it out verbally, try to lift the awful mantle of repugnance and shame he felt toward himself. He turned in desperation to his father, hopped a ride out to the little row house on Seventh Avenue on the N-Judah streetcar and sat down with the short little old man to try and talk it out. As Joe describes what turned out to be one of the most traumatic experiences of his life:

"My father threw me out of the house. He told me he was in THE WAR and he never saw nothin' like that and I must be lyin'. Nobody believed me. And then My Lai comes out and everybody acts like it was an isolated incident, and it wasn't no isolated incident. . . ."

So Joe turned more and more to drugs, and when he made it down to Haight-Ashbury it was in a very stoned-out condition. But that was perfectly appropriate for the Haight, where, just as in Nam, the going medium of social exchange (and change) was drugs. He quickly found that grass was as common here as it had been among the grunts, but there was this *new* experience also to be tried, an experience he'd only heard of in Nam: acid—the great mind-bender, the visionary sacrament thousands of Americans now felt was THE catalyst for massive internal change, the drug Timothy Leary kept saying could do *anything,* could open up your mind and force you to reconsider every premise, every prejudice, every bit of useless baggage and bric-a-brac society had laid on you.

Joe says that when a buddy gave him this little white pill while they were sitting on the floor of the Fillmore Ballroom, he just could not believe there was enough there to do anything to him. "This tiny little pill," he still marvels. "Man, it wasn't *big* enough to fuck with *my* head. I'd just come back from smoking kilos of the best weed in Nam. And then my buddy splits this tiny pill in HALF and hands it to me. Man, I couldn't *believe* him. So I dropped it and I lay there on that floor and the whole world just made itself over in my head. Like, the band was the Iron Butterfly and they were playing 'Anna Godda Dovita.' Man, it was a trip and a *half*."

From that time until the end of his hippie period in mid-1971, Remiro remained a faithful member of the Acid Generation. He began to read the standard acid textbooks, the writings of Timothy Leary and the Tibetan Book of the Dead, for instance. He also got into the poetic novelist Richard Brautigan and read Tom Wolfe's *Electric Kool-Aid Acid Test* and came to admire one of its heroes (and a hero of the Beat Generation), Neal Cassady. Like many other members of the counterculture, he supported Leary for governor of California in 1969, before a well-engineered grass bust derailed the acid messiah's campaign. ("I used to think Timothy Leary was the Number-One Man," says Joe.)

By the time he was nearing the end of his hippie experience, Joe was dropping acid two or three times a week. ("It got so that being high was normal," he recalls. "I didn't know what to do when I came down, so I just dropped some more acid.")

As any drug veteran will freely tell you—that's *overdoing* it.

Since all of this activity and all but a few major incidents in the rest of Remiro's story occur in the San Francisco Bay Area (in the City and in Berkeley, for the most part), and since S.L.A. was decidedly a product of the radical community and the counterculture as it has developed there for the past decade, you need to understand both the culturally oriented Haight-Ashbury and superpolitical Berkeley to make any sense out of Remiro, S.L.A., the Foster killing, or the Hearst kidnapping.

S.L.A. was not some kind of freak outcropping, some totally illogical mutation bred of cultural isolation or political iconoclasm. It grew directly from the bedrock of shared experience that thousands of us went through in the Bay Area. Most of S.L.A.'s members arrived late on the scene, but a few shared the early Haight and Berkeley experiences with Joe and were products of this milieu.

Remember that Remiro's most noticeable characteristic is that he is a joiner, not a leader. From high school on, Joe was the cheerleader, the supporter, the rank-and-file backup man. He got home from Nam looking for a scene to join, and in San Francisco he most certainly *found* one.

What was the Haight like in 1968–70, when Joe hung out there? First let's talk about what it was *not*.

There is a large body of false legend and misimpression floating around today about Haight-Ashbury, a complete mythology. A lot of it is buried deep in the somewhat undifferentiating psyche of Joe Remiro.

A lot of these myths were created by the hippies themselves—most especially the final, killer wave of small-time hustlers and street gypsies who smothered a fascinating artistic and social experiment by the sheer weight of numbers and their itchy, adolescent lust and lethargy. The rest (and by far the greatest portion) of these slanders were the handiwork of a great glop of trendy media-lice who would infest the place for a day or two at a time during '67 and '68, dull hacks who quickly reduced a very complex and hopeful scene to a few blatant graphs of sensational copy, glorified touts who seldom took the time or had the love in them to understand what the counterculture was all about.

Despite what they wrote and what the latecomers (like Joe) misinterpreted, Haight-Ashbury was *not* just eight blocks of scabby teeny-bopper runaways panhandling tourists and overamping on bad drugs. It was *not* a stray harem of needle-dizzied chicks giving eternal head to a conga line of drunken Hell's Angels. It was *not* just a convention of amateur dope dealers whispering, "Speed? Lids? Acid? Bennies? Reds????" as you ambled down that manic thoroughfare between Masonic and Stanyan. This may be the way it ended. It may be the way *Life* and *Look* and *Playboy* painted the ugly, dying, decadent last days of its public suicide. But they missed a lot. There was an important experiment going on in the creation of an antimaterialistic and visionary community which these one-dimensional trend followers never let themselves see. They reported only the very *public* street scene, the carnival mob who had seldom heard of Haight-Ashbury's original residents and leaders—a brilliant generation of poets and visionaries and social reformers who spoke of peace and love in quiet and measured tones, people who had done the studying and thinking to back it up—a mature, cosmopolitan band of intensely dedicated creators who were seldom sought out by Time-Life's roving band of high-school hacks. Which was most unfortunate. Because if mass media had better understood the Haight experiment, they might not have been in such a hurry to kill it.

The Haight has always been a transitional area. Geographically it provides a break between the expanding central-city black ghetto on the northeast side of Twin Peaks and the white working-class and middle-class Avenues where Joe Remiro was raised. It starts on the northern slopes of the Peaks and then cascades down to that craftily replanted strip of sand dune known as Golden Gate Park. The nearby presence of the park lends the neighborhood a certain green, lush stillness and provides an almost wild retreat when city pressures prove too much to bear. The eastern end of the Haight is part of the ghetto, and its western extremity nudges up against the Inner Sunset, which is so dominated by St. Anne's Church.

In its early years, the parkside Haight had been a wealthy enclave of mansions that looked down on a long carriage promenade where the rich and fashionable came out to inspect each other in those raucous but elegant days before the 1906 earthquake.

By the time Remiro was born, in '46, the Haight had changed to a middle-class area much like the Inner Sunset, and then it served as a buffer between the Avenues and the Inner City, absorbing wave after wave of ethnic and racial minorities who came here from ghettoized separateness to find a polycultural interdependence and friendship. (Not a bad time to start using the word "symbiosis." Let's say it was a very "symbiotic" neighborhood.)

The Haight of the '50s and early '60s, with which Joe was familiar as he roamed the streets nearby while growing up, was proud of a strong melting-pot tradition. It had first absorbed and cheerfully integrated a wave of Russians and Eastern Europeans, a lot of them Jewish, who arrived in the '50s from their old Fillmore stomping ground, which was becoming entirely black. Then it had welcomed a really variegated population of Latinos, Samoans, Filipinos, and Orientals who came in the late '50s and early '60s. By the time Joe was ready to go to Nam in '66, the inevitable expansion of the next-door ghetto into the Haight was well under way and the neighborhood was about one-third black. There were pressures and strains clearly evident, but the Haight had a strong leadership of civil-rights activists and radicals who *believed* in integration—a lot of the old-timers were veterans of the great 1934 General Strike, which put labor in a position of power in San Francisco (the City's last two mayors have represented labor). Not many of them were still as radical as they had been in their youth—they had grown more cautious as they gained influence and age—but they still deeply believed in social justice.

So it was clearly an interesting mixture, a proving ground for everything Americans have always called "democracy." Now add to this a mid-'60s immigration of yet another highly outspoken minority, a band of *cultural* rebels who started to move out to the Haight from former bohemian and beat enclaves in North Beach and the central City, and you've got an even wilder combination. The first clear sign of their presence was the opening, in 1963, of the Blue Unicorn Coffee House on the neighborhood's northern periphery. Soon they would be opening a number of stores and coffeehouses on Haight Street itself, which then had a surplus of low-rental storefronts. The area would become home for hundreds of young artists, poets, existentialists, dreamers. Strong links developed between Haight-Ashbury and San Francisco State College, a few miles to the southwest, as many teachers and students from State moved in.

It would be inaccurate to categorize the Haight's new creative minority as "beats"—they were too eclectic for that. But the influence of the late '50s North Beach literary and artistic experiment was clearly evident. Allen Ginsberg remained the area's favorite poet, along with such longtime San Francisco greats as the cranky old anarchist Kenneth Rexroth, Robert Duncan, bookstore owner Lawrence Ferlinghetti, Gregory Corso, Philip Whalen, Gary Snyder, Kenneth Patchen, Michael McClure, and Lew Welch. Jack Kerouac had influenced many in terms of both writing and life style, and his hero, Cassady, would soon project *On the Road* in living acidcolor as he bopped about Haight-Ashbury in person. A strong interest in Eastern philosophy (growing among San Francisco writers since the pacifist-anarchist enclave of the '40s) was most evident, and there was a heavy emphasis on Zen and Tao. The philosopher Alan Watts was widely read here.

It was, in fact, a great hedonist picnic and religious revival called the "Human Be-In" led by many of these same cultural heroes in Golden Gate Park (January, 1967) which nudged Haight-Ashbury into international consciousness. Ginsberg, Leary, Snyder, McClure, Lenore Kandel, and half a dozen other beat and acid saints called together a new intentional community to provide a joyous antidote to the great gray pall of cynical conformity that was then smothering America and burning Vietnam alive. Some 25,000 celebrants joined them.

There were those who called this experiment a "revolution," but it was best described in cultural rather than political terms. Many of its members had tried political activism at one stage or another, and during the mid-'60s the majority took a hand in civil-rights and antiwar work—the pacifist influence of Gandhi and Martin Luther King was strong. But most preferred to get into politics one issue at a time and favored the ad hoc approach of organizing separate committees to handle each controversy rather than enfranchising standing organizations. They were profoundly skeptical about traditional "groups" and "leaders."

(One of the earliest street documents of the Haight warned: "Beware of leaders, heroes, organizers. Watch that stuff. Beware of structure-freaks. They do not understand. We know the system doesn't work because we're living in its ruins. We know that leaders don't work out because they have all led us only to the present. . . . Any man who wants to lead you is the Man. Think: Why would anyone want to lead me? Think: L.B.J. is our leader—and you know where that's at. . . . Watch out for the cats who want to play the system's games, 'cause you can't beat the System at its own games, and you know that. Why should we trade one Establishment for another? Fuck leaders.")

In this respect, the Haight community—as it had evolved by mid-1967—was profoundly different from the other main youth enclave of the Bay Area, the student-activist-led Berkeley scene, which gravitated toward organizing and demonstrating techniques inherited from socialist, Bolshevik, and early labor-movement days. Many Berkeley leaders—like Mario Savio—were veterans of marches, sit-ins and voter-registration drives in the Deep South, but Berkeley exuded much less interest in Dr. King's style of nonviolent confrontation and Leary's politics of ecstasy than in the present-day seizure of power—by any means necessary.

In the early days of Haight-Ashbury, people talked a lot about becoming *internally* free before you can become politically free. They talked about love and tried to live it out daily. They offered the cops who patrolled Haight Street handfuls of flowers rather than clenched fists, rocks, and broken pop bottles. The big argument in those tender and naive early days was not whether you should call them "pigs" but whether the term should be "cop" or "police officer." This kind of thinking seemed to work out before the enormous influx of mindless adolescents during the '67 "Summer of Love" completely changed things. As one Park Station cop put it, "The original hippies were good people, friendly people. They didn't cause no trouble. What's around now is just trash."

Those "original hippies" printed many of their early manifestoes and visions in a fantastically imaginative and colorful newspaper called the *Oracle*. Its first issue (September 9, 1966) contained this declaration of independence:

"When in the flow of human events it becomes necessary for the people to cease to recognize the obsolete social patterns which have isolated man from his consciousness and to create with the youthful energies of the world revolutionary community, the harmonious relations to which the two-billion-year-old life process entitles them, a decent respect for the opinions of mankind should declare the causes which impel them to this creation. . . . We hold these experiences to be self-evident —that all is equal, that the creation endows us with certain inalienable rights, that among them are: The freedom of body, the pursuit of joy, and the expansion of consciousness . . . and that to secure these rights, we the citizens of the earth declare our love and compassion for all conflicting hate-carrying men and women of the world. We declare the identity of flesh and consciousness. All reason must respect and protect this holy identity."

Poet Tuli Kupferberg put it this way:

"The world needs less specialists in force and murder and more generalists in love. . . . Who would want to coerce an individual eight hours a day when he could be walking in the woods, fucking, painting, making a useful and artistic object, growing beautiful food, making music, thinking, writing (even), talking to friends, helping cure the sick, watching movies, reading, teaching the beautiful young and, therefore, learning from the beautiful young. . . . Who wants to order anybody to do anything. . . . The best shun power—they want to play and to love—not to intimidate and to interfere and to control. . . . Love is the freedom of the beloved. . . ."

But in those days Tuli was mostly off in New York, where a similar scene was growing up in the East Village (a nice hip name for one of the rottenest old slums in the world). It was the living presence in San Francisco of a band of very clear, very strong-minded poets and visionaries that set the tone and style of the early Haight.

One of them was the beat-period veteran Lenore Kandel, who gave over her life in these days to handing out free food with the Diggers in the Golden Gate Park Panhandle and operating a free store where all the "merchandise" was given away. Her presence and her actions set the example. As she explained this sort of leaderless leadership which shaped the Haight:

"If you mean it, like, do it and say it plain. There's no room for mythical leadership. A leader is somebody who's doing it right now. Everyone becomes a leader for a moment and it has to be that way. . . ."

"One of the things I have to accept and deal with and carry around," says Lenore, "is teaching people that they're beautiful. I have to convince policemen and judges that they're beautiful creatures, beautiful human beings. I truly know that anyone who accepts the equal beauty and divinity of themselves and other human beings cannot willfully harm them. So I have to reach this kind of people.

"As soon as you say one way of life is the only way you become a fanatic and deliberately blind yourself to the infinite possibilities. I find it physically impossible to be a fanatic about anything. Religion, for instance. The Messiah is everyone. This time I think he has to be born in innumerable bodies—not just one—innumerable. . . . All this chaos, all this searching, all this seeking, all these kids running around the country would not occur if it were not that the established order is unsatisfactory and unfunctional. Finding a new way inevitably has a lot of chaos attached. But there are more and more very truthful people forced to the truth because their need is so desperate. The only way to the truth is to make yourself very clear—inside and out. What is your real desire, what do you want? What do you want to know? What do you want to happen? What is the world you desire? You must decide NOW."

Obviously, this kind of very personal, highly introspective and occasionally diffuse philosophy is not easily mass-marketed or translated into four or five neat and easily memorized slogans (unless you badly mangle it). It is not the kind of thing for traditional politics and movements. The fact that it ever appealed to such large numbers of discontented and rootless kids fleeing from the suburbs, educational "prisons," and the prospect of going to Nam to be ground up in a senseless and immoral war was something of a miracle—a miracle that did not last too very long, although the early hippie philosophy was given lip service and wove itself into thousands of easily influenced young minds (like that of Joe Remiro).

"I tried to be a pacifist for over three years," he recalls. "I didn't even eat eggs for over three years. I used to run around the house and throw out bees rather than kill them. . . . I went to all the peace demonstrations. . . . You know, you go away just tripping from all those moratoriums and you read in the paper the next morning that hundreds of thousands of people did it. . . . You feel great for a while and everybody falls in love, but they end up going back to kicking the dogs and beating the kids, you know. . . ."

Just as grass was the drug that turned Joe's head around in Nam, so it was acid that helped to bring him into a counterculture he barely understood. And it was acid that helped to take him out of it.

For if you want to understand Haight-Ashbury during these years, you must also understand the nature of LSD-25. If you want to perceive why it was that so many rather unimaginative young people so quickly accepted the form and the style (if not the content) of a visionary and ecstatic philosophy, you must understand that most of them were hallucinating while they did it. (Street acid went as low as fifty cents a tab in '67. And, in those days, you got 250 to 500 micrograms in a hit. That's good for a very intense, daylong trip—a trip many kids never returned from.)

Acid is a powerful and dangerous drug. In the right hands it is a useful one. In the hands of a Charlie Manson it is a mind-control agent that enforces absolute authority and a blind helter-skelter of orgiastic blood lust. In the hands of a skilled psychologist (as Tim Leary once was), or used by someone with empathy and strong humanistic concern, acid can save you a lot of wasted trips to your unfriendly neighborhood head shrink.

For all its apparent dangers, and despite the overblown praise and uninformed criticism acid has received, it still retains one amazing and useful quality. It is a great releaser of energy. Anyone who walked up and down Haight Street during the early days or went into one of the great rock halls (where nearly everyone was stoned) can tell you that there was an enormous feeling of *energy* in the air, an aura of unbounded possibility and impending miracle which helped to drive the Haight to messianic self-destruct.

Acid provides instant phone booth for your average meek, mild Clark Kent who has been studiously groping for years in a search for that glorious moment of Superman buried deep within his dull and meaningless life. Acid can make you quickly see your hang-ups, the sick little games and evasions you throw between yourself and the truth. It can also give you a quick and fascinating glimpse of the talent and energy that lie within you, just beneath the surface, waiting to be used and expanded upon once you find the key of direct communication with yourself. It makes you believe that you are much *more* than you had ever hoped to be.

Under good circumstances and if properly used.

But taken with a mob of roaring, nearly incoherent punk kids out for the *wildest* time of their lives, it can lead to a cosmic drunk and a lifelong hangover.

In the beginning of the Haight-Ashbury experience, acid watered a communal, flowery, cosmic hallucination that radiated love in all directions. In the end, it poisoned even the most casual day-to-day circumstances of life.

Too many celebrants began to trust only their hallucinations, their jaded instincts, instant flashes of half-baked intuition. Logic was abandoned and study was frowned upon. History was jettisoned as an unnecessary encumbrance to a "good trip." As one New York *Times* writer summed it up in mid-1968, "Hippies will believe in almost anything that fails the test of reason. . . ."

This was the sort of atmosphere that would in the end produce the manic mob mentality of Joe Remiro, who spent most of his time playing hippie while on extended leaves and then had to check back into Fort Ord to playact at being a soldier from May of '68 to January, '69.

He was proving to be one big, fat problem to his superiors. Although Remiro was willing to take a totally unnecessary "clerk" course while a member of the 4th Combat Support Training Brigade in May of '68, there was little else they could get him to do.

"At Fort Ord I refused to do anything," says Joe. "I said that I felt that painting a latrine wall, you know, would contribute to the killing and murdering that I knew for a fact was going on. . . . They sent me to a chaplain; before the psychiatrist, they sent me to the chaplain. That was after they brought me in with all the officers and they tried to fuck with me. They pulled out a Bible and tried to show me through the Bible that war's OK and shit, you know. But I blew that away real easy. And then they sent me to the Catholic chaplain and I told him my feelings and he said that he respected my moral feelings, my moral convictions. But he said that what I should do is what the Army tells me to do and then, once I get out of the Army, I can ask God for forgiveness. . . ."

This did little to enlarge Joe's already flagging respect for Army chaplains.

"You know," he recalls, "when you first get in the Army, they say, 'Don't call me sir.' They're all officers. . . . 'Don't call me sir. Don't salute me. Call me Father.' I saluted *them*. You know, that's when I used to think there was some credence in the Catholic Church or in mysticism. . . ."

Outside of giving the Army a hard time during his last enforced months of service, and spending the majority of his leave time learning to be a hippie, Remiro also resumed a romance he'd partially started in the sixth grade at St. Anne's Parochial School, where he'd met pretty little Kathy Exley.

Kathy—then nineteen, two years younger than Joe—had idolized him ever since they'd met, and Remiro (having a hard time now relating to *anyone* he did not know) took the easy way out and married Kathy in 1970.

They tried settling down at first in the little town of Pacific Grove, which lies just outside Monterey and within spitting distance of Fort Ord. The marriage was short and stormy—a typical botched attempt by a freaked-out Namvet to calm down after getting back. As Joe explains it:

"Well, listen, if you look at veterans coming back from Vietnam, ninety-one percent of them get married as soon as they get back and divorced within a year. And there's one person I can talk to in the whole world and so I married her. But we're in two different worlds, you know. I mean, she was a fantastic woman but I couldn't talk to anybody else . . ."

While he was living in Pacific Grove, Remiro decided it was time to do more than *talk* about how much he hated the Vietnam war. He took the first steps into political activism.

"I got into nonviolent protest," he says. "I wrote 'Resist the Draft' on the back of my station wagon and the whole block of this conservative little town wrote a petition to have me thrown off the block. . . . I drove through my old company formation with my station wagon with what I'd written on it. I went to all the moratoriums. And that day when they had all the military shit at Fort Ord and they had the big demonstration out in front of the gates, I was there. . . ."

He attends all the big peace marches in San Francisco. They generally begin downtown and proceed a long, weary, uphill eight miles to the Polo Field in Golden Gate Park, where the usual predictable speeches are heard. Like thousands of others who joined in the great "moratorium" demonstrations of 1969 and '70, Remiro is still of the opinion that the issue of "peace" can be separated from other political considerations. He is willing to march and chant and carry picket signs three-quarters of the way across the San Francisco peninsula, and he wants to be physically present to add his energy and vibrations to the enormous, full-blooded spirit of the greatest marches ever seen in the American West, but he gets irritated when black and Chicano speakers seize the platform and start to talk about racism and economic exploitation.

The march of November 15, 1969, in which more than 300,000 people participated, was a classic example of this kind of situation—an enormous popular upsurge of anger and resentment against the war focused on only one issue—getting our troops out.

By the time Joe makes it back to the Polo Field for the second great moratorium march (in 1970), he is married. When he gets home he's feeling good and lights up a joint or two and dreams of a peaceful world just ahead. Kathy is in a good mood, too. But it doesn't last. The marriage is going badly. Separations get long and painful, and Joe spends the latter part of his "hippie years" crashing in pads away from his wife. He occasionally stays with his parents or goes over to sleep at his cousin Barbara's house. He gets into more dangerous and unpredictable drugs. Barbara recalls the sad details of Joe's deteriorating marriage. She says that on one occasion, after the couple had moved into the City, Joe walked barefoot and crying from his apartment on the other side of town all the way out to the Avenues to tell her about the latest marital mix-up.

His very Italian mother gets into it and helps to finish things off. Joe leaves Kathy for keeps a few months after his son, Joshua, is born.

"I'm divorced now," says Joe. "I don't know how long I was married 'cause it sort of went off and on, you know. It was really a shaky thing . . . most of the time I was submerged through dope that I had bought off my GI benefits. . . . You know, over seventy-five percent of the veterans are doing that. And that's what the government wants. It gives them more benefits to keep them more opiated and keep 'em out of the fucking mainstream of politics and the working class—keep 'em away from the conscious elements in our society—and it works, you know."

Joe tries to settle down to a job driving a cab—he gets his permit on February 24, 1970. Although he's long been aware that the intellectual game is not really for him, driving around town makes him thoughtful, and he takes a crack at writing.

"I wrote a little short story once about a little incident that happened when I was a kid," he says. "I wrote a lot of poems, you know. I used to drive a Yellow Cab in the City and I used to sit in the Yellow Cab and write poetry and shit . . . I'm not a poet, man. I'm not a poet and I know it."

It is also in 1970 that Joe suffers his first political arrest. While marching on April 15 in a New Mobilization peace demonstration through San Francisco's downtown financial district, he is arrested by a God-fearing, patriotic cop who objects to the fact that Remiro has sewn a small American flag to the seat of his pants.

He is charged with "defiling the flag." Six weeks later a bored and slightly amused judge hands down a suspended thirty-day sentence, and that's that. But this bust is probably the first clear indication that Remiro is moving away from peaceful protest *within* the system and toward all-out confrontation. He is far from alone in this. The times they *are* a-changin' and things are definitely coming to a head in America. Two weeks after Joe is busted for abusing the flag, hundreds of thousands of Americans will be demonstrating against Nixon's invasion of Cambodia. A few days later, four young students are gunned down by the National

Guard at Kent State University in a massacre that entirely changes the make-up and mood of the movement.

The fact that things are shifting from nonviolence to revolution should have been no surprise to those who have followed the developments in the movement and the counterculture over the preceding two years, as countless young men like Remiro have been making it on through their "hippie years" transition and getting serious again.

Joe has been to a lot of peace rallies. He's getting frustrated, he says, because "hundreds of thousands of people all over the country demonstrate and the President says he's not going to let demonstrations affect his decisions. . . ."

The April 15 protest at which Remiro is busted is a good example of the sharpening division between pacifists and revolutionaries. It is part of a wide range of antiwar activities loosely coordinated by the New Mobilization Committee (the "New Mobe") all around the Bay Area. The mood is tense and, in Berkeley, full-scale fighting breaks out as angry demonstrators rage around the university and are attacked by club-swinging sheriff's deputies.

In San Francisco, pacifists barely keep control as Father James Groppi urges the crowd to stop the rally and "go out and tie up traffic in the streets." Berkeley radical Tom Hayden walks up to the microphone and has only one thing to say before he stalks off: "The only response to Nixon's total war is total revolution." Members of the crowd begin to chant, "Pick up the gun. . . . Start a Revolution. . . . Let's take it to the streets. . . ."

San Francisco's frighteningly tall Tactical Squad, which is heavily armed and generally carries three-foot-long staffs instead of the usual billy clubs, is everywhere. One of them makes the Remiro bust as Joe marches down Montgomery ("The Wall Street of the West") after a rally held at the Pacific Stock Exchange. The cop—an Irishman, naturally—is named Sheehan.

The trip to jail is a humiliating one, and Joe is pushed around and cursed on the way. He makes the mistake of identifying himself as a Vietnam veteran—that just makes the cops madder.

There are several reasons why this bust is a mind-bender. For two years now, Joe has been trying to work out in a peaceful way the load of trauma and guilt and massive insight he picked up in Vietnam. He's tried to reconstruct his life in a fashion that would allow him to love and groove and keep his sanity—to have friends, enjoy a good time, get married, raise a kid, make the occasional peace march to show he still *cared* about a war that had so horribly screwed up his head. Yet he has not confronted the system head-on. Like a lot of the rest of us, he has tried to "do his thing" off in a corner with his stoned-out buddies, tried to work it out with dope and mysticism and vegetarianism and perfunctory peace-marching.

But the April 15, 1970, bust must have shaken his faith in these tactics and made him wonder, as he put it so succinctly: "Well, fuck, man! How much longer can I deal with this?"

His rapidly deteriorating marriage doesn't help things any. "Every time Kathy would get some sort of home going, Joe would have a bunch of his hippie friends move in," says Barbara Lockwood. "They'd just get settled down—they tried to live in a couple places in San Francisco—then they'd break up again. And Joe's family kept getting involved in the hassle. That didn't help either. He was really upset about it—all the time."

Kathy may have thought that having a child would stabilize Joe (then most appropriately driving a diaper truck) and get him to settle down to the business of raising a family. But she guessed wrong—it just set him off. It was the birth of Joshua, in fact, that proved to be the real turning point for Joe Remiro. As he puts it:

"I've already told you what a stone pacifist I tried to be. I used to try to convince myself that if my life was at stake, I would rather die than harm another human being. It might have worked out, but on June 25, 1971, at exactly seven-twenty p.m., I became a militant and helped my wife—as much as possible—give birth to our son.

"I had to ask myself some questions. Yes, I would defend his life to any extent and by any means. . . . Then you go from that to expand your morality to more than just your own family and just your own personal self and expand it to all the people in Angola and to the people in Vietnam and Cambodia . . . you know, the people in India, the Palestinians, the Irish people who are getting murdered regularly. You know, through the actual actions of this country's military or through the funding we give other armies. What would you be . . . would you be a pacifist if you were a Vietnamese living in South Vietnam?"

Despite this rather dramatic explanation, the truth of the matter is probably that Joe has been rethinking a lot of things in the months since his April 15 bust. It isn't just the totally unsettled nature of his personal life that's getting to him—it's the times. It's Cambodia and Kent State. It's Nixon and increasing repression. The '60s had been full of rebellion—but full of hope. Things felt like they were going to *change,* and it wasn't going to take a revolution to do it.

But the Nixon administration and the forces of repression assassinated those expectations in the early '70s, and a curtain of doubt and fear slowly closed off the fruitful vision of an entire reform-minded generation. A rumble of angry and violent frustration began to drown out the sweet-voiced song of peace and reason that had so enchanted Remiro and hundreds of thousands of other young people in the late '60s. Repression breeds resistance. In the 1969 National Violence Commission Report the situation was accurately summed up:

"Little by little, we move toward an armed society which, while not clearly totalitarian, can no longer be said to rest upon the consent of the governed. . . ."

Mantra-chanting poets and acid saints are totally out as heroes by mid-'71. The new heroes are revolutionists like the bad-ass Black Panthers. Months before Joshua is born, Remiro has read *Soul on Ice* by Panther leader Eldridge Cleaver, and he is mightily impressed. He's long been searching for someone to look up to and imitate.

"Eldridge laid it out clear, man," Remiro explains. "He says white kids don't have anyone to look up to. . . . Who—George Washington? Thomas Jefferson? He names all these supposedly heroes, man. He says the white youth, you know, knows too much now. They're not going to look up to slaveholders and racists. They don't want no dogs as heroes, man. . . ."

This kind of thinking is getting him good and ready for the next logical stopping-off place in his troubled life—Berkeley. And Berkeley has always been a totally different world from San Francisco.

"One day I stopped over in Berkeley, man, and all of a sudden I met some political people," recalls Joe. "They started explaining things that I had never had the answer for. Before that I used to really believe that if I could sit down and talk to Nixon and explain to him what was really happening that I could straighten everything out. I really believed that, you know. I didn't realize that the man is very conscious of what he's doing, you know, and that he's very conscious of the system he is part of and the politics he is part of and the oppression he is part of. . . ."

A few months after Joshua is born, Joe leaves Kathy for good. Within six months he will be a true militant.

6

*"After a decade of struggle, we have a deeper sense
of the place Berkeley. It is not just a place we pass through,
enjoying the city's charms in a first flirtatious affair. It is a place
to stay, to live, to struggle. We are learning how local struggle
can take on international significance. . . ."*
—Tom Hayden, 1969

JOE REMIRO'S TORTURED SEARCH for a new identity and purpose shifts from San Francisco across a sunken coastal valley filled with slowly swirling tides of salt-flavored sewage. He is soon spending most of his time across the Bay in Berkeley and in those portions of next-door Oakland favored by activists, militants, and revolutionaries. The area is a unique breeding ground for new ideas, causes, movements, and energies, which first pop up in this wildly mixed multicity centered around a great university, an anarchistic youth ghetto and dreary miles of black and Chicano slums.

S.L.A. understood the East Bay's importance and summed it up quite well in their first communiqué:

"The Black, Chicano and conscious white youth in our communities recognizes the importance of the Oakland-Berkeley area to the liberation struggle of all oppressed peoples. We know that the ruling class must seek to stop the revolutionary community here before the ruling class can regain its arm of control around the struggling and oppressed peoples of the world. . . ."

A bit rhetorical, but a clear indication that S.L.A. realized that the East Bay has long been in ferment and that it is an ideal place to initiate rebellion.

As for Berkeley itself, you've got to consider it from both the conventional point of view—lay of the land, population, percentage of students, styles of architecture, social history, and so on—and in relation to its role as sparkplug, seedbed, maternity ward for the American

[65]

student movement. Since the fall of 1964, when Mario Savio led the Free Speech Movement into Sproul Hall for the first big campus sit-in and massive bust (the true beginning of a decade of student revolt), Berkeley has set the pace for organized rebellion all across the country. It has been a rather predictable reactive agent—that is, Berkeley activists do not dream up their causes out of thin air. They respond—usually first and loudest, to be sure, but only because they speak more directly about what's on everyone's mind, not because they exist apart from what troubles the rest of us.

They react quickly and strongly to the major issues of their time—the Vietnam war, segregation, debasement of women, insane foreign adventures, our stultifying educational system, the repression of free speech on campus, the need for a social system that better fosters full political and personal growth. If there's an orphan cause floating around in need of a home, you can count on Berkeley to adopt it. The pattern is predictable, idealistic, incredibly *earnest* in its wide-eyed belief that something can always be DONE to remedy each new social affliction the nation contracts.

As the National Commission on Violence put it, Berkeley protesters are in the habit of "reacting to events rather than inciting them. The movement has been and remains in the posture of responding to events outside its control; the chief milestones in its growth have been its days of mass outrage at escalations, bombing resumptions, draft policies and prosecutions. . . ."

Action. Reaction. In a way many radicals have never gotten around to acknowledging, the pattern has been profoundly (pardon the dirty word) *reactionary*.

Anyone who first knew Berkeley in those rather effete, ivy-clad days before the Free Speech Movement and then happened to miss out on the intervening ten years of utter commitment, outrage, struggle, and anarchistic celebration would have one hell of a time recognizing the place today.

Certain things have not changed. Berkeley's sophisticated, cosmopolitan faculty has always been a bit bizarre. Back in the first few years of the '60s it used to be said in academic circles that you went over to Berkeley to "beat your friends hello."

The English-teaching hostess at one memorable 1962 Berkeley soiree arrived late after a prolonged S-&-M break down in the sound-proofed basement, where her archaeology-teaching husband donned a long black cape and a satin Halloween mask (nothing else), tied her to an expensive green felt rocking horse, and proceeded to redden her ecstatic backside with a custom-made cat-o'-nine-tails. When she finally got upstairs she found the neighborhood transvestite (a botanist) decked out in basic black and pearls and deep in conversation with a Nazi physicist, who explained away his job at the University of California's deadly Lawrence Radiation Laboratory developing new and more potent hydrogen bombs as simply a means of finishing up the racial purification the last war had so rudely interrupted—it also allowed him to send his three little blonde daughters to the private finishing school of their choice.

While a bored and decadent faculty played out these quaint little parlor games, Berkeley undergraduates were beginning to find ideas and causes with a bit more merit. (Things were not all work and rhetoric at UC—pot was as popular as booze in '63, and dropping acid no longer meant a mess on the chem-lab floor.) But the average student was sincere and dedicated. A strong feeling of commitment born out of the energetic early Kennedy years still hung over this campus.

Hundreds of Berkeley students had recently returned from Peace Corps assignments all over the world, and they came home with an international vision and an unexpected degree of self-reliance. Other undergrads spent the summers of '63 and '64 in the Deep South registering black voters and marching on places like Montgomery and Selma behind Martin Luther King and Ralph Abernathy. They had strong ideals. They believed in massive social change, but, as long as John Kennedy lived, they seemed willing to keep their revolution well within the system.

Kennedy was assassinated in Dallas on November 22, 1963, and in a little more than a year, Savio was leading FSM into Sproul Hall. From then on Berkeley was to be the storm center and main launching pad for all that passed under the heading of "campus revolt" in America.

Before that momentous uprising, the city of Berkeley (113,805 citizens in 1960 and about a quarter of them students) did not differ greatly from any other big American college town. (Except that it was located in California, and everyone *knows* that things are just a whole lot weirder out there.)

Most of Berkeley is built on a slowly rising plain that climbs some three miles from the eastern shore of the Bay to a nearly mountainous range of hills that cuts off the East Bay communities from the dry inland valleys like some enormous Chinese Wall. The campus of the University of California lies just below the first sharp rise of the Berkeley Hills and it is the obvious hub of the entire community.

Its 307-foot-high bell tower is the landmark by which you judge all distances in this part of the world. The educational facility is the town's number-one business, and a vast physical plant has long featured the big, old Hearst Gymnasium, named after Patricia Hearst's great-grandmother Phoebe Apperson Hearst. The Hearsts heavily endowed the university and paid for most of a mining building and a Greek theater as well. There are plaques and memorials to the famous family all across campus.

But, despite the old lady's self-congratulatory largess, the name Hearst has been an unpopular one during the last two decades in Berkeley. Hearst's San Francisco *Examiner,* now a toned-down afternoon shopper greatly admired by race-track oddsmakers and bored housewives in search of a new hamburger recipe, was for many years *the* newspaper in Northern California. And it threw its mastodon bulk behind every know-nothing, redbaiting witch hunt that came along— making it the Big Bad Wolf to a rapidly developing Berkeley left.

Bank robberies and juicy sex murders were its headline stock in trade, and tired patriotism waved like a cloying and deadly shroud across every antique page. The paper was a grim joke to students and faculty alike, and bright young reporters who had the misfortune to represent the "Monarch of the Dailies" in enlightened Berkeley generally stayed drunk as much as possible and kept their identities a closely guarded secret.

Nor was the situation much improved between 1956 and 1974, when Patricia's mother, Catherine Hearst, served out her first appointive term as a regent of the university. The voting record of this devoutly Catholic Deep South Lady of the Old School was absolutely incredible. She faced down even the mildest liberal innovations with the ferocity of Savonarola challenging the heretics. If she had only had the power, Catherine Hearst would gladly have publicly excommunicated Mario Savio, Tom Hayden, Jerry Rubin, Rennie Davis, Dan Siegel, Angela Davis, or any other reformer who troubled her intellectual slumber. The feeling of red-eyed suspicion and downright hatred was quite mutual.

Those residential areas of Berkeley that surround the sprawling UC campus are clearly segregated according to age and income. The hills behind campus are for faculty, San Francisco commuters, and the town's more successful merchants. The North Campus, just above University Avenue (and adjacent to Hearst Avenue—another tip of the civic hat to Phoebe), is also attractive to faculty, well-padded grad students, and undergraduates with generous parents.

It is the South Campus, lying between the university and the Oakland border, with Telegraph Avenue as its main artery, that has always been the joker in the Berkeley deck. Although Tele (or "the Ave," as it is now universally called) was a respectable, student-oriented business street strong on book, clothing, and furniture stores before FSM, it had always harbored a few mild little wine and beer bars, the only nearby hangouts for campus hell-raisers back in the days when a "Big Night Out" meant chugalugging a pitcher or two of draft over on Tele and then staggering home to the frat house singing football pep songs at the top of your squeaky, adolescent voice.

But all that has changed in the past ten years. The Ave is now very definitely where *the* action is, at least the youth-dominated four-block zone between Bancroft (adjacent to campus) and Haste (where Tele widens by two lanes and charges toward Oakland). For the last few years, the core of activity has been in "the Block," that short section between Dwight and Haste which became a liberated zone about 1968.

Today Tele is the last big "hippie" (read that *street youth*) scene left in America. Its narrow sidewalks are always clogged with hundreds of lounging, doped-out drifters, radicals passing out the latest broadsides and proclamations, gawking tourists, students hurrying to class, and a whole fascinating bazaar of craftsmen who sell bangles, beads, belt buckles, ceramics, stained glass, and other bright and innovative handmades right on the pavement. At the Bancroft end there is a No Man's Land of wide sidewalk between the street and Sather Gate, and here you find a dozen or so bright and wholesome gypsy food-carts dispensing hot pretzels, Chinese snacks, vegetarian specialties, and orange juice squeezed on the spot.

The university and its adjacent and dependent areas are not, of course, the whole town. As has become clearly evident since Berkeley elected a black mayor and several black councilmen, there is a large and outspoken ghetto in this college-centered time-warp which the Chamber of Commerce once called the "Athens of the West" but which more up-to-date residents now refer to as the "Moscow of the West."

Berkeley's flatland ghetto is large and nearly encloses the university-dominated areas. It covers all of the land from the freeway-andfreightyard-festooned shore of the Bay east to within about a mile of campus. It also stretches along both sides of the strangely vacant San Pablo Avenue, which echoes all the way into Oakland like some abandoned 1930s movie lot waiting for a retake of *Greed.*

The Berkeley-Oakland black ghetto is the oldest and angriest in the West. It was here that the Black Panther party was formed and its presence has lent a certain realistic cold fury to the Berkeley radical movement.

But none of these energies had homogenized before 1964, and old-timers who were familiar with this scene in those quaint and mostly apolitical days of the '50s and early '60s will tell you that Berkeley was one more "normal" college town where the annual springtime panty raid was just about the wildest demonstration the cops could expect to cope with.

From Berkeley it was straight off the educational assembly line to some "junior executive" job at a boring but well-established corporation, a new car on the installment plan to make the long commute each night out to the suburbs, where a nagging wife had you sour and ulcerated by the time the kids were big enough to hate you. Typical, American, and sterile.

What changed it all?

Utter boredom with this bad excuse for an education. Deep concern for civil rights (or rather the lack of them). The endless, grotesque Vietnam war. The assassination of John Kennedy. A lot of good dope. Everything that bothered the rest of America—but the suckers were afraid to go out and raise hell about it.

A talented writer named Richard Goldstein cruised into the Bay Area in '67, took a careful look at the life styles in Berkeley and Haight-Ashbury, and summed up the difference.

"In 1963," he wrote in the Los Angeles *Times,* "the culture definer was a committed student. Central to his ethic was a socially directed idealism, coupled with a reformer's zeal. This commitment presupposed a potential for good within the existing system.

"Such identification with the establishment was no accident. The vision of the early '60s was very much a product of the Kennedy years. The unprecedented activism that swept the university community during that administration was infectious; the New Frontier had supplanted the beat generation. . . ."

Goldstein went on to say that the students felt betrayed by Kennedy's murder and a lot of them dropped out to become hippies after

Lyndon Johnson came on the scene like some east-of-the-Pecos Ivan the Terrible who forced an entire generation of young men to fight an immoral war and who suppressed all style, all aspiration, all the Camelot bullshit Kennedy had captured our imaginations with.

His thesis seemed to be that "youth ghettos" like Haight-Ashbury were no more than dumping grounds for these once-idealistic students who had been disillusioned by the Great Society. If LBJ could only be vaporized, then everyone could go back to being busted in Mississippi and teaching headhunters in Borneo how to use safety razors, and the Kennedy dream would enshroud us once again.

Not quite that simple.

But he had the first part of it right—the hippie experiment was apolitical at first (although it quickly toughened in the face of intense police harassment, bad drugs, and imported juvenile delinquency). To-day's Haight-Ashbury residents—the ones tough enough to stick out the bad years—speak pretty much the same kind of political language you hear in Berkeley, and the clenched fist long ago replaced the V sign as a generational salutation.

But it ain't true that some sort of invisible cultural wall stood midway across San Francisco Bay, separating the Haight-Ashbury and Berkeley cultures. There was a great deal of interchange, but the styles and goals developed in very different manners. Everyone smoked dope. Clothing and general life styles were often indistinguishable. But on the east side of the Bay people still read books and took politics seri-ously. Those who were students had to keep their drug-crazed brains clear enough to pass a test now and then. It never *did* become unfash-ionable to read newspapers and care about what was happening to the rest of the world. Berkeley was passionately in love with the *future*.

The differences are also geographically evident. Berkeley is firmly attached to the rest of the American continent. San Francisco—although located on the tip of a peninsula and surrounded on only three sides by water—is very much an *island* of the mind. San Francisco has only lately begun to leave the nineteenth century, and it would much rather go back in time than toward a plastic and unpredictable future.

Another factor that gave Berkeley a flavor and style of its own was the development of a whole new youth-ghetto class, which would have an increasing amount to say about how and when to demonstrate —the *non*student who was on hand for the scene rather than for a "formal" education. Defining the "nonstudent" is not simple—he comes in all shapes and sizes, but it's safe to say he's generally a person of more or less college age who may or may not have taken classes on a regular basis at some time in the past. But now he is definitely *not* enrolled in school and yet he is still a member of the college community and lives on its periphery. (In Berkeley, mostly in South Campus.)

He is a person who may "audit" a number of classes—the ones he wants, and for free. He may use the university library and other student facilities, may go to concerts and lectures and enjoy most of the real benefits of being in the highly charged intellectual atmosphere of a great university. Yet he decides for *himself* just how much prefabricated culture he wants to absorb. He may finally give up on attending all the classes and cultural events, and yet he still hangs out on nearby streets like the Ave. He knows a lot of "genuine" students. He participates fully (and often violently) in political events. He may look a lot like a Haight-Ashbury-style hippie, but he's generally tougher—and a hell of a lot more political.

One of these Berkeleyites wrote the following little salute to the dying pipe dream of the Haight in the fall of '68, about the same time the people of the San Francisco community were trying to publicly bury the media-created stillbirth image of "hippie" and declare themselves "Free Men" instead. His poem, tacked up on an anonymous Telegraph Avenue bulletin board and signed with the pseudonym "Ares," was titled "For Those Pacifist Poets," and it went this way:

"ruling guru greybeard bards / having new fun in yr. rolling rock renaissance / have you passed thru the Haight / have you seen yr. turned-on kids? / u promised them Visions & Love & Sharing / clap, hepatitis, fleas, begging and the gang bang / sure, you didn't want to see the scene go that way / but that's how the shit went down / & i do not hear yr howl. / i do not hear exorcising demons. / u told the congress that yr. acid / had taught us how to love / even that blood-soaked thieving swine of a cowboy / the Others call their president. / is there nothing left over for the kids / sleeping on the sidewalks / waiting to be carried off by the bikers / of yr. children's crusade? / yr. disciples are dying in the streets, gurus, / u have been among the philistines too long / u have become their Spectacle. / heal the sores upon thine own bodies, prophets / yr. word has brought them as far as the Haight / can you not carry them to the seashore? / or is it your power and not theirs which has failed? / can it be we warrior poets were right all along? / can it be all the buddhas r hollow & like the Dalai Lama / u have been sipping butter tea upon a peacock throne / as Tibetans perished in the snow? / is it not time to admit that Hate as well as love redeems the world / there is no outside w/out inside / no revolution w/out blood."

Clearly the word "revolution" was not pronounced in Berkeley as it was in the Haight—with the term "cultural" neatly preceding it (and a subconscious prayer mumbled in the background that all those ancient overtones of massive political murder would just go away and stop bothering us). In Berkeley, pragmatists like Mao Tse-tung and Che Guevara were infinitely more popular than wordy dreamers like Tim Leary and Allen Ginsberg.

All of which meant that, in its fascinatingly *reactionary* fashion, you could always count on Berkeley to DO something every time that LBJ or Nixon or the governor of California (His Excellency, the Honorable Ronald McDonald) or some local politico or police chief got out of hand and pushed the citizens to the brink. And when an uprising started in Berkeley, it had a tendency to spread—seldom taking more than a month or two to work its way across the country.

And that's why even the most cautious observers were troubled when the S.L.A. developed in Berkeley.

Joe Remiro and a dozen other East Bay radicals had the temerity to make a formal Declaration of War against the world's mightiest military power while living in the Berkeley-Oakland area in 1973. Had this happened in Peoria or West Podunk, you'd not only have figured they were out of their fucking skulls, you'd have put down the newspaper and gone back to watching Matt Dillon clomping into Miss Kitty's saloon and have forgotten the whole thing before he shot down his first cowboy. But when such an unexpected and outrageous act happens in *Berkeley,* you turn off the TV and read down to the last paragraph.

So much has happened there. So much has changed. And so many people have been profoundly affected.

It was only ten years ago that short-haired, clean-shaven Mario Savio led his revolt on this campus. If Savio could have crystal-balled a look ahead into today's Berkeley and seen the results of his movement, he would have freaked. An entirely new culture was born.

And yet, while it was gestating, the whole thing seemed so natural, so organic. It was just a logical *reaction* to what was happening in the outside world. Things seemed so simple at first. All Savio wanted was the right to set up a few card tables on campus and to slightly improve the quality of higher education. That accomplished, the remnants of

FSM turned their attention to the escalating Vietnam war and used their new "free speech" rights on the UC campus to conduct the first antiwar "teach-ins" of 1965–66.

Troop trains were carrying soldiers right through Berkeley on their way to the Oakland Sixth Army Depot, so the most logical and natural thing was to go down and throw your bodies across the tracks. When that didn't work, it seemed logical to get closer to the contamination itself and march on the Sixth Army embarkation point. Enormous crowds got to the Oakland border before confrontations and arrests occurred. (The Hell's Angels sided with the military. Allen Ginsberg thought they could be recruited, but all they did was take over the acid business instead.)

By October of '67, the peace movement in the East was a snarling adolescent monster quite capable of staging an all-out assault on the Pentagon with little West Coast help, so Berkeley retaliated by staging an extended "Stop the Draft Week" at the Oakland Induction Center, where hundreds of activists—including Joan Baez—were busted for trying to tie up the business of war-as-usual.

Tom Hayden would later say that this was the beginning of "fighting in the streets or, in the rhetoric of the time, it moved us from 'dissent to resistance.' " Concern about the war made Berkeley activists realize that Vietnam was only part of a larger international pattern, and new demonstrations demanded that we get "Out of Korea" and "Out of the Philippines." (Then "Out of Mozambique," "Out of Angola," "Out of West Orange, New Jersey.")

Demonstrating became a way of life, and new causes developed each day. Soon it was *"Viva La Huelga"* in support of the union organizing farm workers. The Black Panther party became the leading edge of armed revolt, and it was "Free Huey" and "Free Eldridge," "Free Erika" and "Free the Panther 21." "Free EVERYBODY!"

By 1968, Berkeley was so in the habit of protest that a week seldom went by without a demonstration of some kind. It was one hell of a good year for it.

Nineteen-sixty-eight was the year the Viet Cong launched not just one but *two* Tet Offensives. (Joe Remiro fought through the first and managed to miss the second.) It was the year LBJ fully unleashed the dictatorial war powers he had extracted from a spineless Congress, the year Lyndon decided he'd never win an election in the fall and so pulled out and left the field open for one Richard Nixon, whose only real competition was Robert Kennedy (canceled out with a bullet in the head that spring). It was the year Martin Luther King was murdered in Memphis and riots followed in a dozen cities, with 46 people killed, 2,600 injured, and 21,000 arrested. It was the year the poor marched on Washington, constructed Resurrection City, and were promptly evicted—like everywhere else in America.

With Kennedy and King dead, Nixon was a shoo-in for President, and all-out political repression assembled in the wings. Sixty-eight was the year they bombed hell out of Hanoi and Haiphong and even brought the world's last live battleship out of mothballs for a bit of gunnery practice on the coast of North Vietnam. The Army logged 10,000 combat deaths in the first eight months (an all-time record) and brought up the level of American troop involvement to 550,000. It was the year 200,000 Biafrans starved to death while a well-fed, crewcut Military Man prepared to land on the moon. And, oh yes, it was the year Jackie Kennedy took on a new last name and a new CIA-patrolled principality.

To all of this, the left responded with an unprecedented wave of protest and confrontation. But pacifists still dominated the action. Laws were broken and violence did occur, but most of the broken heads were on the side of the demonstrators. Nonviolent resistance was still considered morally superior and politically smarter.

Nineteen-sixty-eight proved to be THE year for campus revolt. There were full-fledged strikes and occupations on dozens of major campuses, including San Francisco State and Columbia. In Chicago, a young "conspiracy" managed to derail the Democratic Presidential Express in retaliation for the war. (Four of the eight "conspirators" tried for scuttling Hubie Baby were products of Oakland-Berkeley—Tom Hayden, Rennie Davis, Jerry Rubin, and Bobby Seale.)

Things were getting tough but there was still room for levity.

"POETRY DEMANDS UNEMPLOYMENT" proclaimed one underground broadsheet distributed late in '68 around Berkeley. "Further, The Immediate Abolition of Poverty & The Communal Feeding of All, The Erection of Cities of Light, Wildness & 150,000 Circuses for the Proletariat."

There were fewer smiles to the mile in '69, although the San Francisco *Good Times* proclaimed the year to be one of "Orgy, Armed Education, the Swiss Franc, Quiet Pleasures and Lunar Defilement."

Berkeley will not be the same after '69 has passed. It is not just the fact that Richard Nixon becomes President this year, that Neil Armstrong pollutes the moon's surface with his robotlike footprint, and a few days later Ho Chi Minh dies (probably from embarrassment). It's not just that a new draft lottery begins or that the My Lai inquiry so deftly avoids every real issue except the "guilt" of Lt. William Calley. There is a change of *mood* in Berkeley—a change of style and approach and philosophy. Nineteen-sixty-nine is the year that two slogans begin to appear on the well-marked-up walls of the East Bay. At first they are regarded as a joke. By the time the year is over, no one is laughing.

"ARMED LOVE"

"GIVE PIECE A CHANCE"

And then there's the word "pig." It no longer refers to a farm animal, to the source of well-cured hams and thick-sliced bacon. By the end of 1969 it has completely replaced both "policeman" and "cop" on the tongues and in the minds of the Berkeley left.

A cursory study of the Berkeley *Tribe* turns up such headlines as "It's Time for Pickled Pig," "Blue Swine on Trial," "Mind if I Call You Piggy?," "Roast Pig," and "You Can't Tell the Pigshit from the Horseshit." One Tac Squad unit retaliates with a Porky Pig shoulder patch that says, "*Pride . . . Integrity . . . Guts.*"

The fulcrum upon which this ominous shift in attitude and style balances is called People's Park.

The photograph of the year features an overweight, helmet-engulfed and flak-jacketed cop squatting down in a badly uprooted vacant lot as though he has just finished a long-overdue crap. In one hand he holds a tender green shrub with dirt-encrusted roots dangling helplessly toward the ground. In the other there is a pathetic cluster of dying marigolds. The officer has just ripped both plants out of the earth in a relentless pursuit of "law 'n' order."

The People's Park confrontation of spring, '69, produces a couple of thousand other disturbing photos of police cars upside down and burning on Telegraph Avenue, of helicopters dumping tear gas on playgrounds of helpless children, of rock-and-bottle-throwing mobs of street people facing instant pistol and shotgun retaliation.

Then there is a chilling series showing the vacant lot completely surrounded by high-wire fencing. Inside is a small army of cops and National Guardsmen. The soldiers force back thousands of demonstrators with bared bayonets. There are more pictures to record the following months of arrest and marching and picketing and street fighting. People's Park is indeed the fulcrum, and when it tips toward violence Berkeley moves from resistance to open war.

Between June, '68, and August, '69, there are twenty-three days of street fighting, two thousand arrests, forty days of occupation by "mutual-aid" forces, twenty-two days of National Guard occupation, twenty days of curfew, four months of "State of Disaster," and five months of "State of Emergency." (And there are still people out there who cannot *understand* why Berkeley produced the superviolent S.L.A.?)

Those who go through the People's Park experience never forget it. Things start simply enough. There is a muddy, unused plot of land that the University of California has cleared for "new dormitories," which it never gets around to building. The lot is in an interesting location—just off Tele, between Dwight and Haste streets. Hundreds of young people are already spending so much time roaming up and down Tele in a continual anarchistic celebration of unfocused energy and high spirits that they have come to regard this as a "liberated zone." An unused square block of vacant land right next to their well-established domain is just too great a temptation. It is torn up and muddy. Old cars are abandoned there. Garbage is dumped in great smelly piles and abortions are hidden. The land would be so much more useful if there could be grass and flowers, a barbecue pit, a small campground for those who have nowhere else to sleep, slides and swings for a children's playground. The street people simply decide to take over the land and make good use of it—law or no law. People's Park quickly becomes the hottest issue in Berkeley's history.

As Marvin Garson explains the attitudes that made the park takeover a perfectly natural extension of the scene on Tele:

"All these years leaders have tried to get the masses moving on eighteenth-century issues like free speech and suddenly the masses moved by themselves on twentieth-century issues like free streets and the nature of the city. . . . There are capitalist philosophies of work, of money, of commodities. We know all about that. But there is also a capitalist philosophy of the street inherent in such simple and reasonable notions that streets are for traffic. You live in a box. You work in a box. You buy in a box. The purpose of the streets is to take you from one box to another. Traffic is purposeful movement along the streets from one box to another. The streets are for traffic: NOT for gathering, NOT for celebrating, NOT for spontaneous communicating!"

Tele's street people say *fuck that!* and move onto the University of California's vacant lot to make it their own. For the first time in living memory thousands of people get over their mutual suspicions and dread and willingly go to work together to create something lovely and useful where only a muddy eyesore had existed before. By late April, rubble has been cleared and the land leveled. Some seven hundred square yards of sod have been planted, along with threes and shrubs and flowers. Everyone comes out to cultivate the community garden. A fire pit is dug. Tables and benches are handcrafted on the spot. There's a lot of singing and dope smoking going on. Who says that work has to be unpleasant and demeaning?

The days are sunny and productive for hundreds of kids who'd just been hanging around before. Some of them go out to the Ave and collect money for more sod (at seven cents a square foot). Over a hundred dollars is donated in an hour by people who seldom have enough coins to buy a square meal. The word goes out that Saturdays and Sundays are supposed to be the main workdays, but everyone works every day to improve their very own park.

Watermelons, oranges, wine, and marijuana are passed around freely. A woman's rock band performs from a flat-bed truck complete with its own generator and amplifiers. There's plenty of time for fun, but as soon as someone puts down a shovel the next guy down the line quietly picks it up and continues the necessary work.

Older neighbors join in the fun. They'd been afraid to pass over the torn-up mudhole of land before—afraid of mugging and verbal abuse from the young—but no one is pushed around or abused here these days. If fights start, everyone dives in to break it up. There are no written laws and no cops. They are not needed.

It goes on like this day after day until the university decides that things have gone far enough. (Ronald Reagan is running for reelection next year. People's Park is going to be one of the main issues.)

Before dawn on May 15, 1969, armed sheriff's deputies and construction men move in and evict about one hundred squatters. They put up a big, strong fence and guard it well. As poet Denise Levertov recalls the invasion: "At 6 a.m. the ominous zooming, war-sound of helicopters / breaks into our sleep / To the park: ringed with police. / Bulldozers have moved in. / Barely awake, the people— / those who had made for each other / a green place— / begin to gather at the corners. Their tears / fall on sidewalk cement. / The fence goes up. / Everyone knows (yet no one yet / believes it) what all shall know / this day, and the days / that follow: now, the clubs, the gas, / bayonets, bullets. The war / comes home to us. . . ."

By noon the entire town is in shock and outrage. Thousands rally on the UC campus and march down Tele to Haste before being stopped by police. Suddenly the cops open up with a barrage of tear gas and then wade into the crowd with clubs. The people fight back with rocks, bottles, and street debris. Sheriff's deputies load up shotguns and pistols and fire wildly into the crowd, killing James Rector, blinding artist Alan Blanchard, and wounding at least 150 more young people.

The pacifist spirit that brought People's Park into being is given free reign just once more before Berkeley becomes a permanent war zone. On Memorial Day (May 30), 1969, some 25,000 well-disciplined and peaceful protesters gather to march once more on the park. They first listen to the words of Frank Bardacke, who warns against any violence and then explains that the purpose of this march is "to break through the concrete and the asphalt and build institutions of freedom and brotherhood. . . . The earth wants sun. It wants to break through the concrete and the asphalt and see the sun and . . . it's our duty and it's the spirit of People's Park to help the earth break through the asphalt, to help the earth break through the concrete so it doesn't have to take it upon itself to have earthquakes. . . . The original idea of People's Park was to get back to the earth, to build institutions not dedicated to domination and profit but dedicated to freedom and brotherhood, and that's what we hope to do today. . . ."

The enormous crowd then carefully approaches the fence surrounding their captured park and plants flowers and shrubs *outside* the wire barrier. They offer flowers to the cops and Guardsmen and cover over bayonets and helmets with roses and daisies. Pretty young girls flirt with the uniformed and armed men inside the fence and urge them to throw down their guns and "join us." A few do.

Then the crowd evaporates, hoping that their moral example will bear fruit.

But the fence stayed put for more than a year, and the delicate balance of Berkeley politics tilted irrevocably toward violence as the memory of People's Park—the very last chance for peaceful accommodation—was sadly entombed.

On the first anniversary of the Memorial Day march (in May, 1970) Stew Albert wrote in the Berkeley *Tribe:* "The park is lost and so are its sentiments. We know you can not build happy socialism in a pig's belly. That the relaxed joy we felt on those sweaty Sunday afternoons of work and dope will have to wait until after the armies of money and racism have been defeated. . . . We realize that People's

Park had permanence only in our imagination. . . . Our sisters and brothers must now prepare for a revolutionary war."

These were the sentiments that were dominant in radical Berkeley when Joe Remiro first began to hang out with some regularity along Tele. Very little that Remiro or any other S.L.A. member would write and say four years later would go much beyond the angry rhetoric that followed People's Park. A joint statement put out in 1970 by the Berkeley Commune and Up Against the Wall / Motherfucker summed it up quite well:

The time for talk and accommodation is long past, they said. Only violent action counts. Liberals and "respectable left organizations" sit "righteously clukking like hens, disapproving of 'the terrorists and provocateurs' who are taking care of business. . . . Well, who are the saboteurs and the terrorists??? We are. . . .

"All of us who will sabotage the foundations of Amerika's fucked-up life; all of us who strike terror into the hearts of the bourgeois honkies and all their armchair book quoting jive-ass honky leftists / white collar radicals who are the VD of the revolution. . . . The only thing a liberal or honky leftist is good for is to throw between me and the pig / or jack up for lunch money. And when people on the street realize it they'll run the bastards back to their tv sets. . . .

"At our present stage of development the issue is not whether we should take to the streets, finding some form of mass expression, RATHER than engage in clandestine activity. There is no separation in the revolutionary movement. Every act is assimilated into the struggle, if it furthers revolt. . . . We must be flexible to rally one day and bomb the next. And we must find new forms for massing and moving in the street at the same time we create alternative modes of action when street action is impossible. . . . We do not take to the streets because we want free speech or free assembly (those are liberal demands). . . . We have our own struggle. We are fighting for ourselves / for our community / for our very lives. The issue is not something other than ourselves / we are the issue. It is the liberation of our lives we are fighting for / to liberate ourselves from tight-assed bourgeois life, and it is our experience of the boredom and misery of Amerikan life that drives us to destroy it anywhere it confronts us. . . ."

Listening carefully to this sort of invective is Patricia Soltysik, who has by now dropped out of school to become a radical lesbian feminist. She hangs out a lot on Tele and is living with a new arrival from Minnesota, a gifted poet and artist named Camilla Hall. Also listening closely is Nancy Ling Perry, who has been on the Berkeley scene since '67 and who has long been involved in the prison movement, which really comes alive in 1970 as a new cause célèbre develops.

A white guard is killed at Soledad Prison (one of California's grimmer joints) and three "Soledad Brothers" are charged with murder. They are Fleeta Drumgo, George Jackson, and John Cluchette. Their case focuses new energy from the Berkeley movement on prison *vaporization*—old terms like "reform" just don't make it any more.

Along with these black prisoners Berkeley has a whole new set of heroes in the Weathermen, who become the best-known bombers in a year that is notable for carefully planned explosions. (They claim only a small portion of the 546 blasts reported in '70. The preceding year there had been only 236, and in the year before that, 56.)

On August 7, George Jackson's seventeen-year-old brother, Jonathan, tries to liberate two San Quentin convicts on trial at the futuristic, Frank Lloyd Wright–designed Marin Civic Center Courthouse. He kidnaps a judge, a D.A., and several jury members, planning to use them as hostages to get the Soledad Brothers out of stir.

Jonathan and the judge are gunned down in the parking lot by Quentin screws who ain't *about* to do no bargaining. Angela Davis and Ruchell (Cinque) McGee *—one of the briefly liberated cons—are charged with the killing. Angela is captured in October and is tried and acquitted the next year.

Over on Alcatraz Island the Indians are occupying the grim and windy pile of rock and claim it is theirs by law and treaty. It proves to be a rehearsal for the occupation of Wounded Knee.

On another island, Isla Vista, near Santa Barbara, they're having a hard time keeping their tiny Bank of America branch in business. Student demonstrators have gotten into the habit of regularly burning it down. Hundreds of revolutionaries are now behind bars. They electrify the prison system and, in September of '70, they help to engineer a fantastic uprising at New York's Attica State Penitentiary. They are put down with unprecedented fury as thirty-nine prisoners and hostages are shot down in cold blood.

Nineteen-seventy-one is the year that two mass killers are finally

---

* It was through the Ruchell McGee case that the public first heard of a prisoner with the "reborn name" of Cinque. McGee—like "Cinque Mtume" (Donald DeFreeze) after him—adopted the name and legend of the nineteenth-century black chieftain who rose out of the hold of a slave ship to slaughter his white masters.

convicted—Charles Manson and Lt. William Calley. It's the year the Black Panther party splits down the middle, with Eldridge Cleaver's faction becoming the underground guerrilla Black Liberation Army. It's the year Tim Leary suffers a "revolutionary bust" at Cleaver's hands because Tim still prefers dope to discipline (despite the fact he's now adopted Cleaverite rhetoric and is urging the former Flower Children to "shoot to live." For Leary, happiness is now a warm gun, and "to kill a policeman is a sacred act.")

Nineteen-seventy-one is another year of massive peace demonstrations with little noticeable effect, another year of trashing and street fighting in both Berkeley and San Francisco. But all of this is minor-league compared with the greatest bust in American history as Washington, D.C., cops and marshals march fourteen thousand protesters into a concentration-camp football stadium on the anniversary of the Kent State massacre. (A young University of Florida philosophy student named Russell Little is on hand to see Nixon "law 'n' order" go into high gear.)

Fashions get funkier in anachronistic San Francisco, where "gender-fuck" drag queens imitate the famous Cockettes in high heels, evening gowns, heavy make-up—along with hairy chests, beards, and their balls hanging out. Campy music out of the '40s is *in* on the Frisco scene—all that "June-moon-croon" stuff.

Berkeley has no time for such nonsense. In Berkeley the Fidel Castro look still makes it—big, bushy beards, combat boots, Army fatigues.

The Berkeley hit parade still features "Street Fighting Man" by the Rolling Stones and a little ditty by Speedy Keene that begins, "We've got to get it together / Because the Revolution's *here!*"

By late '71, Joe Remiro has edged deeply into the Berkeley scene. He still does not understand all that he hears, so he crams on Marx, Lenin, Mao, and Stalin.

"You know," he recalls, "mostly Mao and Lenin . . . I was getting into this whole intellectual thing, you know. I was moving into intellectual, political circles."

He takes a hitchhike vacation up the Pacific coast to "get my head clear." He camps out in revolutionary communes up in Oregon, where he sells an underground paper called *Willamette Bridge* on the streets of Eugene. He visits Vancouver and thinks of staying in Canada—skipping out on the whole mess back home and starting all over again in a new atmosphere.

"But I decided my job is back in my own country," he says, "fighting the capitalists in my own country. If I'd have gone to Canada they just would have used me to exploit all that virgin territory, that capitalist wild game preserve."

By mid-'72, Remiro is back in the East Bay for good, and he dives headfirst into radical politics. Two groups take up most of his time and attention through the summer of '72 and up until about the time in early '73 when S.L.A. begins to get itself together.

They are the now-"defunct" Venceremos organization and Vietnam Veterans Against the War.

When he lived in San Francisco Joe had backed VVAW in a rather mild, not-too-involved way. But in the East Bay he becomes a founder and outstanding leader of a new and very vigorous chapter. His work in the increasingly radical veterans' movement will prove that when Joe Remiro gets behind something, he goes all the way.

7

*"The veterans are the only people who really accept direct responsibility
for the Vietnam war. We have to because we were the tools
in that war. We were the cannon fodder, the trained killers.
We pulled the triggers. We were the triggermen."*
—Bob Hood, a leader of VVAW–WSO and Remiro's comrade

BOTH THE HAWKS AND THE PEACENIKS gravely misjudged
the returning Namvets. The Army had strong misgivings
about its hippie soldiers (products of the most unpopular and
most unfairly administered draft in U.S. history), but it did
not generally fear them. The government felt that the vets
would soon "melt back" into the general population.

Peace-movement people often reacted with instinctive revulsion to
these young "barbarians" with so much blood on their hands. Too many
pacifists blamed the vets personally for the war. (One such "nonviolent"
type sent a case of dog food to a group of combat infantrymen with a
note saying that "since you live like animals, you might as well eat
like them.")

But the peaceniks slowly began to see the value of absorbing the
new antiwar vets movement and grudgingly incorporated Namvet contingents into major demonstrations. It was an uneasy marriage of political convenience, and one the veterans often resented.

"They called on us to be in the front lines in all those Trotskyite
peace marches so we could get our heads cracked by the cops first,"
Bob Hood recalls disgustedly. "That way when the local Mafia got back
to the Socialist Workers party, their clubs were so thick with blood
that it didn't hurt so much."

"I went to a couple of demonstrations and marches," says Paul
Halverson. "It seemed like such bullshit. There we were . . . hundreds
of thousands of people walking on the streets, you know, obeying all
the cops' directions. That's why I can understand the emotions that

forced the S.L.A. to pick up guns and try to do it that way. 'Cause you don't *change* anything when you're marching by the thousands. A million people marched in one day and in Washington the President sat and watched a football game and we didn't affect the foreign policy of this country one iota."

No matter how good their intentions, the peace-movement people had not personally experienced the war. They hated it in a very moral and highly abstract way, not with the murderous passion the Namvets harbored. (To them the late '60s slogan "Kill for Peace" was not altogether a joke.)

By 1973, the "movement" was a thing of the past—rather sedate and respectable in retrospect. But the radical Namvets were just beginning to gather steam, and they proved, much to everyone's surprise, to be the one segment of the antiwar coalition that saw through Nixon's "Vietnamization" ploy. Rather than disbanding and going quietly home like the rest of the peace marchers, they became even more militant. They were, in fact, the only group with enough guts to face down the Republican party in its 1972 Miami Beach convention—an act that led to trumped-up charges against the "Gainesville Nine"—charges they quickly proved to be falsehoods.

Namvets, even the ones who took a little time off to play Haight-Ashbury hippie for a while, like Joe, operated on a very different set of imperatives from those of their more easily mollified (and frightened) "youth-culture" buddies. The vets were tougher, angrier and a lot more determined to see to it that America was going to *change* because of Vietnam. They had a number of heavy personal debts to pay. As psychologist and Namvet expert Robert Lifton puts it:

"They did so with the rage of 'survivor-heroes.' . . . To be sure, there is guilt behind their actions. But there is also the bitter rage of men who have been betrayed, the angry insistence that the guilt be shared, and above all, that the nature of the atrocity-producing situation be recognized. . . ."

Some of these guys, like Remiro, quickly hop-skipped over the heads of their less militant buddies who were willing to talk and demonstrate but who felt they'd already *done* their share of the fighting. Joe had opted for violent revolution by late '72, and he was, in Lifton's dialectic, one of those increasingly more common veterans who see their role as that of the "returning hero warrior" whose job is to convey a "new wisdom and freedom to live" to his people.

"For the mythological hero is the champion not of things become but of things becoming, the dragon to be slain by him is precisely the monster of the status quo."

They have rejected the contemporary homily that there *are* no more heroes. Their heroic models are Mao and Che and Fidel and they see violent revolution as the final battlefield, their last chance to expunge their own guilt and to bring massive change to this society. They have come to believe in "war as a means of social revitalization," and through their increasingly fevered activity "the warrior ethos gives way to the myth of the hero."

There are plenty of reasons why the Namvets feel they still have scores to settle.

As Remiro or his buddies will quickly tell you, no group of former U.S. soldiers ever fought in a less honorable war, suffered such great mental and moral disruption, or came home to so little interest and assistance. There were no victory parades, no tears of joy, no heroes' welcomes—just a general pall of icy distrust and avoidance. No veterans have ever had so much trouble getting reintegrated into the life of the country they supposedly laid their lives on the line to preserve.

It has taken the public a long time, but we are finally becoming aware of just how unhappy these guys are and how dangerous their anger and guilt can become. The story of Joe Remiro is extreme, but it is not a total fluke or an exception to the basic rules that apply to the other three million Americans who went to Nam (the youngest soldiers we ever sent to war).

Ask the vets themselves what is troubling hundreds of thousands of them. Ask their psychiatrists and psychologists. Ask the newspapermen who are writing more and more about them these days as Namvets pull a Joe Remiro or break into the headlines with one deadly and bizarre outburst after another.

Like the weird Los Angeles dude who staged a lonely shoot-out from a high cliff above Griffith Park wearing his old GI helmet and hefting an M-16. He thought he was back in Indochina.

Or the strange little black assassin who shot down the mother of Martin Luther King from the "amen corner" one fine Sunday morning and then was taken away yelling, "The war did it to me. . . . The war did it to me."

Or the amputee Medal of Honor winner who came back to a quiet little Illinois town to raise pot in his father's cornfields, got hassled too much, drove wildly down Main Street trying to run down every little old lady in sight, and had to be sent off to the state nuthouse.

Or how about the ex-Marine from Georgia who extended a "normal" Saturday-night barroom brawl with the boys into an all-out massacre?

And then there's the twenty-seven-year-old Wisconsin infantry vet who cannot remember murdering his wife because of drink and drugs and his generally screwed-up head. He told a *Penthouse* reporter that the murder was not his first crack-up. He described a few of the others: ". . . I woke up in a hospital room, surrounded by steel mesh. Some dude told me they bought me in, drunk on my ass, and some shit about marching three pigs, at gunpoint, into the cop shop, announcing that I had attacked and captured two enemy FOs and their radioman. Shit like that happens all the time. A drag . . . I got cracked for causing a public disturbance, once. I was trucking through the alley, when some son-of-a-bitch turned on the shit with a pneumatic jackhammer. I don't know what happened after that, but I woke up in a VA hospital strapped to a bed. Some shrink said some bullshit about me attacking some construction worker, with a shovel. . . . I got two years probation for patrolling the KK River at two o'clock in the morning with a twenty-two rifle. Fucking pigs tried to run me out of town for selling dope, but I beat that. So here I am, trucking town, wired out of my skull, with a thirty-eight Cobra, six hundred dollars worth of junk, and no hard-on. . . ."

A few cold facts explain why we are seeing so many violent, completely alienated Namvets these days:

- More than 20 percent of all returned Vietnam veterans have attempted suicide since they got back. (That's over 500,000.) A lot of them made it. Some 55,000 have died since returning, more than the number of combat soldiers who crapped out in Southeast Asia.
- Namvets suffer a 52 percent divorce rate, way above the average, even in California.
- At *least* 12 percent came home with "serious drug problems." (That means hooked, baby.)
- In 1973, 11 percent of all federal prisoners were Namvets, most were in for drugs and crimes of violence. In San Francisco's county jail, 35 percent were Namvets, and that's probably close to the percentage for prisoners in all of California's jails.
- A Veterans Administration sampling recently showed that one in five Namvets had been busted at least once in the first six months after getting home.

- Their unemployment rate is *twice* that of the national average—10 percent instead of 5 percent in 1973. (Nonwhite Namvets suffer an incredible 14 percent unemployment rate.) The U.S. Bureau of Labor Statistics noted at the end of the first quarter of 1974 that they knew of at least 285,000 nonwhite Namvets out of work, and 63,000 whites. And those are just the guys who are *still* drawing unemployment. Multiply those numbers by three and you've got the total of all the unemployed who have long been off the "official" roster.

- The unemployment problem is compounded by the government itself, which gave 560,000 Vietnam-era vets "less than honorable" discharges and has long been using generally understood codes on even "honorable" separation papers which automatically turn potential employers away from these men.

- Hundreds of thousands of Namvets came back with serious physical and mental health problems. No group of wounded veterans ever met such massive government and community indifference and downright hostility. ("When we got back, the government treated us just like they treated the Vietnamese in Indochina," said one amputee.)

- The Veterans Administration (which runs 170 facilities with 100,000 beds, making it the nation's single biggest hospital system) is most uninterested in taking on Namvet patients. It is filled up with chronically ill older men from earlier wars and likes to accommodate the VFW and American Legion, who have long-established political lobbies. These groups seldom speak up for Namvets. The Indochina war produced a bumper crop of casualties—311,000 wounded, of which 23,000 are 100 percent disabled physically and 13,000 are totally out of it mentally. Four thousand five hundred lost a leg in action and 800 no longer have an arm. One hundred and seventy are lacking at least one hand. Some 1,080 have multiple amputations. From 60,000 to 200,000 Namvets came back with heroin habits (the figure varies because few will cop out on themselves). Veterans caught with habits *before* discharge are, of course, ineligible for *any* VA assistance to cure their habits. Only the shrewd addicts who escaped detection until *after* they got out can get any help, and few work past all the current red tape and roadblocks. The VA no longer even answers its phones in many cities.

- Namvets who would follow the example of 50 percent of World War II's veterans and upgrade themselves through their GI educational benefits are stopped by administrative foul-ups and the low allotments—$220 a month now for a single vet, and that *includes* all tuition and books. You can't make it on that today, when such a figure barely covers tuition alone in most private schools, and only 19 percent take advantage of the totally insufficient bill. Yet no group of vets ever needed additional education more. Eighty percent of the enlisted men in Nam had gotten no further than high school. Despite promises of "career training," few learned much that would get them a job on the outside. ("Who's going to hire a helicopter door-gunner to fix TV sets?") Employers pay little attention to "skills" gained in the military, which has different office procedures and machinery from private industry. The majority of the Namvets, who came from the white working class and racial minorities, ended up in the slums, the ghettos, and the barrios. The lucky ones, those who could find *any* work, ended up washing dishes and as janitors, service-station attendants, and manual laborers.

In Joe Remiro's case it was a series of catch-as-catch-can jobs like driving a taxicab or a diaper truck, selling newspapers on street corners and breaking in as an auto mechanic.

To all of these problems, add the great guilt so many Namvets feel about what they were forced to do in Indochina and their shabby treatment when they got home.

Vets from previous wars also had their nightmares about the killing they had done for "God and Country," but they received some degree of social absolution when they got back—a little honor and respect and help. These are crucial reinforcements as a vet makes the big mental adjustment from murderous combat soldier to law-abiding civilian again.

Namvets came home to find they had fought a war everyone wanted to forget. In Remiro's case, an honest attempt to talk out his guilt with his father led to his being thrown bodily out of the little house where he grew up.

This is bound to scramble your marbles a little.

As psychologist Lifton puts it:

"Sent as intruders in an Asian revolution, asked to fight a filthy and unfathomable war, they returned as intruders to their own society, defiled by that war in the eyes of the very people who sent them as well as in their own. Images and feelings of guilt are generally associated with transgression—with having crossed boundaries that should not have been crossed, with having gone beyond limits that should not have been exceeded. . . . They are survivors who cannot inwardly justify what they have seen and done. They are, therefore, caught in a vicious circle of death and guilt. . . ."

Unlike World War II soldiers, who could be successfully treated for such "guilt" by being shown that their attitude was not logical, that the killing had to be done to stop fascism, the Namvet was suffering from what can only be called "justifiable guilt." He knows damned well what he has done is wrong. How can you convince him otherwise?

Joe Remiro is a good example of this "justifiable guilt" turned inward upon a basically direct and unsophisticated nature to the point where the only possible "atonement" left to him is to become one of the "enemies" he has killed. The Army taught him "we're the good guys and they're the bad guys, the dirty commies." When such a black-and-white assertion is proved utterly false in the eyes of an uncomplicated kid of nineteen away from home on his first big adventure, you're likely to get a case of complete transference.

In Lifton's view, a gung-ho volunteer like Joe, "one who had initially believed in the war and given himself to it," is likely to respond the most violently when he finds he has been fighting the wrong enemy and been suckered into the wrong war. "His resentful critique could extend far beyond the Vietnam war to corruptions throughout society's structure . . . for him, betrayal is greatest."

So what did Joe do? Become a "communist," naturally. A SUPER-communist.

Psychologist Dominic Harveston, a veteran himself who has worked for two years in Hayward with young Namvets, studied one of the interviews upon which this book is based and reached a few general conclusions about Remiro:

"First of all, I think he's confused," said Harveston. "I really feel sorry for the poor son of a bitch. It's tragic. The guy got a raw deal and he tried to work it out, but he just didn't make it. If there had been someone in his life who could have worked with him, he would have gone an entirely different road . . . now he's a suspected murderer."

Harveston, who has worked with more than 150 Namvets, has heard a number of similar stories and feels that Remiro is far from being an exception among the vets he deals with who suffer from "Post-Vietnam Syndrome," that is, the 20 percent who have "serious and prolonged readjustment problems." The most common "PVS" symptoms are guilt, rage, and alienation. The most common response to the feeling of guilt is suicide. Alienation becomes apparent when the Namvet cannot get along with other people who were "not there" with him. (He has a hard time staying married, for instance.) Rage all too often surfaces in acts of incredible violence.

"A lot of them are really, really angry," says Harveston. "A lot of that anger comes up from a situation where they need help, they ask for help, and they don't get any. They say, 'You put me in that situation in Vietnam and you're not helping me deal with it.' "

Harveston regards Remiro as a good example of that 1 or 2 percent of the Namvets who freak out entirely and get into heavy violence. (One percent of three million men is thirty thousand . . . thirty thousand Joe Remiros?) "That's a small percentage," says Harveston, "but that kind of a percentage is enough to raise all the hell in the world. . . . These guys were trained to kill and they were probably the most highly trained and best-equipped killers the world has ever known. If one of them gets out of hand, I'd be afraid to walk down his block. I mean, that kind of a dude is scary!

"I've met guys like Remiro. They haven't done the same things, though. They've channeled it another way, but they're still holding all that guilt in. These guys grew up in a country where they were told to 'love your neighbor, love your friends.' A lot of them came right out of that Flower Child business of 'love each other, care for each other.' So these guys came out of that and they went over there and they were told, 'KILL!' And they did it and now they're having a hell of a time dealing with it. They get pent up. They've got all this anxiety built up inside of them and then they come back to this country, the country they were supposed to be fighting for and they want a fair share . . . love, jobs, help. And a lot of them got nothing. A lot of these guys came home with a lot of very personal things wrapped up in them and they're still hung up on them and they need to talk about it, but their families and loved ones and a lot of their friends don't want to talk. They say, 'Oh, it must have been ugly and horrible over there and I'm sure you don't want to talk about it.' That's a very common response, and these people just don't want to hear.

"So these kids come home and they get all this reaction right away and they say, 'Well, gee, I'd better not tell them about Nam because if I do they won't like me. They'll hate me. They'll throw me out of the house' . . . as Remiro's father did.

"So a lot of times they keep it locked up inside them and they need someplace, some way to work past it, to work through it. They need avenues to work past this stuff because if they don't work it out, there are certain of these guys who have it pent up inside them and then they're going to act it out. And that acting out might come in a way that they're best trained for.

"That should be no surprise to anyone. But people in this country don't want to face it. They don't want to deal with those guys, so they just deny they're there. They don't give 'em anything."

That's the picture. Thousands of Namvets came home jumpy, disillusioned, jobless, lonely. Some were hooked. Many tried to kill themselves. Some succeeded. Half were quickly married and quickly divorced. One in five was arrested in the first six months home. Some got into even deeper trouble and ended up where Remiro now sits—in a jail cell because of a murder.

And when these Namvets go on trial they are usually met by an unsympathetic judge and a bland, slightly frightened jury, people who have heard about these freaky long-haired rebels who smoke dope and live in communes, "good" people who may have been in a war themselves—quite a long time ago and a very different kind of war. ("I went to war and I didn't come back like *that*. What's *wrong* with these young people today?") And they judge these young men with little compassion, without understanding, without even much interest. And they are filling our jails with them.

As Harveston puts it:

"What particularly freaks out these old guys is the fact that so many Namvets came back with strong antiwar beliefs. So many of them came back with political opinions very definitely on the left. And these old guys in their VFW and American Legion hats, all spick and span in their old World War II uniforms, marching in some veterans' parade . . . they see these young VVAW guys with their long hair and all their antiwar banners, their antiviolence ideas. . . . They see some young guy like that wearing a Medal of Honor or a Bronze Star and smoking a joint and they *gotta* acknowledge him as a fellow veteran but it blows their minds. It completely blows their minds."

In 1970–72, Joe Remiro was one of these long-haired, pot-smoking hippie freaks who showed up in Namvet contingents in most of the parades. He supported Vietnam Veterans Against the War all this time, but it was not until he moved to Oakland, in '72, that he became one of the group's real leaders. It was, in fact, Joe's role as one of the "founders" of the East Bay Chapter of VVAW–WSO that was used by newsmen just after his arrest to identify Remiro as a "real radical." Little did they understand how far Joe had gone beyond that group's most extreme commitments.

Bob Hood remembers Joe's early dedication to VVAW:

"Joe and I were members of the San Francisco Chapter of VVAW and I'd been to meetings that were real bad and there was this tight elitist group that was sort of running the chapter, at least that was my conception. Then Joe, who I did not really know at the time, decided that there should be a chapter in the East Bay and he got the contact lists, the names of all the members in the East Bay, and took all the cards with about two hundred names and typed out a letter to all these people saying we're going to start a chapter and we'd like you to come to the founding meeting. And I got one of the letters and I went in late September, '72, to this founding meeting and that was the first time I really got to know Joe.

"He met me at the door of his house over on Harrison Street in Oakland and I was wearing one of them blue Chinese workers' hats, you know, with a red star on it. And I rang the doorbell and he answered the door and I said, 'Hi, Brother.' And he said, 'I'm Joe Remiro.' And he said, 'It's nice to meet you and, wow!, are you a communist?' He looked at my red star. And I said, 'Well, Brother, I'm trying like heck to become one.' And I said, 'It's really a struggle.' And he said, 'Me, too. Right on!' You know, he was really warm.

"It was a very successful meeting. People were getting interested and determined, but the police were outside taking all the license numbers, shit like that. Uniformed Oakland pigs with walkie-talkies, just that blatant. They weren't even cagey about it. It was really a drag 'cause everybody knew they were being spied on by the police and it was like an intimidative factor to try to keep people away. But people came anyway and we had a fairly good time and then we had another meeting there and we decided the pigs were a drag and decided to have them someplace else and we had them at Bill Brennan's apartment. . . ."

Brennan, an eight-year veteran of the Navy, was a late arrival on the Oakland-Berkeley political scene.

"Those meetings were at my place on Jefferson Street in Berkeley," he says. "And then other people started volunteering their houses and finally we got some money together and got an office." He remembers that Remiro was a very strong, "positive, moving, self-confident" sort of guy who got others going. Hood remembers Joe as "high energy."

He says Joe is "a guy who's always UP and looking at the bright side of things, a real positive force in any situation, looking for the positive aspect, trying to stress it and run it for all that it's possibly worth, really flashy and sure of himself, the kind of person who inspires confidence, wins trust . . . a good-lookin' kind of guy, small, wiry, a ladies' man. . . ."

Joe helps East Bay VVAW get its first regular office together in a cheap little storefront on the Oakland end of Telegraph Avenue, about half a mile south of Berkeley. He spends a lot of time working in this Forty-ninth Street and Tele outpost. The phone is listed in his name and he often has to hunt up the bread to keep things moving.

But it is more than low rent that produces a VVAW office south of the Berkeley border. Many radicals who first lived in Berkeley have decided by the early '70s that the freaky youth scene centered around the UC campus is not relevant or revolutionary enough. They want to live and work among the poor and disenfranchised, and the swarming, interlocking ghettos and barrios of Oakland provide a perfect testing ground for their insurrectionary theories.

Many of the leaders of the new VVAW chapter think this way, although few are as intense about it as Joe, who, even at this stage, plunges headfirst into the swirling rhetoric of armed revolution preached in '72 and '73 by such Maoist groups as the Revolutionary Union and Venceremos.

Oakland is not only the East Bay VVAW's headquarters—it is also the home of the main Venceremos contingent at "Montana House." Joe has joined Venceremos, and he is soon shuttling regularly between the Forty-ninth and Tele office and the Venceremos enclave over on Montana Street.

And it isn't just politics that draws him there. Joe is a master at mixing rhetoric and romance, and he is soon going out with a number of women involved in the Venceremos scene. They include the beautiful Alicia Englander, the small but provocative Cynthia Garvey (a strong-minded militant who later will go to jail rather than tell a grand jury what she knows about Joe and the S.L.A.), and Angela Atwood, a very attractive young actress from Indiana who has gravitated toward Venceremos after she and her husband split up, mostly because of politics. It is Joe who brings Angela into S.L.A.

He is really hopping all over the landscape at this point, working with the Farm Workers, the United Prisoners Union, an Oakland election, VVAW, and Venceremos. Whatever inward doubts and hang-ups he went through in '70–'71 as he faced out the trauma of his breakup with Kathy and settled down to self-indoctrination are well hidden now. No more crying. No more half measures.

Everyone who knows Joe at this energetic high point of his life is impressed by his sure touch, his confidence, his complete conviction that he now has THE answer to all of the world's problems.

(As Brennan remarks a bit impishly, Remiro may have had to come on strong to impress the ladies of the revolution: "I think for Joe, being short probably contributed to his feeling that he has to do that much more . . . because you know how women put down men who aren't tall. . . . If you lay back a little from what Joe says and from what other people like him might say, you see they're operating more on fatih than on logic.")

Remiro's rhetoric from this point on becomes progressively more "certain" and flashy. He has entered a stage in his life where he is about to take terrible gambles for what he believes in. He cannot afford to admit he is wrong.

"Look," says Joe," "to have the politics that I have, to go around openly telling everybody—I did, I just went around screaming at everybody, man—I'm *bound* to end up in prison. . . ."

Remiro's style of nonstop, top-speed political harangue can be very convincing—if you ignore shallow thinking and incomplete scholarship. Here's an example, a discussion of "equality," or, rather, the lack of it, delivered with a certain Mixmaster rhetorical sureness, even when caught off base.

"We can't talk about individuals," says Joe. "We've got to talk about groups or organizations. . . . You can't look at things on a perspective of one to one because while we're dealing with them one to one they're killing us ten by ten. . . . You can't look at things from that perspective because you can't deal with a whole society or a whole country or a whole anything on that perspective. You can only deal with individual wants and needs. And if you're going to deal with individual needs and wants you're not going to get anywhere, you know. The whole thing where we're all equals—we should all be treated equally —that's bullshit, you know. Mao said it—I hate to quote Mao or anybody, but Mao said, 'From each according to their ability, to each according to their need.' "

Joe is gently reminded that this is a central bit of the original Marx—from the *Communist Manifesto,* in fact.

"Oh, well, Marx said it," he recovers without a pause. "I'm glad

I'm wrong. I'd rather be wrong about that shit anyway, 'cause I don't think much of it anyway." (A short time before that, he had stated unequivocally that "I have a very definite political line. I'm a revolutionary COMMUNIST and this must be made very clear.")

He resumes:

"So that slogan from Marx points out that we're *not* all equal, that we shouldn't be treated equally, you know, that God didn't create us all equal, you know, that to treat everybody equally means that those who are the smartest, the whitest, the richest, the most influential, are gonna come out on top, you know. People bad-mouth Lenin, you know, because he impressed the ruling class, he impressed the bourgeois, he put 'em in jail, man. Stalin fuckin' killed 'em, man, and they bad-mouthed that, you know. But what should you do? Should you allow them to come back into power by treating everybody equally, you know?"

(To which one can only reply with a big, fat "Huh?" And just how in the hell did *God* get into all this dialectical materialism?)

Brennan, who was nearly recruited for S.L.A. because he admired Joe's style and spirit and looked up to him as something of a hero, finally, with difficulty, pulled away from Remiro's full-speed-ahead "logic." He realized that Joe was not all *that* sure of himself despite the strong front, that he had recently lost a wife and walked out on an infant son, and that he was really at loose ends in the world.

"Much later I saw that Joe was adrift," says Brennan. "You know, no place to go, really. No way to take care of himself. He couldn't get a decent job, no way to offer any sort of security to a woman. And I think at this stage he felt that he just had nothing to lose, that he might as well dedicate his life to a cause. He felt confident enough in himself that when he made the wrong decisions he couldn't realize it and he kept putting a hundred percent of himself into trying to create social change. . . ."

At about this point, in the spring of '73, Brennan, Remiro, Bob Hood, and Rip Miller, who were all Namvets, moved into the attic of an old Oakland house at 3131 Cortland Avenue. (Remiro would later describe this arrangement as a "commune," but the truth of the matter was that it was simply four unmarried young men rooming together until each could work out a cooler arrangement with a young woman.)

"Everybody was on some sort of political trip in that house," says Brennan. "It wasn't just VVAW or Venceremos. It was a house in which all of us had radical politics in common. For Joe, by that time, it was mostly Venceremos. For Bob it was VVAW. For Rip it was also Venceremos. For me, it was sort of several groups I felt interested in, not just one."

Brennan was rooming with Joe for another reason as well. He wanted to observe the make-out master at work with a constant flow of obliging young women who visited Joe in his tight little attic room. Brennan was having trouble getting laid, and he watched Remiro operate with ill-concealed envy.

"We talked a lot about my own confusion," Brennan recalls, "and why I couldn't develop a relationship with a woman and have it last for a period of time. I saw Joe involved with two women at once. He had both Linda and Cathy—the two were friends and both knew what was going on—and I thought, 'Well, he must have some style of living that is satisfying to women.' After a while I tried to pay attention to what was going on and how he did it. I found his apparent openness was another way of controlling them. He manipulated them for his own needs."

Brennan asked Joe how it was done.

"We'd have conversations, you know, with regard to women in the movement that you're attracted to. I'd never made it with movement women although I was once involved with a girl in the Revolutionary Union. And he said, 'Don't forget that they come out of the same system that you did and that they may be fighting against female chauvinism as much as we might fight male chauvinism and male sexism. And you may end up being manipulated also. So you have to be responsible for your own satisfaction. . . .'"

Which is a radically acceptable way of saying that all is still fair in the battle of the sexes.

Brennan continued to watch the attic goings-on with obvious longing. He still wasn't getting any. His relationship with Joe began to deteriorate.

"After a while I heard some conversations that maybe some of the friendships Joe had were cultivated, and I had misgivings about our relationship," he says.

During this period, Joe's ex-wife, Kathy, visited the Cortland house a couple of times (probably hoping to win him back), and Brennan had eyes for her. As he now explains it in acceptable Movementese, "I remember thinking a couple of times, you know, I would be interested in having a relationship with her. But Joe felt she was too liberal, too closed. He felt she was too naive, too much a product of the system, too chauvinized. He felt that if she'd have sex with other men she would be more attractive to him. To me she seemed like a nice person and fairly intelligent and she could hold a conversation and she smoked a little dope with him and she'd probably have been more than willing to grow with him in ways that weren't involved with communism."

Brennan recalls that Joe was a regular pot-smoker at this stage in his life, two or three joints a day, but that he was not dropping any acid. The Cleveland, Ohio, ex-Navy man, who had only recently arrived in pot-wreathed California, was shocked. He thought that smoking that amount of grass was like "being drunk every day."

"I think smoking so much marijuana does damage to the emotional and intellectual growth," says Brennan, "and that frightens me."

Brennan says he remonstrated with Joe about his pot "addiction," and he got especially upset in summer, '73, when all the heavy Venceremos revolutionary leaders were invited over to the Cortland house for a big party and Joe proceeded to stock up on a large supply of extra grass for the event. As Brennan recalls it:

"I said, 'You know, we shouldn't smoke dope. We shouldn't have any dope in the house, 'cause if the police wanted to bust it, this would be fantastic . . . they would have everybody in the house who purported to be the vanguard leadership of the revolution in the Bay Area . . . and here they would all be smoking dope.'

"Joe said, 'Don't be ridiculous. You're being stupid and silly and blah, blah, blah.' Then, just before he moved out in the fall, he said that one of the reasons he was moving was that he wanted to quit smoking marijuana and he felt he couldn't do it around us."

Such contradictions were not unusual in Joe's life. His attitude toward VVAW had completely flip-flopped between September of '72, when he helped to found the new chapter, and the following March, when he effectively dropped out of it.

At issue was Joe's feeling that VVAW–WSO should become more of a general-membership radical organization concerned with a lot more than veterans' benefits and the war in Asia. He felt that VVAW should be deeply involved in many of the same issues that Venceremos was then taking on: disarming of the police, the prison movement, the building of international socialism. Ironically enough, shortly after Remiro left, the organization moved more in the directions he had been urging. As a recent editoral in the *Winter Soldier* newspaper states: "While vets clearly have particular needs and demands, we cannot allow the fight to obtain them to be carried out in isolation from the fight to solve the many problems facing the whole country." The statement urges VVAW–WSO members to fight imperialism, which it calls "the root cause of veterans' problems." It notes that worrying about vets-only issues like medical care, jobs, education, and housing would be "putting a band-aid on a cancerous sore."

As Bob Hood recalls Remiro's parting:

"All these people were saying, 'We only want to do veterans' problems,' and Joe was a combat veteran and he was given leadership and he was saying, 'No. We want to work on Third World struggles. We want to work on this and that and the other, yadda, yadda, yadda.' And people didn't want to follow his leadership and he thought they were being two-faced and liberal. Joe just doesn't have the patience to work with that kind of people right along. He'll go as far as he can with words and then he'll get hot and he'll blow up. He's into action more than words."

A bitter Remiro said later that "I don't consider VVAW or any so-called veterans' organization you read about in the media valid. Most of the VVAW guys had been clerks in Nam, rear-echelon jockeys. I don't consider that representative of Viet vets. As a matter of fact, over sixty-five percent of the combat vets in Nam were nonwhite, and these are the guys the system had better watch out for. But these guys just didn't join VVAW.

"The Oakland Chapter was ninety-nine percent white. I was one of the two combat veterans in a chapter of over twenty-five. And I've got these people who've never been in the service telling me they don't want to do this, they don't want to do that, they want to do things *veterans* want to do. Well, motherfuck that, man! Well, if I'M not a veteran, I'm leaving! I decided the best thing for both was for me to leave and they could go on with their liberal GI benefits thing and I could get off into what I wanted to get into. . . ."

8

"The people will never come to us and say, 'Let's fight.'
There have never been any spontaneous revolutions. They were
all staged, manufactured, by people who went to the head of
the masses and directed them. . . ."
—George Jackson, in *Blood in My Eye*

THE LEADING EDGE OF THE FIGHT for social change in America in the '60s was open confrontation in the streets, first through peaceful protest within the law and then through nonviolent civil disobedience to call attention to the law's injustice.

In 1968–70, the movement was still in the open, but nonviolence had given way to hit-and-run street fighting and trashing. It was a mostly one-sided battle of angry desperation, and the rebels paid a heavy price in arrests and casualties in those violent days after the Martin Luther King assassination and the Chicago "Conspiracy" of '68, the "Days of Rage" and People's Park in '69, the Kent State massacre of '70, and the unprecedented Washington May Day Mop-up of 1971.

"I saw the streets filled with blood," wrote a bitterly battered participant, "all of it *ours*."

By the end of '69, right-wing Republicans had taken full control in both California and the nation. In Washington, the policy became unrelenting "law 'n' order"—arrest 'em first and find out what they're protesting about later. In Sacramento, Ronald Reagan had promised to demolish the Berkeley left "if it takes a bloodbath," and he proved to be dead serious.

Movement veterans who had not retreated into anonymous paranoia by the end of Nixon's first term in '72 were understandably morose about their casualties. They no longer wanted to "take it to the streets." After Chicago's Finest had mopped up the Haymarket with the bodies of the Weathermen in '69, that group went underground and began a long campaign of bombings directed primarily at property rather than human life. The Weather Underground went right to the seat of the political problem in America—almost all of their bombs were planted in public toilets (in the Pentagon, the Capitol building, the Marin Courthouse, dozens of other government facilities).

In Berkeley, the new heroes of the hour were not only these very selective bombers but such out-front total revolutionaries from abroad as the Tupamaros of Uruguay, Brazil's October 8 Movement, the IRA in Northern Ireland, and the Black Septemberists in Palestine. The new textbooks of the Berkeley left were Che Guevara's *Guerrilla Warfare, 150 Questions for the Urban Guerrilla* (by Gen. Alberto Bayo, who had first trained Fidel Castro), and *The Mini-Manual of the Urban Guerrilla* by Carlos Marighella. Not even the Black Panthers seemed radical enough any more and quickly lost popularity. (The Panthers were accused of "going Establishment" after they toned down their "armed self-defense" program and prepared to campaign as "Democrats" in the Oakland city election of 1973. Panther Chief Huey Newton had rented a luxurious $650-a-month apartment overlooking Lake Merritt and hired a personal bodyguard.)

As the Berkeley left moved toward armed uprising, Che's battle cry of *"Venceremos"*—"We Shall Win" became the new rallying point. It became the name of the Bay Area's most extreme revolutionary group of the '71–'73 period. It was to Venceremos that Joe Remiro gravitated as he lost all faith in peaceful social change. Venceremos preached a great deal of what S.L.A. later practiced. Whether or not Venceremos members *acted out* their frequent contention that only armed uprising could bring an end to all they hated in America would prove a sticky legal question that is still being debated.

But there is no doubt that Joe Remiro, Thero Wheeler, Angela Atwood, and Bill and Emily Harris were full-fledged Venceremos members and that Russ Little, Willie Wolfe, and Mizmoon Soltysik were on the periphery of the group's activities. A lot of Remiro's belief that urban guerrilla warfare is the only acceptable alternative to open protest and confrontation was firmed up while he worked with Venceremos, and this kind of thinking is a logical outgrowth of the organization's public position and an even clearer extension of the secret activities with which many members were charged and of which at least six were convicted.

The new tactics boiled down to a policy of hit-and-run attack both on persons and on property by small armed groups where the Establishment least expected it. This would lead, they felt, to a period of savage repression, which, in the end, would polarize the masses and bring millions to the cause of revolution.

As Remiro explains this kind of thinking, he and his friends had decided by 1973 that pacifism, protest, and confrontation in the streets are "finished history. It's a dead end. Everything those peace marches accomplished has been taken back. . . ." As far as "taking it violently to the streets" is concerned, "you don't want a bunch of people who are going to riot . . . they just get murdered. What do you do with riots? You just meet the military army head-on. They know exactly where you are and they can pick the time and the place, man, when to sock you.

"You don't fight the bourgeois military on their own terms. . . . You don't dig trenches if the enemy is all up on trench warfare, you know. You don't have a riot if the enemy is ready to deal with any size riot at any time. A lot of innocent people got killed in those riots in the '60s and I pray people don't go out and riot any more, man. I pray that they use their heads and lay back and study guerrilla warfare. Guerrillas pick their own time and place to strike and even the government admits they have no defense against it. . . ."

The history and politics of Venceremos are, of course, considerably more complex than a philosophy of hit-and-run warfare. The fact that this little-understood offshoot of an offshoot of Students for a Democratic Society (SDS) was able to exist aboveground from January, '71, until mid-'73 is a clear indication that its organizer, Stanford English Professor Bruce Franklin, was more than hip to the political realities of the period.

Venceremos was careful to cloak its clandestine operations beneath a mantle of legal public activity, working to defend and politically educate prisoners, operating a people's medical center and a drug clinic, setting up a defense committee for an active-duty GI war protester, staging antiwar demonstrations that had a tendency to get extremely violent, even running a perfectly legal newspaper.

It was necessary to publicly and legally bring together a membership that might later be won over to clandestine "armed struggle." As Franklin himself put it, "It was impossible to build a base without taking direct action, and no direct action was effective without building a base. It was equally impossible to serve the people effectively without raising the level of the struggle."

Venceremos stood up strongly for Third World causes, and it boasted it had a "majority" of Third World leadership on its Central Committee. It was, in fact, the only white-student-originated radical group to deliberately follow such a policy, despite the fact that its membership majority remained predominantly white.

Venceremos grew directly out of the student left. It developed out of a schism in the Bay Area branch of the Revolutionary Union, which was one of the two halves of SDS that emerged after a 1969 convention in Chicago. The other faction was Weatherman.

The publicly stated program of Venceremos made it appear the most radical aboveground organization of the period. It proclaimed the need for a socialist revolution and a dictatorship of the proletariat. Its five-plank platform (echoing that of the Black Panthers in many particulars) demanded armed self-defense, community control of police (by which they also meant a disarmed police force and an armed citizenry), creation of a "People's Liberation Army," and the right of racial and ethnic minorities to set up their own nations after the revolution if they so chose. S.L.A.'s constitution incorporated much of this.

And, like the S.L.A. philosophy, Venceremos was extremely strong on women's rights, demanding night-and-day child-care centers, free abortion and birth control, total job equality, and true sexual freedom.

Venceremos was deliberately vague about what was meant by "armed struggle." It obviously did not mean taking on the Man with a peashooter, and it went well beyond the strictly defensive Black Panther concept that you've got a right to own a piece to defend your own home should it be invaded by police. Venceremos people did not put it in writing, but they *talked* a lot about going on the offensive through urban guerrilla warfare.

In private, that is.

For Franklin and his well-educated colleagues knew the law, and they knew that to have announced a time and place for armed revolution would surely have gotten them busted. So, in public, Venceremos was most ambiguous about just how and when the revolution would begin. It was their private activities that got them into trouble and led to the group's "demise" in mid-1973.

It's hard to pin down exactly what they *did* do and what they are still doing, for once you enter into this territory—just who stuck what gun in whose face, who made and planted what bombs, how prison guards were killed to aid in the escape of prisoners, the planning of assassinations and kidnappings—you'd better watch your step. This ain't no Sunday-school picnic, buster. You screw up here, and next thing you know you're busted or dead—or both.

Needless to say, only the people who actually got their hands bloody can tell you the full story of just how violent Venceremos actually became and just how much of a direct outgrowth the S.L.A. was of the earlier group. Some of them are dead, and the rest ain't talkin'.

But we have some intriguing clues. The most extensive information on the Venceremos "underground" comes from one of its members, a double-dealing prisoner named Ronald Beaty, who is now being held in supertight custody to save him from the usual fate of snitches in the prison system.

It was Beaty who almost single-handedly dug the Venceremos grave when he appeared as a voluble state's witness against several organization leaders who had helped him escape from Chino prison guards on October 6, 1972. One of the guards was brutally murdered. The conviction in late '73 and early '74 of half a dozen radicals who had stuck their necks out to free and hide Beaty led to Venceremos calling it a day as an aboveground organization. Many California politicians and law-enforcement people claim that segments of the group just went underground and are now raising hell all across the landscape under new names. (It was apparent in the last few months of its legal existence that Franklin and the Central Committee were rapidly losing control of outlying Venceremos collectives. Their restructuring into independent urban guerrilla bands could well have taken place without any cohesive plan.)

Some charge that S.L.A. is no more than a continuation of one of the Venceremos collectives.

In any case, it is Beaty's testimony during the "Chino Escape Case" and at a March, '74, session of the California State Senate Subcommittee on Civil Disorder that provides a quick look into the violent side of Venceremos. (Since Beaty is a proven fink it would be wise to weigh his words carefully before believing him. Nevertheless, what he said in the official hearing is on the record.)

Beaty claims that Venceremos operated publicly with an "open membership" but carried on its clandestine activities with a "closed membership."

"The open membership is for, say, the Stanford Chapter," he says. "They recruit any students that are willing to listen or participate in nonviolent activities like protests or sit-ins or something. And an open member can come and go freely. They never learn or obtain any knowledge of a type that would be damaging to the organization itself. This is the way you eventually move up the ladder, by the way. . . .

"If you start, you start as an open member, and through your participation in activities and your dedication to study, you may eventually participate in a little bombing and you may participate in a burglary for them, the performance they are looking for in addition to dedication."

Those who proved themselves out, claims Beaty, became part of the "closed membership," but few knew many details of the covert operations. Everything was done on a "need-to-know basis."

"Just as an example of my own escape," he says, "there were six members involved. No one of that six knew what the other's job was. If they got caught, they couldn't tell. Only I and Gene Hobson, who is the Central Committee member on the team, actually knew the plan. . . ."

Thanks to Beaty's testimony, Ms. Hobson, forty-five, was convicted of murdering the guard in the Chino escape. (She was captured in December of '72 while driving the escaped Beaty across the Bay Bridge.)

Beaty claims that Venceremos was putting most of its money and energy into working with California prisoners in the hope of helping a number of them escape so they could form an underground organization to bring all-out revolution to America within one to three years.

He says the plan called for him to "set up an underground, illegal arm of Venceremos." He would "set up a training camp where we could train small teams of volunteers from the Venceremos organization and from escaped prisoners that we assisted. We had planned on stopping CDC buses (prison buses) en route, commandeering them with weapons, freeing specific prisoners that we knew were being transferred and attempting to recruit others on the spot with reward of their freedom there. We would have a training camp where we would take these people and train them in illegal activities: sabotage, assassination, kidnap, robbery. And we were preparing at the time I was out, we were actually preparing then a manual of what we had done.

"We had solicited each member of Venceremos if they had any special knowledge, like making bombs. If he was a good explosives man, he was to summarize his knowledge in a workable manner. Criminal elements, like myself, hot-wire cars and things of this nature; burglar alarms, how to get around them. We were summarizing as much information for use in illegal activities as we could, and each member of these teams would be trained in every phase of this. Our plans were set up so that each sixty to ninety days we would have approximately a ten-man team fully trained. And this squad would be trained for a specific mission—for example, kidnap. We would be trained for that one purpose, kidnapping. In that training we would have several other crimes involved. We would, maybe, have to kill a police officer as final initiation rites, or we may have to commit a large burglary or robbery to finance ourselves. But our ultimate mission was the kidnap. Once we had completed this, then this ten-man squad disintegrated and went into five two-man teams and they went into five different parts of the country, five major cities. They created the whole evolution over again. They liberated from the town they were assigned to or recruited another ten people, set them up, trained them for a period of sixty days, taught them everything that they had been taught, again for a specific goal in that town, kidnap or assassination or sabotage or a major robbery. You can see how fast we intended that to multiply. With ten teams or five teams breaking out of each one every sixty days, at the end of the year you have quite a number of cells established."

Testimony by both Beaty and an undercover "Red Squad" cop concluded that, although Venceremos had "officially" disbanded by August of '73 (the month S.L.A. issued its declaration of war), in actuality, they simply split up and went underground in small groups, with its members beginning new activities that were an extension of what they had been doing before.

Beaty testified that the only difference between S.L.A. and Venceremos was the change of name. "Their actions," he said, "are precisely out of the manual that we wrote. They are just six months behind schedule."

Whether or not Venceremos flowed that directly into S.L.A. is questionable. Joe claims that he made up his mind late in the spring of '73 that Venceremos did not suit him.

"Their political line was real nice, but, in practice, it came out as racist, opportunist, and elite, and every time they got a Third World person they threw him into leadership and said, 'Look! We have Third World leadership! It became evident to me that I had no say in what was going on and nobody I knew had any say. It was just a few people dictating to the rest. Venceremos was an experience I had to go through to learn. The experience was good and the best experiences are the ones you get fucked in, because those are the ones you learn most from."

It was the issue of "token leadership" by blacks and Chicanos that seemed to upset Remiro most. He would later duck the issue of whether Donald DeFreeze, the only black clearly active in S.L.A. for a period of time, was also, in the Venceremos tradition, a token general field marshal.

"Black women wouldn't join Venceremos," he says, "because they saw that all the group was doing was grabbing black dudes, giving them a white old lady, and putting them in leadership. They saw it as a threat, and it was. It was bullshit. It was a rip-off. They ripped off aggressive nonwhite people, put 'em in a white organization, took 'em away from their own community, the people they *should* have been leading."

Whether or not Remiro really means all that he says about Venceremos is another matter. S.L.A. members tried hard to take the heat off old comrades by "cutting them off" in late '73.

Whatever the truth of the matter may finally be about S.L.A.'s growth out of the earlier radical group, it is clear that Remiro's activities in Maoist Venceremos put him in touch with the two main issues that created S.L.A.—armed struggle and the prison movement. And Venceremos contacts put Joe in touch with Mizmoon Soltysik, Camilla Hall, Thero Wheeler, and Donald DeFreeze, all "known" S.L.A. members.

It is impossible at this point to piece together all the intimate details of how this core group of at least eleven people created S.L.A. It is apparent that there were originally more members and a "backup" circle of sympathetic friends. But secrecy became an obsession with the new group, so much so that FBI and local police admitted that all the usual informers and plants were totally useless. Reporters for underground publications also found that their normal sources in the traditional Berkeley left had gone dry.

There was a great deal of rumor, conjecture, and theory in the air but damned little fact. As Remiro explains S.L.A.'s need for extraordinarily tight security arrangements:

"If you look historically at the way things happen in this country, anyone who tries to organize any kind of militant organization is framed and infiltrated from the first. But S.L.A. was *not* infiltrated. All those stoolies and all their fuckin' political organizations didn't know jackshit about the S.L.A. All those underground informers, agents and shit, are impotent against groups like S.L.A."

Russell Little puts it even more succinctly:

"There was no contact with all those pseudoleft groups. Who's going to run to Venceremos when they got snitches all through the organization? Half of the people in prison have been sold out by political leadership like that."

(Informed observers who have watched massive government infiltration of the extreme left in America since the early '50s, when one former FBI agent revealed that at least half the membership of the Communist party was made up of informers, would not readily argue with such assumptions. Nixon's secret "plumbers unit" was equally obsessed with spying on the new left.)

So the story of what Remiro went through during that crucial period from about March, '73, when he dropped out of active participation in VVAW, his last aboveground involvement, and his arrest on January 10, 1974, must be pieced together from what he says and implies, from what Russell Little has been willing to say, from the clues provided by one or two of Remiro's friends, like Bill Brennan and Bob Hood, and from what the prosecution has leaked out about their case to newspapers and through reading the transcript of the Alameda Grand Jury proceedings in which Remiro and Little were indicted for murder.

It is not an altogether satisfying way to cover this fascinating period of revolutionary activity. But, in the end, all of the pieces of the puzzle seem to fall together.

As Remiro pulled away from VVAW and decided it was time to turn all that talk about armed struggle into practice, two major events occurred that were to shape the course of his history.

On February 28, 1973, more than four hundred militant Indians took over the hamlet of Wounded Knee, South Dakota. They would hold it for seventy days, until May 8. Joe would be there for the last ten days of battle.

On March 5, 1973, an inmate named DeFreeze would escape from Soledad and come to Berkeley to hide out. He would soon be working closely with Remiro.

Through that spring, Joe kept busy on a number of fronts. He was still living in the Oakland attic on Cortland Avenue, but he also had mail delivered to a nearby little cottage, at 4414 Bond Street, as he prepared to move over there. Late in January, he enrolled at North Peralta College to take a course in auto mechanics so that he might finally learn a skill that could lead to a regular job. (Willie Wolfe went to school there too that semester. Russ Little enrolled that spring at the College of Alameda, another campus of the Peralta Junior College District.)

Joe was heavily into Marxist study groups, along with other members of the Venceremos–VVAW circle, and he had begun to teach his comrades how to use, dismantle, and maintain such weapons as the M-1 carbine, revolvers, automatic pistols, and shotguns. He frequently went out to the Chabot Rifle Range in the Oakland Hills that spring and summer with S.L.A. members Little, Wolfe, the Harrises, Nancy Ling Perry, Camilla Hall, Angela Atwood, and Mizmoon Soltysik.

Bill Brennan is one of the few friends who went through this period with Joe and is now willing to talk about it.

"Joe was as dedicated and intense as ever," says Brennan. "He had a lot of energy that spring, a lot of discipline. He talked a lot of politics. We used to talk a lot about what racism is and what its manifestations are. We talked about the economic basis of racism and how economics control politics. I attended a lot of the study groups and met Willie Wolfe and Bill and Emily Harris there. We talked a lot about Marx, Lenin, the National Question, Mao, and George Jackson. I was into reading philosophical essays a lot then."

As many as twenty to thirty other Berkeley radicals were invited to attend these study groups. Apparently they were used as the first level of screening to check out and recruit people for S.L.A. Brennan did not make the grade.

"I met Russ Little and Angela Atwood when they came around the house," Brennan continues. "None of them seemed particularly crazy to me. They seemed calm and gentle and loving and deeply committed to the idea that the current American economic and political conditions are intolerable."

Late in April, Remiro decided to join in the Battle of Wounded Knee. He had by now completely reversed the John Wayne shoot-'em-up ethics of his youth and wanted to join the Indians in wiping out palefaces. The fight had been going on for more than six weeks, and it had become one of the great causes célèbres of the Berkeley left. It was almost all that Remiro and his Venceremos study groups talked about, and Joe decided, in typical actions-speak-louder-than-words fashion, that it was time to go out and DO something about helping the Indians. He hopped into a truck, along with one of his VVAW buddies, and drove off to South Dakota to enter into his first armed engagement since the Tet Offensive of January, 1968, in Vietnam.

The confrontation had originated when members of the American Indian Movement (AIM) had deliberately taken over the site of the last major massacre of an Indian tribe by the U.S. Army (April 29, 1890).

AIM leaders claimed that provisions of the original treaty of 1868 between the United States and the Sioux Nation had been broken, and they were especially angry about the way the Oglala tribe, who lived in the Wounded Knee area, had been treated. On February 22, 1973, they declared that the Sioux were once again an independent nation, at war with the United States.

After six weeks of battle, trained soldiers were badly needed, and Joe was immediately welcomed when he came in with arms and ammunition.

"I was at Wounded Knee just a little more than a week," he recalls. "I was inside the boundaries of the Wounded Knee perimeter. I went there to find out whether the Indians wanted anything to do with outside agitators—and they sure *did*. It was my job to run from bunker to bunker during the fire fights, bringing in ammunition for them."

"I have nothing but respect for the Oglala Sioux Indians, man. Those Oglala Sioux are HELL!

"Shit, one of their women, she turned an armored personnel carrier around with a twenty-two rifle. The people inside Wounded Knee were eating oatmeal and living in holes in the ground and in bunkers.

"But their leadership was a bunch of bullshit. While the people in Wounded Knee were nearly starving and freezing to death, Dennis Banks was living in a fortified house and eating eggs, and Russell Means was in California saying they were going to 'fight to the death.' Their leadership was a bunch of shit."

Joe says that the "real fighters" came in armed with everything from M-16s to a small automatic cannon, and that he gladly fought beside them. But such true soldiers were few and far between, and Remiro was pleased when he found he was needed and accepted by the Indians.

"A few good guns would have gone a long way, man," he says a bit wistfully. "There those Indians are, out in the trenches at night with these old rifles and shotguns blazing away and hitting nothing." Remiro was standing watch when the second fatality of Wounded Knee occurred, and he had to sneak through the federal lines to go report it to Dennis Banks, whom he found "shacked up in this little house in town with his old lady and they're eating meat and good food while back at Wounded Knee the real fighters are getting some kind of a stew that's ninety-five percent oatmeal."

Remiro stuck it out until the night of May 5, when word came that an agreement was about to be signed.

"The real fighters split, man," he recalls, "and they took their guns with them. They weren't *about* to stick around and get busted! All the feds found was one old guy with one handgun when they came in the next day, and that belonged to one of the people who lived in the place and it was there before the occupation."

Bill Brennan recalls that Remiro limped home from Wounded Knee on crutches in mid-May.

"He said he slipped and fell down an embankment when he was escaping that last night," says Brennan.

"Joe was very open about what happened to him up there—as always," Brennan continues. "He told us about the sniping between the Indians and the marshals and about this ritual he went through with the Indians in something like a sauna bath, and when it was over he was sunburned from the heat of it. He said he had a sort of spiritual experience with a medicine man up there. But with all his Marxist training he was very dubious about what he saw and felt."

Remiro had cut classes from North Peralta College to make the Wounded Knee scene, and Brennan says he had to take a special test to get through his auto-mechanics course. Joe passed but did not enroll in college again.

By early June, Joe spends less and less time at home in the Cortland house. The political study sessions, gun classes, and range practice continue. Brennan feels that something dangerous is building up, but he cannot put his finger on exactly what it is.

In early summer, Joe is still going with Cynthia Garvey. Venceremos is in deep trouble and is facing prosecution in the Chino Escape Case. Brennan says that Joe tells Cynthia a couple of times that he's quitting Venceremos, but he does not seem to actually do it.

He is getting very intense about guns. Brennan remembers his purchase that summer of an automatic pistol. (On July 17, '73, Remiro purchases a German Walther .380 at Traders Sporting Goods in Oakland. He pays $149.95 for it and picks it up on July 24.)

"He bought this three-eighty with a six-and-a-half-inch barrel," says Brennan, "and he had it for a while and then he was making all these movements in this room saying, 'Wow! This gun's not concealable enough, but it feels good!' So he went back and got another one and he said, 'Ya, this is concealable. You know, you can hold this in your hand and no one can see it, you know.' And he was sighting it around the room and so on."

Joe bought the second Walther .380 on September 25, '73, at Seigel's Guns in Oakland. He paid $169 for it and picked it up on September 29. Along with the pistol, he purchased a hundred rounds of superpowered, hollow-point bullets. "They were too strong and expensive for target practice," says the man who sold all of this to him.

Brennan becomes nervous as Joe gets more and more silent. That summer, an Oakland police helicopter had crashed while on patrol and a group calling itself the "August 7 Movement" took credit for shooting it down.

"I guess I said something against the guys who shot down the copter," says Brennan. "I said that action was really fucked, and he had a really strong physical reaction, like, he moved or his face contorted or something. But he was strangely quiet about it. He didn't say anything, which I thought was funny. And then sometime that fall, I think it was around November, he moved over to Bond Street with Willie the Wolfe which I thought was good. It felt more comfortable with him gone."

Brennan says that sometime late that summer Remiro approached him with a plan for stealing a car.

"He said he'd learned how to steal cars when he was in high school," says Brennan, "and that it would be easy. I think he was seeing how far I'd go. I think he was going to try to recruit me for S.L.A. and I'm glad now I backed out of it."

Remiro was later charged in Alameda County with stealing a '69 Chevrolet van on October 12, 1973, from a Berkeley resident named Donald Sullivan. That's less than a month before Oakland Schools Superintendent Marcus Foster is shot on the parking lot of his administration building, and about seven weeks after the S.L.A. has framed its first major document, an August 21, 1973, "Declaration of War" against the United States of America. The declaration is made on the second anniversary of the death of George Jackson in San Quentin Prison.

By this time there are rumors floating around Berkeley that some sort of superviolent new group is forming, but no one knows any real facts. There's also a rumor that it has grown out of a faction of Venceremos and a collective called the "East Bay Commune," that there has been a split among the members, and that the more violent people have walked off with the weapons and some expensive ammunition-making equipment. There's this other rumor that some black dude who's just escaped from the pen has been going around to militant groups offering himself as a paid assassin but everybody is freaked by him and suspects he's some kind of an agent. It's all rumor. There are no names or dates or places. No concrete details of any kind.

The true histories of the known members of the Symbionese Liberation Army tell the story of this period in a more interesting and reliable way.

9

*"The musical accompaniment to the Castro revolution was Chopin
and the spirit of Garibaldi hung over it. It had all the naive
hopefulness and humanitarian faith of the 19th Century. . . ."*
—I. F. Stone, in an introduction to Che Guevara's *Guerrilla Warfare*

*"The composition of the S.L.A. is bewildering, but we can turn to
history to learn why such alliances are possible. I think
especially of the Russian student movement from the 1860's
to the Russian Revolution. . . ."*
—S. I. Hayakawa

THOSE WHO BLINDLY HATED the Symbionese Liberation Army, everything it had come out of and everything it stood for, were utterly appalled when a San Francisco commentator referred to them as "romantics, unbelievable nineteenth-century revolutionary romantics." The forces of law 'n' order could only see this little band as bloody-minded killers and abductors. They had no time or patience for comparisons or apologisms.

And yet there *are* some very strong similarities between S.L.A. and the fantastic generation of student terrorists and revolutionaries, the populist "Narodniki" of the 1860s, '70s, and '80s in Russia. Thousands of these young idealists attempted, like S.L.A., "to work for the people."

Their methods and their rhetoric are amazingly alike. As Pavel Axelrod put it in 1874, every revolutionary terrorist must decide that he will "abandon the university, forswear his privileged condition, his family, and turn his back even upon science and art. All connections linking him with the upper classes must be severed . . . he must transform his whole inner essence, so as to feel one with the lowest strata of the people. . . ."

Like the Narodniki, most of the young S.L.A. members came from the university intelligentsia. (As Remiro summed it up later,

"So what were we—four cheerleaders, two fraternity brothers, a young archaeologist, a philosopher, an artist . . . we were *some* bunch of baddies. . . .")

They came from comfortable, even rich, homes, and they deliberately cast aside their sheltered upbringings to identify themselves with the lowest strata they could find in America, not the now-prosperous proletariat, the employed union workers who old-fashioned Marxists will insist are still the only true revolutionary class, but the blacks and Chicanos and Indians; the unemployed and unemployable, the prisoners, the street gypsies and wanderers, the migrant laborers and punk kids just kicked out of high school, that great, surging wave of the unwashed whom the Marxists uneasily label "lumpenproletariat."

Like the Narodniki, who had little understanding of then-developing Russian dialectical materialism, but an enormous mystical confidence in their own half-informed vision and in "the people," the S.L.A. chose terrorism, assassination, bank robbery, and kidnap to gain the respect and following of this "lowest strata" and to undermine what they felt was an absolutist government.

The Narodniki, in a great wave of naive idealism, went out into the medieval countryside of Russia in 1874 to minister to sick peasants, teach revolution, bring their bodies and their hopeful rhetoric to the people. The suspicious kulaks promptly repaid all of this unsolicited attention by turning them in to the czar's secret police. S.L.A. was betrayed by the black people of the Los Angeles ghetto in much the same way.

A final item of comparison must be guesswork at this stage. The Narodniki (and the S.L.A.) thought in their own time that they *were* the revolution. But, instead, the Russian terrorists proved to be only its first wave, a futuristic irritant and example which led to true insurrection much later.*

The personal histories of all but four of the eleven young people publicly identified as S.L.A. members tend to confirm this striking parallel. They were young, idealistic, raised in comfortable homes and by middle-class or rich families whom they later renounced, turning toward revolution as THE answer with more fervor than reason, hunted down in a wave of savage repression. (The exceptions would include the only two

---

* Lenin's brother, Alexander, belonged to this movement and was executed for planning an attempt on the life of Czar Alexander III in 1887. The event had an overwhelming effect upon one of the men who would finally direct Russia's first *successful* revolution a full thirty years later.

real members of an oppressed race, the two blacks—Donald DeFreeze and Thero Wheeler. And then there were Joe Remiro, who may have been raised "white" but who actually *did* come from a working-class, partly Chicano family, and Russell Little, who is part Indian and also claims a working-class background. If you take Patricia Hearst's conversion to the S.L.A. completely seriously, she also sounds like a latter-day Narodnik.)

Remiro had become deeply involved with all the other Symbionese by early summer of '73. Their meeting ground was Oakland-Berkeley.

First on the scene was Nancy Ling Perry, twenty-six, one of the prettiest and most energetic (as well as the smallest, at four foot eleven, ninety-eight pounds) of the group. An intense, totally committed social reformer, Nancy (who was named Fahizah—"One Who Is Victorious" —by the S.L.A.) began life at the other end of the political spectrum.

She was raised in Santa Rosa, California, about eighty miles north of San Francisco. It is the seat of Sonoma County, a rather quiet, politically somnambulant agricultural area. Her father was Hal C. Ling, an ultraconservative and well-to-do furniture-store owner who thought he had conditioned his daughter well when she became a cheerleader in junior high and spent part of her high-school senior year campaigning for her father's favorite politician, Barry Goldwater. It is said that Nancy became fond of Goldwater's famous maxim: "Extremism in the defense of liberty is no vice."

The recollections of her parents, who later disowned her, are mostly clichés. The "We gave her everything!" and "She had every opportunity a kid could want!" kind of stuff. Her father says that she was "deep rather than frivolous" in high school, where she maintained a straight-A average and became class secretary.

But perhaps he sensed her growing rebellion, for he packed her off in '65 to Richard Nixon's ultraconservative alma mater, Whittier College in Southern California. The place irritated and bored Nancy Ling, and she demanded the chance to study in a more stimulating atmosphere. By fall of '66 she was registered at the Berkeley campus of the University of California.

At first her parents talked her into living in a university residence hall, but Nancy soon slipped out to settle in the swarming South Campus community, and from then on her life melted into that of the radical Berkeley scene. She graduated in '71 with a bachelor's degree in English literature. She reregistered as a chemistry major, hoping eventually to study medicine. She never got the chance.

More than any of the other white S.L.A. members, "Fahizah" gave herself completely over to two of the great causes of the Berkeley revolution—integration of blacks and prison reform. Nancy soon learned to think and act and talk *black*.

In 1967, at the age of nineteen, she completely flipped out her parents by marrying a talented black composer, pianist, and harpsichordist, Gilbert Perry, who was also a UC student at the time. Their stormy marriage ("It was a love-hate kind of thing") lasted legally until her death seven years later, but she was separated from Gilbert in February, '73, and never went back.

Nancy was probably the first member of S.L.A. to think seriously about the prison problem. Her first activities, writing to and visiting prisoners, began in 1966.

Life as the wife of a struggling young musician was a rough one from the beginning, and Nancy had to work. She dealt a watered-down form of blackjack, mostly topless, in a slimy North Beach tourist dive, turned a few tricks now and then, dealt dope, did a lot of shoplifting, and liked living in San Francisco's Fillmore District because, as she once put it only half-jokingly, "it provides quicker access to crime."

She lived through the great early days of the Haight-Ashbury and the first, invigorating splurge of good feeling and wild rhetoric in Berkeley. She liked the freedom of the streets, hitchhiking and living in the immediate present. She wanted to be a person who happened just now.

Although Nancy was a great one for bunching up her tiny fist and yelling "Right on" at political rallies and during discussions (especially with attractive young men), she never struck her Berkeley friends as a political "heavy." Her beliefs, like those of a lot of the South Campus floating population, were a rather amorphous blend of radical rhetoric, astrology (she let the charts guide her life), yoga, and the *I Ching*. She was never a really serious student of Marxism. It was hard if you stayed as stoned as Nancy did after she and her husband split up—"twelve or thirteen joints a day."

It was, in fact, that separation which led directly to her recruitment into S.L.A. After she and Gilbert came apart, Nancy was distracted and despondent. She needed a man.

She moved from one cheap flat to another, staying stoned, and dealing "the best dope in town and the finest hash oil there was." She went through mercurial shifts of mood: "Some weeks she'd look like a beautiful, cocky bitch. On other weeks she'd look like a waif with greasy hair." She told one friend that her separation from Gilbert and her own conflicts had led her into an "incredible self-hatred, that sometimes her mind was completely obliterated by her venom toward herself."

During this time she worked fairly steadily in the very center of the Berkeley street scene, in a portable little "Fruity Rudy" juice stand that sat on the sidewalk at the UC campus end of Tele.

She met hundreds of people but worked hard and didn't converse much unless she felt someone was "political." She had little use for those "dissipated old-timers from the '60s."

She had trouble working inside the tiny juice stand with the bright orange-and-green awning. Her employer was Rudy Henderson, a forty-seven-year-old black man with close-cropped, silvery hair who was once a jazz drummer. He now runs four "Fruity Rudy" stands around Berkeley and gives tennis lessons.

"It took her six months before she could get up enough nerve to work in the cart. She had claustrophobia," recalls Rudy. Nancy apparently fell in love with her boss early in her separation from Gilbert.

"One time she shouted in the street, 'Don't you know I love you?' She was trying to rush me into something and I was a cold fish. But I liked her more after she made her move," he says.

To prove her love, Nancy tried to get Rudy a hot TV set from some guys who had picked her up hitchhiking. Rudy ended up paying $150 for a box of bricks and wood, and Nancy immediately hitched over to the City to turn tricks so she could pay him back. Rudy accepted the money. "She was like a sister to me—but she had to learn," says he.

Their relationship went no further. Nancy was looking hard for a man and suddenly she found *two*. First she went with Joe Remiro and then with a handsome Southern friend of his named Russell Little. A romance blossomed, and Nancy began to pull herself into line with Russ's revolutionary life style.

"She gave up dope and switched to health foods," one friend recalls. "She gave away these 'superlids' to her neighbors and she became very concerned with her own body. She wanted to cleanse herself. She didn't feel she was of any use to the revolution all stoned out. . . ."

In early '73, Nancy became more involved than ever with the prison movement—at one point she contributed $130 out of her weekly $140 salary to needy prisoners.

Russ was also deeply into visiting the penitentiaries, and their dual dedication brought them even closer together. She had long been writing to men at Folsom. In the spring and summer of '73, Nancy began to visit Albert Taylor at Vacaville. Taylor is a prison militant and a friend of Death Row Jeff, a jailhouse revolutionary of great repute whom Russ Little was visiting at about the same time. The two must have traveled to Vacaville together frequently. Nancy also asked permission to join Russ in a number of meetings of a group called the Black Cultural Association. One of the more militant members of BCA was Donald DeFreeze, and, in this way, a small group of white Berkeley militants looking for a black leader found their messiah.

When S.L.A. hit the headlines early in '74, it was Nancy Ling Perry who became known as the group's "propagandist." That English degree was finally of some use to her. She was one of the first S.L.A.ers to be publicly identified, and her rhetorical style was receiving front-page play as early as February 10, '74, when the San Francisco *Examiner* ran an unedited 3,800-word letter in which she described her intellectual metamorphosis from high school to the present. It was probably the most interesting personal document produced in the whole caper. Nancy wrote that:

"I have three backgrounds. . . . I have a work background, a love background, and a prison background. My prison background means that I have close ties and feeling with our incarcerated brothers and sisters. What they have taught me is that if people on the outside do not understand the necessity of defending them through force of arms, then it is because these people on the outside do not yet realize that they are in an immediate danger of being thrown into concentration camps themselves, tortured or shot down on the streets for expressing their beliefs. What my love background taught me was a whole lot of what love is all about, and that the greater one's capacity for love is, the greater is one's longing for freedom. What my work background taught me is that one of the things that every revolutionary does is to fight to get back the fruits of her or his own labor and the control of his or her own destiny. . . .

"When I was in high school in 1963–64 I witnessed the first military coup against we, the people of this country. I saw us passively sit by our t.v.'s and unconsciously watch as the military armed corporate state took over the existing government, and blatantly destroyed the constitution that some of us still believed in. I listened to the people around me deny that a military coup had taken place and claim that such a thing could not happen here. The people that I grew up around were so politically naive that their conceptions of a military coup only recognized those that have occurred in South America and African countries where the military and ruling class took over the government by an open force of arms. But the method of taking over the government was different here. Here the coup was simply accomplished by assassinating the then president John Kennedy, and then assassinating any further opposition to the dictator who was to take power; that dictator is the current president Richard Nixon. In 1964 I witnessed these and other somewhat hidden beginnings of the military/corporate state that we now live in. And I heard my teachers and the government controlled media spread lies about what had happened. I saw the Civil Rights protests, the killings and bombings of my black brothers and sisters and the conditioned reactions of the extreme racism in my school and home. When I questioned my teachers about how these occurrences related to the meanings of democracy and freedom that we were told existed to protect us all, the answer I got was that we were better off not knowing the truth about what was happening. I told my teachers and my family and friends, that I felt we were all being used as pawns and puppets, and that those who had taken over the government were trying to keep us asleep and in a political stupor. I asked my teachers to tell me what happened in Nazi Germany; I asked them to tell me the meaning of fascism; I asked them to tell me the meaning of genocide; and then when I began to hear about a war in Vietnam, I asked them to tell me the meaning of imperialism. The answer to all my questions then was either silence or a reply filled with confusion and lies, and a racist pride and attitude that, 'Well, after all, it was all for us.' "

If this statement is true, Nancy Ling had ceased to be an "obedient and conservative" daughter long before her parents became aware of it. By the time she died, on May 17, 1974, she had become, in the eyes of Patricia Hearst: "A beautiful sister who didn't talk much but who was the teacher of many by her righteous example. She, more than any other, had come to understand and conquer the putrid disease of bourgeois mentality. She proved often that she was unwilling to compromise with the enemy. . . . Fahizah taught me the perils of hesitation, to shoot first and make sure the pig is dead before splitting. She was wise and bad."

Nancy Ling had been at UC almost two years when the next future S.L.A. member hit the scene.

In the fall of '68, when she arrived at the university with a scholarship to study sociology, French, English, and Spanish, she was known as Patricia Soltysik. But within three years, she had dropped out of school to become a radical lesbian feminist and was living with Camilla Hall, who gave her a poetic new moniker—"Mizmoon." She decided in '71 to legally change her name to "Mizmoon Boell" so that her life might become even more like the love poems Camilla was writing to her each day. In the S.L.A. she became "Zoya," and Patricia Hearst remembers her as a "female guerrilla, perfect love and perfect hate reflected in stone-cold eyes. She moved viciously and with caution, understanding the peril of the smallest mistake. She taught me, 'Keep your ass down and be bad.' "

Zoya died on her twenty-fourth birthday.

All accounts agree that Patricia-Mizmoon-Zoya was, indeed, the "baddest" of the S.L.A. women. She was clearly a product of that boiling rage and frustration which, in the early '70s, made the women's movement in Berkeley (and most especially its lesbian contingent) the most unrelenting and intolerant segment of the radical community.

But it had not always been so with this brilliant, highly independent daughter of a small-town pharmacist.

Patricia was raised in Goleta, a conservative little community of about three thousand, near the University of California's Isla Vista campus and, therefore, a part of the university complex.

As she was growing up, Patricia did her best to blend in with these quiet surroundings. She was the third in a family of seven, the eldest among five daughters. She remained close to her mother all of her life, although she is said to have feuded with her father after her parents were divorced.

In high school, Patricia Soltysik was regarded as a "superstraight conservative," an honors student who spent her spare time as president of the "Usherettes" service club, working with the farm-oriented 4-H Club, and training guide dogs for the blind. She went out for cheerleader but was not chosen.

She was obviously evolving a mind and style of her own, but in Goleta she kept things pretty much to herself, dating the local high-school heroes and dressing in "cashmere sweaters, skirts, nylons, and heels."

When she hit the exhilarating atmosphere of Berkeley, Patricia changed rapidly. Her dating habits shifted mostly from boys to girls after a massive misunderstanding with a boyfriend during her junior year. (A bit later in the game, though, she showed a strong bisexual proclivity for black men.)

She entered directly and forcefully into the radical feminist milieu and began work on a major artistic and sociological project, an exhibit of photographs accompanied by interviews with aged San Francisco women in which they described their social roles around the turn of the century. She quit her classes at UC to devote herself full-time to this labor of love.

In 1972, she and Camilla Hall separated and Camilla moved over to Francisco Street, at the other end of Berkeley.

Mizmoon's relationship with her mother and her brother, Fred, began to gradually weaken, although they had long boasted they were a close family. Her disapproving brother returned from Peace Corps duty in '72 to find his sister vastly changed:

"At first she was working on a one-to-one level," he recalls. "But then her sense of reality changed. She thought she could help with what she called 'the masses.' She went from liberal to humanitarian to romantic revolutionary. . . .

"She took a lot of shit and swallowed every word of it," he says. When Fred visited her for the last time, in the spring of '73, Mizmoon had become a "revolutionary ascetic . . . she was studying her butt off reading revolutionary tracts . . . no coffee, no cigarettes, just pure revolution."

At this stage, Mizmoon had become a $3.98-an-hour janitor at the Berkeley Public Library and was busy championing the hiring of more women in such jobs that had traditionally been for men only. She generally wore black-and-white-striped coveralls or baggy Turkish pants "with tons of room in the crotch."

Her brother notes acidly that "when she wasn't in the library, she was privately writing revolutionary theory." (FBI investigators later said that it was in the Berkeley library that Mizmoon and DeFreeze did most of the research and writing needed to put together the main S.L.A. documents. DeFreeze was, at this stage, living in Mizmoon's little house, where he had fled after his prison escape.)

Fred Soltysik, justifiably angry about his sister's final martyrdom, has nothing friendly to say about the politics that delivered her to her executioners. He calls her thinking "a mélange of women's rights and hash-brown rhetoric. She never discriminated against causes. She did the whole leftist trip: boycotting Gallo, the women's movement, writing and visiting prisoners."

It was this last activity that really got Mizmoon into trouble, for out of her visits in late '72 and early '73 to the Black Cultural Association at Vacaville came Donald DeFreeze's escape and the eventual formation of S.L.A.

But it was not the politics of the prison movement that brought Camilla Hall ("Gabi") to her death in Los Angeles at the age of twenty-nine. It was her love for Mizmoon.

A newly politicized Patricia Hearst later claimed that Camilla "crouched low with her ass to the ground" and "practiced until her shotgun was an extension of her right and her left arm . . . an impulse . . . a tool of survival. . . . She loved to touch people with a strong, not delicate embrace. Gabi taught me the patience and discipline necessary for survival and victory. . . ."

"Candy," as her childhood friends once called her, had come a long way from the days when her closest relationship with a gun was sticking flowers down the barrel of an embarrassed soldier's M-16 during a peace demonstration.

No one claims that Camilla was a saint. This bespectacled daughter of a Minnesota Lutheran minister who came from a German-Swedish background was full of driving hungers and needs and angers. Friends who knew her well in '73 felt that she had reached a dead end in one style of life, that of a smiling, gentle feminist who hated no one and who survived from '70 on in Berkeley as a parks groundskeeper and a mendicant poet and artist selling her work on weekends in supermarket parking lots. They felt that Camilla, about to face that crucial turning point of a thirtieth birthday, was either going to have to become a complete rebel or make a number of serious compromises that she was unable to face up to.

Camilla Hall was the oldest S.L.A. member next to DeFreeze, and she was the only veteran of an entire decade of civil-rights and antiwar struggle. She was a living reminder that the movement that finally produced S.L.A. had begun with a firm commitment to pacifism, to a philosophy and practice of complete nonviolence and humanism.

Candy had been pacifistic in everything she did. She was a lover of gently purring Siamese cats. She always had a house full of well-tended green plants and loved fine music and witty conversation. She was a deft and whimsical poet. She created subtle Thurberesque little paintings, etchings, and caricatures, which sold well for a time around Berkeley. If "Candy" could go apeshit for armed revolution, thought her troubled friends, then it could happen to *any* of us. And in the angry and frustrating days of the Nixon '70s, this was a dangerous thought.

Camilla-Candy-Gabi was born in a small, southern Minnesota town, the fourth and last child of the minister and his young wife, who died shortly after the birth. The other three children died before maturity—Terrance at age seven of a heart defect, Peter at eight of a kidney ailment, and Nan at fifteen of the same disease.

Her father took her with him on missionary duty in South America and Africa, where Camilla learned firsthand about hunger, disease, and dictatorial governments.

She returned to attend Gustavus Adolphus College, in St. Peter, Minnesota, where her father was chaplain. She was a bright, highly creative student with a flair for art. She then went to the University of Minnesota, got a B.A. in humanities, and went to work for three years as a social worker in Duluth and Minneapolis. Friends from this period recall that "her happiness came from playing the guitar and singing to neighborhood children." She generally had a kind word for everyone and an almost perpetual smile behind her thick glasses.

In the late '60s Camilla became dedicated to the peace movement and went to Washington to demonstrate. She was later maced while picketing a George Wallace rally. She gave over her spare time to an underground newspaper.

By '70, Camilla had decided to publicly embrace a lesbian life style, and she moved to Berkeley, half a continent away from her father, who "was not pleased with this development but who never interfered."

The early '70s were a time of creativity and some degree of success as Camilla gave poetry readings, held exhibitions of her art, and managed to eke out a living selling her work. But money got tighter and survival as an artist got a lot harder. A schoolmate named Joyce Halverson, whom Camilla used to visit in San Francisco, recalls that "she was getting very frustrated . . . nothing was going anywhere, really."

Her affair with Mizmoon was a happy one before the temporary breakup of late '72. It produced a great flow of love poems.

"I will cradle you/in my woman hips/kiss you/with my woman lips,/fold you to my heart and sing:/Sister woman, you are a joy to me," wrote Camilla at the height of the affair.

She recorded a moment of contentment this way: "strong and warm/beside my body/tender and gentle/next to my soul."

Their first breakup led her into a period of need and frustration.

She wrote: "*One* will do at the moment, but I know *my* thirst—I'll need MANY MANY MORE/before *I'm* through!/if old souls see a-new/ coming through the cry/who's to say we shouldn't try?"

There were times of intense loneliness, when she felt completely abandoned: "Surely out of two hundred/million people there must be/

one . . . two . . . or even *three*/who could love me . . ./where can they be?"

She remained a "goody-goody liberal" in the eyes of many of her more radical Berkeley acquaintances during this period, but in late '72 she took a trip to Europe to rethink her situation. She began again to correspond with Mizmoon, and she vividly imagined their reunion in this love poem, sent from Amsterdam in January of '73:

"I want to wake you coffee with real cream/brewed just like you like it—to go with a croissant or muffin/or some home made sweet./I want to surprise you with it—to see you smile up from your pillow/as the aroma gently wakes you/on a late rainy day. . . ./or laugh when you see me swoosh thru/your room with a blazing candle/chocolate ice cream,/and rich strong coffee—just like you like it."

From Spain she wrote Mizmoon that she soon would be home: "I thought I was free and I was. . . ./free to go/but not to stay away/ so I'm coming back . . ./and I'm glad you are there to sing me home."

Camilla got back to Berkeley in February, '73. There was a lot more brewing than coffee at this point, and her love for Mizmoon would soon take her into a world of gun classes, Maoist study groups, trips to a rifle range, and guerrilla warfare.

Like "Candy" Hall, Willie Wolfe, who was the next future S.L.A. member to hit the Berkeley scene in April of '71, was noted for his gentleness and idealism. At twenty-three, he was to be the youngest of the group's members until Patty Hearst, who turned twenty while in captivity, announced her conversion.

Willie (or "Cujo," as his guerrilla comrades called him) ended up as S.L.A. "treasurer and information officer." He had come to Berkeley to study archaeology and astronomy, but first he went to work in an East Bay factory to get his own tuition money together. This was typical of Willie the Wolfe—he always wanted to make it on his own despite the fact that he came from a family that long had been wealthy. His father, Dr. L. S. Wolfe, is a successful Emmanus, Pennsylvania, an-esthesiologist whose family had been in the habit of sending all of its sons to the better Eastern prep schools and then on to Yale.

Willie was the fifth of six children. He was raised, for the most part, in the well-to-do little community of Litchfield, Connecticut, where his grandparents had lived. They once gave him a model of the whaling ship *Charles W. Morgan,* docked at nearby Mystic, Connecticut. Willie never forgot. He used the name as an S.L.A. alias.

He was a precocious reader, finishing his first volume of Virginia

Woolf at the age of ten and making finalist in the National Merit Scholarships while at the exclusive Mt. Hermon prep school in Mt. Hermon, Massachusetts.

His father was more than willing to send him on to Yale, but Willie, already a strong-minded young idealist who had a tendency to take sudden and passionate interest in social causes, wanted to go out and discover the world for himself.

His father was a liberal who fleshed out his beliefs by bringing poor black kids into his home, and he understood and approved. First Willie moved to Harlem to room with Michael Carreras, one of the black foster brothers partly raised in the Wolfe family. He rapidly got involved in radical politics and began studying Marxist and Maoist thought.

"He was looking for a life of a little deprivation," comments Carreras. "When you've had it easy, maybe you feel guilty because you haven't been able to experience life in the raw."

When he was nineteen, Willie asked his dad for two hundred dollars to make a trip to Europe. He hitchhiked and worked his way across the continent and even spent part of the time digging ditches in Greece to make his own way. When he came home, nine months later, he returned sixty dollars to Dr. Wolfe.

Berkeley was obviously the next stopping-off place for this socially aware kid to bop into, but he made only a brief attempt to take regular classes in the Black Studies Department. By the fall of '72, Willie had moved out of a university residence hall and into an Oakland commune. Over the next year, he would live first with Joe Remiro at 4614 Bond Street and then would join Russ Little at the "Peking Man House" commune at 5939 Chabot Road. The place was full of Maoists, but that's not how it got the name. Those who originally set it up had operated a gypsy food-cart called "Peking Man" at the gates of UC, right next to Nancy Ling Perry's "Fruity Rudy" cart. Chinese health-food snacks had long supported the house.

Willie quickly became the most ardent prison-movement worker among the future S.L.A. members. He spent an enormous amount of time going to see prisoners at Vacaville, Folsom, and San Quentin, corresponding with them, and visiting their families when the inmates requested it. His intense energy was mainly channeled into the Vacaville Black Cultural Association, whose outside coordinator, Colston Westbrook, first brought Willie on in. Little, the Harrises, and other S.L.A. prospects soon joined him. Death Row Jeff would later claim that it was through BCA meetings that he and Willie became the "first S.L.A. members."

Willie's range of interests were very cerebral and diverse. He was a promising archaeologist who found such good fossils one summer in Wyoming that he lectured to a group of professionals about it. He joined radical demonstrations with a true believer's zeal, but, before S.L.A., he spoke strongly against violence and the possession of guns.

"My son," says Dr. Wolfe, "was a pussycat, a gentle kid who even convinced me to give up my hunting rifles."

Although he was not a veteran, Willie joined VVAW–WSO, and that's where he met Joe Remiro. His Maoist associations rapidly brought him into Venceremos circles.

Patricia Hearst, who later fell in love with Willie, remembered him as "the gentlest, most beautiful man I've ever known. He taught me the truth as he learned it from the beautiful brothers in California's concentration camps. We loved each other so much, and his love for the people was so deep. . . . Neither Cujo or I had ever loved an individual the way we loved each other . . . probably because our relationship wasn't based on bourgeois fucked-up values, attitudes and goals. . . ."

It's probable that it was S.L.A. "treasurer and information officer" Cujo (which means "Unconquerable") who became the main instrument in Patty Hearst's conversion.

Angela DeAngelis (translation: "Angel of the Angels") Atwood was brought into S.L.A. by the same romantic twist of fate that snared Camilla Hall. She fell in love with someone. In Angela's case it was not another woman but a virile young soldier named Joe Remiro.

Angela ("General Gelina" to her comrades) was twenty-five, quite pretty, and a talented actress, but, like the rest of the S.L.A. gunsels, she proved a rotten shot.

Perhaps this should not be too surprising, since absolutely nothing in her history up until the summer of '73, when she met Joe, would indicate that "Angel" had the least interest in violence.

When she hit Berkeley, those somewhat snobbish radicals who set taste and style there immediately typecast her as an "All-American College Coed Type." A fellow student in a Marxist study group decided she was "politically naive but very concerned about society. She was just a sweet little chick—no, sorry, I can't say 'chick.' That's a sexist word."

When Remiro brought her over to his parents' house for Thanksgiving dinner in '73, his mother immediately decided Angela was "just a nice Italian girl." She was very pleased that Joe was finally interested in someone from a good, Catholic home, a girl with a healthy interest in raising plants and flowers.

Angela was the daughter of a New Jersey Teamster organizer, Lawrence DeAngelis. Her sister remembers her as a "good girl . . . an A-plus girl" who had a "normal" life and a very "regular" upbringing. Angela later told friends that things were not all *that* normal. Her mother died when she was fourteen, and, as the oldest child, she was expected to immediately take her place and "become housekeeper, maid, and mother to my sister and brother." Her father, she said, was strict and demanding, and she had to become a "child with all the responsibilities of an adult."

Nevertheless, Angela was a "good student" at Manchester Regional High School in North Haledon, New Jersey, from which she graduated in 1966. She was head cheerleader, a member of the honor society, and president of the drama club.

She went to Indiana University in Bloomington to study speech and acting. In 1969, she met a fellow theatrical student, Bill Harris, who had just returned from Marine duty in Vietnam to become an antiwar activist in VVAW.

She also met Harris's friend, Gary Atwood, another Indiana U student of literature and political history. The two were soon living together.

Angela—whose only "political involvement" up to that date had been helping her father organize a Teamster strike—had little to say on her own at first, but she listened intently as Harris and Atwood debated Marxist theory, especially the question of whether "the gun" was the answer. They discussed the Berkeley scene in depth, and both decided to support the Black Panther program of armed self-defense.

"Angela now began to take a stand of her own on political questions," Gary recalls. "She was working as a student teacher at Ben Davis High School in Indianapolis. She discussed with her class the ideas of the Black Panthers and was reprimanded by school authorities."

When the Kent State students were killed in May of '70, Angela wore a black armband to class and refused to remove it after an angry debate with the principal.

In mid-'71, the Harrises moved next door to Angela and Gary, and their political debates got even more intense. Bill was becoming more convinced that only "armed struggle" and "armed propaganda" could solve things, and he gave Gary the works of Che Guevara and Regis Debray to read. At the same time, Gary, faced with the possibility of being drafted, declared himself a conscientious objector and opted to do his alternative service as a teacher in the San Francisco area.

Angela was by now an ardent feminist but, nevertheless, she and Gary were married in May of '71. They decided in June to move to Berkeley.

So that Gary could teach and also attend college, Angela went to work as a waitress in an enormous plastic restaurant in the basement of the San Francisco headquarters of Bank of America. It's called The Great Electric Underground.

The Harrises soon followed them out from Indiana, and the old friendship was picked up. But things had already started to go badly with Angela and Gary. A lot of it had to do with politics. Bill and Emily preached a more violent line than Gary says he was ready for, but Angela bought it entirely. (Gary would later declare himself a Trotskyite totally opposed to "petit-bourgeois terrorism.")

Angela began to devote her energies to the United Farm Workers (a choice that must have upset her father, an official of the rival Teamsters) and to a semiprofessional Berkeley production of Ibsen's play *Hedda Gabler*. She was cast as Thea Elvsted, the idealistic young woman who splits up with her husband so that she might follow her own convictions. The play repeated itself in real life as Gary left her to go back and study in Indiana. Angela moved in with the Harrises.

"I decided to go back to complete some requirements and then come back to Berkeley later," explains Gary. "Angela wanted to stay there. I came to Bloomington in August of '73 and never saw my wife or the Harrises again. The last I heard from her was an angry phone call in which we debated the question of armed propaganda and Angela hung up on me."

At about this point, writer Berna Rauch met Angela, and they acted together in the Company Theater. Berna describes Angela as "delicate, small-boned . . . sensitive face, strong nose, long dark hair, depth and warmth in brown eyes . . . tiny shoulders, a petite, compact dancer's body: small breasts and strong, solid legs."

Berna saw Angela as a "giver" who denied herself so that her friends might eat, a lover of cats who had four of them, named Lalenya, Vagina, Abraxas, and Chagall.

As the production of *Hedda Gabler* continued through early '73, Berna became a close friend to Angela and watched her grow politically as she began to work with Venceremos. Berna describes her at this point:

"There's nothing of 'Angela the Coed' about you now. Your legs remain unshaven. You think it's fine to gain weight and you don't worry about looking fat. The idea is to please yourself, not to please men. You lose some of your delicacy and begin to look more like a sturdy, earthy Italian peasant woman. Especially when you wrap a bandanna around your head and wear your tattered, cut-off blue jean shorts."

This is the girl Little dated and Remiro had a six-month affair with. By the time Patty Hearst met her, the new militancy had taken her over entirely. Said Patty:

"Gelina was beautiful. Fire and joy. She exploded with the desire to kill the pigs. She wrote poetry—some of it on the walls of Golden Gate [an apartment hideout in San Francisco]. . . . She loved the people more than her love for any one person or material comfort and she never let her mind rest from the strategies that are the blood of revolution. Gelina would have yelled 'Fire power to the people' if there wasn't the necessity to whisper the words of revolution. We laughed and cried and struggled together. She taught me how to fight the enemy within through her constant struggle with bourgeois conditioning."

The poem Angela left behind in San Francisco shows that hers *was* a rather schizoid bit of reconditioning. It read:

"Reality/you're hard to find/we've looked a long time/A new born babe could tell/they bid you farewell/and stuffed/Ones of jive in your place/Face it comrade/Now's the time/We're all alive!/Eat it, Pig/in our minds/the bigger the trigger/the better the target!/the cool/calm palm/will smear heavy on the hit/Sucker Pay—MALCOLM/We're here to stay!"

While Angela Atwood learned this sort of violent rhetoric late in the game in Berkeley, the next future S.L.A. soldiers to arrive on the scene, Bill and Emily Harris, who check in late in '72, seemed to be already well indoctrinated. (They later became "Teko" and "Yolanda.")

Emily, twenty-seven, was the stronger and more radical of the two, and she quickly joined the remnants of the Venceremos organization to become a leader of the Oakland Chino Defense Committee, which was working to save what remained of Venceremos after the Beaty fiasco.

Bill, twenty-nine, was a short (five foot seven) former speech and acting major with a master's degree and a good knowledge of journalism. He carried a tremendous load of guilt and political awareness because of a Marine tour of duty in Vietnam. He also possessed a bright and irreverent wit. He busied himself with helping the Farm Workers and setting up study and self-defense classes in the Harris home at 434 Forty-first Street, in a working-class section of Oakland.

Bill and Emily were definitely the "aristocrats" of the first S.L.A. band. Both came from wealthy and conservative families. Both were professionals with impressive academic backgrounds. They had been into the social swim at the University of Indiana, the former Emily Schwartz as a Chi Omega sorority sister and Bill as a fraternity brother.

Emily received an English degree in '69 and went on to teach both French and English in a Bloomington, Indiana, junior high school. Bill originally entered Indiana U in 1963 but left in '65 to serve his Marine Corps hitch. He came back in '67 to get a bachelor's degree in English. In '72 he obtained a master's degree in urban education but apparently used it only briefly to teach in Bloomington.

Emily's family was extremely conservative. Her father, Fred Schwartz, would be the only parent to immediately call in the FBI the minute he got wind of what his daughter was doing politically. Schwartz was an engineering consultant and village trustee in the exclusive Illinois suburb of Clarendon Hills. Emily, who was raised there, was long remembered as the "smartest kid in the class" in her high school, where she earned straight A's. She was active in the school pep club (another cheerleader!) and worked with a service organization that helped the poor.

Those who remember her from those days as a teacher in Indiana say that Emily was "very soft-spoken" except when it came to education. "Em was really into kids. She had strong beliefs of her own, but not what one would classify as radical. . . . She was really concerned about teaching kids not just facts, but how to make a decision from alternatives. Em was a great one for alerting people to alternatives. She would stay after class and informally rap with the kids about alternatives to our form of government. Em looked upon teaching as a responsibility. . . ."

A staunchly conservative young man from Southern California who dated Emily Schwartz in the summer of '67, when she was a sorority sister working at the Disneyland Hotel, recalls that the girl he knew had absolutely nothing to say about politics: "We partied around at homes or at the beach during the daytime and worked at night at the park," says Tim Casey. He recalls her as "a very nice, intelligent, sensitive girl—gentle, witty and fun. She was slim, fresh, blond-haired, very alive and vital. She smiled and laughed a lot. . . ."

Bill Harris was an Army brat. He was born on January 22, 1945, at Fort Sill, Oklahoma, where his father was then assigned as an officer. His stepfather, Jerry Bunnell, is an Air Force lieutenant colonel. (Bill's father, Fred, died in 1965.) The family still lives in a small mansion in Carmel, Indiana.

Harris was an acolyte in St. Christopher's Episcopal Church. He was remembered from high school as the "class cut-up" who won a local journalism prize and joined the golf team. His political education was very much like that of Joe Remiro, a volunteer who went to Nam with rather conservative opinions but who was so shocked there, especially by the way blacks and other minority soldiers were treated, that he came home strongly against *all* war and began to preach pacifism. He would not even allow a gun in his house. He adopted a hippie life style for a while and worked on the underground Indiana newspaper *Common Sense*. He gradually became active in VVAW.

Bill and Emily were married in '72 in a fashionable ceremony that ended with an all-night "mod" dance party featuring a famous rock band.

When the Harrises moved to Oakland, they occupied a neat, clean little apartment furnished in good and expensive taste. Their wardrobes were extensive and fashionable. Emily went to work as a typist at the University of California's research center, and Bill became a post-office truckdriver. Between the two of them, they brought in about twelve hundred dollars a month.

Visitors to their nicely appointed home, including Bill's military stepfather, noticed the Maoist posters in the hall and the revolutionary books on the shelves but put it down as only a "passing fancy." They did not see the guns and ammunition neatly stored away out of sight. (Emily's father had never visited the California apartment. All it took for him to call in the feds was a letter she sent him early in '74 proclaiming that she had entered a new life style and that "I have learned a lot from . . . the people in prison and they, in turn, have learned a lot from me. One person in particular—a beautiful black man—has conveyed to me the torture of being black in this country and of being poor. He has dedicated his life to eliminating the conditions that oppose people's being able to lead satisfying lives and to replace these with conditions that make people truly free. Bill and I have changed our relationship so that it no longer confines us and I am enjoying relationships with other men. I am in love with the black man I referred to earlier and that love is very beautiful and fulfilling.")

She was, of course, referring to Donald ("Cinque") DeFreeze, who, after his escape from Vacaville, provided the focus of energy and aspiration that brought the Harrises into contact with other young radicals on the periphery of Venceremos who were also deeply into the prison movement.

One of the most active of them was Russell Little, twenty-four, a native of Pensacola, Florida, who came to Berkeley to stay in the summer of '72 and was soon living communally in Peking Man House at 5939 Chabot Road.

Little, who would end up being charged as Remiro's accomplice in the Foster murder and the Concord shoot-out and was obviously Joe's best buddy in the late '73–early '74 period, is a swaggering young graduate in philosophy from the University of Florida. He styles his speech to match that of the oppressed blacks, with whom he identifies, but his scientific and philosophic background shows through. He is obviously a very cerebral kind of person who speaks only after long and careful thought and then attempts to give the impression that what he says is loose and down home.

More than any other S.L.A. member (except Cinque), Little ("Osceola" in S.L.A.) was ready to move directly into violent revolution. His transition from redneck Florida youth completely devoid of any pacifist inhibitions or half measures to political activist was abrupt, with no in-between stages. As he tells his own story:

"My dad worked at the Pensacola Naval Air Station as a civilian electronics mechanic. We lived in a duplex in a government housing project until I was eight. Then, in the spring of the third grade, in 1958, we moved into a working-class subdivision on the outskirts of town. I lived there until I was almost nineteen, when I left and went to the University of Florida [in Gainesville] to start my second year in college. I was able to go then because I got a scholarship and loan because of my grades in high school and my one year in Pensacola Junior College [Little was ninth in a class of 600]. . . . I was studying math and science planning to become a major in electrical engineering.

"I got my first shotgun at age seven. I bought it with money I made cutting grass (my sister and I didn't get allowances). It was a bolt-action four-ten. I went hunting for quail, wild turkeys, squirrels, and sometimes deer, with my Dad using a double-barreled twelve-gauge usually. He's part Creek Indian, and we had good times in the woods, going out early before sunrise and getting back late at night. I used to sneak my shotgun out when I was a teen-ager and go off into the woods, which were only about a mile from our house.

"I didn't read the newspaper or books or watch much TV. In fact, I wasn't even aware of the civil-rights movement—it was consciously suppressed. The blacks in our town didn't dare raise much hell because the crackers would come down on them, guns blazing, and everyone knew it.

"There was a black shantytown with houses made of cardboard, tin, et cetera, about half a mile down the road from our house, kind of hid off in the woods. I would see young black kids at the corner store, but we'd just look at each other, it was a colonial situation, apartheid. We didn't know what to say or do, just kind of scared of each other. After I graduated from high school in the spring of '67, it got continually funkier, with more and more ghetto blacks coming into the school, teachers quitting, racial fights, et cetera.

"So I went off to the university in the fall of '68 completely ignorant of what was happening in this country and around the world, but thinking I was smart as hell. I mean, after all, I was the first one from either side of the family to make it to college, and I even had a partial scholarship. Shit, man, I was on my way and it wasn't even hard, I just kept on like I had always done, went to classes, played football, baseball, et cetera, in the afternoons and on weekends. Chased the women around and boozed it up as often as I could afford. My first year at Florida didn't include any real political changes.

"My second year . . . would have to be called the turning point in my life—politically and socially. I took a course in philosophy that fall, 1969, which seemed to drive home some of the contradictions which I had and was experiencing. The course was taught by a young Marxist graduate student with a background very similar to mine.

"This came at a crucial period. I had finally realized that there were many social problems in this country, such as racism and the unjust war in Vietnam, that I didn't have any real understanding of. I also realized that I was literally standing with one foot inside the door of the 'Good American Life.' I was getting engaged to a young woman back in Pensacola whose father was a highly paid chemical engineer, and it looked like I was going to finish in electrical engineering and move into a different social class than I had grown up in, one I didn't really care for.

"Well, I went ahead and got engaged that Christmas, 1969, but it only lasted till March of '70. When I broke off that engagement I was saying to hell with engineering and the 'Good American Life.' I realized I was way behind and started out to catch up. Reading about the civil-rights movement and Malcolm X, studying Marx, Lenin, Mao. Going to marches, rallies, demonstrations. In the spring getting righteously angry about Kent State and Jackson State.

"When I went home that summer, a long-haired, pissed-off radical, my parents and friends didn't know what to think. [That summer Russ joined 300,000 other kids at the Atlanta Rock Festival, where he got stoned out, freaked out, and very definitely into the spirit of the late '60s youth rebellion.]

"The next school year, '70 to '71, I was in philosophy. I started studying those dudes right before Marx—Kant, Hegel, Feuerbach, the German Idealists. I took an active part in organizing left campus politics. [Little's mentor that year had belonged to SDS in West Germany. He told Russ about underground guerrilla fighting and the organization of street gangs.]

"That spring the majority of the Black Student Union was arrested by the racist university president. We rallied, demonstrated, and rioted for a month, then the people got worried about spring exams and copped out. I and the rest of the campus crazies went direct to Washington for May Day, 1971. We were confrontation-oriented, believing that direct experience with the brutality of the pigs was most responsible for radicalizing people. I was never a true hippie, a peacenik or pacifist. I was probably a Yippie at that period of my life." (Little took part in the street fighting that ended with more than eleven thousand arrests. He came away with a strong taste for blood.)

The following summer, Little and his girlfriend, Robyn Steiner, hopped into a sweet little yellow Chevy and headed for California. He had been reading the works of Eldridge Cleaver, Huey Newton, and George Jackson, and he wanted to get involved in the radical East Bay scene centered around the prison movement.

When George Jackson was killed by prison guards on August 21, 1971, Little was all ready to go out and riot in the streets. But the riots never began, and that, plus the fact that neither he nor Robyn could find work, dampened their enthusiasm for Berkeley. They returned to Florida, where Russ finished up his studies and got a degree in philosophy—mostly Marxist philosophy with a little Sartre existentialism thrown in.

"OK," he says, "we waited. We stayed in Florida until March of

'72 and we couldn't stand it any longer so then we split. We were livin' like *Steal This Book* and it didn't cost us any money. That's how we survived like that, doin' things here and there, crashin' with hippies. It's real easy, man. Well, we traveled up and down the beaches a bit in California. And then we ran into some people who were working in the prisons. They had ways of getting in and going twice a week. So we stopped, you know. We'd been travelin' around and havin' a good time, you know. But I'm feelin' kind of guilty, you know. Like, I feel I should be doin' somethin' really constructive. So we stopped there and the people are nice and they're off into Maoist theory an' shit an' off into the prisons. So I say, 'Cool!' you know. 'Let's do this for a while,' you know."

The people Russ "ran into" who were working with prisoners were the residents of Peking House. Among them were Nancy Ling Perry and Willie the Wolfe. There were other friends involved, like Joe Remiro, Angela Atwood, Mizmoon, and the Harrises.

This was Little's entry into the rapidly forming S.L.A. His next step would be Vacaville State Prison and a meeting with a black convict named DeFreeze.

10

"You do, indeed, know me. You have always known me. I'm that nigger you have hunted and feared night and day. I'm that nigger you have killed hundreds of my people in a vain hope of finding. I'm that nigger that is no longer just hunted, robbed and murdered. I'm that nigger that hunts you now. . . ."
—Field Marshal Cinque of the S.L.A., in a communiqué,
February 21, 1974

THE "CALIFORNIA MEDICAL FACILITY" at Vacaville, as it is misleadingly called by the Department of Corrections officials who run it, is neither a hospital nor a loony bin. It's a kind of way station, an entry and exit point for the 23,000 cons who now inhabit the state's entire complex of thirteen penitentiaries, camps, and "training facilities" which constitute the world's largest and most violent prison system.

They evaluate the new cons at Vacaville before assigning them to other "maximum," "medium" or "minimum" security institutions. Many return later for another evaluation, which will decide whether or not they are ready for parole.

Vacaville (translation: "Cowtown") is about fifty miles northeast of Berkeley, a rather pleasant hour's drive up Highway 80, across Carquinez Strait, and over rolling farm country to this little community of eight thousand souls, which lies in the abbreviated shadow of Mt. Vaca (2,870 feet).

The prison is just outside the town, and it was here that at least eight S.L.A. members and friends traveled with some regularity late in '72 and through '73 to attend meetings of a rather extraordinary "self-help" educational group called the Black Cultural Association (BCA).

Like a number of similar programs which sought to get white cons ready for a return to the outside world, BCA was organized in '68 to

[139]

give the black prisoners a sense of pride and hope (as well as to provide tutoring in such down-to-earth matters as English grammar).

BCA gatherings were held twice a week, with tutoring at the Wednesday session and "cultural meetings" on Friday nights, which attracted about 100 prisoners and some 130 outsiders. These sessions opened with a flag ceremony featuring the tricolor banner of the Republic of New Africa and a clenched-fist black power salute. The evening might continue with a number of speeches, or there might be poetry readings, debates, or plays. Most of this was monitored by prison staff members who got a little nervous late in '72, when many of the speeches overflowed with Maoist political rhetoric. The high point of the sessions for most of the outsiders who had driven in from the Bay Area was the social hour of coffee, cake, and conversation following the organized program. It was here, amid the massive static of dozens of individual rap sessions, well out of earshot of guards, that the groundwork was laid for S.L.A. leadership by three tough black cons, and the first discussions were held leading to the escape of two of them and to the eventual assassination of Dr. Marcus Foster.

The informal Vacaville BCA sessions provided an ideal entry through the thick walls of the penitentiary system for white East Bay radicals who had come to believe through their work in Venceremos that they must liberate the prisons and who had decided after reading the works of Malcolm X, Eldridge Cleaver, George Jackson, and Huey Newton that the most logical leaders for a new American Revolution would be the black graduates of California's superpens. Russell Little describes how BCA fitted perfectly into radical plans:

"So I started goin'," he says. "Most of the people there are just socializin' an shit, more like a social club . . . just hangin' out, you know. They get out of their self an' shit, I can dig that. So some real righteous prison revolutionaries come through there every now and then an' so I meet 'em, you know, an' we start studyin' some of these things, you know. We start studyin' Debray and Marighella an' shit. We start talkin' about urban guerrilla warfare an' shit like that, you know. A lot about what happened with the Panthers, man. . . . All the Panthers talk about now is elections. Well, fuck the elections . . . that's the way *these* people feel, you know.

"OK, so we went to Vacaville twice a week. Some of these people think we're really gonna turn them on to Mao by goin' there twice a week for an hour or two and read Mao to 'em. I think the best way we can help these people and not just them but the entire revolution, is by supporting and working with the revolutionaries who are inside the prison. They're the ones who influence people, you know. So that's where my energies started goin'. And through the revolutionary people I'd met there, I started workin' with 'em, rappin' with 'em on a one-to-one basis. As far as the revolutionary people were concerned, the shit that was goin' on at BCA was goin' on in illegal little get-togethers an' out in the yard an' shit. . . . ."

So, little by little, BCA became a front, a ploy for the kind of serious plotting the revolutionaries had in mind.

Exactly which eventual members of S.L.A. came in for the meetings remains something of a mystery. Department of Corrections officials admit that identifications of visitors were not too carefully checked and that some S.L.A. members may have used phony ID.

It is certain that Willie the Wolfe attended BCA frequently. He was the first of the future S.L.A.ers to be brought in, about March of '72, by "outside coordinator" Colston Westbrook, who was a UC Berkeley student of black language and culture. Willie probably met Westbrook while taking black studies courses.

Willie then brought his friend Russ Little as well as Little's girlfriend, Robyn Steiner, into BCA meetings. Nancy Ling Perry applied for permission to attend BCA and finally got in late in '73. Several residents of Peking House, where Russ was living, also came, including David Gunnell, Jean Wah Chan, and Amanda de Normanville. Prison authorities are fairly certain that at least three other S.L.A.ers made it in with switched or phony ID, including Emily and Bill Harris and Mizmoon Soltysik. Remiro says he did not go up to Vacaville at all but visited other prisons and corresponded with a number of inmates at this point instead.

Little had originally come to California because "I knew there were a lot of revolutionaries in the prisons. The moment I got here, I went into the prisons and met a lot of people." The three who would have the most profound effect on his future would be Death Row Jeff (Clifford Jefferson), Donald DeFreeze (whose "reborn" Swahili name was Cinque Mtume, or "Fifth Prophet"), and a former Venceremos member named Thero Wheeler.

All were black. All were in for crimes of violence, and all were self-proclaimed revolutionists who would take leadership roles in S.L.A.

"We're not into some kind of big black leadership thing," says

Little rather unconvincingly. "But the fact remains that a lot of the leadership did come out of the prisons. It *is* black. It did come out of the ghettos and that's because they have practical experience in prisons and riots. It's not because they're black superheroes. It's because they've had experience an' we can keep from making mistakes that they've made. . . ."

Cliff, Cinque, and Thero ended up being the heavies these middle-class whites who had not done thirty days in jail between them had been looking so hard for. Their presence provided the exact catalyst needed to transform all the usual Berkeley rhetorical bullshit into action. For to these three convicts revolution was no game. They lived with cold black fury amid deep hatred and frustration, and they had already demonstrated that they harbored absolutely no mental reservations about using kidnap and murder to accomplish their goals.

The histories of these three black men, and an understanding of the explosive situation that's long been building up in California's super-pens, can quickly explain how S.L.A. made the big leap from theory into violence.

Death Row Jeff was the oldest and most con-wise of the three.

He had spent twenty-seven of his forty-seven years in stir when Little, Wolfe, and Perry encountered him at Vacaville in '72. He had served time for burglary, car theft, and second-degree murder. It was the murder rap that last sent him to prison, in 1949. The conviction was from Bakersfield, a violently racist little agricultural town at the southern end of the San Joaquin valley.

In September of '56, Jeff was involved in a knife fight with three other Folsom convicts—Frisco Willie, Rink Carter, and Sheik Thompson. Sheik was badly injured and Jeff took the rap. Under a strange old 1901 California prison law, any con found guilty of attacking another prisoner, whether the victim died or not, had to be sentenced to death. Jeff was the first person ever sentenced to die in the gas chamber under this aspect of the law, that is, after the victim had recovered.

His case became something of a cause célèbre in the late '50s as Jeff waited out a number of execution dates, stays, and appeals on San Quentin's Death Row. He became a friend of Caryl Chessman (executed in '60) and an enemy of a murderous monster named Stephen Nash, whom he once attacked in the exercise yard.

He was finally removed from the Row after Governor Goodin Knight communted Jefferson's death sentence to "life without possibility of parole." In May of '59, Jeff asked to be transferred from the pen to a mental hospital because his life sentence was a "living hell and death would be a lot easier."

He also was finding life in the pen hazardous, since he'd gotten into so many knife fights that new arrivals wanted to beat him out as the "fastest blade in the yard."

Although Jeff would later claim that he was the "boss" of the S.L.A., outside radicals close to the urban guerrilla group as well as the prison officials to whom Jeff "confessed" were more than a bit skeptical. Despite his reputation as kind of a "grand old man" of the prison system, Jeff was politically naive and barely literate. He attended BCA sessions but seemed little interested in Marxist indoctrination. He was more into the "party-time" aspects of the organization. Jeff does have a good heart and seems sincere in his statements that he wants to be "dedicated to the people."

A prison spokesman calls Jeff a kind of "dean emeritus" of the California jails. "I think that's the way S.L.A. looked up to him. I also think that the reason the outside S.L.A. people related to people like Jeff was so these big old guys would make a place for them and keep 'em safe when they finally ended up coming into the prisons themselves as convicts. . . . It was kind of an insurance policy."

Jeff had been in prison for so long that he had little idea of who the "oppressed people" outside stir really were in the '70s. "He's thinking about the poor at the time he first came to prison. He remembers the Mexican *braceros* he saw driving to Folsom through the San Joaquin valley from Bakersfield more than twenty years ago. I don't think he even knows about the social movements that are now going on. . . ."

Nevertheless, Death Row Jeff would later tell the Vacaville screws that he was "in charge" of S.L.A., along with his two convict friends, Albert Taylor and Raymond Sparks, who would die, supposedly in a hanging suicide, in the fall of '74. Taylor was considered a "psycho" at Vacaville. He was serving a life sentence for a 1970 murder in San Luis Obispo County. Sparks, forty, had been convicted in '70 of murdering two San Franciscans after convictions of burglary, assault, and rape.

"Jeff still felt he was the boss of S.L.A. as late as November, '73, when Marcus Foster was killed," says the official prison source. "He claims that a vote was taken on killing Foster and that he abstained. But after that there doesn't seem to be much to indicate he was consulted about anything. It's fairly apparent that Jeff and DeFreeze didn't like each other, and once DeFreeze escaped to Berkeley he pretty much took things over. The best theory we have around the prisons based on a whole variety of sources is that nobody really dreamed up the S.L.A. until DeFreeze had joined the radicals in Berkeley."

The fact that Jeff and DeFreeze didn't much dig each other should have been no surprise. They had little in common except their race.

DeFreeze, nearly a generation younger than gnarled old Jeff, was an open-faced, big-eyed, and very attractive young man. He was better read than Jeff, considerably more aware politically, and a good example of that enormous shift in consciousness and self-image that had taken place among black inmates in the late '60s and early '70s as more and more of them came to regard themselves as political prisoners. Large segments of DeFreeze's history remain shadowy and contradictory, and it's hard to pin down exactly when he stopped being just one more slick-talking, fast-moving con man and settled down to begin taking himself seriously as a revolutionary. There's no doubt that going to jail in '70 had a lot to do with it.

Certainly the nature of his arrests during the last part of his sixteen-year life of crime would indicate that DeFreeze had entered the fringes of revolutionary activity. When Los Angeles police stopped him for running a red light while riding a bicycle, itself a strange enough occupation in Freeway City, they found a bomb in his back pocket and a gun and second bomb in the bike basket.

At an early stage in his prison career, DeFreeze, like several other members of his family, had joined the Black Muslim sect. He hated whites and boasted he'd "eat them for breakfast" if he got the chance. But by the time he began to meet Berkeley radicals at BCA gatherings in late '72, Cinque had taken a Swahili "reborn" name and had come under the influence of Malcolm X, George Jackson, and other black writers who believed that revolution could be accomplished only through a multiracial coalition.

"He was a strong believer in multinationalism," recalls Russ Little. "But he didn't want to try and force that on blacks or Chicanos or native Americans. . . . He was a very serious dude, very dedicated, a sincere person, man. . . . He didn't use contemporary Marxist-Leninist language, but he studied all that shit, man. He studied just as much as any of those political motherfuckers out on the streets who run their mouth and pass out leaflets, you know. He geared the whole thing down to street reality. He took on all this shit, man, from a ghetto perspective and he related to it from that perspective. He understood it intellectually and he could run it down that way if he wanted to, but he wasn't about to do that. He didn't think that was going to get him anywhere doing that. . . ."

Joe Remiro remembers that in prison Cinque was "quiet and studious. . . . He studied the whole situation carefully before he acted. He didn't get involved in any public political activities until the BCA thing and then he saw what a shuck it was and he got out of it right away. But, on the other hand, he was involved with and respected by the real radicals at Vacaville. He was a quiet, studious, thoughtful, and beautiful brother. . . ."

Such descriptions do not jibe at all with the recollections of other friends and relatives who had known DeFreeze in earlier years. There is such a total disparity, in fact, that he must have changed enormously during his three years in Vacaville and Soledad—prison often does that to impressionable and basically intelligent men.

The story of Donald David DeFreeze (alias Cinque Mtume, Donald DeFrez, John DeFrield, David Kenneth Robinson, Steven Robinson, and Donald David Thompson) is full of enigmas.

He was born on November 16, 1943, in the benighted industrial city of Cleveland, Ohio, the first of eight children in the family of a respectable working-class father (a toolmaker) and a twenty-five-year-old mother who later became a registered nurse to help keep her large family together.

Donald went to grammar school in what was then a mixed black and Eastern European immigrant neighborhood. By the time he got to Empire Junior High School (he quit in ninth grade) there were almost no whites left in his class, and the Glenville District was well on the way to becoming the totally blighted ghetto it is today.

Donald was a rebel, and his furious father nearly killed him on at least three occasions as he tried to beat his oldest son into line. Later DeFreeze would tell a psychiatrist that his father "used to inflict inhuman punishment. He hit him with hammers, baseball bats, etc. . . . Every time he went to the hospital his father would tell them he just got hurt. The time he was first picked up with a gun he had planned to shoot his father. . . ."

Instead of committing patricide, the disturbed fourteen-year-old ran away from home. He soon landed in Buffalo, New York, where he lived with the family of a fundamentalist black minister, the Reverend William Foster. By 1960, when he was only sixteen, he was already into deep trouble and was charged that year with breaking into parking meters and stealing a car. He was sent off to Elmira State Reformatory.

As DeFreeze himself later described his juvenile captivity in a strongly self-serving letter to a judge:

". . . I didn't have a home life in the little prison as we called it. There was nothing but fear and hate, day in and day out. The hate was maddening. The only safe place was your cell that you went to at the end of the day. I only had two fights, if you can call them fights. I never did win. It was funny but the fights were over the fact that I would not be a part of the gangs, black or white. I wanted to be friendly with everyone. This the other inmates would not allow. They would try to make me fight but I always got around them somehow. They then tried to make a homosexual out of me. I got around this, too. After two and a half years, I found myself hated by many of the boys there. . . ."

On going into the reformatory, DeFreeze had claimed he was an "orphan" to protect his relatives, but the long stint at Elmira changed his mind and at the age of eighteen he confessed that his mother was alive and well in Cleveland. He was soon returned to her, after stopping off at Foster's home to ask for the hand of the minister's daughter, Harriet. Permission was denied, but DeFreeze long stayed in touch with his religious foster parents in Buffalo and a later proclivity for writing phony religious letters to sentencing judges and singing hymns to juries can undoubtedly be traced to his short stint in a fundamentalist home.

The year 1963 was a blockbuster for nineteen-year-old DeFreeze. He was back home long enough to attend his father's funeral, then moved to New Jersey, where he met Gloria Thomas, a divorcee with three children, who was six years older than DeFreeze. His troubles had just begun.

"Then one day I met my wife, Glory," he later wrote. "She was nice and lovely. I fell in love with her, I think. I believe I was just glad and happy that anyone would have me the way I was. I was nineteen and in love and life really became real to me. . . . We were married and things were lovely all the way up to a few months. Then seven months later I came home sooner than I do most of the time from work and she and an old boyfriend had just had relations. I was very, very mad and very hurt and I told the boy he could have her if he wanted her and she him before I killed someone. . . ."

A number of violent fights erupt and after one of them, in September of '64, Gloria calls in the Orange, New Jersey, police and they charge DeFreeze with assault. A year later they're back to charge him with firing a gun in his basement. In his pocket they find a crudely manufactured bomb constructed of bamboo sticks, copper wire, and pipe cleaners. He's put on probation until the following June, but that spring he decides to leave Gloria and move out to Los Angeles, where he is arrested on a San Bernardino valley freeway while hitchhiking. The cops find he is carrying a tear-gas pencil "gun," a sharpened butter knife, and a sawed-off rifle in his suitcase. He's charged with burglary and possession of dangerous weapons, but he gets off with a lecture from the judge and the sentence is reduced to the time he has already served while awaiting trial. This is the first of half a dozen weapons offenses in which DeFreeze manages to connive his way around serving any heavy time—he generally gets off with probation or with charges dismissed. He shows a growing fascination with guns and bombs. As he puts it:

"I started playing with guns and fireworks and dogs and cars. Just anything to get away from life and how unhappy I was. . . ."

He gets Gloria to move out to California: "I told my wife I would forget all that she had done to me and everything as if it never happened. I treated her like a man should his wife. . . ."

Things are hard in L.A. DeFreeze is a junior-high-school dropout. He's worked all the occasional, catch-as-catch-can jobs a young, untrained black kid can get—carry-out in a grocery store, house painter, carpenter, construction laborer, hamburger-stand fry cook, auto-body-shop worker, service-station attendant, typist. The jobs are few and far between, and he has a demanding wife who soon presents him with three new children of his own. Two of the six children prove to be asthmatics, and one needs a hernia operation. Gloria gets sick too, and there is no hospitalization. DeFreeze begins to steal. (Some say he did even worse things—like betraying his friends when he got caught.) As he describes this period between 1967 and 1969, which was his year for getting into *real* trouble:

"I worked two jobs and was a thief in between. Gloria had all she wanted, TVs in every room. Her home looks like or better than a movie star's. I tried to hide my weakness and unhappiness in work. I worked twenty-two hours a day and still I had no peace, and she wanted more. . . ."

During '67 DeFreeze is busted three times for crimes of violence. In June he's picked up riding his bomb-laden bicycle through the South Los Angeles ghetto and he tells police he has "found" the bombs and gun and is out trying to "sell them" to raise money for his family. A most unlikely story, but he gets off with three years of probation.

On December 2, DeFreeze is captured after a ghetto prostitute is robbed and beaten and detectives find a revolver on him that is part of a cache of 240 pistols and rifles recently stolen from a Torrance, California, Army surplus store. A few days later, De Freeze is taken to his apartment building by cops looking for the rest of the guns. He dives through a window and escapes. Four days later he's captured on a South L.A. street, taken back to the same building heavily chained and handcuffed, and directs the cops to the apartment of his friend, Ronald Coleman, who has the stolen weapons neatly stockpiled.

During his trial on this offense, DeFreeze fires his legal-aid lawyer and conducts his own defense. The prosecutor recalls that Donald has studied the law diligently and files a stack of correct legal documents. He presents a good defense, and, in his summation to the jury, he reads the Bible, weeps, and sings Christian hymns. Nevertheless, he and Coleman finally do a bit of plea bargaining with the prosecutor, and DeFreeze gets off with a highly suspicious five-year probation.

Members of the Black Panther party will later charge that DeFreeze has been working for the police and that the big arms rip-off was intended to supply weapons for a running gun battle between the Panthers and Ron Karenga's United Slaves organization. The Panthers say that "US" was no more than a police front, but these charges have not been proven. Court records do reveal, however, that DeFreeze unsuccessfully attempted to subpoena former Los Angeles District Attorney Evelle Younger to testify as a defense witness about his past "cooperation" with authorities. And Gloria DeFreeze wrote a letter to the trial judge saying that her husband had "helped recover weapons for the police and they promised to help him in return."

In November of '68 a court-appointed psychiatrist concluded that DeFreeze was an "emotionally confused and conflicted young man with deep-rooted feelings of inadequacy. . . . His disorganization and impaired social adjustment seem to suggest a schizophrenic potential. He seems to be a passive aggressive individual. He appears to have a fascination with regard to firearms and explosives. . . . It is felt he is in need of a structured 24-hour program of treatment. . . . His fascination with firearms and explosives makes him dangerous." The psychiatrist, Dr. Frederick J. Hacker, recommends that Donald be locked up, but the trial judge doesn't see it that way.

Perhaps Gloria should not have been in such a hurry to get Donald off the hook in '68, for the following spring he is again arrested for brandishing a weapon. This time it's a semiautomatic M-68 rifle with a thirty-two-round clip firmly in place. His object: killing Gloria and the children, "to keep them from leaving me."

Sixty-nine is to be a banner year for this kind of thing. DeFreeze will finish the year facing a long prison sentence after four charges have been filed involving him in everything from kidnapping to attempted bank burglary and a shoot-out with the police.

The first of the charges involves Gloria and the M-68. She's really getting scared now and starts hiding out from Donald. On May 9, DeFreeze is supposedly all the way across the country in Newark, New Jersey, kidnapping the caretaker of the B'Nai Abraham Jewish temple. His accomplice is supposedly a leader of the local Black Panther party. It's all done to get a phone number that's available in the directory. (The Panthers will later charge this is part of a police conspiracy to frame them, but, again, nothing has yet been proven.)

DeFreeze skips out of Newark just ahead of an indictment for the kidnap and is next busted in his home town of Cleveland, a few blocks up St. Clair Avenue from his mother's house. When discovered late one night atop the roof of a local branch of the Cleveland Trust Company, he is busily chopping a hole in the ceiling with a complete set of burglar tools. He is carrying a knife, a .38-caliber revolver, a .25-caliber pistol, and a hand grenade. He gets himself bailed out for five thousand dollars on the burglary charges (which are later dropped) and then skips town.

He's back in Los Angeles on November 25, in time to slide into a car next to a young Filipino woman, smack her on the side of the head with a gun, and steal a thousand-dollar cashier's check from her purse. He goes to a local Bank of America to try to cash it (dumb—it's made out to a woman). A bank clerk smells rip-off and calls a guard, who chases DeFreeze out the door with gun blazing. Donald fires back seven shots but misses. When the cops catch up with him a few blocks away, DeFreeze has been hit in the hand and the foot, and he surrenders meekly. This time his luck has run out. No more probation.

He pleads insanity and writes strange Biblical warnings to the judge, who decides DeFreeze is loco, but not all *that* crazy, and slams him into Vacaville under a five-years-to-life sentence.

The judge writes a note to the jailers asking them to "consider this defendant's mental state. . . . I do not now declare a present doubt as to his sanity but I do feel he needs help—and lots of it."

The prosecuting attorney writes: "This man is a high-danger risk to society. As soon as he is released from prison he will return to the same violent career. It is also my opinion that this defendant will eventually kill someone. . . ."

DeFreeze writes back:

"My Father has said that in the day that the walls are to be built around me, in that day the decree be far removed. There is nothing more to be said than this, so we'll know when it comes to pass that I am not alone. You can smile and laugh at me and call me a fool for you think the Power of my Life is in your hands. But your Power, MY GOD WILL TAKE: FOR I AM NOT ALONE."

So whammo, slammo, right into the high-risk stress unit at Vacaville, where the prison alienist notes that "DeFreeze is fascinated with firearms. . . . He has a schizoid personality. . . . We have not had any problems with him, but he has not volunteered for work of any kind. . . ."

At about this time, early in '70, he briefly embraces Islam. Within two years he will be enrolled in the BCA program, where he will greatly impress visiting Berkeley radicals. He has not done nearly so well with old friends, the cops, or fellow convicts, who sum up DeFreeze this way:

"A cheap, undependable, turnover punk. . . . I knew he was dead as far as his psychological state was concerned. . . . I just couldn't deal with him." (An L.A. undercover cop who may have briefly used De-Freeze as an informant.)

"I felt he had a mental problem. The only persons he trusted were me and the kids . . . but I lived in constant fear of him. I thought he was going to kill me." (Gloria DeFreeze, who divorced her husband of seven years while he was in the slam.)

"He was a jerk . . . a small-time hustler with no interest in the black struggle." (A black New Jersey cop who once busted DeFreeze.)

"I got the impression he'd do anything for a buck." (A New Jersey attorney who works with the Black Panthers and who once accused DeFreeze of working with the cops against them.)

"A hip shooter who rapped without thinking and without being able to back up his own con." (A fellow Vacaville inmate.)

"He was not lily-white. He was a bit of a showboat and a little crazy. But as far as I know personally, all the time he was in the joint, he was righteous. He was no snitch." (Another Vacaville inmate.)

Conspiracy freaks, who pop up out of the superparanoid left like fresh muffins out of a hot toaster, will later charge that DeFreeze was a "highly valued and protected informer" for the Los Angeles Police Department, not only before '70, when he was sent to Vacaville, but later in stir, even after he'd been put away by these same stern law-enforcement types. They would claim that any political actions DeFreeze would take part in with the S.L.A. were no more than "a plot to discredit the left," even though it is apparent that if DeFreeze had conned his way out of serving time before '69 by snitching and double-dealing everyone in sight, the cops had surely abandoned him by '70, when it was decided that Donald was altogether too crazy and unreliable to keep out of jail any more.

It is much more probable that the Donald DeFreeze who had been in stir two years when he met Willie Wolfe, Russ Little, Nancy Ling Perry, and other incognito S.L.A. types was a considerably sobered and more centered kind of nut. No *agent provocateur* could have dreamed up the almost hallucinatory and very deadly S.L.A. caper that Cinque would soon export to Berkeley. He may not have entirely deserved Patricia Hearst's later glowing tribute, but the DeFreeze who became an urban guerrilla leader had changed greatly. As Patty put it: "Cinque loved the people with tenderness and respect. They listened to him when he talked because they knew that his love reflected the truth in the future. Cin knew that to live was to shoot straight. He longed to be with his black sisters and brothers, but at the same time, he wanted to prove to black people that white freedom fighters are comrades in arms. . . . Cinque was in a race with time believing that every minute must be another step forward in the fight to save the children. He taught me virtually everything imaginable but he wasn't liberal with us. He'd kick our asses if we didn't drop over a fence fast enough or keep our asses down while practicing. . . . Most importantly, he taught me how to show my love for the people. He helped me see that it's not how long we live that's important, it's how we live, what we decide to do with our lives."

So, despite all of the vitriolic conjecture about Donald DeFreeze being no more than a "paid informer" and a "police agent" before and after his Vacaville incarceration, those who knew him well and those who have studied the conversions of other freaked-out, violent, young black cons in stir do not find it surprising that three years in the penitentiary might have been just the lesson necessary to bring a basically intelligent and believing young man like Cinque around to an angry and determined belief in revolution. So many other well-recorded cases of behind-the-walls conversion have emerged from these same snake pits over the past decade that such a conclusion does not seem the least bit illogical. The testimonies of Eldridge Cleaver and George Jackson well describe how the jail experience can turn a violent young punk into a dedicated revolutionist. As Cleaver put it:

"I was very familiar with the Eldridge who came to prison, but that

Eldridge no longer exists. And the one I am now is in some ways a stranger to me. You may find this difficult to understand but it is very easy for one in prison to lose his sense of self. . . . During my last stay in prison, I made the desperate decision to abandon completely the criminal path and to redirect my life. While in prison, I concentrated on developing the skills of a writer. . . ."

George Jackson described the metamorphic quality of his own incarceration this way:

"Blackmen born in the U.S. and fortunate enough to live past the age of 18 are conditioned to accept the inevitability of prison. For most of us, it simply looms as the next phase in a sequence of humiliation. . . . I was captured and brought into prison when I was 18 years old because I couldn't adjust. The record that the state has compiled on my activities reads like the record of ten men. It labels me brigand, thief, burglar, gambler, hobo, drug addict, gunman, escape artist, Communist revolutionary and murderer. . . . There are still some blacks here who consider themselves criminals—but not many. Believe me, my friend, with the time and incentive that these brothers have to read, study and think, you will find no class or category more aware, more embittered, desperate or dedicated to the ultimate remedy—revolution. . . . Very few men imprisoned for economic crimes or even crimes of passion against the oppressor feel that they are really guilty. Most of today's black convicts have come to understand that they are the most abused victims of an unrighteous order. . . ."

Thero Wheeler also experienced this kind of behind-the-walls re-education. But he differed from Donald DeFreeze in that his innate pragmatism and a strong sense of self-preservation made him abandon the revolution when his own ass was up for grabs. Cinque ended up paying with his life for his political conversion.

Wheeler, a twenty-nine-year-old native of Texas, first got busted in San Francisco at the age of sixteen for robbing and stomping a middle-aged white man. He was sentenced to the penitentiary in '62 but paroled five years later. His parole was revoked in '70, after he was convicted of assaulting a Los Angeles cop. In December, '71, he escaped from Soledad Prison, was recaptured and sent to Folsom, and was then shifted, in September of '72, to Vacaville, where he was to be evaluated for parole in that institution's infamous "stress program."

A racist British reporter later told the world that Thero was just a dumb-dumb, a "stuttering illiterate with the muscles of a Sonny Liston." He said that when Wheeler joined S.L.A. "the guerrillas got a gorilla."

Such a bigoted and one-dimensional appraisal does not match up with the facts.

It is probably true, as prison spokesmen have implied, that Thero Wheeler saw involvement with outside radicals as a means of escaping. He was right; it worked. But there seems to be no question that Wheeler had brains and dedication. He was one of the only two penitentiary prisoners with the guts to publicly join Venceremos in '72, and he took his Marxist indoctrination seriously.*

Thero had shown no signs of social consciousness before making his first jail trip, but soon after he joined Venceremos he got involved in a number of projects that got him labeled as an "organizer" and "troublemaker" by his jailers. In '72 he filed a class action suit demanding that the prison allow San Francisco's respectable black community newspaper, the *Sun Reporter,* to be mailed in to convicts. He began to challenge small injustices and demand investigations and hearings. He became a competent jailhouse lawyer and helped other convicts with their legal work.

In April of '72, Wheeler wrote an article in the Venceremos newspaper which said that the ultimate goal for prison activists is to "keep our revolutionary commitment under all the harsh forms that repression and mounting fascism are taking. . . . I call for a stronger base within the cadres," he wrote, "and the immediate release of all prisoners, many of whom are political prisoners."

His Venceremos membership was a thorn in the side of prison officials, and they made it clear to him that he would not even be considered for parole as long as he belonged. He obligingly quit Venceremos in the fall of '72 and was then moved from Folsom to Vacaville for parole evaluation. He was due to go before the board late in '73, but he "paroled" himself by escaping on August 2.

In the last few months before Wheeler walked away from a gardening crew working on a complex of Little League baseball diamonds just outside the prison gate, he had been adamantly protesting against his treatment at Vacaville.

In the spring of '73 Wheeler almost died because he could not get adequate medical care in the prison's Stress Assessment Unit, where inmates who are being evaluated are put under intense and often sadistic psychological and physical pressure to see if they can control their anger and violent tendencies. Wheeler suffers from a peptic ulcer, and he still

* The only other out-front Venceremos member in stir was the ill-famed Ronald Beaty.

has two bullets inside his guts which occasionally cause inflammation and bleeding.

At about midnight, Wheeler complained of pains in his belly. He got a quick check-out from a prison medical technician, who gave him a couple of aspirins and told him that "nothing was wrong" with him. Thero returned to his cell and vomited blood for more than two hours. Medical help was called for but refused until the other prisoners telephoned in that Wheeler was dead and threatened a riot unless the medical technicians came down to get the "body."

More than an hour later, the technicians and fifteen guards came into the stress unit, decided Wheeler *was* seriously ill, and removed him to the hospital. He had lost three pints of blood by then and was on the verge of death.

Wheeler continued to suffer from internal bleeding all through the spring and summer, and just before his escape he filed suit to be removed to an outside hospital so that he might receive adequate care. His continuing illness along with the fact that very few "political" prisoners can expect to gain parole in California these days were thought to have been the motivations for his escape.

Although Wheeler claimed he'd quit Venceremos, a number of his visitors just before the escape were members of a Peninsula law commune closely tied to the radical group. One of the visitors was Mary Alice Siem, who came to Vacaville the day before Thero split.

The Vacaville facility from which Thero Wheeler walked away is far from being the worst or the most dangerous of the thirteen California state pens, but the same increasingly disturbing conditions exist here as are now becoming endemic in maximum-security joints like San Quentin, Folsom, and Soledad.

Prisons are in an uproar all across America today, but California has the largest and most politicized system anywhere, and what causes no more than a ripple of back-page commentary in Pittsburgh and Des Moines tidal-waves into headlines on the West Coast.

Medical conditions (as Thero's case indicates) are worsening. There is now almost no inmate contact with prison doctors, and outside physicians cannot touch their patients without a court order. There is no such thing as regular physicals for California's cons—they're quickly scanned on the way in, and coming out it's the same kind of perfunctory look-see or an equally routine autopsy.

Two circumstances have brought greater violence and frustration than before. California's court system is screening out most of the "good guys" charged with minor, nonviolent offenses these days. They get probation. That means the pens are filling up with violent prisoners.

Then the Adult Authority seems to have decided that the "indeterminate sentencing" procedure gives them a license to hold any convict unpopular with jailers or showing signs of political awareness for the rest of his life, no matter what the original charges were against him or how short his basic sentence was. The lack of a definite release date means that a California prisoner can be held until the day he dies unless he totally debases himself before his keepers. Prisoners are no longer "rehabilitated" or left to quietly do their sentences if they still have some pride left. They are totally broken as men when they get out. Those who cannot be broken will die in stir.

Needless to say, these conditions are likely to make a man angry and frustrated. The screws prefer, of course, to let them take it out on other cons rather than on the prison personnel, and they have covertly encouraged the spread of a bloody race war between four main prison gangs—the Aryan Brotherhood, Nuestra Familia, Emme (or the "Mexican Mafia" as the screws like to call it), and the Black Guerrilla Family, which has incorporated portions of Eldridge Cleaver's Black Liberation Army and the Republic of New Africa organization. Some Black Muslims also support BGF but, officially, they try to stay out of it.

In 1972–73, the California prisons experienced "the worst siege of violence in their history." They racked up three hundred stabbings, with sixty fatalities—six of them were screws.

It is estimated that nearly three thousand California cons, about 15 percent of the entire prison population, belong to the four major gangs. A lot of the knifings are directly attributable to rumbles between these groups, but a lot more of them are the result of rebellions among inmates against squealers who would regularly inform on their buddies to the jailers. With this sort of retribution now hanging over everyone's head, the old divide and conquer techniques used by a small handful of prison guards to hold down an enormous convict population just don't work any more. The terrified jailers are now resorting to system-wide "lock-downs," in which all normal work and recreational activities are curtailed and prisoners are caged in their cells twenty-four hours a day. This has brought even more frustration and anger.

Escapes, like those of Donald DeFreeze and Thero Wheeler, have been increasing. In 1973 there were thirty-seven escape incidents, involving sixty-one persons.

All of this was well publicized. All of it leads careful observers to one conclusion—the California prison system is seething with revolt. It's a damned good place to recruit revolutionaries. The young white Berkeley radicals who founded S.L.A. didn't have to be clairvoyant or even exceptionally well informed to see all of this. It was obvious.

They plucked Donald DeFreeze out of Soledad and Thero Wheeler out of Vacaville. From that point on, only bullets could stop them.

11

*". . . We can be sure that if the blacks, by the use of their violence,
their intelligence, their poetry, all that they have accumulated
for centuries while observing their former masters in silence and
in secrecy—if the blacks do not undertake their own liberation,
the whites will not make a move. . . ."*
—Jean Genet, from his introduction to George Jackson's
Soledad Brother.

I T IS IRONIC THAT OFFICIALS of the medium-security prison at
Vacaville should have decided in December of '72 that Donald
DeFreeze would be under better control in the maximum-security
hellhole known as Soledad, some 120 miles south of San Francisco and Berkeley. For Soledad had been in ferment since
January of '69, when a white guard shot down three black inmates in
an exercise yard, and, in less than a week, a second guard was sum-
marily executed in retaliation. Out of this crossfire were born all the
events that inspired a fresh wave of radical concentration on the prison
movement—the trial of three black convicts known as the Soledad
Brothers and the exoneration of two of them long after Jonathan Jackson had died at the Marin Courthouse in a desperate plot to free the
by now famous Soledad cons, and his brother George had been annihilated during an "escape attempt" at San Quentin.

Soledad (the name translates to "solitude, loneliness, lonely retreat") is set just in sight of Highway 101 as the road progresses slowly
down a relatively empty, uninteresting stretch of agricultural valley
below Salinas. (Another sixty miles to the southwest lies San Simeon,
William Randolph Hearst's mad transplant of a European barony to
a windy coastal cattle range. Tourists on the way down to visit the state-
supported vestiges of Hearst's most massive megalomania generally drive
past the forbidding gun towers of Soledad too fast even to ask,

"Whazzat?" But such ignorance is one-sided, for the name and legend of the Hearst empire are well known, and hated, inside these prison walls.)

DeFreeze would not long remain in Soledad. He had apparently been plotting an escape for months after hearing through the prison grapevine that a job would soon be open tending the heating system down at Soledad. He had applied himself to a course in boiler maintenance, was transferred, and was then chosen for a job refurbishing a heating system on the midnight-to-8:00 A.M. shift. He arrived on March 5, 1973, for his first night on the job with a lone guard in the furnace room of Soledad's mostly unused South Facility, an area the prison system was about to revamp into a training school for new screws.

He made his escape that first night. The guard, treating DeFreeze like a trusty (which he most certainly was *not*), left him alone shortly after midnight. When he returned forty-five minutes later to check up on his charge, Cinque Mtume was gone. Only a low fence separated the convict from open fields between the prison and the highway. A search was quickly begun, and a car that had stopped on the road with its blinkers on was surrounded, but it proved to be only a motorist with mechanical trouble.

No one in the prison system can say for sure just how and when Cinque escaped. Some think he took off as soon as the guard's back was turned and was quickly picked up by an accomplice outside with a car. More than a year later, a communiqué from S.L.A. claimed that Cinque had escaped "alone and on foot." The matter will probably never be clarified, since DeFreeze is no longer around to talk about it.

Several visitors to the BCA meetings at Vacaville, and other members of the East Bay black community who are active in the prison movement or have relatives in stir have hinted that they were approached early in March by the newly escaped DeFreeze but they refused him refuge. He turned for help to the white radicals who had come to idolize him a few months before at Vacaville and was quickly taken in. It's probable that one of the first of these S.L.A.ers he visited was Russell Little, who had continued to correspond with him at Soledad and had even written letters to the parole board in an effort to obtain Cinque's release.

Other members of the old Venceremos circles Little hung out with were soon recruited to hide the escaped black leader they had awaited so long. Since Little, Wolfe, and Nancy Ling Perry had been on the BCA visitor's list and might be checked out by authorities, it was decided to stash DeFreeze with a friend whose name was not then known. Mizmoon Soltysik was chosen, and Cinque became her tenant and lover. Chris Thompson helped to move him in.

The arrangement was apparently an open one, and Cinque was soon dating Cynthia Garvey, Nancy Ling Perry, and Emily Harris as well— a not too uncommon situation in radical Berkeley, where making love is considered a dandy way to get to know some interesting strangers (a fact attested to by a massive gonorrhea epidemic recorded there that spring).

Mizmoon's house was just a few blocks below Telegraph Avenue, in an area that has long housed more than its share of revolutionists. The neighborhood is kind of a "free zone" where pot is grown and smoked openly, a section Berkeley cops and visiting state and federal narcs have learned to avoid, since the entire community rises to intimidate the police when there's a raid. Red tin stars and Chairman Mao buttons, sold at cost at the Little Red Book Store just the other side of Tele, are as common as dandelions along these streets. A five-foot-high "power" fist made of red papier-mâché once dominated the front yard of the area's most militant commune, and a nearby bulletin board surrounded by boxes of free used clothes and piles of books, records, and household items to help out a largely indigent population keeps everyone well informed on radical current events, rallies, and demonstrations. It faces a neighborhood coffeehouse set up in the back room of a rambling Victorian house that is a prime meeting place and control room for life in the neighborhood. There is a strong sense of community spirit and revolutionary purpose here.

The week before Cinque arrived, a street near Mizmoon's house was closed off for a block party, at which the Red Star Singers performed revolutionary classics along with old labor songs. One ballad went: "There's a war in Vietnam/People's revolution in Vietnam/People fighting to be free." Onlookers soon were singing along and adding new names with each verse. First it was Ireland that was fighting to be free, and then Mozambique, Puerto Rico, Angola, and Chile. This went on all afternoon.

On the opposite side of the street, a continuing chess tournament competed for attention with political booths manned by Venceremos and the Women's Health Collective. This section of South Campus was not only an excellent place for Cinque to hide out but also an absolutely perfect locale for the first serious meetings of S.L.A. in the late spring and early summer. Not only Mizmoon and Camilla Hall lived here, but at one point they were within walking distance of the apartment occupied by Russ Little and Robyn Steiner.

Those who attend the first meetings are already up to their necks in radical politics, and the spring of '73 is an extremely busy one for all of them. The Harrises are conducting self-defense classes in their Oakland apartment and helping the Chino Defense Committee raise money to keep Venceremos leaders out of jail. Angela Atwood has just finished acting in *Hedda Gabler* and is looking for something more exciting to get involved in—revolution, for instance.

Camilla Hall has returned in February from her trip to Europe. She had tried, and failed, to forget her affair with Mizmoon, and she is soon back visiting her lover and jealously observing Mizmoon's dual affair with Cinque and Chris Thompson.

Russ Little, Nancy Ling Perry, Robyn Steiner, and Willie the Wolfe continue their frequent visits to the jails as well as their incessant letter writing both to convicts and to parole boards. There are a number of superstar prison-movement trials to keep an eye on this spring: Ruchell (Cinque) McGee is being tried for his part in the Marin Civic Center shoot-out. (He will beat the main charges after a jury deadlocks in early April.) The first hearings begin for the "San Quentin Six," the convicts who stood up against the screws the day George Jackson was killed.

The antiwar movement had become a thing of the past on January 27, when a Vietnamese cease-fire finally arrived. That was only seven days after Nixon's second inauguration, but the word "Watergate" had already begun to pollute the airwaves.

With America's direct involvement in the war over and Nixon about to scuttle himself, radical Berkeley turns to domestic issues, and Joe Remiro faces his busiest spring as he dives headfirst into a dozen causes.

He continues working with the Oakland office of VVAW until late March and is involved in two of their major activities, backing the United Farm Workers and campaigning for Black Panther leader Bobby Seale, who is runing for mayor of Oakland (a task Remiro must find distasteful, for he has begun to violently disagree with the Panthers). Joe is also taking a course in auto mechanics at North Peralta College and is learning a lot about machine-shop work—the kind of skills necessary to become a good gunsmith.

Remiro commutes across the Bay occasionally to visit his folks in San Francisco and to work as VVAW's representative with a group being formed by Popeye Jackson of the United Prisoners Union. Jackson had organized a Coalition Against Racism and Repression in January—only a month after he received his parole and walked out of jail to breathe freely for the first time in years. Jackson, like Joe, is a member of Venceremos and says he works well with Remiro.

"He was quiet," says Popeye, "a really good-working guy, man. . . . Everybody who knew him had a lot of respect for Joe. I didn't get much of a chance to talk to him, though. Joe was doing so much good work, man, around the movement, and he never really had time to sit down with me. . . . He was a really quiet dude. If he had something to say, he said it. He didn't pull no words. It was brief, precise, and to the fucking point, man. There wasn't no bullshit about it . . . not what I heard of it."

Remiro goes to Wounded Knee as a volunteer soldier late in April. Marxist study sessions, gun classes, and range practice continue through the spring and summer. They provide a marvelous way to attract and screen potential recruits for the now-forming S.L.A.

The ideological groundwork for the new group is well under way by May. It is completed before August 21, 1973, when the Symbionese Liberation Army goes whole hog and issues its "Declaration of War" against the slightly larger United States of America. Thero Wheeler does not escape from Vacaville until August 2, and he's too late on the scene to add many ideas to the initial war declaration and constitution. But he's on hand quite soon enough to back up friend Cinque's lethal talents with a few choice tricks of his own.

The study and gun sessions attract some thirty to forty friends and fellow partisans who drift through the gatherings held in a number of Berkeley and Oakland locations between late spring and early fall. Only a few are trusted enough to be recruited into the fledgling urban guerrilla army. In the meantime, Mizmoon, the Harrises, Nancy Ling Perry, and other members with extensive academic and radical training are hard at work researching a wide range of ancient and contemporary documents to produce the "symbiotic" blend of ideas and images that will flesh out the four major documents of S.L.A. Their sources include black nationalist manifestoes, the goals of the Black Panthers, Venceremos, and VVAW, the writings of all the major American prison revolutionaries, and even mythological studies like *The Sacred Symbols of Mu,* from which they borrow a seven-headed cobra as the S.L.A. emblem. They will later claim the multiple-fanged serpent is "170,000 years old . . . one of the first symbols used by people to signify God and life." This strangely mutated mixture of black nationalist theory, ghetto hustle and jive from Cinque, reshuffled guerrilla tactics from Joe Remiro, half-baked mysticism from the muddled head of Nancy Ling Perry, and cold dialectical materialism from the well-educated Harrises and Mizmoon whirls around in a discussion Mixmaster as dozens of meetings are held. Thero Wheeler's old lady, Mary Alice Siem, will later say she attended twenty such gatherings in the three months she was involved from August to October of '73.

The inputs are many and fascinating. The new group immediately attracts several dozen Berkeley radicals who have had it with "just talk" and the ineffectual protests and confrontations of the early '70s. As one of them explains:

"We joined the S.L.A. separately, not knowing each other at the time, but for similar reasons, as we later discovered, namely that we could no longer tolerate the quality and conditions of our private and public lives—repressive education that was no more than an assembly line for making obedient slaves, boring and humiliating jobs, declining 'standards of living,' and a polluted, ugly environment. And, as far as we could see, things were getting worse. All the reforms we fought for in the '60s had failed or been taken back, and were inadequate to start with. All of us were frustrated with the divided factions of the so-called revolutionary left.

"That movement was based on guilt, on always making the revolution for somebody else, in the name of somebody else's oppression, supposedly greater than our own. It was dominated by egotistical leaders—bureaucrats and leader-stars—who cared only about their own 'revolutionary' careers. They led a mass of follower-lackeys who proved their own decrepitude by tolerating and, in fact, creating such leaders. The confusion of antiwar groups, sexual liberation groups, and national liberation groups were all presenting the image of militant opposition, but we wanted to do more than merely talk back to the TV screen. We were looking for brothers and sisters who felt as urgently as we did that the time to seize back our lives was now.

"The Symbionese people we contacted were self-disciplined, serious, and efficient revolutionary cadres, willing to risk anything in order to gain everything. When we joined the Symbionese Federation we thought we had found a place for ourselves in a revolutionary organization that was on its way beyond the left, old and new. . . ."

Joe Remiro put his reasons for joining S.L.A. this way: "I saw that white people shouldn't join the revolution because they want to help the poor black people or the poor brown people. White people are into the revolution because they realize that their own security is very flaky and they're revolting in their own best interests, in their own interests.

Hear what I'm saying? I'm saying that the reason that white people should revolt and join the revolution is not for the black people, is not for the brown people, is not for the native Americans. It's for themselves."

Remiro was obviously one of those who were most completely won over. A number of the other early S.L.A. members were not as absolutely convinced as he that the answer to the political and personal problems they faced in 1973 was guerrilla warfare. But S.L.A.'s very direct and total dedication to a violent attack on all they hated in American society appealed greatly to the rising level of hatred so strongly felt by many former humanists and pacifists who had completely given up on old-style movement tactics.

They had discovered the ancient paradox that love is a two-sided coin. What you care about deeply enough, you may also learn to hate, and the level of hatred and frustration running loose around Berkeley early in '73 was frightening. As Remiro would put it:

"The dialectical relationship between love and hate cannot be denied. If there weren't anything we could classify as hate, if hate didn't exist, could you define or prove that such a thing as love existed? Love and hate do exist—together. We can't know love unless we also know hate. Anyone who claims to only love and not hate is being dishonest with themselves."

It became fashionable in Berkeley to quote Che Guevara on the subject. Revolutionists, said Che, are motivated in their man-killing careers by "great feelings of love." Some of the salutations S.L.A. members began to use in their correspondence from this point on included "Love and FirePower," "In Revolutionary Unity and Internationalism through Criticism, Self-Critcism and Love," and "Dare to Struggle, Dare to Win, Dare to Love."

The most lethal variety of this brand of revolutionary "love" was reserved for the Establishment and its police. By spring, '73 no true Berkeley revolutionary ever referred to them as anything but "pigs." It was, in fact, the adroitness with which you used the term that either won you acceptance into groups like S.L.A. or immediately aroused suspicion. A recent conversation about the use of this pungent term among a group of people who may have attended the early S.L.A. meetings went this way:

First radical (a thirty-year-old mother who had been through the peace movement and Venceremos): "If you can't use the word 'pig,' you don't understand fascism or repression."

Second radical (an equally intense younger woman, myopic, bespectacled, rather academic—the kind who would most certainly have joined the Communist party twenty years ago): "Anyone who is squeamish about it belongs back in those old student days, those nonviolent days when you had to avoid using the word 'rock' because someone might throw one."

A black ex-convict: "The people we're working with in those concentration camps, they don't have no trouble usin' the word 'pig.' "

First radical: "There's no fuckin' difference between a fuckin' fascist and a fuckin' pig."

First liberal (a middle-aged man soon to be expelled from the group): "But we're trying to relate to lawyers and old-left radicals like the National Lawyers Guild. We need them to defend prisoners. The word 'pig' scares them off."

Ex-con: "Fuckin' lawyers don't care what you call 'em just so you lay some money in their fuckin' hands."

Second liberal (also on the verge of expulsion): "But I don't know if you mean cops or prison guards or corporation heads when you use that term."

Second radical: "That's right. They're ALL pigs!"

First radical: "It doesn't matter whether the Man is dressed in suit and tie or a uniform when he's arresting you. It doesn't matter whether he's a poor pig or a rich pig. He's a pig."

Second radical: "Anyone who's turned off by the word 'pig' is a liberal, anyway. And they've *gotta* be fucked."

Get the tone and style? Those who take the command in such discussions are angry, fighting mad. For them, the time to talk of peace is long past. It's not a question of *whether* to fight any more, just *how*. Since they view contemporary politics as just one more form of warfare, those who do not agree with them are the enemy. Everything then boils down to "which side are you on?" Are you one of *us* or one of *them?*" And since "them" constitutes the government and its millions of agents and supporters, this kind of absolutist thinking leads to an intense degree of paranoia. You're never sure just who you're talking to. He might be a fink. He might agree with you today and betray you tomorrow. This led to the formation of S.L.A. under a thick cloud of secrecy and distrust.

Central to this increasingly conspiratorial attitude (the conversations were heavily into armed uprising, and that *is* illegal) was the conviction held by the escaped convicts and many of the white former university radicals, like Nancy Ling Perry, that a revolution was legally and morally justified because the U.S. government was *already* a dictatorship, what S.L.A. frequently referred to as a "corporate fascist military dictatorship." Fascism, in the eyes of the S.L.A.ers and thousands of other American radicals, was already *here,* so it was absolutely absurd to continue talking about changing things through peaceful, legal methods. Dictatorships pay no attention to petitions and demonstrations; they simply arrest the petitioners and machine-gun the demonstrators.

Ms. Perry asserted this very strongly in her fantastic letter of January 17, 1974. She claimed that democracy in the United States ended when John Kennedy was assassinated, that massive, shadowy forces of repression run by and for the benefit of the giant corporations and cartels had taken over in this country, and that Richard Nixon was only their front man. Events like Watergate, with its revelations of a secret-police plumbers unit, have done little to contradict such conclusions.

Those who believe that a dictatorship is already here then jump to the next conclusion (one that is verified by the U.S. Declaration of Independence)—that Americans have an "inalienable right" to rebel against tyranny as well as to "alter and abolish" such states and to "institute a new government."

Skeptics may laugh at the enormity of these assumptions. But in trying to understand the S.L.A. or any of today's armed urban guerrilla terrorist groups, the observer would do well to remember that these young people are absolutely *serious* in their beliefs. Serious and totally committed.

The fact that they are reacting to a set of political conditions that have not yet occurred but which could loom with angry forboding just over the horizon does not change their rather futuristic convictions nor alter their belief that the worst has already occurred in America.

It is true that for most of the citizens of this nation, the republic does still exist, does still function. There is still a Constitution and a Bill of Rights. There is still free speech and free press. The law does still apply, albeit unequally, as the forced Agnew resignation and the Nixon pardon so well indicate. But for a man in prison (which most cons now call "concentration camps"), there is no liberty. To a man out of work, the depression has already begun. To a fourteen-year-old black kid shot in the back by a drunken, racist cop there is no equality under the law.

And the phenomenon that S.L.A. and the whole American guerrilla movement represent is simply this:

You do not draw your political conclusions from any sort of statistical overview that takes in *all* the people. You relate only to your own experience and to the experiences of those who are at the bottom—the blacks, the convicts, the most unskilled, unemployed, and despised in the land, the punk kids who drop out of school because there really is nothing there for them but confinement. Revolutionists who are now operating in such groups as S.L.A., the Black Liberation Army, the Black Guerrilla Family, and the New World Liberation Front regard *these* experiences as the absolute truth of the matter. And anyone who disagrees is simply a "racist liberal" or a "white bourgeois blinded by his skin and class privileges." Very neat, very intolerant—and very lethal.

So the major questions that had to be resolved in the founding meetings of the S.L.A. were these:

Not *is* there a dictatorship, but how bad is it? Not *should* we take up arms against it, but only when and how? How do we relate to the revolutionary experience of the past? In particular, how can we utilize the guerrilla tactics of Che and Mao, Alberto Bayo and Carlos Marighella?

What allies can we hope to bring into this struggle? Most especially, can we hope for strong support from black radicals, who are truly the forefront of revolution in America? How can we get these blacks to trust new and untried white revolutionists like ourselves?

How do we relate to the old-left and new-left politicos—if at all? We say we are socialist revolutionaries, but do we simply accept all the pedantic teachings of Marx and Mao, or do we create a new hybrid revolutionary philosophy and guerrilla practice to better suit conditions in America? Is it true that there is a "particularity" in the American experience that makes it different from that of other nations, and are we different from revolutionists in other countries? Are we, in fact, really internationalists? Do we think of world revolution or only about revolution in one nation at a time?

How do we structure our daily lives while we are waging the revolution? How do we live among ourselves, and how do we raise the necessary money? Most especially, how do we resolve the issue of complete and absolute equality for women among our ranks (a prime consideration in any group that is dominated by feminists)? How do we feel about culture and spirituality? (An artist-poet and at least one mystic were involved.)

How do we structure our new organization to bring in many other militant groups and to create a united front and a federated coalition of other people from the Asian, black, brown, Indian, white, women's, gray, and gay liberation movements?

How will this lead to the creation of a fighting army whose existence is the central purpose of all we do? ("The people always organize to fight the enemy; and when leaders fail to start the fight, then the people fall from that organization.")

It is doubtful that a dozen or so young Berkeley radicals, or even a larger, more mature group, could have come up with concrete, realistic answers to all of these perplexing and complicated questions. But they tried, and very hard, as their four major documents and their proclamations, letters, and communiqués indicate. Probably the clearest reflection on a very personal basis of their experience and thinking comes from Joe Remiro. Here are some of the answers to the main questions the S.L.A. founders had to consider.

About fascism: "Fascism is here. It's more obvious every day—the politicos even admit it," Little and Remiro jointly respond. "Civil rights, even on paper, are dead. Political grand juries, preventative detention, stop and search laws, search and seizure laws, and a host of other such laws which legally overrule a person's constitutional and human rights were designed specifically to encourage and support frame-ups. It is fascism, loud and clear. And we've been aware of it for some time now because of our relations with revolutionary prisoners who are always the first and hardest hit by repression."

Says Remiro: "The only ones who've got civil rights now are white people. Go to the prisons and look at those concentration camps. I mean, the thing is, man, that these things exist and that they are out front to anyone who wants to look and check 'em out. They're right there to see. It's fascism, but it's not like German fascism—it's so much more sophisticated that there's no comparison, there's no motherfucking comparison at all. You just can't wait for those signs they had in Germany. The Social Democrats sat on their asses while the Nazis instituted fascism. You can't expect the American government to do the same thing that they did in Germany, 'cause this government's more sophisticated, more organized. They've got statewide and national computer banks, man. You know, it's completely different. . . ."

On taking arms against this "fascist state":

Says Remiro: "You just can't sit around and wait. You've got to organize a people's army now, a trained and armed people's army. The only way you get that is from practice, you know. I mean, it's going to come down sooner or later. Fact of the matter is, when it comes down you want to have something to fight back with. You don't want a bunch of untrained people who don't know how to fight the enemy. You have to fuckin' have some kind of training, and it doesn't come out of books, you know. You have to raise people's consciousness to fight, you know. I'll tell you one thing, man—the masses aren't alienated by armed struggle. I'm talking about the oppressed masses, not the white middle class. And I'm not talking about the working class that makes over five dollars an hour. The real oppressed masses are not alienated by violence. The exact opposite is true. A lot of people are sitting on the fringe waiting for something to happen, and they're going to go with *us*. I used to admire the ideals of pacifism but I think they're dead now. I believe that if the Vietnamese people had been pacifists they would all be slaves right now. If the people of Mozambique had been pacifists they would have been slaves. What would a pacifist have done against Hitler? They're going to play hell trying to get me to walk pacifistically into the gas chamber. Martin Luther King wasn't very pacifistic when he was killed. By then he was saying that pacifism doesn't work. There has to be revolutionary violence to combat the reactionary violence that the government set loose."

Nancy Ling Perry summed it up this way: "I believe that whenever people are confronted with oppression, starvation, and the death of their freedom that they want to fight. It has been the history of many political leaders to suppress this will of the people, and to pretend the people do not have the right to fight, and to pretend that the people will somehow achieve their liberation without revolutionary violence. But the truth is that there has never been a precedent for a nonviolent revolution; the defenseless and unarmed people of Chile can testify to that. Revolutionary violence is nothing but the most profound means of achieving internal as well as external balance."

On the use of urban guerrilla warfare tactics to launch this violent revolution:

"The theory that's going to work is clearly the foco theory," says Remiro. "You know, it's the theory of small armed bands of guerrillas, you know, developing the struggle to the point where over a long period of years the guerrillas actually do end up with the majority of the power and the strength, you know. That's not a theory that calls for mass uprising and insurrection, you know. . . . When guerrillas are on the offensive, they pick their own terrain and tactics and the enemy simply doesn't know where they're going to hit next and in the cities they'll never catch 'em. The fucking urban centers in America are jungles. They can't find 'em and they don't know where they'll hit next. You can see that in the Bay Area with S.L.A., but when you spread that out all across the United States they're going to have to employ half the people and police to try and watch out for what the other half is going to do. The government is terrified this urban guerrilla thing is going to catch on, and if it does they know they cannot stop it. They have no defense against this type of guerrilla warfare. If you took just six groups like the S.L.A. and let them loose in six different cities, operating all at once, they couldn't stop it. It could not be contained and it could not be defeated."

The allies S.L.A. sought to bring into their guerrilla war were all of those groups who have long been in the forefront of dissent in America. The inability of previous revolutionary movements to bring together any kind of wide spectrum of dissenting groups has been the main stumbling block to insurrectional success in the past. The concept of a "united front" on the left has been talked about since the turn of the century. Says the S.L.A. Declaration of War in explaining their approach (and the reason for the name "Symbionese"):

"The Symbionese Federation and The Symbionese Liberation Army is made up of the aged, youth, and women and men of all races and people. The name Symbionese is taken from the word symbiosis and we define its meaning as a body of dissimilar bodies and organisms living in deep and loving harmony and partnership in the best interest of all within that body. . . . We of the Symbionese Federation and The S.L.A. are the children of all oppressed people, who have decided to redefine ourselves as a Symbionese Race and People . . . to die a race, and be born a nation, is to become free. . . ."

The Declaration of War also indicates that this federation was to be brought together under black and minority leadership in much the same way Venceremos tried to recruit all of its chiefs from Third World communities.

Cinque Mtume was already on hand to lead at this point (with the consent of the women, who actually made most of S.L.A.'s major decisions), and the new group was desperately trying to get backing from such notorious armed fighting groups as BLA and the BGF (who were mostly in the California prisons). They were getting nowhere. S.L.A. was all too apparently a bunch of white Berkeleyites, and the militant blacks did not trust them. They also had to overcome their *own* feelings of guilt about even being white and having grown up with "privileges." This proved to be a very important and central psychological issue—this need to prove themselves to the blacks as real guerrilla fighters, fearless revolutionaries willing to die a grim and blazing death rather than to retreat an inch.

Camilla Hall expressed the personal agony of this dilemma as the need to "battle the enemy within . . . the putrid disease of bourgeois mentality is in all of us. We are consciously working to rid ourselves of it so we can be better soldiers, fighters for the people. . . ."

Other S.L.A.ers repeated this theme so often that it became a kind of requiem for those who died or went to jail. Remiro and Little frequently said that the most important single accomplishment of S.L.A. was that it finally proved, once and for all, to the black revolutionists that whites are brave and can be trusted. . . . They won't run home for dinner in the middle of the battle.

It is, in fact, this intense repentance and guilt over being white and the concomitant avidity with which they idolize and imitate the black insurrectionists (to the point of changing speech patterns to match genuine ghetto dialect) that most confuses and irritates parents and childhood friends of the S.L.A.ers. These kids, from "good" and even "rich" homes, from the comfortable, child-breeding hothouses of suburban America, are so often the brightest, most attractive, and most energetic products of a youth-oriented culture in which good looks and sexuality of the kind Berkeley overflows with will almost automatically land you a "promising" job and a one-way ticket into all that passes today in America for the "good life." The fact that their kids dumped all this for a life of danger and privation, that they even denounced their own race and upbringing, still adds up to one big fat enigma to the parents.

"How? Why?" ask the stunned and still unbelieving survivors. "Why did they go out murdering and kidnapping, fucking and blindly imitating a bunch of wino niggers from the slums? Didn't they have every chance? Didn't we give them everything?"

The question answers itself.

Their kids ended up realizing that they had received too *much*. The resulting feelings of guilt—most especially guilt toward blacks—has been a prime motivation for fifteen years of civil-rights marching and sitting-in, for unselfish involvement in Peace Corps work and poverty programs, for demonstrating and trashing, and finally for conversion to a philosophy of violent revolution. It is a crucial part of what becoming "hip" has been about since the early '30s in America, a full twenty years before Norman Mailer stereotyped that phenomenon in "The White Negro." Mezz Mezzrow, a white reedman who had to join the most despised and depressed residents of Harlem to find out what being "hip" was all about, explains it in *Really the Blues*. He found a kind of funky, existentialist reality that, for him, was more direct and honest than anything he had grown up with as a white. Like previous generations of "hip" Americans, the S.L.A.ers became negrophiles, and they studied, imitated, and learned prodigiously. They soon were imitating all that their parents most hated and feared in the black side of American culture. They repudiated all the advantages of being educated and white. They decided they must join the truly wretched of the earth, and our black ghettos were a perfect place to find them.

But the blacks did not often return their interest and love. Remiro describes the dilemma this way:

"If I was black and raised in this society, you know, I don't think I'd like white people very much myself. White people say, 'Well we don't have to *prove* anything.' Well, they *do* have to prove a lot. And I don't hold it at all against black people for not trusting white people. The white people of S.L.A. realized that, and they realized that they *did* have to prove something because all whites have been proving historically is that they're a bunch of assholes that shouldn't be trusted, you know. I don't even have any argument with Black Muslims, you know. I can't argue with them how they're not justified in feeling that the white man is the devil. All I can do is point out how they very we*ll *may* be justified in feeling the white man is the devil, you know. I can't argue with them, man, I cannot argue with them. I don't feel that white people are going to lead the revolution. I don't feel that it's historically possible for white people to lead anything in this country, you know. I don't think that there are any black or brown or red revolutionaries in this country who are going to allow themselves to be led by any white people. They've been ripped off too much. But what *has* happened now is that white revolutionaries have come of age and been recognized as revolutionaries. They came down to cases. They dealt with it as class rather than races. The government would like nothing better than if all the blacks would say, 'Fuck the whites!' and start a revolution alone. Why, the government would like nothing better, you know. The S.L.A. was working toward averting a racial war, which is probably inevitable still. And if it happened, just where would I be? I'd be joining the race war on the opposite side, man."

Remiro feels that blacks and revolutionaries now share a common consciousness, a "revolutionary consciousness," and this explains why their style of speaking is so similar:

"The undisputable fact that most revolutionaries are black is not because of their color," he says. "It's because of what black people in this country have had to live with and live through, you know. So we can't bring it down to, well, the blacks are revolutionaries and the whites aren't. Revolutionaries are people who understand and feel it. The fact that most revolutionaries are black is just historical, and looking at what they've lived through, at what's been dealt out to them, what they haven't gotten, how many times they've been fucked over, you know, it makes sense. Up till now blacks are the only people who've really been talking revolution—people like Malcolm X and George Jackson. It's a new experience to hear white people really talking revolution. What was needed was some white revolutionaries to prove they were really revolutionaries, and up to now all that has happened is—the only thing that's come out nationally in a revolutionary way was the Weather underground, and all they've done is put their own white brand of revolutionary activity out, which was a complete contradiction to the Black Liberation Army's brand of revolutionary activity. What the S.L.A. has done is move in from the middle and use 'em both. I mean, the only way it was going to be united was by the white people, man."

Says Russ Little: "When you come right down to it, generally speaking, the white people in this country have always just said, you know, stood back and said, 'Ya! We support you! Right on with the Black Panthers! Ya! That was a far-out gun battle, man!' And they write songs about it or some ol' shit like that. But when it came right down to it, you really couldn't depend on them for any concrete support. I mean, they can rationalize that, 'Well, according to Marx and Lenin, they're the most oppressed segment of the society, so naturally they're going to be the ones who are the most heroic,' and blah, blah, blah. And that's a bunch of horseshit, you know. Just realizing that makes it worse, sitting there and saying that kind of shit, you know. You're saying, 'I'm going to keep my class privileges and shit, and I'm going to let them fight. . . .'"

Bill Harris puts it this way: "Contrary to what many of us may think, the special privileges white men as a group have gained for themselves through the oppression of all other people has never secured for us the freedom we desire. White men must understand that they will live under the threat of death as long as they continue to oppress the members of any class or group who have the strength and determination to fight back. White men themselves have only one avenue to freedom and that is to join in fighting to the death those who are and those who aspire to be the slavemasters of the world. Many of us have been bold enough to intellectualize about revolution, but far too chickenshit to get down and help make it. Most of us have been nearly fatally stricken with the vile sickness of racism. Again, most of us have been immobilized by our sexist egos and have watched and done nothing as our sisters have rushed by us into battle. We have fooled ourselves into believing that Madison Avenue piggery will bring us eternal bourgeois happiness. If we haven't bought into the sexist, racist, capitalist, imperialist program, we have 'greened out' in Mendocino and New Hampshire. To black people who lead our struggle to freedom, we have proved to be the racist punks of the world when we kick back and live off the blood and lives of the people."

Emily Harris puts it even more succinctly: "Our past as middle-class white Americans was meaningless. It was truly wasted potential, filled with desperate pessimism. It was desperate pessimism that could feel the emptiness of capitalist America even before we could understand it. Our lives now are not easy or full of joy. We may die. But our lives are real, because we see the truth and the future. . . ."

The quesion of relating either to the Marxist old left or to the more anarchistic new left, all of whom were contemptuously called "politicos" by S.L.A., was not long debated. It was assumed that all of these groups, including the loosely organized Black Panthers, were heavily infiltrated by government informers. The real lessons, they felt, would be learned from guerrilla movements abroad, most especially from the Cubans and the Chinese.

Bill Harris explains that "the S.L.A. came into being because many people refused to wait for so-called revolutionary groups and organizations to lead them into a revolution which would, therefore, never come. We grew tired of waiting for mythological North American revolutionaries with the necessary expertise and skills we lacked to teach us. . . ."

"Politicos go and do things dogmatically," says Remiro. "They go around saying, 'Uh, well, the skilled workers were the vanguard in Russia and China' and all this. They don't realize that in Russia and China those people weren't making more than anybody else, you know. Here those people are making more than college graduates. Man, you know, those people have been bought off by THE imperialist country. They've been bought off, man, intentionally. I hope they join the revolution. But the ones that do aren't going to join until their wages are fucked up and their unions are closed down. Till, you know, they actually *feel* the oppression that's going on, and they don't feel it, man. The ones who have to start the revolution and will probably be in it to the end are the ones who are the most oppressed. And then these politicos jump up and say, 'Oh, that's only the *lumpenproletariat.*' Fuck that lumpenproletariat shit, man. The lumpenproletariat in this country is a hell of a lot different. . . ."

"The new left?" says Russ Little incredulously. "I'd say all that campus shit was dead by the end of '71. I knew all that shit was dead when I came to Berkeley in '72 the first time. I knew that there had to be something new come out. Grandstanding, rioting, and all that shit is dead, man. As far as we're concerned, the new left is dead. We think that another stage is coming on, a period of spontaneous, serious revolutionary activity. It takes more than handing out a few leaflets telling people to boycott a grocery store. People are tired of that kind of shit. People are tired of these guys getting up and sayin' they're revolutionaries. They're just not serious. They're white kids out for a thrill. They're so chickenshit they can't even say no when the FBI comes to the door. As far as armed struggle is concerned, they support it in Vietnam, in Mozambique, somewhere else in the world. Just don't come around us. There wasn't no one in S.L.A. that was so stupid or naive to talk to people like that. Angela Davis has sold out just like Huey Newton and the rest of them. They're pissed off at S.L.A., the leaders of these little organizations that don't have any members left, 'cause all the militants left their organizations. Who the fuck wants to consult them? When they can't even see the validity of things that are being done. Why should they be consulted, man? That's a security risk. You don't deal with those people who are fronting people off. There was a lot of fronting off with the Panthers. The cowards have two lines: if something is unsuccessful, it is adventurist. If it is successful, it is a government conspiracy to bring down the heat on them. They talk, talk, talk and wonder why no one listens except their white politico buddies. They're hypocritical liberals, counterrevolutionary punks who spout leftist rhetoric when they're absolutely sure nothing will come of it."

S.L.A. members spent a lot of time studying Marxism, and Remiro, for one, frequently insists that he's a "communist revolutionary internationalist." But the home-blended mixture of ideologies and practical solutions to contemporary guerrilla problems that he has put together to suit himself would probably confound other communists he might encounter in China or Cuba or Russia. In much the same way that the Cuban revolution brought a new style of Marxism into being to fulfill the needs and style of that torrid, emotional, and very Hispanic little island, so the developing urban guerrilla movement in the United States is altered by the "particularity" of the American experience.* "The first stage of revolutionary warfare is what we're in now," says Remiro. "We're in the beginning of the first stage and it's the most dangerous stage, 'cause revolutionaries are going to make a lot of mistakes. A lot of us are going to get killed, like Jonathan Jackson did. Who would have thought the pigs would sacrifice a judge rather than turn a few convicts loose? But, in fact, the only way they're going to develop a more flexible fighting tool is by learning from their mistakes, you know. You can't learn out of books. You have to learn by doing it. You got a theory, put it into practice. If it fucks up, the next people have learned something, you know. You're not going to see anybody running off into a courtroom any more and grabbing a judge and a D.A. and think the pigs are going to let 'em drive away in a van. It's a period of trial and error, a period of making fatal mistakes, and a lot of people are going to get killed, a lot of dedicated people killed by making dumb mistakes. But it's a very necessary period so that we can get rid of this dogmatic bullshit and formulate our own strategy for a revolution in this country. Improvising seems the wisest thing to do. . . .

"You see," Joe explains, "that's what separates the politicos from the revolutionaries. The politicos are dogmatic and don't realize the particularity of this country as compared with the contradictions with other countries. They expect to have a Chinese revolution or a Russian revolution, which is not possible here. It's a completely different country, completely different circumstances, and it's going to take a completely different kind of revolution. I mean, there isn't no place like America, man. Where else would a guerrilla army decide that only

* Speaking of Cuba, it is a fundamental truism among America's "internationalist" revolutionaries that the United States entered the ranks of "imperialist" powers with the Spanish-American War. A previously continental republic, whose citizens had the right to vote and select their own representatives, for the first time acquired extracontinental colonies and "subjects" who would be denied the franchise. It is also a radical "truism" that William Randolph Hearst was primarily responsible for starting that imperial war over the question of Cuba and that his newspapers did more to create the "American Empire" than any other agency. Hearst—and his heirs—have been viewed as absolute hobgoblins of a jingoist, ruthless campaign of "manifest destiny" and empire building by the extreme left since well before World War I.

half of a fighting unit could get stoned at one time? Where else would a guerrilla soldier tell you that the main thing he likes to do for entertainment is to fuck?"

The latter remark had come from Russ Little, who sums up his approach to blending old and new revolutionary styles this way: "I couldn't say we were Maoists, 'cause Mao and them were involved in rural warfare. We're North American revolutionaries. We're trying to apply all these ideas to the North American continent. . . . We study revolutionary movements all over the world and try to apply whatever we can in the States and try to reevaluate things. We can't just say we're Maoists or Guevarists or Tupamarists. We've learned a lot from all of them, but none had to deal with a country this massive and this heavy into a police state. . . ."

As far as S.L.A. being essentially "internationalist" in its thinking:

"Sure it's an international conspiracy," says Little, "with freedom fighters all part of an international proletarian revolutionary movement, and we're winning! We've never met, but we know each other, have the same enemy, suffer the same setbacks, enjoy the same victories, get killed by the same U.S. Grade A bullets. . . ."

Remiro expands the point saying that true "democracy" does not consist in the people of only one nation choosing leaders who will take care of them but exploit the people of other countries. He would not, for instance, countenance a Richard Nixon in power even though his election had been approved by a true majority of the American public.

"A nation doesn't have the right to come off and become capitalist and imperialist. When they do they have no rights," he says. "They lose their rights. If we allowed a free election in this country and a Nixon were elected again, I'd say, 'Well, bullshit! There ain't gonna be no more motherfuckin' free elections.' And you ask what if all the people voted for him. What about the people in Harlem and the people in the Fillmore? Those people didn't want him? The people in the Philippines, the people in South America, the people in Asia, you know. They didn't want him. We gotta think of the majority, and the real majority in the world is nonwhite. The real majority is oppressed by imperialism. Lenin said he didn't give a piss about Russia. He said, 'Fuck Russia!' He wanted a world revolution. . . . I say, 'Fuck the United States, man!' If the United States wants to support a Nixon, fuck 'em. The majority shit is international as far as I'm concerned. The majority of the world has made their choice, man."

The next major question that comes up, just how S.L.A. members were to live from day to day while organizing an eventual revolution, would obviously involve a certain degree of communal living, as much as security would allow. Remiro says that he believes in living communally because he believes in communism, but that the kind of rather apolitical, pacifist communes now common in cities like Berkeley are "far from true communism. It's far from the solution, you know. It's like all these communes going around and all these people thinking it's going to spread until it spreads all over the world, which sure isn't giving much credit to the people of Cambodia or the people of Chile. While these people are going around spreading communal life one by one, they're killing the people of Chile ten by ten."

Communal families, like all others, have their housekeeping problems and their hassles about who's going to take out the garbage and cook the dinners. Remiro says he wants to live with a "guerrilla woman —the highest form of woman." Being a rather notorious romantic, it's apparent that Remiro's "guerrilla woman" might change in name and face from time to time, because, as he says, "I fall in love all the time."

When it comes to raising children, he says he's all for it. The first thing a revolutionary parent must do, he says, is to "arm them . . . just as soon as they're old enough to hold a gun." Remiro first took his own son, Joshua, out for firing-range practice at the age of three.

All decisions in revolutionary households must, of course, be made with the full agreement of the participating women. S.L.A. was feminist-oriented from the first. The group's constitution calls for laws "that will neither force people into nor force them to stay in personal relationships they do not wish to be in"—like marriage or any lasting contractual relationship between men and women. Such a loose situation suits Remiro, who readily admits that he's lost enough arguments with militant feminists to say in front that he is a "sexist—raised and programed. Feminists have talked to me about their rights and have only moved my consciousness forward and left themselves in the same place. After hours of mouthy struggle they have ALL walked away labeling me a sexist pig. If that is all they wished to do they could have saved a lot of time, as I would have readily copped out. With 'revolutionary women' there is no struggle. They took their rights and left me with mine. They didn't bore me with feminist rhetoric. They completely won me over, won my support, and then made it clear that my support wasn't needed."

S.L.A. decided that the use of heavy drugs in its ranks was definitely out. The prohibition was written into S.L.A.'s "Codes of War" with fascinating exactness: "This rule applies to the use of such drugs as heroin, speed, peyote, mescaline, reds, pep pills, whites, yellow jackets, bennies, dexies, goof balls, LSD and any other kind of hallucinatory drug."

But that old American "particularity" reared its funky head a bit later in the ruling. A certain amount of boozing (Cinque liked plum wine) and pot smoking (everybody else had been a head at one time or another) was OK. The Codes say that "permission is granted for the use of only two types of relaxing drugs: these are marijuana and/or beer and wine and other alcohol."

The only catch is that no more than half of a fighting unit can get stoned at one time and true revolutionaries were expected to soon "get over" the need for even booze or pot. As Remiro puts it:

"Acid, booze, any kind of narcotic, all it does is shield you from the realities of life. I didn't start to become political till I cut loose drugs, man. Drugs didn't make me political. I'd never advise anyone to take acid. I'd never advise anyone to smoke grass. I don't think anyone should. I think that if people haven't done it, fine. If they have, fine. You know, once you get completely involved in the revolution you don't need any of that stuff."

As to getting the money together to keep an organization like. S.L.A. moving, it was decided that the most attractive methods were to be the same "revolutionary" forms favored by the Irish Republican Army and Joseph Stalin—bank stickups, burglaries, and other rip-offs from the Establishment.

Anyone who got out of line or violated house codes could count on a bit of self-denial or KP such as "the cleaning and maintenance of all cell arms, ammunition and explosives for one week, the upkeep of outhouses, the full suspension of wine or cigarettes and extra duties such as additional watches, practice and study periods, correspondence, filing, typing, washing, cleaning, cooking and physical exercise." Everybody got a turn at washing the dishes, making the beds, and sweeping the floor.

The group gave considerable thought to its positions on "art and culture." As the use of the ancient mystical symbol of the seven-headed cobra demonstrates, several members (like Nancy Ling Perry) had a considerable interest in the occult as well.

"We embrace the concepts of art and spiritual consciousness in material, relevant terms based upon the common conditions of all oppressed peoples," she wrote. "We have begun to re-define art as the natural creative reflection of our desperate struggle to survive. Art for us is the total process of sharing and communally using what we learn in order to live and to fight. We recognize Cinque as an artist for what he teaches the people, but we also recognize as he himself has said that truth has no author. Another thing which we feel is necessary to clarify is the word 'spirit' and all that which is called spiritual. The spirit is the bodies and souls of all the people, and the spiritual is the intensity of our common instincts, as reflected throughout history, to fight for the freedom of all oppressed peoples, to save the earth and the children from the putrid disease of bourgeois mentality and the putrid disease of the corporate fascist military state."

Once-Catholic Joe Remiro gets very uneasy about the word "spiritual." "I ain't fighting for no advanced spiritual awareness," he says. "I think spiritual awareness was at its most advanced stage when they had the Crusades, when they had the fucking imperialist Crusades. As far as culture is concerned, I see a real need for a revolutionary type of art form that relates to oppressed people, you know, rather than a bourgeois art form which is mostly what dominates right now, you know. The way poetry expresses itself today in a lot of cases is very intellectualized and only middle-class white people can relate to it."

The questions about forming an organization that would attract a number of divergent racial and cultural minorities are best answered in the texts of the Declaration of War and the Constitution.*

In essence, the S.L.A. proposed to set up a sort of tentative "federation," hung together mostly for the purpose of immediately fighting a revolution, and "not a government, but rather a united and federated formation of members of different races and people and political parties who have agreed to struggle in a united front. . . ."

The heavy emphasis on an essentially independent role for each racial and cultural group included in this temporary federation was designed to bring in black nationalists who might wish to jointly rebel against the American system but who would want to have their own independent nation after the revolution had been won.

Adding an ingredient or two of black nationalism to their symbiotic stew, S.L.A. members also decided that since their new dedication to revolution constituted a personal "rebirth" for each of them, it would be appropriate for each to receive a "reborn name." Donald DeFreeze, who had been "reborn" as Cinque Mtume while in prison,

* See Appendix for complete contents.

probably initiated the custom. So monikers like Teko, Cujo, Fahizah, Gelina, Zoya, Gabi, Yolanda, Tania, Bo, and Osceola were considerably more than code names. They represented new psychological and historical identities.

Remiro feels that blacks and other "minority" people should be allowed to live in completely separate states if they wish. "Integration is a rip-off, man," he says. "It's ripping off some very beautiful and important cultures. If all the nonwhites say they want to integrate with the white people, which I doubt, I'll say 'Right on!' with that. It's not up to me to make the decision. I support the right of national minorities to do whatever the fuck they want to do—to self-determination. If the black nation decides they want to separate completely, that's their right. And as a white revolutionary I'll support that right and I'll fight for that right. But the revolutionaries in S.L.A. don't say they're *supporting* segregation. It's not up to them. We're not pushing secession. We're just saying that their rights do include that. As Stalin said about self-determination for national minorities, which he was part of, you know . . . he said, 'We support the right of national minorities to the point of secession,' but then he used the parallel of divorce. He said, 'We support the right of women to be allowed to divorce their husbands, but we don't encourage it. But if they decide they want to, they have got the right.' "

Separate from the Symbionese Federation, but growing out of it, there was to be a Symbionese Liberation Army, a force governed by a War Council made up of federation representatives and regulated by the S.L.A. Codes of War.

Since the whole purpose of the federation was to put an army in the field against the U.S. government, continued membership in the federation was to require some participation in the armed actions of the S.L.A.

"The War Council may disagree upon a particular action or strategy," says the Constitution. "When in disagreement, that particular membership need not participate in The S.L.A. action, but membership on The War Council is maintained only as long as all commitments made to the collective Symbionese War Council are continued to be fully adhered to."

This last provision was obviously the product of heated debate that broke out among the founding members of the federation when it was decided to assassinate Oakland Schools Superintendent Foster.

Tentative discussion of the Foster hit probably began early in the summer. What Foster was doing in the heavily black Oakland schools was discussed as early as May at BCA meetings at Vacaville. One participant now out of stir remembers a BCA leader saying that "if you want to eliminate the problem in the schools with the man stepping on your kids' necks, you eliminate the problem by eliminating Marcus Foster."

S.L.A. did not definitely zero in on Foster, though, until at least late July, after the Alameda County Grand Jury had asked the Oakland School District to come up with a plan to cut down on violence, vandalism, and truancy. Foster's response turned out to be his death warrant. In September, he endorsed a plan that would have brought armed police guards into the halls of Oakland's fifteen junior highs and six high schools and would have required students to obtain identification cards with their photos inside. It also would have authorized the compilation of what the S.L.A. called "bio-dossiers" on all Oakland students to provide police agencies with early warning about their "criminal tendencies." Funding to the tune of $255,000 was to be provided for this plan by the California Council on Criminal Justice, an agency of the state. By October, Oakland was in a furor over the proposal, and an October 8 School Board meeting was nearly mobbed by angry parents and left organizations. Black Panthers Bobby Seale and Elaine Brown led the opposition. S.L.A. had apparently decided long before October 8 to rub out Foster for the "Forced Youth Identification Program," the cop patrols in the halls, and the new dossiers; they claimed the plan was "patterned after the system of apartheid in South Africa" and would lead to many students being jailed "from age 15 for an 'indefinite' period of time."

Thero Wheeler was on the scene by mid-August, and his brooding presence gave the group the kind of additional proven kill-power that made them confident they could successfully play the role of assassins. It was time to start arming up. Another irritant that apparently drove them headlong into the murder was the November 1 killing in nearby Emeryville of a fourteen-year-old black youth, Tyrone Guyton, who was shot in the back following a joy ride in a car that later turned out to be stolen. The black community was in an uproar over the matter, and S.L.A. later decided to "even the score" with the "black pig" Foster.

By midsummer, Remiro had begun to visit his favorite Oakland gun shop, Siegel's, at 508 West MacArthur Boulevard, at least every second week. He would walk in "to look over and occasionally buy new guns." He brought a lot of friends with him, white revolutionists who made absolutely no attempt to hide their identities as they purchased lethal weapons. Said an incredulous store owner: "Most professional criminals would not come into a gun shop and buy firearms. They probably would steal them or get them in some other way. But this S.L.A. crowd didn't seem to care."

Remiro had purchased his first Walther .380 automatic pistol on July 17. He picked up a second copy of the German gun on September 25. On August 17, he bought a 12-gauge Ithaca shotgun. On July 28, Mizmoon got a Browning 30.06 rifle. On August 23, Willie Wolfe picked up a Mossberg shotgun in San Lorenzo's Gemco department store. On November 7, Angela Atwood purchased a 9mm Mauser pistol at Siegel's, and on November 27 Bill Harris also went in to get a 9mm Mauser. Sometime in late spring, Russ Little had purchased a .38-caliber Rossi pistol from Chris Thompson, a Brazilian gun much favored by the Tupamaros and other South American revolutionists. During that same spring, Remiro had experienced an odd stroke of luck. He won a fancy 30.30 Winchester commemorative rifle during a Siegel's drawing, but he told the shopkeeper, "I don't have any use for it" and sold the gun back to the store.

The S.L.A. had begun to conduct their lethal preparations in a number of locations. Nancy Ling Perry, Willie Wolfe, Russ Little, and Robyn Steiner were living at communal Peking House. Remiro was rooming with Hood, Brennan, and Rip Miller on Cortland Road. He began moving with Willie over to nearby Bond Street sometime in October. They would only occupy the place until December. Mizmoon, Camilla, and Cinque were shacked up cozily on Parker Street, although Camilla still was paying rent on a separate cottage some distance across Berkeley. Thero Wheeler and Mary Alice Siem were living rather privately in a well-hidden apartment in Oakland. Everyone kept busy.

Their homework was of an extremely unusual variety. Some S.L.A. members drew up "hit lists" of possible assassination victims.

Those to be honored with cyanide-bullet executions included Marcus Foster; Raymond Procunier, then head of the California prison system; another Foster, Richard, who, strangely enough, was also a schools superintendent, in next-door Berkeley; fourteen manufacturers and business leaders, including representatives of Kaiser Industries, ITT,

Bank of America, Standard Oil, and Safeway Stores; and possibly William Knowland, publisher of the extreme right Oakland *Tribune* and a former redbaiting senator of the Eisenhower era.

Other plans for violent actions required the preparation of intricate maps showing the locations of possible kidnaps, burglaries, and armed robberies. Another such map showed a Sonoma County farm where a demolition contractor stored large quantities of dynamite, handy for making bombs.

Some maps contained full information on store burglar alarms and the locations of cash registers, mirrors, and employee stations. One showed the route usually taken by a courier who brought deposits from an Oakland bar into a nearby bank branch. Oakland cops would later tell the press that S.L.A. had used this plan on January 7, '74, to stick up the bank courier.

Also in the works was the rip-off on October 12 of a '69 Chevrolet van from young Donald Sullivan, who told the cops that someone who looked a lot like Joe Remiro walked behind him that night as he went into his apartment on Berkeley's Telegraph Avenue and demanded the keys to his white van. Sullivan said the man had a gun in his right hand and said, "Give me the keys . . . I'm in a hurry." The truck was found a few months later near an S.L.A. hideout in Concord with everything stripped out from front to back except the steering wheel. A good auto mechanic had apparently pulled out all of the guts to be transferred to another Chevy van. Remiro would later be charged with this car theft.

Other previews of things to come were flashing across the cerebral cortex of busy Nancy Ling Perry, who rented two new hideouts in October. One was a scummy apartment (Number 12) on Oakland's rundown, racially mixed Seventh Avenue (Number 1621). It was six-tenths of a mile from the Oakland Schools Administration Building, where Foster worked.

The other one was at 1560 Sutherland Court, in the Concord area, a location that Fahizah would later call an S.L.A. "information-intelligence" headquarters. In keeping with the group's well-thought-out policy of setting up a hideout near the site of an upcoming action, the chances are good that the Concord location was chosen because it was close to the scene of some job they had long considered.

All this activity was making some of the more timid recruits nervous. These were the guys who sounded serious at first, as long as it was all *talk* about guerrilla warfare. But by fall, it had become apparent that this was not going to be just one more of those endless Berkeley yak circles, not just a lot of stoned-out theoretical arguments while you were stretched out on the floor of some South Campus pad with a joint in one hand and a can of beer in the other, ogling a willing sister who might be in your sack that night. This was for real, and when the final decision to kill Foster had been made, a lot of these "talk" revolutionaries dropped out. As one of them later explained it:

"Contradictions had already begun to emerge among the membership. Although some of the brothers and sisters asserted that to create a positive vision of a new society required serious thinking, a clear and comprehensive theory and strategy, others insisted that all that was necessary was to put yourself into situations where your ass would get kicked and armed bravery would do the rest. Some of the brothers and sisters were complaining about the lack of democracy within the organization. The justification for this was always that we were in a 'state of war.'

"It increasingly became apparent to us that the Symbionese Federation was not fundamentally opposed to the errors of the left we had known, but was rather the culmination of all its defects. The process of the organization was totally top-down. The War Council made decisions in secret and the members were expected to obey orders without question, just as in a capitalist army. Serious conflict developed over the subordination of the support units, as of all nonmilitary activities of the organization to the combat units: that is, the 'Army' came to be seen as the chief agent of the revolution."

Dissension even developed between Cinque and Wheeler. At one point that fall (the date is not too clear), Cin, Nancy Ling Perry, and Mizmoon arrived at Thero's Oakland hideout and, according to Mary Alice Siem, said they were going to kill her and Wheeler, because "they were unreliable and knew too much." The three gunsels were talked out of the internecine hit, but Mary claims they walked out with six hundred dollars that had been in her purse.

Things were getting downright *hot* in an otherwise chilly fall for S.L.A. Eight pistol shots and two shotgun blasts later, they would get even hotter.

12

"You see, the first S.L.A. action cleared up a lot of things. . . .
The Black Liberation Army talks about people coming down on them
for shooting black pigs, you know. And they point out right up
front, you know, a black pig or a white pig, the motherfuckers, you
know, are all gonna get killed and they ain't gonna accept any
criticism about shooting black pigs."
—Joe Remiro

THE CENTER OF OAKLAND, CALIFORNIA, is largely devastated by the twin blights of ghetto strangulation and urban renewal. Vast stretches of once-swarming downtown are now ghostlands of vacant buildings and parking lots. The occupied houses that remain are shabby, delapidated frame buildings that provide a creaky, temporary refuge for blacks, Chinese, the old, and the disenfranchised, who know they will soon be "redeveloped" completely out of the area.

The outlines of the kind of "Future Oakland" that the slowly progressing city planners envision here can be seen growing up around Lake Merritt, a prettily landscaped former salt-water marsh that juts into the Oakland Estuary, that old refuge of sailing ships, whale-oil manufactories, whorehouses, opium dens, and deadfall saloons that provided a rowdy and down-to-earth home for legendary roamers like Jack London and Joaquin Miller. It was just about the only part of Oakland of which native-born Gertrude Stein much approved. She summed up her opinion of the rest of the town very plainly. "Oakland?" she said. "There is no *there* there."

The west side of Lake Merritt is anchored by a great aluminum skyscraper built by Henry Kaiser. The southeast side is held down by an enormous luxury apartment house where Panther leader Huey Newton long occupied a $650-a-month suite complete with a four-hundred-pound bodyguard and a personal tailor. In between these two monuments to the American Dream Come True stands a ten-story, pyramid-topped courthouse and jail, which handles those who have resisted all that Henry Kaiser and William Knowland wanted Oakland to become.

Just around a slight bend of the lake from the courthouse stands the three-story poured-concrete headquarters of the Oakland school system. It's a quick, two-block walk away and within easy view of anyone looking across the corner of the lake from the jail or down from Huey Newton's aerie. In a small indentation between the main building and a smaller annex fronting on Eleventh Street lies a dimly lit parking space just big enough for two cars. Until November 6, 1973, one parking stall was plainly marked "Superintendent" and the other "Deputy Superintendent." To get from the back steps of the main building, where the Oakland Board of Education regularly meets, and over to the little parking lot, you must pass through a narrow, boxed-in courtyard and then through an even narrower defile between the main building and a small, wooden, temporary structure about thirty feet wide that lies between the administration center and the annex.

It is an ideal spot for an ambush, an easily observed and well-contained killing ground where few strangers or even school employees will pass.

It was here one wet and gloomy Tuesday evening on November 6 (Election Day), that fifty-year-old Marcus Foster met his death under a barrage of cyanide-filled bullets, and his assistant, thirty-eight-year-old Robert Blackburn, who had followed him to Oakland from Philadelphia, was gravely wounded by a shotgun blast.

Joe Remiro and Russell Little were accused of the crime two months after S.L.A. publicly took credit for the savage attack.

Foster, the first black superintendent of any major California school system, was (if the publicity put out about him is to be believed) a progressive, liberal educator, a persistent integrationist who was working hard for the largely minority student body of sixty thousand kids in the Oakland schools.

November 6 had been a busy day for him. School Board meetings were not usually held on Election Day, and they generally did not start as early as this one (at 4:00 P.M., with a potluck dinner about 6:00 and adjournment before 7:00). Foster arrived late. Until 4.30 he'd been lecturing the Oakland City Council at nearby City Hall on the need for more money to keep gymnasiums, playgrounds, and other recreational facilities in the city's ninety schools open after class so the kids would have someplace to go. The big East Bay community contains the oldest and angriest ghetto in the West, and Foster spoke up mostly for those ghetto kids who are likely to get into even more trouble than usual without organized recreation. He warned that a plan to cut back such activities would lead to desperation and trouble. "I shudder to think about all the violence we will see," he warned. He had cause to shudder. He would be dead in less than three hours.

Foster then made it over to the Board of Education meeting, which proved to be rather routine—not at all like the stormy October 8 session, which had debated identification cards, "bio-dossiers," and armed cops in school hallways. S.L.A. was apparently not aware of it (they had no clipping service), but Foster had tentatively withdrawn his support for the identification and policing plan at the October meeting. Bobby Seale had won out, and the rather canny and politic superintendent had retreated in the face of all that violent and well-organized community opposition. His feelings about the matter were obviously mixed. Like a lot of liberal superintendents trying to mollify an essentially conservative school board (and Oakland's was anything but progressive), Foster was the man in the middle. He found it expedient to publicly take a line that would keep the board happy but privately (or talking to liberals and reformers whose help he also needed), he was known to express different opinions. This wavering kind of attitude cost him his life.

On the ID/cops issue, Foster continued to make public statements that lined up with the board's affirmative position. In the first week of November he'd met with a roomful of high-school journalists who had quizzed him on this explosive matter, and he'd told them he favored the program and that it would "reduce truancy, vandalism and get reduced bus fares." He claimed that the card was "first and foremost for your protection."

A few days earlier and in private he had taken an entirely different position while visiting an old friend, the prominent San Francisco civil-rights lawyer Charles Garry. Garry claims that Foster stated he was "definitely against the plan and that he considered it a police state action . . . an example of fascist forces trying to take over."

Perhaps this kind of double-talk had proven a necessity during Foster's years as an administrator in the racially troubled Philadelphia schools and in the ticklish position he had occupied as head of the Oakland system since July of 1970. For he was best known, both nationally and in the Bay Area, as a great compromiser, a kind of black Henry Clay in urban education, a voice of reason, a man with enormous talents for bringing people together cooperatively to solve problems in peaceful ways. These tactics worked well with normal, reasonable, political people. It was most unfortunate that the warmongering extremists of S.L.A. did not prize such attributes.

Most of the business was over by 6:30 P.M. at that Election Day meeting, and all of the board members had left the room before Foster and Blackburn gathered up their papers into attaché cases and prepared to leave. Foster also carried an umbrella, for it was raining. Now down to the car—only one of them, since Blackburn had been driving his boss to work for several weeks. The space usually occupied by Foster's car had been filled this night by board member Melvin Caughell, who had hurried on home a few minutes before the administrators walked to their parking lot. Caughell said he'd seen nothing unusual.

Shortly before 7:00 P.M., the two executives pulled up the collars of their raincoats to fend off the cold and steady drizzle. They squinted out into the dim fall evening and surveyed the seemingly abandoned area just behind the administration building, which, for reason long forgotten, all of Oakland still likes to call the "White House."

They hurried down a steep flight of stone steps into the asphalt courtyard. They were deep in conversation and hardly noticed two slight figures standing out there in the rain between the big administration building and the old wooden portable structure. They almost brushed up against the two loiterers as they made a slight left turn to enter the parking area.

It's true that these two did not seem so very remarkable, either to Foster and Blackburn or to other witnesses who had passed them by a few minutes earlier when the meeting had broken up. They were generally described as very young, possibly black or Chicano, with "tan or olive complexions . . . at least not pasty white." Blackburn would have a hard time deciding whether or not Russ Little could have been one of them. They were said to have long, shoulder-length dark hair, nothing too unusual among the young these days. They were of "medium height—five feet six inches to five feet eight inches" and of "slender build—110 to 120 pounds." They wore almost identical costumes, a kind of proletarian uniform, so to speak, blue knit watch cap, dark pants, blue denim jacket with some sort of a matching white emblem patch over the right breast—no one paused long enough to examine it closely. And, oh yes, the somewhat hazy witnesses would later add, they *might* have been women.

As Blackburn recalls these two ominously waiting young people out there in the rain:

"As we left the door, proceeded down the stairway which occupies this indentation, walking down the stairs, I noticed on my right, somewhere at about this point at the back of the building, two persons leaning against that building. It occurred to me I had never seen anybody in that position before and I thought it wasn't a serious concern, but I thought it rather strange.

"Then I thought immediately . . . well, presumably these are stragglers from the Board of Education meeting which had just been completed, and people waiting for a ride, or who were just chatting, leaning against the building. So then we came down those stairs and turned to our right, and then proceeded to walk along this area and through the passageway. Once again, as we drew near the two persons, I glanced up and looked at them again and then kept walking. We then walked along together in the area between the main building and this single-story portable. . . ."

The small parking area seemed strangely narrow and deadly this night, and the educators grew quiet as they entered it. On the wet pavement waited Blackburn's little economy car, a 1971 white Chevrolet Vega. It was parked facing inward toward the portable wooden building with its peeling layer of gray paint. Bushes and shrubbery covered a corner of the lawn between the annex to the west and Eleventh Street. A second narrow passageway between the shrubbery and the car led back to the rear of the main administration building.

Blackburn strode quickly around the rear of the auto, followed a few steps back by Foster. He was heading toward the passenger side to open the door for his boss. Foster had barely reached the front of the car on the driver's side. He had gone less than twenty feet past the two waiting gunmen, and they must have fallen immediately in behind him. Then it happened—cold, fast, and without warning. They opened up at point-blank range into Foster's back. Blackburn describes the vicious wipe-out:

"I saw the muzzle flashes of the guns," he says. "I had my briefcase in one hand, my keys in the other. They seemed to be repeated shots in very fast sequence. My first impression was that two weapons were being fired and almost simultaneously. But, you know, a split second later than that I saw Dr. Foster. He seemed to stumble forward."

The bullets, eight of them, popped out of the barrels of two pistols blazing away in the steady hands of the two long-haired youths who had followed Foster and Blackburn onto the parking lot. The first seven slugs hit Foster in the back. He whirled to face his assassins, and the last shot tore through the front of his body. The hollow-pointed slugs simply ripped him apart. They chewed up his entire torso. Several passed clean through his exploding flesh to bury themselves in the left front fender and door of the parked car.

Now it would be Blackburn's turn. At least one assassin awaited him behind the bushes to his right. Crouching low in the wet foliage, he cocked the hammer of his 12-gauge shotgun and aimed.

"We were by then, you know, I would say there must have been almost twenty feet, eighteen, a good distance between us at that point," says Blackburn, trying to calculate how far he stood from the dying Foster. "And, as I indicated, I must have then continued to turn around and then attempted to move up the passenger side of the car."

He only got a little past the right rear fender when the first shotgun blast cut loose. It missed him by inches and buried a dozen hunks of double-ought buckshot into the Vega's right rear fender. He was not so lucky on the second blast. Ten to twelve hard steel balls cut into Blackburn's flesh. They entered his liver and spleen, his left kidney, abdomen, and left arm. He screamed in surprise and pain and then ran for his life.

It was more than two hundred feet from the parking lot to the only door he knew was open where there might be help in the mostly dark administration building. Blackburn put everything he had into it and outdistanced his pursuers. He managed to get inside the door before falling into the arms of David Tom, a school-system printer who had been working late in the basement of the building when he heard muffled shots from the nearby ambush. He had rushed up the steps to open a rear door and found Blackburn standing there screaming for help.

"Marc's been shot! Marc's been shot!" Blackburn yelled.

Tom ran to the parking stall to find Dr. Foster spread out on the wet pavement. His briefcase and umbrella lay on the ground. Tom knelt beside him and felt for a pulse. He thought he felt a faint stir of life and began to give mouth-to-mouth resuscitation. Too late. Foster was a D.O.A. when an ambulance brought him into Highland Hospital a few minutes later.

But Blackburn was alive and talking quite vividly. His recollections would fill in whatever blank spots S.L.A. incompetence and poor planning had left in the case.

The school center was soon crawling with cops, but the killers were long gone.

As physical evidence and eyewitness testimony filled out the rest of the story, it became apparent that the S.L.A. executioners had escaped on foot from the bloody little parking lot. Footprints from a pair of deeply grooved jungle boots showed that at least one gunman, probably the shotgun man behind the bushes, had walked up to the assassination site over a wet and muddy path that begins in the parking lot of Oakland Civic Auditorium—just a stone's throw away from the courthouse jail where Remiro and Little would spend so many months—and passed through a wooded children's playground beside an isolated channel of Lake Merritt, which provides a lonely, seldom-used sanctuary just behind the school administration center, an echoing, mossy lagoon full of snakes, trash, and a soggy memory or two.

The person wearing the distinctive boots, and possibly several companions retreated down this dark path past deserted but fanciful slides and swings shaped like mythical tigers and lions. They went at top speed, tripping occasionally on the rotted crossties which were all that remained of an abandoned children's railroad. They ran so fast and so recklessly, in fact, that a number of rounds of unspent .45-caliber ammunition fell from one of their pockets, leaving a nice, neat trail for the pleasantly surprised cops to later follow. The trail ended on the black-topped auditorium parking lot, where a car probably awaited them. Where the assassins had gone from there was pure conjecture until the end of November, when a curious landlord at 1621 Seventh Avenue discovered that half a dozen mysterious tenants who had been holed up for weeks less than a mile from the assassination scene were actually the S.L.A. Neighbors identified Cinque, Nancy Ling Perry, and Russell Little as being among them. No one seemed sure about Joe Remiro's photograph.

For months the Oakland cops had no suspects to hang the murder raps on, but they had plenty of clues. There were the extraordinary slugs removed from Foster's body, the car, and the wooden building. There were eight .38-caliber pistol shells, most of them apparently fired from a Walther automatic and a few out of a Rossi. There were two empty shotgun shells with some distinctive writing on them.

The .38-caliber shell casings were quickly identified as being of a special kind—"Super-Vel" ammunition, which a gun specialist later described as being "hotter and more powerful" than standard rounds, and a lot more lethal. Super-Vel bullets are hollow-pointed. Such rounds mushroom out on impact and do horrible internal damage, much more than the kind of jacketed, solid slugs that "civilized" armies use in warfare. Hollow slugs, like dumdum bullets, are outlawed on the battlefield, but revolutionists and a great many American police departments are fond of them because the victim almost certainly dies from the impact.

The slugs pulled out of Foster would also yield another interesting clue—the most unusual aspect of the case, in fact. Not only had the manufacturer hollowed out the tips of these lead bullets, but some other craftsman had gone the original one better and, with a fine drill, had cut through the thin wall that usually covers over the hollowed-out point to open up the little chamber for an even more deadly purpose.

Into each of the eight slugs that had entered Foster's body they had poured a small quantity of a famous and easily obtainable poison, potassium cyanide (7.1 milligrams, to be exact). The opening through the end of the bullet had been covered over with a little plug of wax, which shot out on impact.

Oakland autopsy surgeons had never seen this trick attempted before, and initial reports on the Foster case contained no data whatsoever about the cyanide modification of the Symbionese bullets. They would later testify that they had "smelled" the strong almond odor of cyanide when removing the slugs from Foster. Whether they had investigated further and found the cyanide mixed in with the lead remains in doubt.

It quickly became a moot point when, less than sixteen hours after Marcus Foster was murdered, the S.L.A. left its first calling card on the doorstep of the world.

"Communique Number One" was found in the mailbox at KPFA, the Berkeley radical community's favorite radio station. First discovered and read at 10:30 A.M. on November 7, it appeared to be a kind of revolutionary "true bill" or indictment as well as a death warrant for Foster. Its fantastic contents would immediately turn this totally unknown band of terrorists into the most hunted, and least understood, band of outlaws in American history. It read:

"Symbionese Liberation Army Western Regional Youth Unit Communique No. 1.

"Subject: The Implementation of the Internal Warfare Identification Computer System.

"Warrant Order: Execution by Cyanide Bullets. Date: November 6, 1973.

"Warrant Issued by: The Court of the People.

"Charges: Supporting and taking part in the forming and implementation of a Political Police Force operating within the Schools of the People. Supporting and taking part in the forming and implementation of

Bio-Dossiers through the Forced Youth Identification Program. Supporting and taking part in the building of composite files for the Internal Warfare Identification Computer System.

"Target: Dr. Marcus A. Foster, Superintendent of Schools, Oakland, California. Robert Blackburn, Deputy Superintendent, Oakland, California."

From there, the communiqué freely admitted the Foster murder and then warned "the fascist Board of Education and its fascist supporters that The Court of the People have issued a Death Warrant on All Members and Supporters of the Internal Warfare Identification Computer System. This SHOOT ON SIGHT order will stay in effect until such time as ALL POLITICAL POLICE ARE REMOVED FROM OUR SCHOOLS AND ALL PHOTO AND OTHER FORMS OF IDENTIFICATION ARE STOPPED."

This outrageous admission and not-too-subtle warning electrified the Bay Area.

The Oakland police put four teams of homicide inspectors on the case, along with every investigator the district attorney could spare. This brought together a group of thirty trained men, who followed up every imaginable clue to initiate the biggest manhunt in Oakland history.

Although the S.L.A. communiqué made clear the political motivation of the killing, including the tit-for-tat aspect of Foster's death being a retribution for the murder of young Tyrone Guyton, most officials and plain citizens still could not comprehend the reasoning behind the bizarre assassination. Their consternation was shared for a change by all of the radical groups who normally could be counted on to applaud any frontal assault on the system and its leaders. The Black Panthers condemned the killing and its perpetrators, as did most other left groups. It was, in fact, the Foster assassination which almost certainly doomed S.L.A. to a lonely and little-lamented extinction in the end. It also proved that an unquestioning devotion to textbook definitions as to who is and is not "the enemy" does not always match up to political realities. They killed the wrong man.

Marcus Foster may have had too much compromise in his system to be any kind of a hero to the left, but he was not a "black pig" by any means. S.L.A. failed to study the true politics of the case, despite long and loudly proclaiming that they were first and foremost a "political" group. The lack of this study and understanding would doom them politically. This is a fact that Joe Remiro and Russ Little were still unwilling to admit a full eight months after the killing and a good many months after their comrades had apparently realized that the Foster caper had become a dead end from which they had to move on to bigger and better-publicized things, like the kidnapping of Patricia Hearst. But, of course, Little and Remiro could not simply *forget* the Marcus Foster matter. Their lives were at stake because of it.

Perhaps a good part of S.L.A.'s confusion about Foster grew out of the enormous ideational and generational gap that must have existed between these violent young rebels who arrived in Berkeley long after its first passionate affair with integration and civil rights, and an older black man whose career was clearly the product of that profoundly moral movement to bring the races together in America without bloodshed.

After Foster was dead, a number of politicians who had little use for him alive suddenly decided that he had been the East Bay's "answer to Martin Luther King" or that he had been "our Moses." Their self-serving eulogies, as well as the volume and anguish of more sincere public mourning, were rather extraordinary when you consider the history of Foster's difficult three years in Oakland. It seems almost as though people were lamenting the passing of an era rather than a man, the assassination of compromise and commitment to peaceful change rather than the wipe-out of an educator whose activities both in Philadelphia and Northern California were progressive but unremarkable.

Marcus Foster was a competent administrator and fairly glib politician. He was a black man of that generation long accustomed to emphasizing the similarities rather than the differences between the races, a supporter of NAACP and the Urban League rather than SNCC and CORE and their even more radical offspring. He was honestly committed to giving a fair first shake in life to the thousands of minority kids for whom he was responsible. But with six thousand staff members and sixty thousand students to keep in line, it was a big and very political order. He was good at his job, but it wasn't a Martin Luther King kind of a gig and he was no utopian, no wide-eyed idealist.

Foster had to spend a lot of his time mollifying the local Birchers, holding hands with the Kaisers and the Knowlands and the other ruling reactionaries, soothing ruffled feathers at Kiwanis and Lions Club luncheons, balancing a knee full of coffee and doughnuts at PTA and YMCA meetings, wringing the last possible nickel out of his underpaid staff for the United Crusade and the Boy Scouts. He got along well with ministers and businessmen. He'd paid his academic and professional dues and was in good standing among the nation's top educators, who know that to make out these days as a big-city superintendent you need more than conscience and fresh ideas—it's also necessary to have a direct line into the offices of the giant Eastern foundations and a friend or two in Washington.

Foster's major speeches and communications were adequate if uninspired. They occasionally contained an innovative idea or two, but everything was carefully balanced and subdued so that no one would get upset about it. He knew his job was to keep things together, to maintain a big school system in running order without too much dissension or bind. He was the chief oiler, a greaser of the ways. Under the circumstances, that's all you had a right to ask of the man. He did all that he *could* do under difficult circumstances in Oakland.

That may be the ultimate irony of his murder. Marcus Foster was neither the "fascist" the S.L.A. accused him of being nor the "saint" his eulogists so extravagantly sketched for the weeping multitudes. He was just a strong-willed black man doing a routine job in a competent way. Knocking him off was like sabotaging a piece of machinery or defacing a building. It was more vandalism than an act of revolutionary justice.

Nevertheless, when poor Foster died mayors, congressmen, and assemblymen rose in unanimous wrath to demand the heads of his killers. He was put up among the "visionaries and prophets" in the next morning's newspapers. He was called "a family man . . . a man's man . . . a people's man."

"God and Marcus Foster have left in our hands an unfinished task," said one minister, promoting him into the heavenly Administration Building in a single bound. It was claimed that he had given his "whole life to Oakland," an exaggeration that extended three short years into fifty.

But it was not just the quality of the extravagant tribute that was extraordinary. The quantity was also unprecedented. There was not just one memorial service for Marcus Foster, there were dozens.

On the Friday after his death, Oakland's Catholic bishop eulogized him at a high mass, assisted by fifteen priests. More than eleven hundred of the faithful crowded into the city's cathedral. On Saturday, all the Jewish synagogues in Oakland held memorials. On Sunday, it was the turn of the Protestants and long-bearded, black-robed Greek Orthodox priests to lay him to rest.

The funeral itself was held at Beebe Memorial CME Church on Monday, November 12. At least three thousand people attended, including the mayors of Oakland, Berkeley, and San Francisco. They were joined by delegations of politicians and educators from all over the country. Some fifteen thousand programs were given out to those in the church and the even bigger crowd that followed Foster's coffin to the cemetery.

That evening, another five thousand mourners attended an enormous memorial service in the vast concrete Oakland Coliseum Arena. For probably the first (and certainly the last) time in history, extreme rightist William Knowland would mourn beside Black Panther Bobby Seale. A thousand-voiced choir of Oakland schoolkids managed to nearly overcome the echoing bad acoustics of the cavernous chamber. Foster's widow, Albertine, brought the affair to an emotional climax in the best tradition of early civil rights Christian charity when she urged the multitude to "pray for Dr. Foster's assassins." The place absolutely came apart, a fantastic send-off! (And a dirge for all of S.L.A.'s political ambitions.)

13

"Inexperience makes one underestimate the enemy's intelligence,
or assume some tasks to be 'easy,' thus leaving evidence
which may be fatal. . . ."
—Carlos Marighella, in
The Seven Deadly Sins of the Urban Guerrilla

"In order to deal with the enemy, we must reduce our mistakes to
absolute zero. . . . All underground units should by now have
learned to stay off the streets and highways late at night. . . .
He who travels while the sun sleeps will stumble many times."
—Communiqué on the S.L.A. from the Black Liberation Army

O N JANUARY 10, 1974, partly because of dumb chance and partly because of his own errors, the game was suddenly up for Joe Remiro. He and Russ Little became the S.L.A.'s first "prisoners of war" after an incident that proved to be a catastrophic checkmate to all of the group's planning up to that date—an arrest that may have been a prime motivation for the kidnap of Patricia Hearst less than three weeks later.

It happened at 1:20 A.M., in an almost too quiet and very suburban bedroom community some twenty-five miles northeast of the central Oakland area where Marcus Foster was killed. The unincorporated section known as Clayton Valley was, in fact, probably one of the last places police would have looked for Foster's assassins, had they still been looking. The unsuccessful search had bogged down after two fruitless months, and the Oakland cops were discouraged and frustrated. Only a stroke of luck could help them now.

It came in the form of a children's prank and the presence of an observant and highly intuitive cop named David Duge.

Sergeant Duge had been on the Concord police force for seven years. He was patrolling that night through what his department called "Sector Two," a wildly gerrymandered morass of fairly new subdivisions that include some blocks that are part of the City of Concord, some that belong to the smaller village of Clayton to the south, and other hunks of real estate that are completely unincorporated—like Clayton Valley.

The area has little claim to fame outside of the fact that it immediately adjoins an enormous naval magazine. Thousands of tons of shells and bombs pass through here on their way to nearby Port Chicago, where they are shipped to Southeast Asia to be used in the now "Vietnamized" war. The port has been well known in radical circles since Berkeley antiwar activists staged a long vigil at the entrance to the shipping area, where they were frequently arrested for organizing lie-downs in front of bomb-carrying trucks. A group like S.L.A., planning revolution and in need of munitions to fight it, might regard such a naval magazine as a very enticing target indeed.

It's not easy to find your way around this neck of the woods late at night. Most streets dead-end in deliberate culs-de-sac. The one-story, ranch-style houses (many in the forty-to-fifty-thousand-dollar class) are generally set well back from the road, and few show street numbers. There is little lighting. To make things worse, some of the neighborhood kids had turned all of the street signs around just the day before. The names at east corner for blocks around Sutherland Court were transposed.

But Sergeant Duge knew the area well. He'd been patrolling it alone and in an unmarked "supervisor's car" for months. He had seven other cops working for him patrolling the sector, each alone and in a similar Concord police car. They kept in close radio contact, since it's dangerous to work without a partner at night. As soon as a cruiser decides to stop a suspicious car or person he radios for a backup unit to rush over and help him out. Sometimes they arrive immediately; sometimes there's a delay.

This January 10 at 1:20 A.M., Sergeant Duge was driving down Ayers Road, a main artery that dead-ends at the naval magazine. One of the cross streets is Sutherland Drive. A smaller dead-end byway is called Sutherland Court. Here, on October 8, Nancy Ling Perry, posing as "Nancy DeVoto," had rented Number 1560, a $31,000, three-bedroom ranch house, for $250 a month. Joe Remiro and Russell Little were apparently looking for this S.L.A. "headquarters" when Sergeant Duge spotted them moving slowly west on Sutherland Drive in an orange-red 1965 Chevrolet van. Russ was driving. The cop's suspicions were immediately aroused:

"This is a residential area," he later explained, "and, during the week in the City of Concord, there is virtually no traffic other than that of the folks coming home from swing shift. They usually come home between midnight and 12:30 and after that the normal flow of traffic through the residential area ceases in our city because it's basically what is termed a bedroom community. I hadn't seen this van in the area before, and I had worked it for the past eight months during these nighttime hours, and we do become familiar with the cars that are normally out at this hour and are looking for cars that we are not familiar with.

"So the car moving up to this stop sign in the slow manner, coming out of an expensive residential area, and then proceeding across the intersection at another slow rate rather than as if it were going specifically to someplace—and coupled with the fact I hadn't seen the van before—I made a U-turn and looked for it again to see where it was going and what it would be doing."

Duge switched off his headlights and fell in behind the van about a block back. He watched it make a complete slow circle up and down Sutherland Drive and several adjoining streets, as if it were looking for something, and then he threw on his headlights and his red spotlight and raced up just behind it.

"I pulled into a normal traffic stop position," says Duge, "and pulled into a position fifteen feet behind it. I raised the front red spotlight and shined it in the driver's side, hitting the truck-type rear-view mirror. The driver looked into the rear-view mirror. I could see his face in the reflection of the lights. I felt at this time that he knew there was a police car behind him, and he did stay stopped for the red light, my red light."

Duge then called in by radio, telling his dispatcher that he was making a traffic stop, giving the license number of the van, and asking for Officer Lee to come over right away to "back me up." He then got out of his unmarked patrol car and walked over to the driver's side of the van to ask Russell Little for his license.

"In the same sentence," says Duge, "I asked him what he was doing, that I felt his movements were suspicious, and I asked him for the driver's license. And he told me that he was looking for a friend's house."

Duge also asked for Remiro's license, which was handed to him from the passenger side. He tried to sneak a look into the back of the van but discovered that the windows were all covered with curtains and that another set of curtains hung just behind the front seat, blocking his view past Little and Remiro.

"I asked the driver for the name of his friend and where he lived," says Duge. Little responded that the man's name was DeVoto and that he lived on Sutherland Court. Duge walked back to his squad car and read the names off the licenses into the radio. The phony license Little had handed him bore the name "Robert James Scalise." Duge also asked his dispatcher to check out the street directory for the name "DeVoto" on Sutherland Court. The response crackled back quickly. No warrants were out for either Remiro or "Scalise." And there was no listing for a DeVoto in the year-old street directory. Duge began walking back toward the van, which still had its engine running.

"At that time the thought ran through my mind that this is an awful little bit of conversation for two people that are lost," Duge recalls. "No extra requests. Most people at nighttime, when they're lost, seem happy to see a policeman. Other than the little they had said it was a void."

Duge says he began to feel real danger in the air. He began to listen for the distinctive sound of the souped-up motor of his backup patrol unit. Nothing. He edged slowly over to the passenger side of the van and tapped on the window. He asked Remiro to step out for a moment.

"He made no verbal reply," says Duge. "He just stepped out of the van and closed the door. I felt for officer safety I should frisk him. I asked him, 'Do you have any guns or knives on you? I'm going to frisk you.'

"I took a half step toward him and was just going to place my hands down his side. He took his jacket and took one good step back, opened it up, and at this time I turned facing him and I observed on his right hip, underneath a shirt that was out of his pants, a bulge. And being a policeman for as long as I have been, that bulge was exactly the same shape as the handle of an automatic pistol. I ran to the rear of my patrol car and crouched behind the trunk of the car. I saw Remiro, saw an automatic pistol in his hand, and heard two explosions and saw the muzzle blast of two shots being fired at me. I don't know where the projectiles went.

"I drew my pistol and returned fire, two shots. I fired at the muzzle blast. It's very similar to flashbulbs going off in your face in the dark."

Duge says that at least one of Remiro's shots smashed his car's windshield but neither hit him. He says that he could see Remiro standing at the van's left front side and, again, "two muzzle blasts, two loud reports, and aimed right at me. I raised up over the corner of the car, my patrol car, and returned two shots. After firing the two, I again went back for cover and then again looked around the left side, saw no one, went back behind my car, and looked around the right side and saw Mr. Remiro running from the front of the van in a direction which would be to my right. He fired one shot as he was running and then disappeared from sight.

"I stayed under cover, hoping that he wouldn't return and, at the same time, the van pulled over and went straight ahead, driving across Ayers Road to Sutherland in an easterly direction, and I lost sight of it and it went through this curve."

Duge again radioed for help, and two backup cars screeched up beside him. He explained about the escaping van, and just then it reappeared, lost again and heading straight toward them. The two patrol cars quickly blockaded the street, and the van bumped to a halt. It couldn't have gone far anyway, since one of Duge's shots had punctured a tire. Another bullet had cut through the van's rear window, passed clean through Little's shoulder, and smashed through the front windshield.

"We exited our cars with shotguns," says Duge, "and called the driver out."

Little got out with his hands in the air. He was bleeding profusely from the shoulder wound. The cops frisked and handcuffed him. They found he was wearing an empty gun holster on his belt.

Concord Officer Bruce Brueker then searched the van.

"I approached the vehicle, and the driver's door was open," he recalls. "I observed a pistol laying on the engine cover, which is between the two front seats of the vehicle." It was a fully loaded and unfired .38-caliber revolver with a short (2-inch) barrel. In the back of the van Brueker found another gun in a paper bag, this one a 9mm rifle that had originally been purchased in Los Angeles. There was also a telephone-book-thick stack of 8½-by-11 inch fliers wrapped up in a paper bag from the Gemco department store ("America's Finest," proclaimed the bag proudly). A quick unrumpling of the curled-up bag produced a neat stack of newly printed literature, about two thousand copies of the Symbionese "Goals," complete with cobra symbol and an explanation on the back of the symbol's mythological and historical meaning. The print job had been done in brown ink on yellow paper. It was the only printed propaganda that S.L.A. was ever known to produce, and fear of its discovery must have driven Remiro into his desperate gunfight with Sergeant Duge.

Officer Brueker gave a long, low whistle as he unwrapped the fliers. As he recalls the discovery: "I observed a rather unusual drawing. Then

I saw printed on top of this, 'Symbionese Liberation Army.' " The Foster case had finally been broken.

In the meantime, the area filled up with cop cars with their whirling red lights. Within a few minutes, dozens of heavily armed policemen were fanning out across the surprised suburban community, seeking Remiro. They were to search for him until just before dawn—5:30 A.M., to be exact.

As Concord Officer James Alcorn recalls the capture:

"We had officers on foot checking through various residences and backyards. Others were on the street looking for any activity or movement. Then I saw someone running, and I drove down Sutherland to investigate. As we started up this driveway, a figure appeared from in front of a parked car and at the same time the figure appeared we heard the words 'I give up! I've had it! I'm coming out!' He had his hands raised. And, at that time, we ordered him, Officer Sansen and myself, to back down the driveway, come down walking backwards with his hands in the air.

"I held him at gunpoint while Officer Sansen searched the individual," says Alcorn. "We found a three-eighty automatic pistol and also removed a holster, which contained a packet of cigarettes."

The gun was the Walther automatic that Joe had purchased on July 19 at Traders Sporting Goods. Ballistics experts would testify that it was the same weapon which had fired most of the lethal, cyanide-laden slugs into the body of Marcus Foster. It would become the prime link between a previously unheard of young radical named Remiro and the infamous Foster assassination.

At the time of the arrest, nervous Concord cops were happy enough just to have captured both of the suspects from the shoot-out. They did not bother to ask Joe where he'd been hiding during the preceding four hours. A semi-informed guess might indicate that Remiro had made his way from the shoot-out site two blocks over to the S.L.A. "information/intelligence headquarters" at 1560 Sutherland Court. At least three of his comrades—Cinque, Nancy Ling Perry, and Mizmoon—were probably there. A council of war might then have been held, with frequent glances out the window at the approaching line of flashlights and squad cars. The place was absolutely loaded with evidence that had to be destroyed, and things were altogether too hot around the little one-story house for the S.L.A.ers to escape without a diversionary move. Was it decided to let Remiro sacrifice himself by going back and surrendering to take the heat off his comrades so they might destroy the evidence and escape? Remiro's not saying, and the other participants are dead, so the real answer may never be known. But it is recorded that Joe's apprehension *did* pull police away from the neighborhood.

That same day at a little before 6:00 P.M., only twelve hours after Joe's bust, the remaining S.L.A. members made their escape in a '67 Olds registered to Willie the Wolfe. They had no sooner backed out the concrete drive as fast as possible (the heavily laden car's rear bumper went CRASH! onto the street as it shot out the drive) than 1560 Sutherland Court burst into flame.

A next-door resident, who describes herself as a "nosy neighbor," saw the flames suddenly leap up in the front rooms at 1560 and immediately called the fire department. They arrived so quickly that very little damage was done, despite the fact that the departing S.L.A.ers had splashed gasoline and left incendiary bombs around the place. There was only a superficial scorching of the living room, kitchen, and one bedroom. Another strike-out for S.L.A. They left so many clues behind that even the dumbest detective could make out like Sherlock Holmes.

The full extent of the inventory of goodies discovered on Sutherland Court was still something of a police secret at the time this book was being prepared. A lot of questions remain unanswered about the three months S.L.A. occupied the place. Why had they chosen this exact location? Was it because they planned to swipe some bombs from the nearby naval magazine, or was it because one of the executives on their "hit list" lived nearby? And what was really behind a strange shooting incident that occurred at 1560 Sutherland on November 12, 1973, just six days after Dr. Foster had been snuffed?

Neighbor Janice Damstra reported that around 10:00 A.M. on that day a young man of about seventeen came up to the front door of the residence of "George and Nancy DeVoto" and asked for the man of the house. "And when Nancy asked who was calling, the boy panicked and pulled a gun out of his pocket. So she pushed the gun aside and kicked him in the back of the leg. A shot rang out, and he, in turn, ran up the street. . . ."

Nancy, whom neighbors regarded as "no more than a nice, average suburban housewife with a nice, average suburban husband," did not want to call the police, but Old Nosy Neighbor insisted. A photograph made by a newspaper photographer that day—the one the FBI later used on her "Wanted" fliers—shows a short, black-haired little woman with her face wrinkled into an annoyed frown and her cardigan-encased arms folded defensively against all inquiry.

She told the police she simply could not understand why anyone would want to shoot a nice suburban housewife or her recently discharged Army veteran husband. They had just come from New York. They had no enemies. The cops let it drop there, although they later busted a suspect in the case and let him go. They never revealed just why he had wanted to kill "George DeVoto." Was this kid a member of S.L.A. who disagreed with the Foster killing and wanted to retaliate in kind? Perhaps someday we'll be told.

But not all of the Symbionese history locked up in that house was hidden away from the public eye. Thanks to the incomplete January 10 fire, a great many clues were identifiable. Amid the wreckage, investigators and newsmen found:

A cache of weapons and explosives, including at least two pipe bombs, black powder, fire bombs, bullets with their tips drilled out and packed with cyanide, empty chemical vials, ammunition cartons for 12-gauge shotguns and .380-caliber rifles, two boxes for 9mm ammunition, the sawed-off barrels of shotguns illegally modified, and stocks for carbines. Neighborhood kids were later seen carting off bayonets and "B-B gun target pistols" from rubble the cops did not properly search.

There was also a typewriter believed to be the one used to create the first S.L.A. communiqués on the Foster killing. Number One explained the killing. Number Two rescinded a "Shoot on Sight" order against Board of Education members, because a few days after Foster died they chickened out on their police patrol and "bio-dossier" program and canceled out the works. There was a copying machine the cops thought had been used to reproduce S.L.A. communiqués. There was a citizen's band radio, two walkie-talkies, tools, and a dinner plate (called the "cyanide plate" by investigators) that contained traces of potassium cyanide. There was a lot of typed and printed literature, radical posters, and a stack of texts on warfare and politics.

One of the most interesting and incriminating items found at 1560 Sutherland Court was a hand-drawn diagram labeled "Ambush," which showed the exact layout of the Oakland schools administration building parking lot where Foster and Blackburn had been gunned down. There were also original copies of the first two communiqués and a third and fourth communiqué, which had not yet been acted upon.

These dandy little items had to do with the proposed kidnap and/or execution of two business executives because their firms were felt to be guilty of "murder, genocide, robbery and supporting and taking part in crimes against the people of Ireland, Brazil, Rhodesia and South Africa, the Philippines, Angola, Mozambique and Guinea-Bissau." The two named execs were D. E. Stanberry, of the Colgate-Palmolive Company in Berkeley, and Charles W. Comer of South San Francisco, who was president of the T. A. White Candy Company, which S.L.A. claimed was a "subsidiary of ITT." Later evidence indicated that surveillance had already begun on these two and that more than a dozen other businessmen were being considered for warrants of "arrest" and/or "execution." It is probable that plans were also being made to kill Oakland *Tribune* publisher William Knowland and Raymond Procunier, head of the California prisons.

Twelve names that definitely were down on S.L.A.'s hit list were Donald T. Lauer, of Wells Fargo Bank; D. S. Langsdorf, of Bank of America; Theodore Lenzen, of Standard Oil; Arthur P. Shapro, of Liberty National Bank; Robert T. Shinkle, of Crocker-Citizens Bank; James H. Woodhead, of the Kaiser Corporation; Willsie Wood, a retired banker; Calvin T. Townsend, of ITT; UC Regent Joseph A. Moore, Jr.; Robert A. Magowan, of Safeway Stores; Edwin A. Adams, of Bank of California; and the late John E. Countryman, of Del Monte Foods, who had been dead several months before the always well-informed S.L.A. decided they wanted to kill him.

Mizmoon Soltysik and Nancy Ling Perry were not the least bit ashamed of the somewhat amateur quality of their research and surveillance. Admitted the two in a memo that accompanied one of the wipe-out lists:

"Understanding that we are all just learning how to do this, and that it takes practice, and that the list is suggestions of things, the most important, that we'd like to know and realizing that many of them are difficult to obtain, and wanting to remind you to be extremely cautious and as inconspicuous as possible, also to let you know that the maps and drawings do not require that you be an artist . . ."

The maps (in addition to the Foster "ambush" sketch) included a number of the older stickup and burglary diagrams as well as newer drawings of the Richmond–San Rafael Bridge, which ends next to San Quentin Prison and the Berkeley Post Office. The fingerprints of Joe Remiro were supposedly found on several of them.

Notations found on one of the documents said that "a map of industry and business would be different since it would show alarm systems, kinds of window, times of security patrols, walk distances, roof tops, how close other businesses are, etc. In addition to maps we would have work sheets about area, times when traffic is heavy, habits around areas, doors, lites, walkways, bus stops, cars in area, dress in area, opening and closing time of stores, pig patrols, security patrols. . . ."

Another fascinating document, entitled "Security Around the Pad," advised that should an S.L.A. headquarters be abandoned, "Molotov cocktails should be ignited to burn down pad." Other precautions itemized included checking out prospective hideouts for "thickness of fence, position of trees and places pigs could fire from." There were warnings that "guerrillas should watch all curtains—don't brush against them, be sure they are FULLY CLOSED" and that "a radio or record should be on at all times when there is activity or discussion."

Some other rules for day-to-day living underground included: "Keep your handgun with you at all times. Keep your ammo and rifles, etc. together and ready to carry out at all times. Always know where your shoes are. Always know where your Molotov cocktails are. Notify comrades when going in or out of the pad."

Extremely paranoid rules were made regarding visitors, who were to be frisked in the bathroom before sitting down to converse. All visitors were to be relieved of their pieces and searched for "bugging and beeping devices."

Equally interesting was a little green notebook, which contained the name of Patricia Campbell Hearst along with some quick notes obviously taken down during a telephone conversation. The notes said: "At UC—daughter of Hearst—Junior—Art student" and "on the night of the full moon of January 7 . . ." Somewhat red-faced investigators were later asked just why the Hearst family had not been notified of this find *before* the famous February 4 snatch, but they just mumbled and pointed a fat finger at the next cop down the line.

Those interested in the intellectual inputs of S.L.A. got some solid information from a list of books found both at Sutherland Court and, a bit later, in a strange old hideout in downtown Oakland occupied by Bill Harris and unknown friends for only a few weeks in January. They included standard revolutionary texts like Marighella's *Mini-Manual of the Urban Guerrilla* and a variety of radical classics by Marx, Lenin, and Mao. There was even a copy of Machiavelli's *The Prince,* along with technical reference works like *Chemical and Biological Warfare, The Biological Effects of Radiation, Germ Warfare,* and a classified Army manual on the making of improvised munitions.

Closets held a variety of good-quality middle-class clothing, which seemed to indicate that some of these former hippies had decided on a little protective coloration while moving through suburbia. There were a number of women's wigs and a revealing theatrical make-up kit heavy on potions for dark complexions, along with a how-to-do-it book on TV and movie false faces.

Notebooks and odds and ends of the group's working papers contained the names of at least nine S.L.A. members and supporters who were never publicly identified by lawmen during the later course of the investigation. They included a "Sarah," who may have helped bankroll the organization, as well as Shago, Sodium, Aikla, Seara, Arco, Brother Hi, "M," and Zolla.

Tacked up on the walls of one bedroom, police found newspaper clippings about the activities of another shadowy urban guerrilla group, the August 7 Movement, which had taken credit in five late-'73 communiqués for such actions as shooting down an Oakland police helicopter, killing two cops, and abducting a taxi driver in an attempt to make Yellow Cab close down until the San Quentin Six were released. (August 7 was the day Jonathan Jackson was gunned down at Marin Civic Center.)

The helicopter attack had resulted in considerable civic furor, with the police chief immediately offering a forty-thousand-dollar reward for the culprits, despite the fact that a coroner's report indicated that neither of the two copter pilots had been shot after all. Careful observers of the East Bay radical scene felt that the August 7 baddies were probably, like S.L.A., an underground offshoot of disintegrating Venceremos. But sensationalist crime reporters, always quick to blow up a minor angle, began to write that S.L.A. and the August 7 Movement were one and the same.

It was probably this journalistic conjecture, most certainly a slander in radical circles, which prompted Nancy Ling Perry to write her public "Letter to the People" on January 17, just a week after the burning of the Sutherland Court place and six days after police had issued a warrant for her arrest, charging her with arson and setting her bail at an unusually high $200,000.

Nancy said she wanted to set things straight. In this lone communication between the Foster wipe-out and the Hearst snatch, "Fahizah" clarified her motives and announced to the world that Joe Remiro and Russ Little most definitely *were* Soldiers of the S.L.A. It would be the beginning of a practice in which the guerrilla group would mention Remiro and Little in nearly every communiqué or message they put out from that point on.

Wrote Nancy:

". . . I am now being sought for a political action, and in spite of the fact that two of my closest companeros are now chained in the Adjustment Center (the prison's prison) at San Quentin Concentration Camp, I am still with other members of the S.L.A. information/intelligence unit, and I am hiding only from the enemy and not from the people. . . .

"Although it is the practice of the Symbionese Liberation Army to act rather than talk, I am compelled to speak because I wish to make clear my position and why I am fighting, what it is I am fighting for. . . ."

After examining her own history and beliefs, Nancy said that "I would like to correct and clarify the information given to you by the regime-controlled media and police-state reports associating the Symbionese Liberation Army with the August 7th. First of all, statements about August 7th literature and original communiques being found in the Concord house are completely untrue. The Symbionese Liberation Army is NOT the August 7th; in fact, the August 7th is a counter-revolutionary Oakland City and California State police plot to discredit revolutionaries and confuse people. As a member of the S.L.A. I can tell you that the S.L.A. takes full credit and responsibility for its actions, we acknowledge everything that we do, and if we had shot down a helicopter, we would say so."

To prove her point, Nancy then freely admitted to the arson with which she was charged, saying that "the house was set on fire by me only to melt away any fingerprints that may have been overlooked."

She next set out to defend Remiro and Little, claiming that they were innocent of the Foster killing because they had not belonged to S.L.A. "combat forces" but only to an unarmed "information/intelligence unit."

"We can easily verify that the ballistics on the .380 now in the hands of pig agents [the main piece of evidence against Remiro] do not match those of the weapon used in the attack on the Oakland Board of Education." (It was true that S.L.A. had *two* Walthers in their possession. These guns are so finely tooled that it is sometimes very hard to tell the ballistics of a bullet fired out of one from a slug that passed through another Walther barrel. In addition to that, Oakland investigators admitted that "someone had passed some coarse substance through the barrel" of the Walther found on Remiro in a effort to "change ballistic markings." They had apparently, to some degree, succeeded, since a great deal of additional evidence was presented to indict Remiro, involving markings on the *casings* of the shells found near Foster rather than markings on the slugs themselves.)

Nancy Ling Perry closed her letter with a word for Joe and Russ: "I would like to convey the word to my two captured companeros: you have not been forgotten, and you will be defended because there has been no set back and all combat forces are intact. There really are no words available to me to express what I feel about the capture of my two companeros. They are in a concentration camp now because none of us were offensively armed, and because I was not aware that they were under attack. But, my beautiful brothers, as we have said many times, we learn from our mistakes, and we learn from our active participating in struggle, not from political rhetoric. So we don't cry, but simply fight on; and right on with that. A comrade of mine, Bo [Remiro], says something that I'd like to leave you with: 'There are two things to remember about revolution: We are going to get our asses kicked and we are going to win.' "

Her extraordinary missive closed with the standard S.L.A. byword: "Death to the Fascist Insect that Preys upon the Life of the People."

Fahizah's implied threat of an armed jailbreak for Remiro and Little did not plant any new ideas in the minds of the police who were holding them. The security precautions taken by their captors were extraordinary from the beginning. At this stage, the size and fighting capabilities of the S.L.A. were still threatening unknowns to the cops, and an attempted jailbreak was feared from the first.

Russ and Joe were no sooner booked into the Concord City Jail on the morning of January 10 than an extra shift of guards was called in to surround the place. No one got in or out of the building without being carefully frisked and checked out. The place swarmed with patrolmen and detectives. These were the prize captives of the century, and Concord was not about to lose 'em. Both prisoners were kept chained and under constant observation in their cells. Every item that had been in their possession at the time of arrest was carefully examined.

It was quickly found that each had carried a key that fit the door to the S.L.A. hideout on Oakland's Seventh Avenue, from which the Foster hit had supposedly been staged. Other keys fit the triple door locks at Sutherland Court. At least one key fit the ignition and door locks of the Chevy van the two had been riding at the time of their capture. These locks, the cops said, had come out of the '69 white Chevy van stolen at gunpoint on October 12 in Berkeley. (The stripped remains of that van had been found on October 20 in Concord, less than three-quarters of a mile from the Sutherland Court house.)

Remiro and Little were so thoroughly cleaned of all "incriminating evidence" that bailiffs hauled Russ into Martinez Municipal Court the day after his capture (January 11) without his shoes on—they were still being studied by detectives. Obviously they felt Little could have been the "shotgun man" who had left clear boot marks on the muddy getaway path near Foster's corpse.

Even the normally staid and uninterested public defender representing Little had to get up and protest when he saw his wounded client being led into court in his stocking feet. Judge John Hatzenbuhler agreed that this was a bit "improper" and ordered the guards to find a pair of shoes for Little before his next court appearance. But this was only the beginning of a period of unprecedented "special measures," which would nearly end with the two "soldiers" being interrogated in San Quentin's gas chamber. No prisoners in California history had ever been accorded such treatment.

Their first appearance in Judge Haltzenbuhler's Contra Costa County Court dealt only with charges stemming from the shoot-out with Sergeant Duge the day before but, nevertheless, a record $250,000 bail was set for each. The charges included attempted murder and assault with a deadly weapon on a cop.

Radical attorney Robin Yeamans represented Remiro at first. Within a few days she would send out two rather unusual "investigators" to comb the ashes at Sutherland Court for evidence—they were Venceremos leader Ray Hofstetter and Robert McBriarty. After checking their finds with cops on the scene, the two split with a load of goodies.

Despite the extraordinarily high bail on the shoot-out charges, friends of Remiro and Little said they might be able to raise enough ransom to spring the two, but their hopes were immediately dashed by the filing of murder charges in the Foster case. The Oakland cops were wasting no time now that they finally had their accidental breakthrough.

They made absolutely sure the two would stay safely in jail. First Remiro and Little were transferred from the nervous little holding facility in Concord to the more "secure" Contra Costa County Jail in Martinez, where armed guards on the roof were joined by constant patrols in the streets. The two were no sooner booked into Martinez than new and considerably more serious "no bail" holding charges were lodged against them in the Foster case. Bail on the Alameda County matters would total $500,000 for each prisoner. With such an array of charges in two counties to face and three-quarters-of-a-million bail set on each of them, it appeared unlikely that Remiro or Little would get out of stir before years of hearings and trials were over, if then.

Not content with these stringent measures, the state's highest law-enforcement officials, who were by now deeply involved in the S.L.A. case, ordered an even more extraordinary precaution taken. Although neither Joe nor Russ had yet been convicted of *anything,* not even a parking ticket, it was decided on January 11 to move them over across the bay to California's grimmest and most "secure" penitentiary: San Quentin. (Under normal holding procedures, a "suspect" in a criminal matter is considered innocent until he has been tried and is kept in less forbidding city or county jails before the trial. Only *convicted* persons are shipped off to do heavy time in the penitentiaries.)

To accomplish this rare feat, the state invoked a seldom-used ruling that allows county sheriffs to legally transfer untried prisoners to a penitentiary because there is danger they might be "forcibly removed" from a county jail. This antique statute was created in the nineteenth century, when mobs of vigilantes sometimes broke down jail doors to lynch particularly unpopular cattle rustlers and horse thieves. It had not been used in decades.

By January 12, Remiro and Little were securely locked away in that "jail within a jail," San Quentin's Adjustment Center. This was the "hole" where George Jackson had been gunned down, the place they locked up convicts who were so "incorrigible" that no normal joint is strong enough to hold them. It was a bit inconvenient for Remiro and Little, to be sure, but for two radicals who had worked so long and hard in the prison movement it was something of an honor, too. They had made the big time.

With the slam of a prison door, Joe and Russ were caged beside the real heroes of the California pens. Near them were the San Quentin Six (including the legendary "Soledad Brother" Fleeta Drumgo), who had stood up against Adjustment Center guards on August 21, 1971, along with George Jackson. As a slightly awed and star-struck Remiro would later put it:

"These are the guerrillas of the prisons. These are the combat veterans. . . . We had a chance to talk to a lot of really fine comrades in San Quentin. . . . Fine comrades . . . fine comrades."

Prison officials would quickly tell a rather incredulous press that Remiro and Little had been put into this most maximum of all security setups "for their own protection. They wouldn't last a flat minute on the Mainline. Marcus Foster was a very popular man."

Remiro's reply was right to the bitter point: "This is just another way to take away the rights that we do have," he said. "We have less rights than the inmates that have been convicted. . . ."

Conditions in the Adjustment Center were stark and stringent. There were constant body searches, and Little and Remiro were held twenty-three hours a day in solitary-confinement "strip cells" with almost no furniture and only a hole in the middle of the floor to serve as a toilet. They were constantly watched, and the lights in their cells were never turned off. (This proved to be a real torture for Little, who suffers from glaucoma.) Each prisoner was allowed less than an hour a day of solitary exercise in a small Adjustment Center courtyard.

No visitors were allowed except an attorney or two, who found it almost impossible to consult with their clients to prepare their defenses in the normal manner. One of the first to visit Joe was a distant cousin (and a cousin of San Francisco Mayor Alioto), the attorney Sal Balistreri. He'd been urged to come by Joe's sister, a rather conservative young woman who was terrified she might end up with her name in the papers, but nevertheless was a true sister who cared about Joe.

Since the address of Joe's parents over on Seventh Avenue in San Francisco had been on the driver's license he'd given to Sergeant Duge in Concord, the press found it easy to locate Charles and Antoinette Remiro. Only the father would talk to them, and only once at that. In a quick interview conducted with a reporter just outside the half-open door of his little row house in the Sunset district, Charles Remiro half sobbed out his reaction to Joe's arrest.

"He wouldn't have harmed anyone," he said of his son. "He wouldn't even hurt a bird. But ever since he came back from the Army, he's never been the same."

The message that Joe had tried so hard to relay to Charles Remiro five years before, when he had told him about the massacres he'd participated in during the Vietnam war (the day Charles threw him out of the house), had finally begun to sink in. The father mumbled something else about the Army having given Joe "some pills" that changed his personality. It was apparent that he thought Joe had come back a drug addict.

"I don't know what to do," he continued. "Do you want me to commit suicide over this? It's all I've been thinking about. He was such a gentle boy. I love my son and he loves me." End of interview. The door was quickly closed and it would not again open for a member of the press. And, despite his unusual expression of concern, Charles Remiro could not bring himself to act it out in person. He did not visit Joe in jail or show up for his initial court hearings.

But Joe's comrades in S.L.A. did not forget him. Bill Harris used his contacts in San Quentin to send messages to Joe. One letter that did not get through (meant for a member of the Black Guerrilla Family) noted that "conditions are certainly not good for our getting together. I want you to know I am fine and stronger than ever, despite some recent setbacks. We intend to overcome the setbacks in a powerful manner. Communicate my greetings to the soldiers there."

On January 18, Remiro and Little would attempt to tell the world about the incredible conditions of their confinement in a communiqué, which their jailers seized. A copy finally reached the *Phoenix* newspaper, which quickly published it. The two jointly proclaimed their innocence of the charges against them:

"We are not guilty of crime and will not become so by failure to stand as politically conscious and socially motivated men," they wrote. ". . . Our crime is the realization that as revolutionaries it is our duty to totally support and recognize all those struggling for national liberation and the construction of a more humane and egalitarian society. This is our only crime. We have already been convicted and sentenced to one of their worst hell-holes, San Quentin's 'Adjustment Center' even before railroading us thru court. But we still grow stronger every day—the spirit of Lolita Lebron and George Jackson thrives here! We feel like the rabbit who was thrown into the briar patch for punishment."

Remiro would later say that he was thrilled to find that everyone in the Adjustment Center remembered Jackson. "Nobody says, 'I knew George Jackson,'" he would later recall. "Nobody says, 'George said this or George said that.' They pass the Bible around, you know, *Soledad Brother* and *Blood in My Eye*. That's the Bible. In the hole, too, they've got it. The pigs rip it up every chance they get. But they get it back. But nobody ever says, 'I knew George, or George said this, or I saw George do that.' Nobody says that. The fascist prisoners, you know, the Nazi prisoners, they won't say anything bad about George. The guards won't say anything bad about George. He's that sort of a *threat,* you know. Somebody says something bad about George, that person's going to get killed. Well, I'll tell you, no guard will come into the Adjustment

Center and say, 'George Jackson was a motherfucking fool,' or anything like that. They won't even think of it. I swear to God, man! The Nazis, the fucking Nazi prisoners, won't even say it. The only way people in prison can do anything now is getting a firm hold on guerrilla warfare and guerrilla tactics. I think guerrilla tactics are very possible when you're in jail, especially when you have some of the most revolutionary people in the world sitting right next to you, you know."

Outside the walls of San Quentin, investigators were having a field day with the now-unfolding Foster case. No sooner had Remiro and Little been busted than search warrants were issued for their last known addresses. Thorough investigations were begun on everyone known to be connected with them. It proved to be a fascinating crew. Those who were actually S.L.A. members saw it coming and, in nearly every case, went immediately underground as soon as they heard the news of the Remiro-Little arrest. Willie Wolfe, who had been visiting his father in Pennsylvania, received a phone call from California on January 10 and quickly dropped out of sight. The Harrises and Angela Atwood disappeared from their Oakland apartment at 434 Forty-first Street the same day. Emily walked out on her job at UC Berkeley's Survey Research Center, and her husband failed to again show up for his post-office job. Mizmoon Soltysik disappeared once and for all from her Berkeley apartment. The heat was definitely on.

The raids the following day were direct and to the point at Peking Man House on Chabot Road (Russ Little's last "known address"), at 4614-16 Bond Street (Remiro's pad), and at the Oakland apartment of Nancy Ling Perry's brother, an address she had used to register the '65 Chevy van that Russ and Joe were captured in.

The most thorough and fruitful search was conducted at the Chabot Road commune, where investigators walked away with a trunkload of books, posters, typewriters, an M-1 carbine, boots belonging to Russ, and an electric drill and a number of bits (possibly connected with the cutting of holes for cyanide bullets). Almost nothing was found at Bond Street, where police searched both the cottage in back once occupied by Remiro (4614) and the little house in front (4616) occupied by his old VVAW friend, Bob Hood, and Jeanie Dolly, a former Venceremos member who had been working in the Oakland VVAW office that Remiro had helped to set up.

Jeanie, a strong-minded young blonde who had once been one of Ken Kesey's band of Merry Pranksters and a close friend of Jack

Kerouac's hero, Neal Cassady, told a crowd of reporters who had come to witness this altogether public search of her home that she had not seen Remiro "in months" and that the cottage in back had been vacant for at least "four or five weeks."

Despite their extensive search, the Bond Street investigators walked away with nothing more than "three white unused typewriter paper sheets, a sales slip" for some other paper, and a copy of *American Rifleman* magazine, to which Joe Remiro had apparently once subscribed.

Over at Chabot Road, Peking House landlord David Gunnell served tea to the press while a six-hour search went on, but he declined to discuss either Russ Little or Robyn Steiner with them. He got his advice from a young lawyer who had become something of a legend in radical Berkeley, Dan Siegel, the former UC student-body president who had once set off a small street war by advising students to go take back People's Park.

Siegel also followed the cops and press corps over to Bond Street to advise Hood and Ms. Dolly on their rights while their house was being torn apart. He was joined there by another well-wisher, Reese Ehrlich, who had lived with his wife in this very same house early in '73. Ehrlich had been a strong radical student leader at UC and had helped to organize the violent Washington, D.C., antiwar protest of '69. His latest political activities had centered on organizing the Coalition to Save Our Schools, the most violent and effective critics of the much-hated plan to set up police patrols and an identification system in the Oakland schools.

The presence of these well-known radicals simply reinforced the presupposition of the invading Oakland cops and FBI that the S.L.A. was the culmination of everything they had always feared and hated in the East Bay left. The radicals' growing fear that the Symbionese caper (which most of them publicly condemned) would thus bring down the heat on everyone left of Wendell Willkie was promptly actualized January 17 (just a week after the Concord shoot-out), when Oakland Police Captain John Lothrop went way off base to announce that "Vietnam Veterans Against the War could be involved in S.L.A." Placing himself directly under the limelight and loving it, Captain Lothrop went on to say that "I have evidence it [the S.L.A.] is more than just a handful. I have twenty-five names. . . ."

Such an announcement was exactly what District Attorney Lowell Jensen did *not* need. Jensen had his heart set on trying Remiro and Little for the Foster murder *himself*. He said he was trying hard to hold down adverse pretrial publicity, which would allow the defense to move the case to another, "less prejudiced," county through a change-of-venue motion.

Statements like those made by Lothrop pretty much guaranteed such a move. They were also a giveaway that, evidence or no evidence, everyone on that Oakland S.L.A. "suspect list" was about to find himself in a heap of trouble.

One of the earliest busts happened to Bob Hood, who caught it on February 6, after weeks of intensive surveillance both at his home and at the Telegraph Avenue VVAW office. He says he was "framed" after a traffic-stop confrontation with police, in which he supposedly opened a small pocketknife with one hand to attack a heavily armed patrolman.

The heat also descended on such peripheral S.L.A. "suspects" as Popeye Jackson (who nearly had his parole revoked) and others working in the prison movement. Radicals, including Angela Davis and Jerry Rubin, had already become quite critical of the Foster killing. Now they began to *really* take the guerrillas to task for bringing on such a wave of "repression." The leaders in this building barrage of criticism were the Black Panthers, who made it clear they had no use for S.L.A. whatsoever. The feeling was mutual, according to Joe Remiro, who added that Huey Newton was not only at the top of the S.L.A. hit list—he was "on the hit list of *every* true revolutionary."

Remiro and Little went even further in a communiqué they finally managed to smuggle out of prison, which said that the "politicos" were trying to "subvert unity thru their historic use of rhetoric, factionalism, dogma and just plain bullshit. . . . Being of no more use to the 'State' these 'legal revolutionists' will be attacked and imprisoned as scapegoats replacing the true guerrillas whom all the king's horses and all the king's men can't find. This is also historical and past the point of meaningful political struggle. Stated plainly: The games are over—the Revolution is on!"

That declaration would be spoken even more clearly in S.L.A. style, action rather than words, on a moonlit February 4, when the guerrillas would enroll a new member the hard way.

14

*"Radicalism has its value but excessive radicalism is dangerous.
Conservatism has its uses. . . ."*
—William Randolph Hearst

"You furnish the pictures and I'll furnish the war."
—*Ibid.*

R IPPING OFF A HEARST is, for many and complex reasons, considerably trickier than seizing the brat of some bigwig politician or the spoiled heiress to a rubber-goods fortune, especially if the snatch will then be recorded as the "First Political Kidnapping in American History" and you plan to use it to make the world's media dance to your revolutionary tune.

First, you've got to consider all of the legal and public-relations angles. Every ambitious cop in the country will want in on the case. But, then again, as long as you've got the "kidnap victim" securely stashed, they'll be leashed and muzzled by a worried patrician family that still calls a lot of the political shots in both California and Washington. Since this is to be an exercise in "armed propaganda" (as first conceived by Carlos Marighella), you've got to pump every important concept you want the people to hear into captive newspapers, which will reluctantly run your unedited proclamations only as long as you've got the victim. You must drag out this outrageous story for weeks and months to get every bit of possible coverage. It helps to have a prize-winning journalist and an English major or two in your ranks to pound out the copy.

There will, of course, be surprises and imponderables to deal with. One that was obviously overlooked at first was the *genetic* problem. When S.L.A. decided to kidnap nineteen-year-old Patricia Campbell Hearst, they did not realize they were tampering with Mendelian law. Dominant genes have a tendency to skip a generation before they reassert themselves, and William Randolph Hearst (barely asleep beneath his granddaughter's tender skin) was not only a querulous megalomaniac, but a damned shifty one at that. He had an unlimited imagination, was totally independent of tradition and pubic opinion (except when they suited his purposes), and was known to change sides at the drop of a circulation audit.

Patty Hearst had already exhibited a few of her grandfather's famous qualities, most notably independence of mind and stubbornness. She even looked and thought a little like him. The conditions of her staid upbringing had diluted and temporized much of "the Chief's" opportunistic brilliance, but old WRH was still in there, locked firmly into Patty's thoroughly Hearstian genetic structure.

His great sense of showmanship, his natural instinct for politics, his love of the dramatic and the coarsely spectacular, none of these other qualities would have surfaced in Patty Hearst had it not been for the S.L.A. But dump this "pampered princess" from Hillsborough into a drawn-out, tense, and superpublicized situation like a revolutionary kidnapping, and the resurrected spirit of William Randolph Hearst might come bursting forth once again—that indomitable and frenetic spirit which sank the Maine, floated a whole new era of American imperialism, stamped the word "yellow" for all time on pop journalism.

Patty Hearst would prove to be a genetic time bomb.

As the little green notebook in their charred-over Concord hideout indicates, S.L.A. had apparently been thinking about seizing her since late '73. Bill Harris's January letter to a San Quentin convict, written just nineteen days before the Hearst snatch and less than a week after the Remiro-Little bust, promised that S.L.A. would overcome the Concord setback in a "powerful manner."

The whole operation was to be a carefully staged commando raid. It was a do-or-die number for a desperate S.L.A., with at least five members involved. It had to be well planned and quickly executed.

Three weeks before the caper, about the middle of January, three S.L.A.ers crashed a party at the two-floor town-house apartment where Patty Hearst lived with her fiancé, Stephen Weed. Steve was a teaching assistant at UC and a graduate student in philosophy. He'd invited a few other grad students over for some fine wine and a few joints. They were a sedate, quite dependable lot, and the three unknown visitors to the nicely furnished $250-a-month South Campus pad at 2603 Benvenue just didn't fit into the scene, but nobody had the nerve to ask them to leave. A friend who attended the party later described them as "rough types, not college students—sinister. . . ."

A second careful casing of the kidnap scene was staged a few days before the action itself was to take place by two S.L.A.ers who rang the apartment bell and asked Steve Weed if any of the four units in the building was for rent. They sized things up once more and gauged his reactions.

One thing was obvious—Stevie Weed wasn't going to be any problem. A rather vague, mealy-mouthed sort of twenty-six-year-old who had lucked into an affair with a Hearst heiress mostly because he was young and the only really eligible instructor in a private girls' school she'd attended near her Hillsborough home, Weed could always be counted on to temporize rather than act. No-o-o-o-o-o problem.

The fact that Patty, who had met Weed when she was only sixteen and was shacking up with him within a year, was about to settle down with this walrus-faced philosopher for *keeps* (a marriage had been announced for spring, '74) was something of a mystery to everyone who knew the unlikely young couple. But who has the right to question love?

Patty's parents did.

But her mother got nowhere (as usual) and her father (as usual) quickly caved in beneath the absolute determination of this favorite of his five daughters.

Randolph A. Hearst, the fourth of William Randolph's five sons, was a very clear example of Mendel's proposition that a father's more prominent characteristics often by-pass his sons. He had obviously inherited little of the Chief's outrageous willfulness. He'd been raised Episcopalian, by his mother, the ex-showgirl Millicent, who was long estranged from WRH, and immediately gave way to a grimly determined young Catholic Southern belle named Catherine Campbell he met and married in her native Atlanta in 1938. "Convert!" said Catherine, and Randolph immediately obliged.

It is also true that Randolph Hearst (twin brother to David and considered the "brightest" of Hearst's sons) had not lived close or long enough with his famous father to really absorb much by example. When "Randy" was only seven, Hearst made public his legendary affair with actress Marion Davies and sought a divorce from Millicent. It was the one thing she could refuse him, and refuse him she did. But Hearst moved in with Miss Davies anyway, and he provided her with a number of her own estates and pleasure resorts as well as incomparable accommodations at the fabulous San Simeon, that most grandiose example of personal extravagance since Versailles.*

Randolph Hearst did get a chance to visit with the "Old Man" from time to time, and, as one of the heirs, he most certainly would have the benefit of a part of the Hearst patrimony. He "worked his way up" through the organization as a reporter and editor, but this traditional publishing farce had little to do with his true economic interests, the perpetuation of a diversified empire that not only retained the few successful remnants of a once-great newspaper chain and published thirteen magazines, but also was deeply involved in mining, real estate, newsprint production, and other industries. For this, the instincts of a banker or an accountant were more appropriate than those of a politician or a newsman.

It was not the job of Randolph Hearst or his brothers to go out and pioneer in new fields as their father had done (and lose and waste a number of fortunes in doing it). It was their preordained role, stringently guided by several trusts and foundations whose boards they generally chaired, to keep and expand upon the millions WRH had left on his demise in 1951.†

Randolph and his kin were only careful shadows of this extravagant and ruthless spirit. But Patricia, third of five daughters, began to show signs of true Hearstian obduracy as early as age fourteen, when she absolutely rebelled against the strict discipline at Catholic Santa Catalina Girls School in Monterey. (Rumors that she was thrown out for smoking pot are untrue. At this stage, Patty strongly disapproved of marijuana, hippies, and anything vaguely left in politics.)

She simply could not stand the dreariness of it all, could not tolerate

---

* At least thirty million dollars were spent establishing this twin-towered, castlelike monstrosity, with dozens of outbuildings, that sits on a lonely coastal foothill of the Santa Lucia Mountains overlooking a 48,000-acre cattle ranch without another building in sight. That figure does not include the cost of the art masterpieces inside, the statues and waterworks outside, the Medieval and Renaissance buildings brought intact from Europe to tack on to the ever-growing "castle," and the complete zoo stocked with nearly every animal on earth. Hearst spent more on housing and decoration than any man since the time of Louis XIV.

† Probably the most accurate obituary written after that passing came from author Adela Rogers St. John, who knew Hearst quite well and said that "no other press lord ever wielded his power with less sense of responsibility; no other press ever matched the Hearst press for flamboyance, perversity and incitement of mass hysteria. Hearst never believed in anything much, not even Hearst, and his appeal was not to men's minds but to their infantile emotions which he never conquered in himself: arrogance, hatred, frustration, fear. . . ."

another *bit* of the continual KP imposed upon her for her uncontrollable high spirits and her inability to fake the necessary degree of "humility" required in this semiconvent. She was tired of endlessly scrubbing out the nuns' toilets, dumping garbage cans, and saying ten thousand Hail Marys as penance. About the only activity Patty apparently enjoyed there was cheerleading. (Right. *Another* damned cheerleader!)

Like her salty old grandfather, Patty took a strong and early interest in sex, another reason for getting away from conventlike Santa Catalina in 1970 to experience her junior year of high school somewhere more interesting.

True, Crystal Springs, a liberal, nonsectarian, and very exclusive academy only a mile from the twenty-two-room Hearst mansion in Hillsborough, was a girls' school. But you could get on and off campus easily, as Patty did quite rapidly in a brand new MG sports car her dad bought for her sixteenth birthday, and there *were* several young male teachers on campus.

The youngest and most interesting of them was the then-twenty-two-year-old Stephen Weed, a blond, blue-eyed, slightly built recent graduate of Princeton. Weed, son of a Palo Alto stockbroker, had flirted casually with SDS politics while in college but had backed off into a sort of fuzzy liberalism by the time he'd begun teaching math at Crystal Springs. Neither he nor Patty Hearst would join contingents of peace marchers who drove into San Francisco from the college. Weed seemed mostly interested in looking out for himself.

And life *was* a ball with two hundred rich young girls hot after your white and hairy bod. Patty was neither the richest nor the most attractive of the competitors, just the most determined. She *did* stand out, refusing to wear the school uniform and driving her sporty new car onto campus in violation of all the rules. She was more than worth looking at, this nicely built, petite sixteen-year-old—five foot three, 110 pounds, sparkling white teeth and a wide, winning smile, brown hair (occasionally dyed to blonde). She obviously decided early in the game that she *wanted* Stephen Weed, and, like her grandfather, what she wanted too much she would frequently have the misfortune of ending up with. Steve wasn't really that hard to get. (One does wonder what would have happened had the choice been a bit wider, had Patty been enrolled in a coed high school with lots of attractive boys to choose from.)

By the end of her second semester at Crystal Springs, the Hearst heiress had begun an affair with Weed. On an Asian Studies tour to

Japan (the rich don't have to settle for textbook descriptions), she'd confided to another schoolgirl that she was already "on the pill" and had to keep a close eye on her watch in order to take her contraceptives on time.

Patty worked hard through the summers of '70 and '71, taking extra courses so she could graduate a year early, still aged sixteen, from high school. She wanted independence and she wanted it fast, so she worked hard and got good grades. She was an apt student, not the kind deeply interested in ideas, just an extremely bright young girl who knew how to use the system energetically to get what she wanted out of it. Early graduation would get her out of a live-at-home situation in Hillsborough and into a college dorm where she could come and go as she pleased.

It would not be fair, though, to imply that Patty Hearst was an entirely selfish hedonist without convictions of any kind. She had refused to go through the usual rich-girl "coming-out" party to take her place as a debutante in Bay Area society. In the election year of '72, she supported George McGovern despite the fact that her father's newspapers were editorializing for Nixon. She once told Randolph that his papers, most especially the San Francisco *Examiner,* which he was then "editing," were completely out of touch with the reality of the times and that no one she knew ever bothered to read them.

She was aware that there was poverty and injustice in the world, but it simply didn't *touch* her. Her own life had for so long been sheltered and privileged, she was so far away from the ugly part of life. She could look forward to a life of assured financial independence because of a long-established trust fund. She could get ready cash—like the eight-thousand-dollar check her dad gave her on her eighteenth birthday, like the unlimited use of his credit cards and a three-hundred-dollar-a-month allowance in college—from an indulgent father simply for the asking.

She knew that there would *always* be money available for her pleasures and needs. She knew she was a Hearst. It's true she had the good sense to be embarrassed about it in public, but privately she admitted it *did* have its advantages. It was a first-class trip through life with vacations in the private family compound at San Simeon or out at an enormous deserted estate her great-grandmother had built north of San Francisco—a wooded barony along a cool, deep-running river, where Patty and her guests had the pick of five empty mansions to settle down and relax in. Patty knew she had it made.

The turning point in her life, the moment to strike out on her own despite everything, came in the fall of '71 for Patricia Campbell Hearst. Her mother, with whom the girl had never gotten along particularly well since Catherine had packed her off to a Catholic boarding school at the age of ten, was determined that her dangerously headstrong daughter should go to a safe and sane college. She had Stanford, a rich man's playground, in mind. It was about twenty miles south of Hillsborough, and most of the *best* families in the Bay Area send their daughters and sons down to the former estate of Leland Stanford for a gentlemanly (and ladylike) education.

Catherine Hearst, a regent of the University of California for more than a dozen years at this point, would *never* have seriously considered sending a child of hers onto a campus of this college system whose affairs she regulated. *Least* of all to Berkeley, that hotbed of radical politics and anarchist life styles.

But Patty quickly made herself equally clear. She *was* going to attend UC Berkeley as an arts major in the fall of 1972. But first she would spend a year at nearby Menlo College, in the posh suburb of Atherton, a coed facility quite close to Stephen Weed's apartment. Could she live at home, since she was going to school so close to home? Most certainly not. Patty was going to live in a dormitory and that was that.

She did not explain all of her reasoning to her outraged mother in the fall of 1971. That would come later. But her secret thinking was simple. The cool, diffident Weed planned to continue teaching at Crystal Springs through to the summer of '72. Then he expected to move over to Berkeley to pursue a graduate degree in philosophy at UC. Patty planned to stay close.

Her year at Menlo College was a happy one, according to at least one roommate, a young Iranian girl named Nasrin Rohani-Yavari, who helped to cover for Patty on those nights when she would slip out of the dorm and go over to sleep with Steve. The love affair blossomed, to the point where Weed felt no compunctions about encouraging Patty to take a summer tour of Europe in '72.

Randolph and Catherine Hearst were delighted with the idea. They breathed a joint sigh of relief, for the dimensions of Patty's intense affair with this bland underling were becoming altogether too clear. Rich parents have *always* squelched such importune alliances by sending their daughters off to Europe, and they hoped the traditional formula would work once again—but no luck. Eighteen-year-old Patricia came back in the fall ready to move over to Berkeley. And then she dropped the *real* bombshell, the one that nearly gave the staid and proper Catherine apoplexy. Patty was going to live with Stephen Weed quite openly, marriage license or no marriage license.

She said that she was *thinking* of eventually marrying him but had decided it was more sensible to live with him first. This was not an entirely unheard-of approach to love and marriage in the sexually liberated year of 1972. Most of Patty's generation would make a similar choice—she just did it younger than the rest.

Catherine Hearst was angry beyond words. Weed was not the sort of person she favored even as a *suitor!* But to live with him in sin . . . unthinkable! And in *Berkeley!*

There was angry talk of immediately disowning young Patricia, but her father cooled things out for her. He took a somewhat more worldly view of affairs of this sort. He did not see much in Weed, either, but perhaps a short shack-up might enlighten this headstrong but basically intelligent daughter of his. Randolph was not the roaring hedonist his father had been, but he'd read a French novel or two.

So, in the fall of '72, Patty was off to the decidedly upper-middle-class town house at 2603 Benvenue to begin life as a Berkeley undergraduate cohabiting with an older, more sedate and accomplished teaching assistant and graduate student. In December of '73, she publicly announced that she planned to marry Weed in the spring, and Catherine Hearst gave one huge sigh of relief and began to think about expensive china and matched cookie cutters. She just *loved* big weddings.

Randolph Hearst's reaction is not recorded. It was probably a tired and piteous groan.

Her studies and Weed completely absorbed Patty. Campus was only four blocks north of their elegant little pad, and she could walk directly to school over quiet College Avenue without encountering the Telegraph Avenue scene just a few blocks to the west. She avoided Tele, since she had little use for the street people and their dirty, radical ways.

She and Weed immersed themselves in the kind of quietly informed life they expected to be able to continue when he became a professor of philosophy, a position he'd have no trouble obtaining with a Hearst for his wife. They bought fine wines and refinished antique furniture. They enjoyed Patty's increasingly epicurean cooking and then lay back to smoke a dynamite joint or two while listening to the mellowest of sounds from an expensive stereo. The world might rage outside in anger and despair, but life was cosy on Benvenue. Until the night of February 4, 1974, that is.

The evening's more memorable activities begin a little before 9:00 P.M. about a mile and a half north of Patty's place and on the other side of the sprawling UC campus. Peter Benenson, a bearded young mathematician who works in the Lawrence Radiation Lab, is unloading a bag of groceries from his blue '63 Chevy convertible and is about to carry it into his apartment at 1304 Josephine Street. Two more bags wait in the back seat.

Suddenly, strong hands reach out of the darkness behind him and throw him against the car. His groceries fly across the sidewalk. A carton of ice cream splashes onto the pavement and begins to melt.

"Shut up! Don't make a sound! Do what you're told and you won't get hurt!" says the determined voice of a large and mature black man. Benenson has been around the Berkeley scene enough to immediately figure it's a rip-off. They want the car and the contents of his apartment. He ain't about to argue. He does not resist as they pull his wrists together and tie them tightly. The cords cut into his flesh, but he's too frightened to protest. Behind him stand Cinque, a second black man, and Mizmoon Soltysik. All are armed and very deadly.

Benenson is thrown onto the floor behind the front seat of the convertible. His captors force him to lie tightly cramped with his legs curled up against his chest. Two of them sit in the front seat and a third hops into the back to order the captive to keep his head down—or else! He decides he will be *most* cooperative. He cannot see their faces too well, but he hears whispered conversations. They notice he is listening and order him to "stay down or we'll kill you." The car bumps down the streets of Berkeley, heading south. (Within half a dozen blocks, they cross Hearst Avenue, named after the great-grandmother of the girl they are on their way to kidnap.)

It is a rather quiet Monday night, and the moon is just beginning to rise. They cut across nearly vacant Tele. The street people have abandoned their favorite turf this cold winter night, it's more comfortable indoors. With so little street action, even the cops are staying home. There are few patrol units on the street.

Shortly after 9:10 P.M., the convertible stops at 2603 Benvenue. Unbeknownst to the freaked-out Benenson, his captured auto is to be the leader of a three-car convoy. Parked behind the convertible stands another Chevy, a white '60 station wagon probably driven by Nancy Ling Perry, and behind that sits the little blue Volkswagen that belongs to Camilla Hall. Benenson is again warned to keep down as the occupants of his car get out, quietly closing the doors behind them.

The woman leads the two black men around the side of the brown-shingled, two-story building and into an enclosed garden-patio at the rear onto which Patty's unit opens through a big, sliding glass door. There are potted bushes and plants everywhere—some hang from pots suspended around the glass doors. They see bamboo, ivy, ferns, and philodendrons.

The woman, who is wearing a long, black wig, knocks lightly on the glass door. No response. She knocks again. (She holds a loaded .38 automatic in one hand, just out of sight in the folds of her long and tattered old dress. All three of the night visitors are wearing combat boots. The two men carry automatic rifles, probably M-1 carbines.)

Inside the apartment, Patty Hearst has just gotten out of a warm shower. Her hair is still damp and hangs loosely over the back of an expensive, dark-blue robe from I. Magnin's. Underneath, she wears nothing but a pair of nylon panties.

Steve Weed is stretched out on a long sofa just across from the sliding glass door. He's listening to the stereo, which is turned up fairly high, and he does not hear the first rapping on the glass. After the second knock, he gets up and moves slowly toward it. He looks at Patty quizzically. She shakes her head. She doesn't expect any visitors tonight, either. She stands just behind him as he slides the door open a little.

The woman outside says something barely audible about "an accident" and needing to use "the phone to call help." Weed doesn't like the looks of her and is reluctant to let her in. But while he hesitates, the matter is decided for him. The woman comes crashing into the room with the men directly behind her. Weed is thrown onto the floor. He sees the long, shiny barrels of their guns and thinks, "Oh, God, we're about to be robbed. . . ."

The larger of the two men orders him to keep his face down or "you're dead." He glances up just long enough to see one of the men grab Patty's wallet, which contains all of her father's credit cards and her own ID. Then they take Weed's passport. One of the invaders decides Weed should be put out of action, and he forces his face into the thick rug on the floor.

A moment later, Weed is smashed over the head with a full bottle of one of the fine wines he and Patty had so carefully selected. He is bleeding and dizzy but not really unconscious yet; he decides to play dead and see what's next. He can hear Patty struggling and screaming in the kitchen: "No, please! Not me! Let me go!" she screams.

They begin to drag her out the open doorway and toward their waiting car. Her robe falls open in the struggle, and she is naked except for her briefs. Weed, who is definitely no fighter, claims that at this stage he hears the click of a rifle bolt being snapped back and the woman saying "He's seen us. We'll have to kill him."

"I thought I had nothing to lose," he says. "I jumped up and screamed and ran around the living room overturning furniture and lamps and screaming." An amazed Cinque stands there watching these antics with a rifle pointed at Weed. He begins to smile. This white cracker is just too *much*. Weed runs out of the back door and leaps three fences before he ends up half a block away, still screaming. Alarmed neighbors finally grab him and hold him down.

(Later, a furious Catherine Hearst will accuse Weed of doing too little to save her daughter: "Whatever happened to all the Clark Gables in the world?" she would demand quite seriously.)

A next-door neighbor, Steven Suenaga, twenty-one, turns out to be a bit scrappier. He dives into the fray after Weed retreats and is severely beaten by the slowly departing S.L.A. commandos.

Patty is still yelling "Not me! Oh, please, not me!" as she is hauled out to the convertible and unceremoniously dumped into the trunk and locked in. Aroused neighbors come running, and the S.L.A. team fires a volley of bullets in the general direction of the apartment house. Everyone ducks for cover, and the convertible and its two escorts race off into the dark.

Benenson, still on the floor of his car, hears all of the racket and the slam of the trunk lid. He feels the car accelerate for a rapid escape for a few blocks and then slow and curve around until it is on a quiet, somewhat isolated street of old mansions known as Tanglewood Drive. They are about half a mile from the kidnap location and just at the foot of the Berkeley Hills. The other two cars stop behind, and he hears the trunk lid snap open and a still-whimpering Patricia being pulled out and thrown into the white station wagon. Mizmoon joins her, and the two black men get into the Volkswagen. Before they leave, they warn Benenson to stay down and "you won't get hurt."

The cars take off. He lies there a long, long time before he finally gets up the nerve to slide off the floor and peer around. Things are absolutely quiet up Tanglewood Drive. Benenson manages to get untied, but he is still terrified. They might come back. They know where he lives, and they might kill him if he talks. He walks four miles to his sister's house and hides out till the following day, when he finally decides it's time to talk to the cops.

His part of the story adds little to what the police have already figured out. They had discovered the spilled groceries and the abandoned convertible. They have the testimony of the slightly injured Weed and the flabbergasted neighbors.

They're even pretty sure they know who has pulled the snatch. They found a box of ammunition with cyanide neatly stuffed into each slug in the hallway of the Benvenue apartment. They're looking for the Symbionese, but there's a news embargo on the story until that afternoon, when crusty old Senator William Knowland orders his Oakland *Tribune* to go ahead and print this fantastic yarn. (From this point on, Knowland feels he is a marked man.)

On Tuesday, February 5, the world begins to intently follow the Kidnap of the Century, a drama that will eat up as much newsprint as William Randolph Hearst expended to start an entire war and create a new colonial empire. It's a story with more ups and downs than a runaway roller coaster. It will have an ending that no fiction writer in his right mind would try to palm off on an incredulous public.

Although he is in jail when it begins, and he'll still be locked up at the end, Joe Remiro becomes a central figure in this legend. His presence hangs over it from the moment the cyanide bullets are found in the disordered mess on the floor of the Patricia Hearst apartment.

15

"We are never completely contemporaneous with our present. History advances in disguise; it appears on stage wearing the mask of the preceding scene. . . . The blame, of course, is not history's, but lies in our vision, encumbered with memory and images learned in the past. We see the past superimposed on the present, even when the present is revolution."
—Regis Debray, *Revolution in the Revolution*

IT WAS IMMEDIATELY ASSUMED by supersleuths working on the Hearst kidnapping that S.L.A.'s prime motive in snatching Patty was to trade her off for Remiro and Little.

This assumption was based on a cursory reading of contemporary events rather than on intimate knowledge of the East Bay guerrillas. It was assumed that since this *was* the first true political kidnapping in U.S. history, and since the abductors were plainly students of such famous foreign revolutionists as the Tupamaros of Uruguay and Argentina's ERP, they would simply adhere to tradition and swap the newspaper tycoon's daughter for two of their own captured "compañeros."

So, with that in mind, a great deal of the official activity between Patty's kidnap on February 4 and the arrival of S.L.A. "Communiqué No. 3" explaining the action on February 7 was based upon an erroneous presupposition.

The communiqué itself proved a bit disappointing in that it did not immediately propose an exchange of prisoners, which would have quickly settled the matter.

But the FBI and local police were soon to discover for the first time, but not for the last, that *North* American urban guerrillas make up the rules as they go along. S.L.A. would quickly prove to be the least predictable phenomenon cops and newsmen had ever seen.

The February 7 "Hearst communiqué" made absolutely no mention of Remiro and Little. Like the Foster communiqué (Number One), it was couched in the form of a "Warrant Order" issued by some mythical "Court of the People" and ordering S.L.A. combat units to "arrest" Patricia Campbell Hearst.

The "warrant" resembled the message explaining the Foster wipe-out in that it had obviously been written *after* the action it claimed to authorize. In this case, the burst of rifle fire at Steve and Patty's neighbors was explained away as "warning shots," and a grim notice was tacked on that, in the future, citizens who got in the way of S.L.A. activity would be "executed immediately."

"The prisoner is to be maintained in adequate physical and mental condition and unharmed as long as these conditions are adhered to," it said. "Protective custody shall be composed of combat and medical units, to safeguard both the prisoner and her health.

"All communications from this court MUST be published in full, in all newspapers, and all other forms of the media. Failure to do so will endanger the safety of the prisoner. Further communications will follow."

And that was it. No ransom demands. No prisoner-exchange proposal. But a clear indication that S.L.A. was determined to seize the media.

It was the beginning of the longest, most drawn-out kidnap caper on record, a mammoth stand-off that, by the time it was done, would involve thousands of police officers, at least 150 FBI agents, a small army of volunteers who would deliver free food to more than 100,000 of the poor. All of this would cost Randolph Hearst and his enterprises over $2.3 million and the public would end up with a law enforcement bill in excess of $10 million.

The rich would tremble and the poor secretly rejoice. Politicians would froth and gesticulate and propound insane new laws. Old enemies would cross formerly immovable lines of theory and practice to unite against the "terrorist menace." Fascinating personal confrontations would occur and life in the Bay Area would never again be quite the same.

All because S.L.A. did not do what it was *supposed* to do and simply exchange one prisoner for two.

It was apparent that Remiro and Little also originally expected a trade-off proposal from their old comrades. But both were aware that

conditions were rapidly changing for S.L.A., and they knew that imagination and flexibility were the group's main advantages. There was just no
predicting them. As Remiro put it:

"How do I know what they'll do next? I'm here locked down. A
few weeks is like ten years in the life of an urban guerrilla group. Everything changes completely."

Those who planned on eventual negotiation with S.L.A. did not
forget about Joe and Russ. They were the Establishment's ace in the
hole, and the extraordinary precautions taken with them at San Quentin
became even more stringent after the February 4 kidnap.

S.L.A. showed that it was still concerned about its captured soldiers
in the first of seven famous tapes, delivered to radio station KPFA on
February 12. It detailed the logic behind the abduction and proposed
that a fantastic "good faith gesture" be undertaken by Hearst before any
real negotiations for Patty's release could begin. S.L.A. demanded a gift
of seventy dollars' worth of food for every person in California who had
"welfare cards, social security pension cards, food stamp cards, disabled
veterans cards, medical cards, parole or probation papers and jail or bail
release slips." This "gesture" would have cost Hearst at least $400 mil-
lion. He quickly said it was beyond his capacity to provide but promised
to come back with a counteroffer in a few days.

The February 12 tape—which opened with the voice of Cinque
and then switched to a badly frightened Patty, made extensive reference
to Remiro and Little and indicated that once the "good faith gesture"
had been completed, their freedom was definitely going to be an issue.
Said Patty:

"I am a prisoner of war and so are the two men in San Quentin.
I'm being treated in accordance with the Geneva Convention . . . one
of the conditions being that I am not being tried for crimes which I'm
not accountable for. I'm here because I'm a member of a ruling-class
family, and I think you can begin to see the analogy. The men in San
Quentin are being held, and they're going to be tried simply because
they are members of the S.L.A. and not because they've done anything.
Witnesses to the shooting of Foster saw black men, and two white men
have been arrested for that.

"You're being told this so you'll understand why I was kidnapped,
and so that you'll understand that I am being held innocent in the same
way the two men in San Quentin are innocent, and they are simply members of the group and have not actually done anything themselves to

warrant their arrest. They apparently were part of an intelligence unit and have never executed anyone themselves."

Patty then made it clear, in a voice that wavered between terror and exhaustion, that she did not consider S.L.A. "just a bunch of nuts. They've been really honest with me, but they're perfectly willing to die for what they are doing."

Cinque justified kidnapping Patty with an Old Testament kind of vindictiveness, visiting the sins of the parents upon the child: "The S.L.A. has arrested the subject for the crimes that her mother and father by their actions committed against the American people and the oppressed people of the world," said this angry escaped prisoner in his media debut. He indicated that the Symbionese would kill the Hearst girl if they had to, and he loosely enumerated the Hearsts' sins, saying that Randolph was "the corporate chairman of the fascist media empire of the ultra-right Hearst corporation, which is one of the largest propaganda institutions of this present military dictatorship of the militarily armed corporate state that we now live under in this nation. . . ."

Catherine, he said, had been responsible as a UC regent for "the loaning of funds and the investments of our California monies in corporations which have interests and do gain profits from the robbery, oppression, and genocide carried out by fascist and racist governments around the world and within the United States itself. . . ." (He blamed these investments for the mess in South Africa, Ireland, and the Philippines.)

"The UC Board of Regents," continued Cinque, "one of California's largest foreign investors, supports through its investments the murder of thousands of black women and children of Mozambique, Angola, and Rhodesia, murder being designed to destroy the spirit that all humanity longs for. . . . For these acts and others, the Court of the People hold the Hearst family accountable for their crimes and hold that they are enemies of the people."

Now that the first hand had been dealt and a few of the face cards were on the table, an astounded public began to vaguely comprehend the dimensions of the kidnap. It was obvious that this was no ordinary crime in which a specified amount of money would be demanded for the victim's release. The abductors were clearly political creatures. They had asked nothing for themselves except the best media coverage such a small, previously unknown group had ever received. They had set out, as "General Gelina" (Angela Atwood) would later put it, "to show by example what can be done: That this goodwill gesture was intended to give some food to the people while at the same time point out our understanding that the people can never expect the enemy to feed them. We did this to point out how the enemy can easily afford to feed the people if it were forced to, but what the enemy cannot afford is to reveal to the people the total extent of the sum of the wealth that it has robbed from the people."

Hearst's February 13 announcement that the size of the original S.L.A. food demand was beyond his capacity brought a quick modification from the guerrillas, who sent a second tape on February 16 in which Patty stated that "it was never intended that you feed the whole state. . . . So whatever you come up with basically is OK."

The message also revealed that the public media (radio for S.L.A. and television for the Hearsts) would be the prime communications link between the two parties. Few aspects of their negotiations would be private. And, to a degree that amazed and amused many spectators, the media themselves became a kind of "third party" in the matter. (Associated Press would later claim it had been a "hostage of the Hearsts.") Printed and electronic coverage had never been used so massively and matter-of-factly as a tool by which both sides sought their own ends— and tried to flood the world with their own self-serving propaganda.

It reached the point where Patty would soon be using a radio-broadcast tape to advise her mother what kind of clothing she should wear during televised news conferences at the Hearst mansion.

The media were also frequently used to express instant alarm when FBI agent Charles Bates (in charge of the case in San Francisco) or U.S. Attorney General William Saxbe made threatening noises about doing something positive in the matter.

The big issue seemed to be whether or not the feds would "rush in" on the Symbionese hideout and shoot everyone in sight, including Patty. By the time Patricia had made the February 16 tape, her abductors had apparently convinced her that she was more in danger of meeting her doom in this kind of a police raid than from an S.L.A. cyanide bullet. "I'm sure that Mr. Bates understands that if the FBI has to come in and get me out by force they won't have time to decide who not to kill. They'll just have to kill everyone," said Patty. "I don't particularly want to die that way."

She really had no reason to tremble. The cops didn't have the least idea where she was. It would appear that she was probably held for the first five weeks in a quiet little bungalow in a racially integrated portion of Daly City. Another bedroom community like Concord–Clayon Valley, this rather sedate community just south of San Francisco was probably the last place the cops would have looked.

On February 19, Hearst announced his counteroffer, a two-million-dollar food giveaway called "People in Need" modeled after a program that had been operating successfully for some time in the state of Washington. The S.L.A. thought this was a skinflint proposal, and in their third tape (February 21) demanded an additional four million dollars in food. Hearst said the next day that the matter was "out of my hands," since he could not personally come up with that much loot, but the Hearst Corporation (his alter ego) quickly stepped in to say it had the funds available and would provide two million dollars on Patty's release and another two million dollars in 1975 to make the food program an ongoing proposition. There was no immediate response from S.L.A., so on February 22 the initial giveaway of a portion of Hearst's first two million dollars in food began in both San Francisco and the East Bay. Things were handled so badly that rioting and looting broke out in East Oakland, and thousands of the poor waited hours in line to be turned away empty-handed because the supplies ran out. In some cases the food never even arrived. The papers were full of news of this fiasco and the continuing search for Patty, and the public was now paying very little attention to Remiro and Little.

But S.L.A. had made reference to its captured soldiers in both the February 16 and the February 21 tapes. In the first, Patty assured her parents that "I'll be OK as long as the S.L.A. demands are met, and as long as the two prisoners at San Quentin are OK."

In the February 21 message, Cinque reminded the other side that Patricia was being held as a prisoner of war just like Joe and Russ and that this would continue to be her status "until such time as the status of our captive soldiers is changed. . . ." (A clear hint that a prisoner trade-off still was likely to be a part of S.L.A.'s final terms.)

News that Remiro and Little were undergoing extraordinary conditions of confinement had obviously reached the Symbionese, and Cinque warned that if the two soldiers were "injured" Patty would be "executed immediately."

Over in the antique stone-walled Marin County Penitentiary, some twenty miles north of San Francisco, Little and Remiro were locked down in two so-called quiet cells on San Quentin's now-abandoned

Death Row, just outside its infamous "Little Green Room" gas chamber. (Prisoners called the cells Joe and Russ occupied "the hole.")

"We spent a little more than a month in the Adjustment Center and a few days short of a month in the hole on Death Row," says Remiro. "In prison time this is hardly mentionable. . . . To find out about the Adjustment Center and the hole, ask those who have spent precious years locked down, those who have been regularly and indiscriminately gassed and beaten with pick handles," he continues, "those who have witnessed countless other murders, in the name of 'rehabilitation and adjustment.' Some have been beaten into insanity, while others have been beaten into the objective reality which has led to the birth of organizations such as the Black Guerrilla Family. . . ."

Only two days before nine thousand persons received $100,000 worth of groceries in the first catastrophic People in Need handout, Remiro and Little started to have some food problems of their own. The two suspected that tranquilizing drugs had been added to their meals and both promptly went on a hunger strike.

By the night of February 21, they were on a new plateau of hunger and fear. News of the stand-off between S.L.A. and the Hearsts had reached them and they feared they might be tortured in an attempt to find out where Patty was hidden.

The atmosphere of Death Row was still heavy with the misery of the hundreds of condemned men who had walked down the corridor to their suffocating doom in the Little Green Room, and this did not help Remiro's anxious state of mind.

When a "goon squad" of strange guards and investigators unlocked their two cells at about 10:30 that night and silently led them into the gas chamber, the two young men feared the worst—summary execution without a trial.

"They wanted to stop right there by the gas chamber and interrogate us," Remiro recalls. "They really wanted to psyche us out. We hadn't confessed. I hadn't told them anything except my name when they booked me. They hadn't even talked to me up to then—they knew better. Fuck them. But now they figured they could scare us into talking. They told us we belonged in the gas chamber and that we'd end up there if we didn't cooperate. They chained our hands to a belt around our waist and put us in a car and drove us into the courtyard inside San Quentin's second gate. Then they moved us to an area just inside the first gate, and who the hell should drive in but Death Row Jeff and

Raymond Procunier and six or eight dudes in civies. They drove up in four cars and then we went into some kind of a little room right next to the prison souvenir shop.

"They wanted us to do something about Patty, they said, but Jeff says, 'Hey, these guys haven't eaten for days. Why don't you feed them first before you talk?' So Procunier runs out and gets a couple of cheeseburgers and he starts to unwrap them but I stop him. . . . 'Don't do that, punk,' I say. And then I eat for the first time in a couple of days."

Vacaville prison psychologist Wes Hiler claims that as a result of the San Quentin meeting and a later long-distance telephone call between Jeff and the two captured soldiers, a kind of tentative "agreement" was worked out which would have urged Cinque and his buddies to release Patty in return for their safe conduct out of the United States and the release of the second installment of four million dollars' worth of food to the poor in Hearst's People in Need program. For reasons that Hearst, prison officials, and the FBI have never revealed, this "agreement" was never publicly released.

Remiro and Little also wrote out a statement describing the conditions of their confinement and demanding they be moved back to an ordinary county jail like other prisoners who had not yet been convicted. Then they hit on a novel idea: whatever they had to say, it must be made public through a live and unedited television news conference featuring Joe and Russ. It was that or nothing.

The "agreement" and the list of demands for better conditions of confinement "disappeared" into the prison bureaucracy. The request for a live TV interview was debated for weeks by officials and judges before it was finally rejected.

"They allowed Jeff and us to meet together in the hopes that we would unconsciously aid them by just making a simple statement such as 'Release Patricia Hearst,' " says Joe. "Once they realized that we intended to expose their true colors, they put Jeff in the hole in Vacaville and us in the hole in San Quentin and tried like hell to stop us from communicating with the public. Another aspect of this meeting which seems to have been overlooked is, where did our handwritten suggestions go? When we gave them to Procunier, he would not even look at them, said they were for 'higher-ups'—sounds familiar, doesn't it? The FBI denied any participation or knowledge of the meeting, so who read our suggestions? Statements that no one knew what we intended to say are outright lies."

Philip Guthrie, spokesman for the prison system, tells Procunier's side of the story:

"The reason we had them on Death Row was we didn't want anything to happen to them at that time," he says, "because, as you remember, there were messages coming out of the S.L.A. saying that they were going to do to Patty according to what we did with those two guys, so we sure as hell didn't want to get them killed or hurt or anything, so we had a special watch on 'em."

Guthrie claims that the two were taken through the gas chamber only because this route was the quickest and the most private way out of Death Row. He acknowledges that among the party who met with Remiro and Little were several investigators from the state attorney general's office—men who were working on the Hearst case.

He says that Procunier did not participate in the two-hour meeting between the "soldiers" and Death Row Jeff, but stood outside the door the whole time.

"Afterwards he talked to them a little," says Guthrie, "and then he took the piece of paper from them that had to do with their demands and talked to them about their living conditions and like that. But Procunier's position is that he was not there to negotiate. He arranged the meeting hoping that something might come out of it helpful to bringing back Patty."

Randolph Hearst, who now had a couple of hundred newsmen, television cameramen, and still photographers camped on his front lawn in one of the biggest media conventions ever seen in America, also realized that some sort of a gesture had to be made to convince S.L.A. that the conditions Remiro and Little were complaining about were not so horrible after all. He was not eager to have them duplicated on his daughter. On February 18, he announced that he was appointing an old family friend as a sort of "ombudsman" to visit San Quentin and look in on Joe and Russ as well as to guarantee that they received a "fair trial and due process at all stages of the proceeding."

Attorney William Coblentz, nephew of one of William Randolph Hearst's most faithful friends and editors and a UC regent who had worked beside Catherine Hearst for ten years, was told to go have a look-see.

Coblentz reported that the prisoners were receiving "even-handed" treatment, and, as far as the media were concerned, that was that. (By this stage Hearst was clearing every major story that concerned the kidnap. No local paper or wire-service bureau would release anything without his approval.)

Remiro and Little, who claim they never saw Coblentz at San Quentin, were now working through the courts to get out of the grim penitentiary. Life was getting harder for them. No move beyond their cells could be made without an escort of half a dozen shotgun-carrying guards. Remiro says that one guard told him, "I'll blow your fucking head off the first time I get a chance." He says the same guard later promised to kill him after he'd been "convicted and sent back there."

Finally, on March 8, an Oakland judge, Stafford Buckley, visited San Quentin and decided that conditions the two prisoners faced were more than a bit "unusual." He ordered them transferred to the Almeda County Jail, near the courtroom where their initial hearings would soon begin in the Foster case, and he also guaranteed them a number of un-usual privileges, including five telephone calls a week (of almost any length) for each prisoner, extensive visiting rights, and the opportunity to send out messages and "communiqués" to newspapers and radio sta-tions. (Cynics might suspect these "favors" were granted in the hope of gathering badly needed intelligence information through whatever Remiro and Little wrote and said.)

The pair quickly took advantage of this situation and, early in April, sent out a message that contained their basic position on the Hearst kidnapping.

"We do not hold Patricia Hearst responsible for the actions of the Hearst Corporation or the part it plays within the ruling class," they wrote. "We do, in fact, admire the level of courage and objectivity she has displayed and send her our warmest regards.

"Patty, we feel that we have already done the most concrete thing we can do to assist in your safe release, by exposing the true intentions of the FBI, etc., to the public. We feel confident that the S.L.A. will release you unharmed. We realize, as you do, that the S.L.A. has con-sistently referred to our safety and well-being but, that in reality, you will not be harmed for anything that might happen to us. Actually, you're in a better position only as long as the S.L.A. can protect and keep you well hidden, until you can be released and returned safely to your fiancé. Who knows, you might even look back on this as a worthwhile experi-ence, where people were fed and you and the public were exposed to the cruelty and inhumanity of the corporate powers who rule this country. We look forward to receiving a visit from you, Patty, after you are released."

In the meantime, the food program was getting itself a little more together and, on February 28, some thirty thousand bags of groceries (worth between eight and fifteen dollars apiece) were given out in locations around the Bay Area.

The pandemonium that resulted from the first giveaway was now replaced by an almost too careful and tediously slow passing out of the food packages. In a typical food line in San Francisco, a few blocks from an apartment on Golden Gate Avenue where the S.L.A. would be hiding out from mid-March until the last week in April, it took almost four hours to get one skimpy bag of food.

Massive quantities of the groceries "disappeared" en route to the distribution centers (in one case, an entire truckload of meat) and tons more ended up in the private pantries of the "unselfish volunteers" who were supposed to give it to the poor. None of the procedures originally outlined by S.L.A. were followed, either in the manner of distribution or the requirement that certain forms of identification be asked for. Anyone who showed up got a bag of food—and as many times as he had patience to get in the line for.

Nevertheless, as long as the good weather held, the spirits of the thousands who came out for the long wait were high.

Direct press coverage of the handouts had been forbidden by Hearst and friends. There had been official threats and innuendos, and thousands who came out to wait in the food lines were understandably nervous. At the first handout, a television cameraman who ignored the media ban was severely beaten. (California Attorney General Younger had reluctantly given the People in Need program his blessing after making some remarks about those participating being "parties to an extortion." Humanitarian ol' Governor Ronald McDonald got up after an expensive luncheon for well-fed and powerful Republicans, surveyed his bloated constituents munching their rich pastries and sipping their imported brandy, and expressed himself freely on all those ungrateful poor people who'd had the nerve to accept free food from Hearst: "It's just too bad we can't have an epidemic of botulism," said he.)

A few writers for the underground papers who speak the language of the streets and who are generally as poor as the mostly black lumpenproletariat that made up the food lines simply joined in and got their story of the food program firsthand by waiting out the interminable delays and screw-ups during the five giveaways between February 28 and March 25, when Hearst's first $2.3 million ran out.

Wrote a San Francisco *Phonenix* reporter after he had ingested "a bellyful of revolutionary food . . . a stomach full of Hearst blood money": "It had been a warm, sunny day. The wait was long but the crowd (about three-quarters black) was in good spirits and a lot of good-natured kidding and horseplay went down. A number of the men arrived already stoned and got even higher on handy little pints of Ripple and Thunderbird and tall cans of Ranier and Colt 45. Nothing passed around, though. Nobody had enough for that.

"There's a little pushing and elbowing as people get close to the front of the line. A few cheaters are caught trying to cut in and are half-seriously jeered as they are ushered to the tail-end of the two-block-long crowd. One quick scuffle between a monitor and one of the cheaters who ends up on his ass in a vacant lot. It is done quickly and rather off-handedly by the tall young athlete who obviously knows his street fighting. He barely breaks his stride as he dumps the punk.

"No evidence of cops or photographers here. A few patrol cars and metermaids drive quickly by and are jeered by the crowd. 'Better get yo' ass OUT o' here, muthafuckah!' yells a fist-clenching young black six and a half feet tall who wears an African burnoose and a tight-fitting, brightly colored knit cap. 'We tole you muthafuckahs to stay WAY!'

"The cops eye him narrowly, slow down a bit but decide to keep moving. They obviously have their orders. Things will move the way the S.L.A. has demanded so long as the Hearst girl remains their captive. After that, then it may be a very different story.

"A sweet-faced, bespectacled old black lady barely five feet tall (who is raising her six grandchildren all by herself) tells me about her morning's work:

" 'Left my house over in Bayview 'bout nine-thirty,' she chirps up happily. 'Went on over to Hunters Point first an' got a big bagful. Then down over to Capp Street down 'n the Mission. They got turkeys 'n' HAMS down there. Just givin' tons o' them out. People lined up three blocks down Mission. Then on over to Mission High for another bagful an' finally over here. They gives it out Tuesday an' Thursday this week but I only wants to go shoppin' one day. Thas' enough.'

"We now begin to inch forward about a foot every ten minutes or so. More good-natured joshing and people begin to get to know each other and tell each other their tales. Now this *is* a revolutionary situation. The barriers that really count—walls of mutual suspicion and personal isolation which normally keep people apart and make it easier for the cold, antihuman industrial society to deal with them—*those* barriers are coming down and people in this line are beginning to feel a certain *oneness.*

"I hear the words 'sister' and 'brother' more and more frequently. People begin to help each other out. A woman arrives in a wheelchair and is immediately propelled to the front of the line. Two guys get news of a bedridden old man who cannot come down himself and stand in line for him so they can take bags of food up to his sickroom.

"There is a surge of energy and purpose here just waiting to be harnessed, just waiting to be pointed in some direction of overthrow and change. It is an exciting feeling and one the government is aware of and increasingly nervous about.

"You hear what people are doing and thinking. The schoolkids in front of me talk the usual cars and dope and girls. Two tough-looking dudes in back of me compare notes on San Quentin, Vacaville, Soledad, other joints they've been in. I remember that the only true revolutionaries running around loose in this society are guys like this, the ones who have had *everything* taken away from them by the system, guys who have nothing to lose.

" 'Man, they had me locked down like a DOG down there," one ex-con confides to the other, "like a fuckin' DOG!'

"A few lucky ones at the front of the line who have gotten their groceries already come back and show us their share of the Hearst Ransom: a frozen chicken, a two-pound can of Spam-like luncheon meat, a frozen pound or two of something called 'Beef and Textured Vegetable Protein.' There are a very few oranges, a few carrots, a box of buttermilk pancake mix, two cans of condensed milk. Maybe $12 to $15 worth of food in each bag.

"By the time I get to the front of the line, they're out of frozen chickens and oranges. They give me an extra roll of beef/vegetable protein crap. . . ."

By the time the third food handout is over, on March 5, grumbling about the People in Need program has reached the S.L.A. It's probable that the guerrilla army's members, and Patricia Hearst, have stood in line at the third handout and have seen for themselves how things went. They come away extremely pissed off and, on March 9, the Hearsts receive the fourth S.L.A. tape, which claims the PIN program "intended to shame the people by trying to distribute hog feed instead of top quality dry stuffs. Many people stood in long cold lines for only a bag full of cabbages while others stood in line and got nothing at all. The people know words don't make no bag of cabbages into meat."

S.L.A. rejected the offer of an additional four million dollars in food on Patty's release as no more than "trickery" and implied that the money had to be converted into food and given out *before* her release and not after.

"The Hearst empire has attempted to encourage division among the people by giving them crumbs to fight over," said S.L.A.

They reminded the Hearsts again that they had stated that "Patricia Campbell Hearst would be kept in accordance with international codes of war regarding prisoners of war and that she would be maintained in protective custody. It was further stated that the captive S.L.A. elements who stay at San Quentin would also have to be kept in accordance with such codes because of their legal POW status.

"The S.L.A. requested that Randolph and Catherine Hearst and the Hearst empire see to it that our comrades' conditions follow those guidelines. It was stated at that time that Patricia Hearst's condition would correspond at all times with that of the captured brothers. The S.L.A. has waited with disciplined patience for the agents of the fascist state, including the Hearst media empire, to deal with the conditions of our comrades' confinement.

"The Symbionese War Council, the Court of the People, had considered transferring Patricia Campbell Hearst to a security area which would physically correspond to a strip cell on Death Row in San Quentin concentration camp. This would be an obvious response to barbaric conditions which our comrades are forced to endure.

"However, after extensive nationwide intelligence and analysis by the Symbionese War Council, it became clear that the fascist corporate state and its chief domestic police agency, the FBI, and other police-state agencies and institutions intended to set up Patricia Hearst for execution in order to discredit and isolate the people's forces.

"This is shown by the deliberate disregard for the health, life and safety of Joseph Remiro and Russell Little and the plans of the police state agencies to see to it that Patricia Hearst is killed. . . .

"In response to Randolph Hearst's public request that Patricia Hearst be allowed to communicate periodically with her family in conjunction with international codes of war regarding prisoners of war, the Symbionese War Council has determined that communication between POW Patricia Hearst and her family will come only after the immediate creation of the necessary mechanisms whereby Russell Little and Joseph Remiro can communicate via live national TV with the people and the S.L.A. concerning the full scope of their physical health and all the conditions of their confinement."

Patty Hearst, who had turned twenty a little more than two weeks before the March 9 tape, had been a captive for more than a month now, and the strain was beginning to show. She had been listening to their revolutionary propaganda, reading such basic texts as George Jackson's *Blood in My Eye,* and apparently falling in love. She now echoed S.L.A.'s attitudes about a possible FBI "break-in" during which she would be deliberately killed, and she made it clear for the first time that she felt betrayed and abandoned by her father. It was obvious that she felt he had more than enough money to comply with S.L.A. food program demands but that he valued his money more than her life.

"I don't believe you're doing everything you can, everything in your power," she said. "I don't believe that you're doing anything at all. You said it was out of your hands; what you should have said was that you wash your hands of it."

Like Angela Atwood, who had opened the tape, Patty Hearst made a point of talking about Remiro and Little before she closed her eleven-minute portion of it:

"I have been reading a book by George Jackson," she said. "I'm starting to understand what he means when he talks about fascism in America. Joseph Remiro and Russell Little, the two men in San Quentin, haven't even come to trial yet and already they are being held in strip cells on Death Row. It's very hard to believe that this obvious violation of the Constitution is taking place, but it's true.

"How can people think that these men can get a fair trial? And if there's any doubt in people's minds of what the verdict will be, members of the federation are studying intelligence reports gathered by the S.L.A. on the activities of the FBI.

"These, combined with discussions the members of the federation have had with me and my own observations of the way my father's been conducting himself, have made me afraid because I realize that the plans are coming from the FBI and the attorney general's office in Washington to execute the two men in San Quentin.

"They want to hear what the two men have to say in a live nation-wide broadcast so they can hear all the conditions of their confinement. . . ."

Cinque, in another portion of the March 9 tape, again made it clear that S.L.A. considered the real bottom of society its natural following. "I call upon the robbers, the pimps, the drug addicts, the prostitutes, and all those who have been used as pawns against the people to turn their rage and violence toward the true enemy of the people," he said.

This angry outburst forced People in Need to completely revamp the original plan, which called for a continuing series of small food handouts. It was decided, instead, to give away the remainder of the original $2.3-million budget in one giant handout on March 25 in an effort to placate the Symbionese. Big boxes of food, containing generous quantities of decent but not really good meat, were handed out to over thirty thousand persons. The Hearsts had even printed up little two-by-three-inch stickers bearing the S.L.A. seven-headed cobra and had them pasted on the food boxes in a final attempt to reverse the tide of taped abuse.

But by this point it didn't really matter too much what the Hearsts did or did not do. They had already lost Patty, not just her body but her mind as well.

About mid-March the group had moved into the little three-room flat at 1827 Golden Gate Avenue, in an all-black neighborhood on the northwestern edge of the Fillmore district and a short walk from Haight-Ashbury. About a mile down Golden Gate, just east of Sacred Heart High, where Remiro had gone to school, stands the giant black marble-and-glass Federal Building. Inside its fancy suite of FBI offices, one of the biggest manhunts in history was being coordinated by Charles Bates. On a clear day he could have looked right down Golden Gate and seen the building where the S.L.A. lived for more than six weeks.

To be fair about it, Bates was having his problems. The barrage of publicity about the FBI's inability to "find" the Symbionese was making Washington nervous. And a money-hungry little man in Georgia was so inspired by S.L.A.'s example that he set up an imitation "American Revolutionary Army" and kidnapped another prominent media personality, Atlanta *Constitution* editor Reg Murphy. Murphy was soon found, but the fact that editors, publishers, and their progeny now seemed fair game to the revolutionists had made Oakland *Tribune* publisher William Knowland increasingly distraught.

On February 23 he was found dead near his country home. The coroner's report said suicide, but there was still talk around town that it had been the work of an urban guerrilla group. So the FBI was under great pressure from a growing body of rich and powerful citizens to quickly capture the Symbionese and make an example of them. But Bates just wasn't having any luck, and the rather hip population of San Francisco wasn't helping things any.

Marcus Foster had been completely forgotten by the street people by mid-March, and, despite screams of jealousy and rage from established left organizations, the Symbionese were really *in* by mid-March among both revolutionary blacks and the city's enormous white radical community. They had captured the imagination of thousands with the Hearst kidnap and the food program. This "victory in armed propaganda" was especially apparent in Haight-Ashbury and the Fillmore, where hundreds of "S.L.A. Lives" and "S.L.A. Feeds the Poor" slogans had been spray-painted on every available wall. There were a *lot* of sympathizers.

Clear evidence found later at Golden Gate shows that Patty had definitely joined the group before the end of March and that she was issued a weapon and ammunition and allowed to stand watch along with the rest of her "comrades." She was even occasionally allowed to go out shopping in the neighborhood by herself and it's probable that she stood on Divisadero Street just a few blocks from her hideout and watched the food program fuck-up in anger and disbelief. Dozens of black Fillmore residents recognized her and other prominent guerrillas wandering around the neighborhood. Nobody finked.

One of those who did more than her share to help S.L.A. was a tiny, intense, young black mother named Retimah X.

Originally a Black Muslim who thought "all white people were devils," Retimah says Cinque came to her home and asked her to go out and take care of details S.L.A. members could not attend to because of the real danger. By early April she was buying groceries, renting another hideout, even buying a car for them. She says they offered her money to do all of this, but she refused it.

"All these white people came from good homes," recalls Retimah with genuine admiration. "They didn't have to become revolutionaries, but they chose it themselves. Fahizah talked a lot about how important it was that blacks and whites get together, and every time I came up to Golden Gate she embraced me—they all did. I had never embraced a white before, but the S.L.A. changed my thinking about the race question."

Retimah, who would later have to face a grand jury and possible criminal charges for her role as an S.L.A. supporter, said that she saw as many as thirteen Symbionese Federation members at the little flat in the Fillmore and she was told that the group had, at that time, about twenty members and "dozens of sympathizers" who offered support of various kinds.

"Cinque was quiet and serious. He was clean-shaven and good-looking," Retimah recalls. "He was very believable. The women were all such small people and I sympathized with that, 'cause I'm small, too. The two white men, Teko and Cujo, kept saying that it was important that blacks finally believe that white revolutionaries would stand up and fight.

"Tania [Patty Hearst's "reborn name"] was also a little woman and she was really pissed at the way her parents had acted. She really thought they had betrayed her. She kept talking about what pigs they were."

All the S.L.A.ers were aware that the heat was getting heavier and heavier in San Francisco. The normal patrol of two San Francisco Police helicopters had been augmented by two to three unmarked FBI choppers. Plain-clothes and FBI units were stopping every car they saw driving through the area with both blacks and whites inside.

Sometime before May 1 the Symbionese decided they might have to move into an even more solidly black area, the Bayview–Hunters Point District, which had staged an armed uprising in '67 when ghettos in the East had also exploded. They got Retimah X to pay the landlady two months in advance on a $150-a-month dump in this area where no cab drivers will go after dark and even the cops are afraid.

In the meantime, the Symbionese had expanded their newspaper-reading habits. They started to study a scraggly underground paper I edited called the *Phoenix*. We began to run front-page notices late in February asking that "S.L.A. Please Contact."

On March 7, the paper printed a list of twenty questions addressed to the guerrillas seeking to get a better understanding of the group's "goals, attitudes, plan of action and personal philosophy." A rather audacious request when S.L.A. was the hottest band of fugitives in the country, but *Phoenix* had always been something of a maverick. The paper was definitely left of center but not self-consciously socialist or revolutionary. It concentrated mostly on cultural events and commentary from writers who were more often iconoclastic than militant. The request for answers on just *who* the Symbionese were and *what* they believed was a serious one.

The revolutionists, who then lived only a dozen blocks from the old Victorian house where *Phoenix* was put out, read the requests but did not, at first, respond. Then (stronger on imagination than good sense) I decided to run my *own* answers to the twenty questions, prefaced with a lot of double-talk about how this "may" be an interview because "the style and content is so similar to other S.L.A. communications that we consider it a distinct possibility." I had every reason to believe this, since I'd spent two weeks carefully splicing and rewriting portions of the already voluminous Symbionese communiqués and tapes together to provide answers that were faithful to the style, spirit, and philosophy of the group. It was such a good job that S.L.A. later would incorporate portions of what I'd written into their own pronouncements. They fit perfectly.

Nevertheless, the guerrillas took their public image too seriously to let this mini-scam get by. They decided to call me on it, firmly but not in the lethal way they might have. For they'd also read a second, analytical, article we'd run alongside the "interview," and they dug it. It was the first accurate historical piece on S.L.A. and writing it saved my ass.

Over in Alameda County Jail, Joe Remiro was also reading the twenty questions and the "maybe" interview that supposedly answered them. Later he'd say:

"Those twenty questions, man, Russ and I went through them once and never read them again, although I *did* think the interview was real. We read the article you wrote after that ten times each . . . I tell ya, it was one of the most fantastic things I've ever read."

On April 6, Remiro telephoned *Phoenix* and dropped a *real* interview in my lap. He spoke for more than an hour, and he would soon be calling me every second or third day with hours more of the same.

But S.L.A. beat him to it.

On April 2—a few hours late for April Fool's Day—the Symbionese dealt the *Phoenix* a real joker.

16

"The twenty questions and answers you came up with were there for anyone who cared to take an objective look. That was no great feat nor is it something to be ashamed of—the S.L.A. didn't contact you because of that—the follow-up article you wrote in that same issue was fantastic. Your analysis put these intellectuals—Marxists, Leninists, Maoists, Dogmatists—to shame. You told it like it is, put it where it's at and had the courage to publish it. . . ."
—First letter to the *Phoenix* from Joe Remiro

"CLICK-CLICK-CLICK. Click-click-click."

It sounds like a key rapping nervously against the thick beveled window set high in my front door. By the time I get out there, the messenger has split. His tacky old florist's truck pulls away from the curb and bumps down steep, old Beaver Street.

I'm a little sleepy, been up writing all night. I pad out onto the front porch in my stocking feet to blink disbelievingly into the late-morning glare and discover the guy has left me a green-wrapped package of flowers.

I sniff the hard-blown wind of a fresh spring morning and pick them up. It's overcast, as usual, but it looks as though the sun will burn through by noon. A dangerous day, with an overlay of surprise on it.

"Who the fuck sent these?" I wonder.

I pad half-awake across the living room–office of the comfortably sloppy Victorian flat, past the paste-up tables, the overpriced cold-typesetting machine from IBM, the stacks of ancient books and magazines that provide us with instant collage every publication day.

I'm mildly curious about the flowers, but my mind is still locked on to the present issue, which must be put out, as usual, nearly single-handed and damned fast. Final typesetting is tonight. Paste-up's to-morrow, and printing is Thursday. Not much time. No help but it looks like a quiet issue. Not a bad issue, but nothing special, not the kind of thing they taught you was "good and solid and newsworthy" all those years you worked on the dailies. But it will have to do. A good issue to turn on what's left of the old "liberal-intellectual community," which still forms the backbone of the subscription-buying readership. It will bore the younger, more radically political types. But all that S.L.A. stuff has been getting a bit heavy and it's time for a break. Besides, that scam you did the last time with the resurrected "interview" was going a bit far. It's time to back off.

I amble distractedly over to the groovy old maple bookkeeper's desk, the kind Bob Cratchit would have loved, and plop down the package of flowers. Now who in the hell . . . ? I decide it's just a many-petaled apology from the old socialist film critic who is now two days late with her copy. She probably wrapped the reviews inside. Maybe she got that job doing PR for the Opera and this is a thank you for turning her on to it.

I open the green wrapping paper and a dozen long-stemmed American Beauty roses roll out, looking and smelling like dewy-eyed apology. Underneath the roses I spot a long, fat envelope. My name and address are written inside a big valentine's heart. Ya, it's gotta be Margo. She's just that corny.

I think about other things as I open the envelope—the usual lack of advertising, the hassle I've had with my wife that morning, mostly my fault. I'm tired again. Inside there are several pages of typewritten copy, about as expected—only it doesn't look like *Margo's* copy.

And there's one of those silly, two-bit, so-called humorous greeting cards. On the outside it says, "Guess What?" There's a badly done clip-art drawing of a stork with a baby bundle in his bill. (Oh, for Chrissake! At *her* age?)

I flip the card open. Inside it says, "Happy Birthday." (But it's *not* my birthday. Although yesterday *was* April Fool's Day.) It also says, "Scared the hell out of you, didn't I?" A little piece of photo paper floats down out of the card as I open it, and I have to stoop and scrape it off the floor. It's a funny-looking little triangle—half a driver's license, as it turns out.

ooops!

Suddenly I wake up. There in my hand is just enough evidence to rapidly convince me that I've really *done* it this time. Me and my fucking fake interviews! It's the right-hand half of a California driver's license. I can still read two letters of the middle name—"ll"—and the last name, Hearst. There's just a portion of an address on the top. Then I study the signature—"Patricia Campbell Hearst." There's a neatly sliced photograph of the young woman on the bottom. Not all of the face is there, but it's enough to recognize quickly. The lady has been in the headlines lately, and this is most decidedly her driver's license.

My stomach explodes and I race through the four sheets of copy. Top sheet: "Communiqué No. 7" from the Symbionese Liberation Army. Second sheet: Directions on how to handle the release of the top sheet and the two pages underneath. They are "Codes of War." I glance at them . . . finks and traitors will be executed. (Do they mean *me?* Now you've done it!)

I call my wife:

"Joan! Joan! For Chrissake, come here! The fucking Symbionese are at it again. They sent me a communiqué. And a birthday card. And some roses. Come here!"

There is really no need to yell at her. She's disgustingly psychic and knows at once what I'm hollering about. She's been plugged into the S.L.A. story for months now, with that crystal-ball TV-news mind of hers whirring out possibilities, angles, conjectures. She got me into this mess in the first place and I wish to hell I'd never even heard of these fuckers. What's next, a cyanide bullet?

Joan runs in barefoot and grabs the handful of documents and sucks them into her raging mentality by instant osmotic flush-drain. She knows immediately what's happened, and she explodes with ideas.

"We've got to do what the S.L.A. wants," she says, "get copies of all of this to the three radio stations, release the messages to the rest of the media, get our own act together, and headline this story ourselves. We've got to completely tear up this issue of the paper!"

I read the communiqué again more carefully. They've really dropped a jewel in our laps, the first good news to come out of the whole affair—they're going to release Patty Hearst! Says Communique No. 7, dated April 1:

"SUBJECT: Negotiations and Release of Prisoner.

"Herein enclosed are the Codes of War of the Symbionese Liberation Army, these documents, as all S.L.A. documents, are to be printed in full and omitting nothing by order of this court in all forms of the media.

"Further communications regarding subject prisoner will follow in the following 72 hours. Communications will state the state, city and time of release of the prisoner."

The signature is "I.I. Unit 4, Gen. Field Marshal Cin, S.L.A."

Another sheet contains only one paragraph of instructions. It reads:

"This communication is to be sent through you to the people. You are hereby directed by the Court of the People to notify immediately radio stations KPFA, KSAN and KDIA concerning the complete contents of this communication, understanding that you must not cooperate with the F.B.I. by turning over this communication or by providing them with any information. Protect your rights as reporters by refusing to reveal your sources of information."

And then there are two pages of the "Codes of War," the fourth major S.L.A. document to be released and obviously a statement of basic principles that must go into the media before the group can announce any disciplinary actions against those former members who have betrayed it.

The "Codes" (to be found in full in the Appendix) order death for S.L.A. members who surrender, kill a comrade or cause the death of a buddy by disobeying orders, desert a fellow soldier on the "field of war," inform to the cops, or split without orders. It says that all paid or unpaid informants will be executed, and it gives specific day-to-day rules for discipline within the "Army," including laws on the use of booze and drugs, handling of prisoners, and relations with the general population during the "war" S.L.A. has declared against the United States. It's a very important document and one which, by hook or by crook, they obviously want published immediately. That's why they're using you.

Problems:

1. How do you release *all* this stuff to the three hip radio stations and portions of it to the rest of the media without handing over the documents themselves and providing any information to the feds on how it landed in your hands?

2. What does this mean in relation to the dumb scam you just pulled, running a rewrite of old S.L.A. documents and calling it an "interview"? Will their next communiqué be a volley of poison bullets?

Nerves.

OK. You answer the first question fairly fast. You make Xeroxes of everything, keep the driver's license but put the original documents into the safe of a radical lawyer you trust. You'll fight for their possession in court before giving them to the feds. That's your right as a newsman.

The S.L.A. didn't have to tell you the rules about protecting your working papers and refusing to reveal your sources. That's a basic civil-liberties fight you've been waging for years, for you know that no reporter should cop out on his sources. It's not only immoral—they'll never again trust him, and then he's useless as a journalist. If the FBI wants this information, let them go out and spend two bits for a newspaper like everyone else.

As to releasing the stuff, you give everything to KDIA (the black station), KPFA (the radical Berkeley outlet), and KSAN (the "underground" San Francisco wavelength), just as the Symbionese have instructed. As for the rest of the media, many of them junior G-men who hang out with the cops because they like to, forget it. Give them the wordage but don't let them photocopy anything but the driver's license. Photocopies would show the typewriter used and could even reveal fingerprints. They could end up as evidence.

As to whether the S.L.A. is setting you up for something, who knows? Let's see how things develop. But don't forget—yesterday *was* April Fool's Day. The Cobra People take themselves seriously, and they bite! They obviously read your last issue and there may be a few surprises ahead.

In any case, it's turning out to be a *very* interesting day.

By 1:30 that afternoon (two and a half hours after the flower-drop), I've got the details attended to and have called the three radio stations. Then I tip Associated Press and the dailies (but not UPI, which is on strike and operating with scabs).

The medialice are down upon us by 2:00 P.M., and it's pretty much routine press-conference nonsense. The TV boys (more actors than newsmen) try to take over like they always do, but I make sure the print media get the first break. TV "reporters" take longer anyway. They keep forgetting things and asking for repeats, so I have to read the communiqué and the attached instructions over and over again. It gets to be a bore, but the free advertising is most welcome and I'll do it all day if I have to.

An aging peroxide blonde who has somehow landed a job on the town's only noncommercial television station (that once-liberal bastion of cool, clear Adlai Stevenson fairness) barges in and starts to throw her plastic-gutted weight around.

She can't *understand* why we don't want the FBI in the house. *She* always tells them everything, even if she has to make it up. She throws a childish fit on the spot.

In saunters the Mod Squad hack from the big morning sheet. He's more together than the raging blonde lady but quickly makes it clear that the urban guerrillas are *beneath* him socially. All the revolutionaries he knows joined SDS for kicks while pursuing a course in business administration at some elegant Eastern university. This is the guy who's supposed to represent the "new left," and his grand illogic has led to the dailies' attacking S.L.A. because it offends the sensibilities of Rennie Davis and Jerry Rubin. They've even begun to speak fondly of the Weather Underground. The Hearst paper finds Weather leader Bernadine Dohrn infinitely preferable to Donald DeFreeze and his buddies. Bernadine laughs her ass off.

The afternoon *Examiner* (Hearst's ailing mastodon) sends out a nice, sweet-tempered old guy I used to work beside on the court beat— the dude who almost got us both busted one morning in the summer of '64.

He'd smelled me toking up in our private little toilet right next to Department 33, Superior Court, City and County of San Francisco.

"Hey, John!" he yelled through the antique frosted glass of the bathroom door. "You got some GAGE *in there? Hey, man, I ain't had no gage since nineteen-and-forty-three down in some* TEA PAD *in li'l ol' Harlem."*

Naturally, I rolled him a couple of numbers. It was good weed, and old Hank sucked it in like there was no tomorrow. He hadn't been high in twenty years, and the effect was really comic.

"Hey, MAN!*" he yelled, loud enough for the judge and jury next door to hear every word. "That's dynamite* GAGE! *Why don't you roll up a couple more o' them* MUGGLES *an' we'll just stroll over to the State Building an' cover a li'l ol' pension hearing?"*

Figuring it was going to be some boring and inconsequential affair— just a bunch of retired typists or janitors demanding a few more bucks for their doddering senility—I rolled up a handful of nice, thick numbers and stuffed them into my trouser pocket. Sure, I was holding, but who was going to bust a nice, respectable young reporter like me?

Hank and I made it across the street flying low.

He kept rushing up to prominent judges and politicians he'd known for years, whooping and hollering and throwing his wide and friendly arms around them. They gave him their best shit-eating grins and went away shaking their heads. "Drunk—and at this *hour of the morning!"*

We highballed into the sedate old State Building, and Hank unin-

*tentionally knocked down the armed guard who stands just inside the
entrance. Luckily they were friends, and the guy smiled sheepishly and
put his gun away as he got up off the floor.*

*The hearing room was to our left, and Hank crashed through the
double doors like the Schlitz Malt Liquor bull looking for an open
icebox. Every eye in the room turned toward the intrusion.*

*And then it hit me! Man, I'd seen at least half these dudes before.
They were* NARCS! *It was the* entire *State Narcotics Squad, down
here to lobby for bigger pensions because they had to deal with all of
these really* dangerous, *vicious, Commie Dope Fiends. Like us.*

*I remembered the pocketful of reefers, thrust my hand deep down
into it as though I were trying to crush them out of existence, and cast
my dilated pupils toward the floor. I wanted to disappear, but Hank
was still whooping and hollering as we made it down the aisle to the
very front of the room, where the press table was set in such a way that
we half faced this whole room full of narcs.*

*I got Hank into his seat and whispered, "For Chrissake, Hank,
cool it! We're right in the middle of the* HEAT!" *He toned down a bit,
and, at the first break, I managed to sneak into the men's room and
flush my pocketful of joints down the toilet. What a waste! But, boy,
that was close! At the end of the meeting, the Chief State Narc marched
over to the press table and told Hank he'd bust him if he ever came into
the State Building that stoned again. Then he turned to me: "And who's
your friend?" he asked, totaling up a twenty-year sentence in his cold,
gray eyes. After that, Hank wanted to wander around a bit—visit his
old buddy the attorney general and then make a side trip over to the
FBI. I begged off. I had an unbelievable headache.*

This is the grand old dude the *Examiner* has sent to get the story
and then take me down to Hillsborough so I can give Daddy Hearst a
firsthand report on what the S.L.A. is into these days. I also decide to slip
Hearst the hunk of driver's license they've sent me. It belongs to his
daughter, and I decide that, legally and morally, it's my obligation to
put it in the hands of her family. So, as soon as we've gotten rid of the
last of the TV and radio latecomers, we go out on the front porch for
a quick confrontation with the FBI and then off to Hillsborough in an
Examiner camera car.

(They are pissed I won't hand over their "evidence." The one who
introduces himself only as "McCloud" is courteous but insistent. "Mc-
Cloud?" I say. "Oh, are you that lawman I see on television? That

cowboy I see riding his horse down Fifth Avenue every week?" He just glowers. "And what's your first name, Mr. McCloud?" I ask, taking out my notebook to get the facts. "Ay-junt," says he in that delightfully broad Texas accent of his. "An' ah can get downright naaasty when ah has to!")

We bid the FBI a fond adieu and head south toward Hearstonia. It seems like old times—I'd ridden almost identical camera cars day after day when on assignment in '60–'63. Even the photog is an old buddy. We begin to reminisce about all the drinking we did a decade ago and nearly say "Fuck Hillsborough" and head over to Breen's to see if they still know how to make a triple martini. Hank talks us out of it.

The sun is just setting as we pull off the freeway and wind around some nicely wooded and increasingly affluent suburban streets to the two-story Hearst mansion—not a castle or anything like that, but twenty-two rooms will do nicely for starters. It's my first trip down here.

I'd worked for Randolph Hearst's family for a total of nearly five years as both a reporter and an editor, but, needless to say, I'd never met the man or his brothers. The publishers of the big Hearst papers don't consort with the hired hands any more than Jefferson Davis was in the habit of running down to the cotton fields to sip mint juleps with his slaves. ("Oh all us nigguhs, we just *love* workin' for you, Massah Hearst! An' you, *too,* Miz Catherine.")

The roadside next to the high brick wall in front and the lawn just within are jam-packed with a lazy swarm of reporters and photographers. There are big TV vans, miles of power cables, lights, and tripods set up all over the grass and driveway awaiting the next press-conference extravaganza. We carefully negotiate our way through all of this and the mediamen (who have no idea what we're here for) grudgingly let us past with an irritated buzz like a swarm of fat blue flies being chased off their favorite dog turd.

Inside the front door I am met with an atmosphere of careful elegance—dozens of really fine antiques and art works straight from San Simeon mixed somewhat haphazardly with contemporary overstuffed furniture from a high-class but tasteless department store. It is obviously a well-lived-in house, but there is a certain cold formality in the air, a humorless rigidity.

Randolph Hearst reminds me of Nelson Rockefeller. He is media-wise and always on his political toes, but he's much too rich and powerful to really *care* what is said or written about him. He's about the same age and height as Rockefeller, also wears horn-rimmed glasses, seems alike in temperament, and comes from a somewhat similar economic and cultural background, although Randolph exudes a more calculatingly informal Western style—he's definitely a Californian.

Hearst seems to take up a lot of space, even in a large room, but he manages to gracefully dominate without intruding. He's widely built, with large bones and a rather square and placid face. His clothing is tweedy and well tailored—correct but not uncomfortable. Those large glasses seem to imprison a somewhat saddened pair of tired and world-weary eyes. He's seen too much already.

He had been drinking when I get there, and this may have made him a bit more hearty than usual. I realize that, despite the cordial reception, Randolph Hearst would not normally be caught dead giving me the time of day. But these are not ordinary circumstances. We are in the midst of a superpublicized personal and political crisis that alters everything it touches, and Hearst bends over backward to be agreeable and make a good impression on a normal enemy he now believes can help him get his daughter back.

The whole thing strikes me as a little weird. It is as though the revolution has already been won and here we sit among the Hearst antiques like October soldiers getting stinko in the winter palace of the czar. Yet we have experienced no real change, just the stop-time quality that seems to permeate the entire drama of the S.L.A. All of the characters in this extended play are in a state of temporary suspension like some frozen celluloid hero in an ancient Keystone Komedy the moment after someone has pulled the plug on the projector. There they wait, one silly foot raised skyward, one awkward arm thrust into nothingness, half a smile beginning to form on an idiot face, three-quarters of a thought hanging in a time-locked brain. You know that all of these people will, at some point soon, get back into their regular lives. The Hearsts must soon go back to making money. Stephen Weed must now trudge forward into full professorship—with or without his darling Patty. Even Joe Remiro must go *somewhere* once judgment has been rendered. But, at the moment, you feel this strange and terrible overtone of waiting that engulfs Hillsborough like a coldly tidal dream. Sooner or later someone is going to find the switch. Sooner or later these lives must plug back in.

So there I sit with Randolph Hearst. Instinctively I like him, but this seems a good time to move with caution. Within that velvet glove he now so graciously extends lies a fist of steel, and he still possesses the power to deliver a lethal blow to anyone foolish enough to cross his certain plans.

Catherine Hearst joins us, and it's hate at first sight.

She may or may not have been briefed as to who and what I am (I've been introduced as a "former employee"), but Catherine exudes all the charm of a matronly iceberg looking for the *Titanic*. It is probably more of an instinctual than an intellectual reaction, for she *senses* the heresy within her pious home.

From the moment she enters the room in an expensively tailored wool suit, her heavily made-up, over-fifty face fixed in an immovable mask of frigid propriety, her well-lacquered coiffure holding every hair in regimented place, I feel her horrified eyes locked upon my embarrassed face. It would be impolite to say she stared. It is, after all, *her* home, and she has every right to carefully regard this underground editor with suspicion. But after these cold and unforgiving eyes have pierced me for ten or fifteen minutes, I find I can no longer look tactfully away and soon our eyes are locked into a mutual glare that is anything but loving. I know very little about her background, just that she met "Randy" while he was doing the obligatory stint as a reporter on the Hearst paper in Atlanta (the *Georgian*) in the mid-'30s. That this daughter of a telephone-company executive, a debutante and Junior Leaguer, was noted for her piety and extremely orthodox frame of reference. I get the impression that she's a little dull but no one has ever had the balls to tell her so.

My words at this point are careful and as considerate as I can make them. I tell the Hearsts that I feel intense sympathy for them, that I have a daughter, too, and that if anyone were to kidnap her I'd be out of my mind by now and I'd do *anything* to get her back. I say I'm glad to be bringing them some good news for a change, and then I read the exact language of Communiqué No. 7 with its promise of complete data on Patty's release within seventy-two hours.

I also read them the instructions I have received from the Symbionese, which, I note, sort of put me in the middle. I am charged with giving out the *content* of what they sent but must withhold *the papers themselves,* all except the driver's license, which I say belongs to them.

I hand it over to Randolph Hearst and prepare to leave. I'm glad to be getting out from under those twin guns that Catherine calls eyes. But Randolph wants to talk, and talk he does. Two or three very strong and generous drinks later—he keeps calling them "stirrups," like some

English country gentleman—our conversation becomes well lubricated. We have to interrupt the discussion to take care of some pressing business. First there's a typing job to do, copying the communiqué and Codes of War so that the *Examiner* will have a careful and exact duplicate to print the following morning. That takes nearly an hour, and I work in the Hearst family room with Randolph, Catherine, and several of their daughters and sons-in-law hanging over me. Hank and some other Hearst newsmen help me set things up and do the copyreading. It's like old times, grinding out a story with these guys again.

Then there has to be a press conference. The twirpy little TV newsman who has become a family retainer and the "go-between" to the press insists upon it. A lot of the Hillsborough media crew did not make it up to San Francisco to get the communiqué at the *Phoenix* office. They simply sat on their well-paid asses down in this comfortable retreat of the very rich and waited for the Hearsts to hand the news to them on a platter. This has become the "normal" way for most to cover this complicated story. Some of these reporters have come halfway around the world to cover events from the front lawn of this house. They report only what they are told and end up docile serfs encamped loyally around the ramparts of Hearst's Media Manor, resisting all intruders, and all serious questions, for months on end.

So we get up and begin to walk out onto the front porch for a conference in which I will explain what I've gotten and Hearst will comment on the message itself and attempt to interpret it. The whole situation seems surreal as I amble out there between the two Hearsts, out that door and onto the front pages of the world.

Hearst has also become aware of the incongruity of this situation. It has begun to sink into his weary brain just who and what I am. A few minutes before we walk out to face the reporters, I make it clear that I am one of the three men who founded the underground press in America. I stand for all that he suspects and hates. I have long and loudly opposed everything his newspapers support. I represent a way of thinking and living that is almost beyond his comprehension. To Catherine Hearst, I am clearly the enemy.

So it is more than strange that we should meet this way and then appear so publicly together, and I sort of want to get it over with. The publicity is great, but I feel uncomfortable down here. I do not want to bring any more grief into a bad situation—just hand over the driver's license, make a quick statement, and get the hell home.

But it just doesn't work out that way. I'll be in the house for almost three hours before all this is done, and with that much time involved a confrontation is bound to occur. Randolph brings things out into the open just before the press conference. I've been introduced as a former newsman who quit two good jobs on Hearst papers. He wants to know why, and I begin to tell him about it. I've gotten as far as the famous "Castration of Christ on Christmas Day Caper" in Los Angeles when we reach the front door and prepare to go out.

(I'd resigned because a Jesus Freak art director on the Herald-Examiner *had insisted on airbrushing the cock and balls off the infant Jesus, who appeared on several pages of a special Christmas rotogravure section in 1966. I'd chosen the photos and laid them out. The "offensive" pictures happened to include a Rubens and a Veronese that originally had been owned by one William Randolph Hearst.)*

Catherine overhears the story and looks as though she's about to croak. The old man is laughing. He thinks it's amusing.

She bites her lower lip. He stifles a belly laugh and we're out the door. We face a truly Daliesque scene.

The sun has set by now, but there is still a faint red afterglow on the western horizon. An enormous crowd of media covers the entire front lawn. It is the biggest such gathering I have ever seen, and for a moment they frighten me. They seem more like a lynch mob than a journalism convention. They swarm in upon us as we appear on the front porch, and a sea of expensive cameras click in unison like an orchestra of angry crickets. Reporters scurry back and forth between the front of the house and a long line of red-and-white princess telephones that seem to grow organically out of every tree along the roadside. So much television lighting is focused upon us that it's soon as hot as midday.

But it's not really worth worrying about. It turns out to be just one more of those dumb canned conferences where nothing meaningful is said. There are no interesting questions—questions seem, in fact, to be discouraged. Any attempt I make to bring in something controversial is squelched. I make the suggestion, for instance, that as reporters we should all resist efforts on the part of the government to seize our working notes and force us to reveal our sources of information—we are newsmen, not unpaid informers. I am met with a giant hiss of outrage and find myself grateful that no one has brought a rope. It is quickly obvious that this gathering totally identifies with Hearst and the FBI and unpopular ideas will not be tolerated here. I have never seen so many reverent and uncritical people posing as journalists.

The press conference over, I shake Hearst's hand and start to split. The *Phoenix* is now running a day behind schedule and I have to get home and get a paper together. Certainly this is a problem he'll understand. But he stares at me in disbelief. I have not been dismissed. He stands just inside his front door beckoning me with an insistent index finger. Ooops, sorry boss. I zip back in.

Time for another "stirrup" or two? Sure. Catherine is not pleased to see me back and soon retreats. Her place is taken by a fat, jiveass black man who gives out some nonsense about once being a "radical" in L.A. He's obviously a bodyguard and/or an FBI man, and he keeps a very close eye on me. He occasionally interrupts the conversation when we get into areas that displease him.

Nevertheless, it's good to finally talk without the emotional drain of Catherine's frosty presence. Get a drink or two into him and old Randolph comes on like one of the boys. (Up to a rather carefully defined point.) But when Catherine's around, things are different. This family is obviously a matriarchy. Randolph Hearst seems to have basically fair instincts, and you begin to wonder whether the whole S.L.A. story would have gone down differently if Catherine had not been involved. But then you look hard at Randolph and remember that little of the real harm in the world is done by easily identifiable villains. Most of it comes from well-intentioned and powerful men who bumble through life unable to see themselves or the havoc they spread around them.

The conversation turns again to my earlier criticisms of the Hearst press. It is not the first time Randolph has heard this kind of talk. But I am surprised to find that he has never read the more important critics of mass media. He has not, for instance, even *heard* of A. J. Leibling's famed "Wayward Press" column that ran for so many years in the *New Yorker*. He seems to know very little about his father's notorious history. I get the impression that this is a man who has spent more time worrying about his bank balance than the editorial content of his newspapers.

A lot of the criticism I lay down was first put on Randolph Hearst by his favorite daughter. It was Patricia who told him more than a year ago that his newspapers are now relics from another century and that no one of her generation even *bothers* to read the *Examiner*. She urged that Hearst papers be redesigned, that they finally seek out some of the true social issues of their time.

I remind him of Patricia's opinions as gently as possible and try to explain my belief that her kidnap was definitely a product of the *Examiner*'s stodgy, socially irresponsible attitudes. I try to explain why

Berkeley radicals might feel that Hearst is the enemy, why it was *his* family the S.L.A. has chosen for their outrageous attack.

I do all of this politely and rapidly because he has *asked* me to, not because I want to upset the man or bring more trouble to an already troubled house. I want to get it done with, for I long ago gave up thinking I could instantly change the opinions of a fifty-nine-year-old millionaire who runs the country to suit himself.

Yet it *is* a fascinating opportunity, and Hank, a Hearst hack for nearly thirty years, moves in close to catch every word. You can see his eyes widen as you put out these heresies and the excitement rises, along with the booze, to flush his gentle old face. This is the kind of talk every honest newsman the two of you have ever known would like to lay on the management. It's the kind of talk you traded in a City Hall pressroom ten years ago. But neither of you ever expected to say it to the *boss.* Yes, it is too good a chance to miss, and you start to warm to the task even though you do not expect to alter one molecule in Randolph Hearst's prefabricated brain.

You then talk about the real issues today. You say that America is on the brink of a depression that will make the '30s look like a temporary shortage of butter 'n' egg money. The international situation is strongly against us. The world has gotten sick of American military and economic aggressiveness. Vietnam has outraged mankind. The world will no longer allow us to play the cops of the planet for our own amusement and profit. The Nixon Watergate fiasco has drained what little confidence remained in the national government. Never has the system been so distrusted. The '60s dream of peaceful integration has turned into a separatist '70s nightmare, with more ghetto-burning and full-scale race war just over the horizon.

The big cities have become racial and economic battlefields. (Oakland, for instance, has reported an unemployment rate of over 10 percent. Double that for the true level of misery just across the Bay.) Our prisons are jam-packed, and they spew thousands of dedicated revolutionaries back onto the streets. The Establishment responds by hiring more cops and buying more armaments. All hell is about to break loose.

Hearst answers with a long and pointless story about a recent tour he's taken of black schools in the South. He wishes to appear liberal, a concerned gradualist, a believer in political evolution but completely within the present system. Wait, he says. Take your time. Nothing can be changed in a day.

He can afford to wait. A hungry family on welfare living in a rat-infested tenement cannot. An ex-con going nowhere but back to jail will not. A freaked-out and jobless Namvet whose prime skill is mass murder has already had it with waiting. The time is past for this kind of gradualism, I say. The time is here for immediate and meaningful change. He says that things are not really *that* bad. (Not for him, that is.) I suggest he forget to pay his next parking ticket and then take a one-night "tour" of a big city jail as a prisoner. I suggest he move back into Central City if he's to earn the right to edit a San Francisco paper, that he send his children to the public schools, ride the busses and streetcars instead of a long, black limousine, try to walk the streets at night and then tell me what he thinks of "law 'n' order."

He respectfully declines.

I begin to get a little carried away with an outrageous idea. I begin to wonder if this whole insane S.L.A. experience might not produce something important after all, at least for one family named Hearst. I begin to believe that maybe, just maybe, the S.L.A. number might so shock and outrage Randolph, his board of directors, his editors and writers, that some significant and socially meaningful changes could occur at his newspapers.

What makes this idea grow strong is our discussion of the dramatic and unprecedented series of meetings Hearst has undertaken with dozens of radicals and reformers who sought to serve as "middlemen" in the delicate negotiations with S.L.A., people Hearst would never have otherwise met.

I suggest that he certainly *must* have learned a little something from his visits to Vacaville to confer with Death Row Jeff; he must have absorbed a bit from Popeye Jackson and Dennis Banks of the Indian movement and Cesar Chavez of the Farm Workers. Certainly all of this intense and highly dramatic conversation must have made him think. Certainly he's going to change a few things in his own life and at the papers he dominates. He nods his head in agreement, but it is more a matter of politeness than conviction.

I start to leave again. He wants me to talk and drink some more, and, though I sense a certain loneliness in the man, I have to decline and remind him that I've still got a newspaper to put out. Perhaps another day.

I leave, hoping that maybe, just maybe, this man will change. Maybe the impossible *will* happen and the Hearst newspapers will join the twentieth century.

Perhaps I put too much emphasis on this, perhaps it's because I worked for so many years on two of those papers and I so badly wanted to improve them. It's strange to discover I still care.

I get home and plow into my greatly enlarged load of work. I'm up all night and most of the next, and we get out an interesting issue. I never see or hear from Randolph Hearst again, and nothing ever changes at the San Francisco *Examiner*.

17

"I have chosen to stay and fight."
—Patricia Hearst

I N LESS THAN TWENTY-FOUR HOURS, the S.L.A. would make all of the bustle and confusion caused at the *Phoenix* by Communiqué No. 7 utterly pointless. Patty would take care of that all by herself.

At about noon on April 3, station KSAN received the fifth and most famous of the S.L.A. communications, the incredible "Tania Tape," in which Cinque would announce that "the subject has been freed but has refused to go home or take part as a member of the enemy fascist state. There is no further need to discuss the release of the prisoner under this condition since the prisoner is now a comrade and has been accepted into the ranks of the people's army. . . ."

The announcement, which amounted to one of the greatest propaganda coups in American history, left the Hearsts and their small army of media retainers absolutely flabbergasted. This was the one thing they had not imagined possible. Every conceivable excuse and apology was offered to explain away Patricia's action, everything from "Chinese brainwashing" to a devious James Bond sort of plot in which the girl had been forced to make the tape and was then killed. Every reason was offered except the obvious one, that she was young and romantic, had fallen in love with one of the guerrillas, had come to accept their politics, and was outraged at the way her parents had screwed around while her life was at stake.

The two things that enraged her the most were the mishandling of the food program and her mother's acceptance, a few weeks before the "Tania Tape," of a reappointment by Ronald Reagan to a second sixteen-year term as a UC regent. Such an act was really *cold*.

S.L.A. had made it clear shortly after the kidnapping that Catherine's acts while on the Board of Regents had been one of their prime motives and justifications. A mother who really cared about her child would have resigned immediately from the board, hoping to get the girl back safely. Instead, Ms. Hearst had the nerve to publicly accept reappointment as a regent while Patty was still a *captive* and while everyone at Hillsborough was (publicly) crying, wringing their hands, and worrying out loud about all the danger she was in. As Patty put it:

"My mother's acceptance of the appointment to a second term as a UC regent, as you well knew, would have caused my immediate execution had the S.L.A. been less than 'together' about their political goals. Your actions have taught me a great lesson, and in a strange kind of way, I'm grateful to you. . . ."

With bitterness overflowing, she called her father a "corporate liar" and said "it should be obvious that people who don't even care about their own children couldn't possibly care about anyone else's children. The things which are precious to these people are their power and money. . . ."

The best-publicized family spat on record then focused on Stephen Weed, who also struck out in Patty's newly revolutionary ball game.

"You don't know what's happened since then [February 4, the day of the kidnap]," said Patty in a voice that alternated between militant stridency and adolescent rage. "I have changed—grown. I've become conscious and can never go back to the life we led before. What I'm saying may seem cold to you and to my old friends, but love doesn't mean the same thing to me any more. . . ."

A disbelieving Weed would make one last attempt to win his lover back, an abortive trip to Mexico City to meet with Regis Debray to obtain a letter from the master revolutionary urging Patty to see her family once again and not to defame the name "Tania" she had taken in honor of Che Guevara's one-time mistress. S.L.A. ignored Debray completely.

With the question of Patty's gun-toting future settled, S.L.A. sought to use this last tape, the contents of which would definitely be printed in full, to try to gather recruits for the revolution. Angela Atwood said that Cinque, now installed not only as General Field Marshal of the guerrilla forces but also as "Chairman of the United Symbionese War Council," had only one word for the people: "COME!"

More recruiting slogans were uttered by Bill Harris. Then Nancy Ling Perry came on heavy with an introductory speech for Cinque that would have made the average Kiwanis Club toastmaster green with envy.

"Cinque Mtume is the name that was bestowed upon him by his imprisoned sisters and brothers. It is the name of an ancient African chief who led the fight of his people for freedom. The name means "Fifth Prophet," and Cin was many years ago given this name because of his keen instinct and senses, his spiritual consciousness, and his deep love for all the people and children of this earth. This does not, however, mean that Cinque is from God or someone that is holy or that he has an extreme ego problem. . . ."

Nancy went on to proclaim Cinque as "another prophet and leader. This leader comes not to beg and plead with the enemy, he comes not to warn of violence, but is himself the bringer of the Children of the Wind and the Sound of War. . . ."

After the imaginary cheering had died down and the brass band had been silenced, Cinque himself came on to urge an all-out war on the system and to get down to some of the "business of the revolution"—to be exact, a list of people who had crossed the Symbionese and should be rubbed out "by any of the people's forces when found. . . ."

At this point, the editor of the *Phoenix,* who was listening intently to the tape over the radio, could see why the April Fool's Day communiqué had been sent to him with a little less than friendly intent as a means of justifying the upcoming order to rub out a few enemies. I took a deep breath, for I expected my name to appear on the list of the condemned.

The names listed were Russ Little's old girlfriend, Robyn Steiner (who was called an "informer to the FBI"), Chris Thompson, also labeled a "paid informer," and Colston Westbrook, the Black Cultural Association leader, who was accused of "working for military intelligence" and the FBI at the same time.

(No John Bryan. Whew!)

Cinque followed form and addressed part of the tape to Remiro and Little. This time he apologized for not doing anything to prevent their capture. Said he:

"To our two soldiers who are in the hands of the enemy and to all our comrades behind the walls: as you know, we have learned a hard lesson from our mistakes, and will learn from this for the future and the war that we the people will win. I am sure that you understand that under our codes of war there can be no surrender to the enemy, at any time or at any price. You both have shown correct actions in recognizing that even though you are innocent of any crimes it is not possible for you to receive a fair trial in the enemy's arena. I deeply regret that you were not offensively prepared to attack rather than be seized by the enemy. I send you my love, and the love of all comrades, and courage in your determination to carry on the struggle even from that side of the wall, and we will NEVER relent from this end. In this way, we do expect to meet again. . . ."

(Few outsiders realized what this meant at the time, but it must have been crystal clear to Remiro and Little. Since Patty had joined S.L.A., the group could no longer barter her for the freedom of the two captured soldiers. In effect, Cinque was saying, "Sorry boys, but it looks like you're just going to have to stay in stir. Nothing we can do about it.")

Patty tried to soften the blow a little with a love note in her portion of the tape. Said she:

"Osceola [Little] and Bo [Joe], even though we have never met I feel that I know you. Timing brought me to you, and I'm fighting with your freedom and the freedom of all prisoners in mind. In the strenuous jogs that life takes, you are pillars of strength to me. If I'm feeling down, I think of you, of where you are and why you are there, and my determination grows stronger. It's good to see that your spirits are so high in spite of the terrible conditions. Even though you aren't here, you are with other strong comrades, and the three of us are learning together— I in an environment of love and you in one of hate, in the belly of the fascist beast. We have grown closer to the people and become stronger through our experiences. . . ."

The tape had no sooner been broadcast over KPFA and KSAN than the front page of the *Phoenix* was torn up to accommodate a fascinating new picture of Patricia Hearst, this one showing her in a guerrilla beret, dark pants and shirt, with long, obviously dyed black hair. She was holding what looked like a modified M-16 with a sniper scope on it. Military experts would later claim that it was only a cheap and inaccurate M-1 carbine with a three-cell flashlight taped on top.

The *Phoenix* headline would say PATTY SETS SELF FREE, with an overline calling her "Our Guerrilla of the Year." There would also be a long story that told about the receipt of the April Fool's Day communiqué and the fact that I had run a semifake interview in the preceding issue. Time to fess up.

For, once the true situation had come out with the Tania Tape, I realized that I was walking on very thin ice with both the FBI and S.L.A. I was caught in the crossfire between them. It was now time to get the absolute truth on record and damn the consequences. I'd been outscammed by experts and I'd better admit it while I was still ambulatory. From that point on, I could report on every aspect of the story with an absolutely clear conscience.

I apparently made the right decision, because, within forty-eight hours after we hit the streets, the *Phoenix* telephone rang and Joe Remiro was calling from jail to give us our biggest scoop of all, a complete tape-recorded interview that took more than an hour of phone time and filled three pages in the next issue. S.L.A. also sent *Phoenix* a short thank-you note for releasing the Codes of War as they'd instructed and for not finking to the FBI.

Russ Little soon got into the act as well, and in the issue following the Remiro interview we were able to run Little's handwritten biography and philosophy, which had been forwarded to us from jail.

These two exclusives constituted a first that other journalists had been trying to get for months. But the two prisoners had refused to talk with the "straight press." It took absolutely candid, if embarrassing, admissions I made in *Phoenix* to open their hearts—and their mouths.

Said Remiro:

"You didn't get those roses and the communiqué because you wrote those 20 questions and answers. You got sent it because of the thing you wrote after that [the analytical piece]. It was fantastic. I probably got more insight into you from that thing you wrote in the last issue than you got into the S.L.A. from the documents and communiqués."

Part of the arrangement I made with Remiro after he'd given me the first extensive interview since his arrest was that I would make full transcripts of this "exclusive" available *before* I published it to all the other media. I presented the transcript to the New York *Times,* the Los Angeles *Times,* Associated Press, and United Press (where the strike was now over). Not one word was picked up by these outlets, who had been publicly saying for months that they were desperate to get an interview with Remiro and Little. The first-person article by Russ, in answer to my extensive questions, was also given to the big papers. Again, nothing was used. I was flabbergasted, and more than a bit suspicious. There was absolutely no question about authenticity. I had Remiro's interview on tape. Little's story was in his own handwriting. Their jailers were aware the phone call had been made and the letter sent out. Later I found out that no major story on S.L.A. was appearing in San Francisco, or being accepted by the AP or UPI bureaus, without an OK from Randolph Hearst. He apparently had turned thumbs down on what Remiro and

Little had to say. The public was only going to get his side of the story from here on out.

My talks with the two "captured soldiers" continued until June. They cleared up a lot of basic questions people had been asking about the Symbionese. The two also made it clear that they did not approve of the "superstar" status now being accorded to Cinque.

"We don't want to come on as being romanticists," said Russ Little. "We don't want to come off as being superstars. We don't want to come off as being mystics. We're socialist revolutionaries. We studied all this shit for years. We've been involved for a long time. . . ."

They felt that the other S.L.A.ers, many of them rather unsophisticated street people, were letting Cinque's leadership trip get out of hand. They regarded this as a "counterrevolutionary trend."

"S.L.A. has had a lot of firsts," said Joe. "They seized the media for instance. . . ." But he went on to say that getting on a "superstar trip" was definitely a mistake. "S.L.A. is not the vanguard," he said. "They took a vanguard role and they gave vanguard leadership. They did fantastic military-political action, fantastic propaganda. But there's other groups, other organizations, other people, there's militants all over this country that are capable of the same thing. And for anyone to claim they are the vanguard is really a farce."

Cinque, he said, has "proved his ability as a revolutionary leader. True revolutionaries and lovers of the people have no doubt that he is a military-political genius. Those who attempt through mystical rationalization to build a superstar jeopardize everything. The people have learned through lessons of blood that such superstars, uncriticizable images, can lead toward counterrevolutionary opportunism. The people do not want one prophet, one revolutionary leader—they want a revolution! There are many capable revolutionary leaders, in the ghettos, the prisons, the BLA, the S.L.A., the people want and need them all."

Both Remiro and Little were ecstatic when they got the news of Patricia's conversion to Tania.

"There's absolutely no doubt that she's a member now," said Russ two days after the arrival of the famous tape. "It's obvious from reading her statements. She's aware of all the bullshit that's coming down from her family. There's never been a political kidnapping in history where the victim joins the revolutionary forces. It's crazy, but it could only happen in America. . . ."

Joe had a few words to say on the matter, too:

"All these people who don't understand how Patty Hearst could join the S.L.A. just aren't thinking. I mean, if I were being held by the S.L.A. and they made a demand that was within the ability of my parents to pay, like it would be like asking my parents for two hundred or three hundred dollars, how would you feel about how your parents *really* felt about you if they didn't come up with it? I mean, she was really scared. She said, 'Please get me out of here,' and they did nothing."

As public disbelief reached record heights and every "expert" in America offered new theories to prove that Patty had not actually said what she'd said or done what she'd done, Remiro and Little asked, "Is it really true that people are still running around trying to negotiate for Patty's release? Don't they understand that Patty has been released? Do they expect the S.L.A. to turn Tania over to the FBI? Cinque said the action was terminated. Don't people have dictionaries?"

The public furor continued until April 15, thirteen days after the Tania Tape, when the rich girl turned revolutionary delivered a very clear and convincing statement on the matter while participating in a bank stickup.

In the sixth and next-to-last of the Symbionese tapes, Tania explained the motives behind the $10,660.02 robbery and tried to justify the shooting of two elderly passers-by who had been blasted away by S.L.A.ers who walked into a Sunset District Hibernia Bank hefting loaded automatic weapons. Said she:

"Our action of April 15 forced the corporate state to help finance the revolution. To those clowns who want a personal interview with me—Vincent Hallinan, Steven Weed, and Pig Hearsts—I prefer giving it to the people in the bank."

That "interview" with a crowd of terrified customers, clerks, and guards had been short but to the point:

"Get your motherfucking heads down or we'll blow you away," Patty had stated in a cultured but convincing tone of voice.

She'd made a point of posing throughout the robbery in front of automatic bank cameras, which took thousands of shots of the heiress turned desperado. (Much cheaper than running down to your neighborhood portrait photographer.) S.L.A. meant the pictures to provide a complete and final statement on Patty's conversion, and Remiro and Little were joyous.

"It was bodacious," said Remiro. "Absolutely bodacious," said Little. "That's a prison word that means 'just too much!'"

Remiro explained the revolutionary logic that made S.L.A. follow in the well-worn footsteps of the old Irish Republican Army and Joseph Stalin to become bank robbers.

"Look, man, this is beautiful for practice in guerrilla tactics. And we have to live, you know. We're not part-time revolutionaries."

As to the shooting of the two bystanders:

"I think the S.L.A. was just as sad about it as you or I were, that it had to happen. It's too bad they didn't have time to stick around and help the people who were shot down, like the Tupamaros once did in a stickup in Uruguay. But what would have happened if they'd have left that bank just three minutes later, just three minutes later, man? That's when the pigs arrived. There would have been a carful of pigs out there and there would have been one hell of a motherfucking battle and there would have been all these innocent people killed, man. See, you can't apply revolutionary tactics dogmatically from one country to another."

Between April 15 and May 17 no new word was heard from S.L.A. On May 4 the "deadline" set by the Hearst Corporation for the return of Patty passed, and four million dollars they had put in a trust to be used for the food program if she were safely back home by that date reverted to the corporation.

On the day before, May 3, Death Row Jeff released a somewhat finky statement, motivated apparently by promises that he might finally obtain his freedom, and urged S.L.A. to return Patty in time to meet the May 4 deadline because "these other poor and oppressed people need to be fed." He urged that Patty come back aboveground to "go around the country and around the world teaching to the people."

He got only silence in response. The location of the Symbionese remained as much a mystery as ever.

An extremely embarrassed FBI continued to make pathetic statements about being "hot on the trail" of the fugitives.

It was obviously no more than idle chatter. Until May 16, when Bill Harris went shoplifting just once too often.

18

"This is not a good place. They'd be much better off to go back up to Berkeley. . . . Southern Californians have never flipped out like the Bay community has. . . . The only kind of support they might pick up here is other crazies who have spent a lot of time in Berkeley. . . . They might get some of these Bay Area white crazies down here to die with them. . . ."
—Los Angeles Police Chief Edward M. Davis on the Symbionese

S. L.A. HAD SAID THAT THEIR ACTIONS would speak for them, and guerrilla watchers kept close to their radios and TV sets from mid-April, when Hibernia Bank was knocked over, until mid-May, when the next action-statement was made. The cops found gunpowder in the Golden Gate Avenue pad shortly after May Day, and everyone figured that whatever went down next, it would go off with a bang!

On May 16 the newspapers poignantly asked, "What Ever Happened to Patricia Hearst?" It had been more than three months since she had been kidnapped. The following day they would find out, and that day would prove to be a sociological milestone for America in a number of ways.

On May 17, 1954, just twenty years earlier and in the same year Patty had been born, the Supreme Court released its famous school integration order in the case of *Brown vs. Board of Education*. At the time, it had been called the most important decision of the century, the end of segregation in this country, the beginning of true racial justice and complete integration on every level.

Twenty years is a long time to wait for something that has supposedly already been given you, and a lot of energy and aspiration had gone down the drain after two frustrating decades of bumping head-on into a massive roadblock of entrenched privilege and prejudice. It had been a battle of attrition and it had dispelled all illusions about "racial equality" in America.

A famous black commentator editorialized on the morning of May 17, 1974, that not even school desegregation had been completed in those twenty years, and as for *true* integration, forget it! The South, wrote Carl Rowan, had merely lifted itself to the level of the surreptitious and sleazy racism so long practiced in the North. A few more blacks were finishing high school and going to college, but more and more of them were attending black-dominated central-city schools that had been abandoned in the white flight to suburbia. Once he got out of school, it was as hard as ever for the average black kid to get a good job. And as for housing, "we are more ghettoized than 20 years ago with our cities virtual black prisons ringed by hostile white suburbs."

It was on this troubled anniversary, and within a still-burned-over ghetto where thousands of blacks had risen in overwhelming denunciation of bigotry and half measures not nine years before in the Watts riots, that S.L.A. would give May 17 still another dismal significance. It would be the day a band of urban guerrillas would take on the armed might of the Establishment for the first time in an all-out fire fight. And it would be the day that Cinque, Cujo, Fahizah, Gelina, Zoya, and Gabi would die amid unparalleled violence and notoriety.

They got into this mess in an absurdly casual way and because they let paranoia and textbook geography get in the way of gut wisdom and the well-proven historical fact that politically repressive Southern California, which wanted to go with the Confederacy in 1861, has always been a dead end for reformers and revolutionists.

Bill Harris would explain that, by late April, the group had begun to fear capture on the peninsula tip of land occupied by the City of San Francisco, an area he called a "natural defile, a trap . . . surrounded by water and with limited choices for breaking a major encirclement."

So S.L.A. pulled out a road map or two and, relying on Cinque's rather ill-informed and hazy recollection of what life was like in the Los Angeles ghetto, they decided it would be "safer" to move south, where they could lose themselves amid crumbling stucco slums on the endless smog-shrouded plains.

"We decided to move our base of operations to Southern California, concentrating on the Greater Los Angeles area with its vast oppressed communities and more favorable terrain," said Harris. First a "reconnaissance team" was sent down for a brief look, and then the whole unit "slipped out of San Francisco and into Los Angeles on May Day, 1974."

On May 9, the group of nine, which now called itself the "Malcolm X Combat Unit" of the S.L.A., rented a rundown little white cottage at 833 West Eighty-fourth Street, less than two miles (and the other side of the Harbor Freeway) from the center of the Watts uprising. The tiny house was well within what was known in 1965 as the "Riot Zone," an area where enormous mobs completely took control, burning hundreds of white-owned stores (and altogether too many of their own houses), looting and drinking and celebrating in an anarchistic flood that almost swept over downtown L.A. before terrified police and troops could contain it.

Dozens of lots in this area still sit vacant after the mass incineration and, here and there, burned-out frame buildings no one has ever bothered to tear down are vivid reminders of the immense fury that sizzles just beneath the surface of the biggest black district in the West.

The appearance of this slum community is a bit deceptive at first. Unlike the jam-packed old brick tenements of the Eastern ghettos, built before the advent of the automobile, South L.A. incorporates street after street of once-tidy little bungalows and ranch houses with ample yards and a fair number of trees and shrubs. It takes a closer inspection of unpainted walls, broken windows, and dozens of people packed into two or three rooms to make the visitor realize this is truly a ghetto. It's also an interesting prophecy of what will eventually happen to the hundreds of square miles of jerry-built "suburbs" now surrounding central Los Angeles once their plaster fronts cave in and the "middle class" flees to newer ticky-tacks.

Just what luck S.L.A. had in organizing a revolution in South L.A. in its first two weeks in town is not fully known, but a little extended observation may have hipped them to the fact that the "Southland's" black population, more recent arrivals from Dixie than ghetto San Franciscans, were in no mood to screw around with any "integrated" revolution. White faces are a rarity in South L.A. and instant race hatred is the norm. The militants of the area had long ago told white reformers to go home and work on their own people, and, among the less-than-political majority, whites with a price on their heads are fair game no matter what kinda bullshit they're putting down.

By May 16 there were clear signs that S.L.A. had decided the climate down here was definitely unhealthy and that they planned an excursion into the mountains, perhaps even a trip down to Mexico to link up with the Revolutionary Armed Forces, a guerrilla outfit whose origins go back to Pancho Villa and Che Guevara.

In any case, they had begun to purchase camping equipment, dehydrated food, and thick woolen clothing of the kind outdoorsmen favor. All the rations were proportioned to handle nine—Cinque, Camilla Hall, William and Emily Harris, William Wolfe, Angela Atwood, Nancy Ling Perry, Mizmoon Soltysik, and Patricia Hearst. (At the Eighty-fourth Street cottage the now-reliable "Tania" was assigned late-night guard duty, "all night till light.")

Ignoring Carlos Marighella's stern warning that an urban guerrilla must never "boast about his actions and broadcast them to the four winds," the Symbionese now began to reveal themselves to complete strangers, on the totally erroneous assumption that no black would turn them in. Perhaps it was because of their misunderstanding of the Los Angeles scene, or perhaps the game had gone on for too long with month after month of hiding; perhaps they were subconsciously tired of it all and simply wanted to get it over with.

The same day that Emily Harris rented the Eighty-fourth Street house, her black "General Field Marshal" ambled next door to see Kyle Jones, who had rented them the pad. "Hi," he said, "I'm Cinque."

Jones, a crusty old codger who is known around his neighborhood as "the Prophet," said, "You don't look like your pictures."

"How do you think I've stayed free for so long?" replied the guerrilla chief.

Jones was invited next door to meet the rest of the gang, and he said he saw seven or eight of them sitting around in a circle drinking beer. In the middle of the circle was an impressive-looking pile of guns.

Cinque introduced the old man around: "That's Patty Hearst, Tania," he said. "Does she look like she's been kidnapped? We've just given her a haircut. How do you like it?" Tania shook her newly trimmed locks out and laughed at him.

"Patty seemed a little nervous for a while," said Cinque, "but she's toughening up."

"The Prophet" soon got into the habit of running errands for S.L.A., mostly beer and wine runs down to the corner store. One day he asked Cinque to do him a small favor. "When you leave, don't leave me bloody," said the old man in a good-natured way.

"Don't believe all that bullshit," laughed Cinque. "None of that bullshit you hear on the radio and TV. Our shit is as heavy as theirs."

With a major expedition into the wilderness clearly in the near future, Bill and Emily Harris decided on May 16 to run down to nearby Mel's Sporting Goods Store in Inglewood to pick up some more warm clothing.

Late that afternoon, they took a red-and-white Volkswagen bus—one of the three vans they'd brought down from San Francisco—and went out to pick up $31.50 worth of thick flannel shirts and socks. Patty drove them over and waited in the Volks parked just across the street from Mel's as the couple went in to make their purchases.

A gung-ho twenty-year-old store clerk named Tony Shepard saw them come in at about 3:45 P.M. He didn't like their looks—the place has a bad shoplifting problem—and decided to keep a close eye on them. He would later claim that Harris walked out of the store with a cloth cartridge bandolier that he had not paid for draped over his arm.

Shepard stuck a revolver in his pocket and grabbed a pair of handcuffs. He signaled a second employee to follow him outside, and he then confronted the Harrises on the street.

"Why don't you pay for that bandolier on your arm?" Shepard asked a highly antagonistic Harris, who claimed he *had* paid for it and made several less than friendly remarks about Shepard's ancestry.

The clerk-detective decided to make a pinch and approached Harris with open handcuffs ready to snap on. He managed to get one cuff on Teko's left hand before a pushing and shoving match landed both of them on the sidewalk. In the struggle, a .38-caliber revolver flew out of Harris's clothing and landed on the street. Shepard and Harris were fighting for its possession when suddenly their little stand-off was interrupted by the sound of twenty-seven bullets smashing into the plate-glass window and sign across the front of Mel's Sporting Goods. Patty Hearst had seen the sidewalk action, pulled out a modified M-1, and sprayed the place with red-hot slugs. She shot high, but it was enough of a warning to get Shepard up and off of Harris, who was joined by Emily in a race across the street to the Volkswagen. The second store clerk, being of sound mind, got the hell inside the store and gave up the cops-and-robbers business entirely. But Shepard was only slightly fazed. First he took a couple of shots at the fleeing van, and then he bolted into his car and pursued the Volks through the streets of Inglewood.

His part of a long and complicated escape ended less than a mile away, after the Harrises and Patty had abandoned the van and commandeered two other cars at gunpoint. Harris began to approach the clerk's car with his M-1 quite convincingly pointed at Shepard's head, and the junior G-man finally decided it wasn't worth all this for a lousy shoplifting pinch and split.

Not sure they'd lost him, the S.L.A. trio apparently reverted to an already agreed-upon contingency plan and traded cars once again, this time snatching an eighteen-year-old baseball player named Tom Matthews who had a "For Sale" sign in the window of his '69 Ford van parked out in front of his house. Emily Harris walked up to Matthews's front door and asked for a demonstration ride. Before it was over, he had been made an S.L.A. prisoner on a random twelve-hour trip around town. Matthews got so completely over his initial fear that he ended up chatting amicably with Patty Hearst for several hours about her entire involvement with the guerrillas, thereby scoring a scoop any newsman in the country would have given an arm and a leg for.

She verified once again that she had *not* had anything to do with setting up her own kidnap, and that she most definitely *was* pissed at her father for his handling of the food program and at her mother for the UC regent number. She said that she had joined S.L.A. willingly and that she was now out to revolutionize the world.

The group sat for several hours in a drive-in movie awaiting a contact that apparently never materialized; then they drove up to a deserted road in the Hollywood Hills, where Matthews promptly went to sleep. As the star second baseman of the Lynwood baseball team, he had to be ready to play in an important game the next day.

About 6:30 A.M., the S.L.A. trio once again switched cars, this time taking a Lincoln Continental at gunpoint after leaving Matthews alone in his truck with the keys in the ignition and a warning that he'd better keep down and keep his mouth closed. They dumped the owner of the Continental and sped away, thus providing the last authenticated sighting of the three between May 17 and the time this book was put together early in 1975.

Matthews obliged his new friends by waiting until he drove some thirty miles to his home in Lynwood before calling the feds. He went on that afternoon to win his baseball game. Much to his surprise, Patty Hearst, legally a kidnap "victim" herself up to this point, would later be charged with the "kidnap" of Tom Matthews. Another first for the S.L.A.

Meanwhile, back at the hideout (as they say in the whodunits), Cinque and his buddies had grown restive by 8:30 P.M., some four hours after the Harrises and Patty had gone out to make a quick shopping trip. They should have been back by *now*.

Acting on what was apparently another of the group's contingency plans, they hastily abandoned the cottage (even leaving a fresh-cooked and uneaten hot dog on the stove). Their departure was well considered, because police had by now impounded the red-and-white Volkswagen bus and discovered it contained a parking ticket tissued a few days before at 835 West Eighty-fourth Street, right next door to the guerrilla hideout. Had the police and FBI not gotten into a heated jurisdictional dispute and held off an assault until late the next morning, they might have nabbed the fugitives right there and then.

As it was, their flight only put things off for about twenty-two hours.

At 2:00 A.M. on the morning of May 17, the six Symbionese had settled down in their second known Los Angeles hideout, a one-story, two-bedroom frame cottage with a stone porch foundation, composition shingles, and an unusable attic. It was at 1466 East Fifty-fourth Street, well within the Watts Riot Zone. Whether or not they bought their way in with a fat hundred-dollar fee for a night's lodging or were welcomed by sympathizers who had long expected them is a point still being debated by police and press. But the move to the east side of the Harbor Freeway, which cuts the ghetto in two like a concrete river, and about three miles north of the center of Watts was to prove a bad choice, indeed.

Horrified white reporters who rushed right home and washed their hands after a trip into the slums would refer to 1466 East Fifty-fourth Street as "some kind of a crash pad," because two young unmarried mothers were raising two teen-agers and five small children in four rooms with the help of a steady line of "uncles" and friends who kept things hopping day and night. "It was a good place to go for a game of dominoes and a drink or two," one of the more frequent visitors fondly recalled.

"They always party over there—every day," said a disinterested neighbor. "Folks goin' in and out all day."

None of this is so unusual in the ghetto. You live hard and fast if you're poor with no past and very little future. You swing and jive and booze and smoke whatever dope you can find and drop the pills that are handed to you. Ain't nothin' special. True, the traffic through the house occupied by Christine Johnson and Minnie Lewis was a bit heavier than most places, and, as Sam the Hamburger Stand Man down at the corner of Fifty-seventh and Compton would put it, "Man, one thing's for sure, those S.L.A. people picked the wrong house on the wrong street in the wrong town. Ain't nothin' secret around here for long."

When Cinque, Willie the Wolfe, and the four girls arrived, there were four adults sitting around the house boozing and watching TV. They were Ms. Johnson and Ms. Lewis, Freddie Freeman, and a seventeen-year-old neighbor named Brenda Daniels, who had supposedly come over from across the street to help "baby-sit" Minnie Lewis's five kids but ended up so stoned that she stuck around all that night and most of the next day to watch the action.

As Brenda recalls the beginning of what would become the most memorable day in her life:

"I went down to Minnie's every Thursday evening to play some cards and drink a little. I fell asleep early and when I woke up around two A.M. I saw four white women and three dudes—two blacks and one white. I saw guns spread out all over the floor, an' I asked them why they had guns, more than I'd ever seen in my life. They didn't answer, and, instead, the black dude asked me my name and then introduced me to everyone."

Still believing their immense publicity had endeared them to all blacks and that they would not be betrayed, Cinque gave the hung-over young girl all the correct names. That press they'd been getting had to be good for *something*.

But Brenda wasn't overly impressed, and she just went back to sleep. When she was asked just whom she was introduced to (and was Patty Hearst among them?), she gave the naive white interviewer one of those profoundly knowing ghetto smiles and replied sweetly, "Man, how can I tell? All white women look the same to me."

She did recall their costumes, though. Cinque was wearing a standard Army surplus guerrilla uniform—a khaki shirt and pants and a knit cap. The women all wore turtleneck sweaters, either dark green or dark blue, and more than one to a customer—they would later start peeling them off as it got hotter. Their "commando" uniforms also included dark pants with bulging holsters strapped to their belts and special pockets sewn onto the legs to hold big hunting knives.

A somewhat irreverent British reporter who once covered the fighting in Northern Ireland would say that "they looked like a women's auxiliary of the Provisional IRA invented by Hollywood."

(This same wit would also label them "a bunch of muddled romantics who probably owed far more to Hemingway than to Ho Chi Minh.")

Brenda awoke a little after dawn the next morning to watch Minnie Lewis scurry around getting her children off to school. At about 6:00 A.M., "the black dude gave me twenty dollars to go to the store for some beer, food, you know, lunch meat and two packs of Camels. He told me to be cool 'cause he was goin' to watch me, an' he did, too, through the alley. So I came back with the stuff from Sam's."

Cinque had taken care of another minor problem a little earlier when he and Freddie moved the two S.L.A. vans from in front of 1466 East Fifty-fourth Street to a parking lot behind a partly burned-out apartment house a block and a half away, at 1451 East Fifty-third Street. He had no way of knowing that this was a notorious "drop spot" for stolen cars, a location regularly checked out by police units that cruise the neighborhood.

On this particular day, they were looking hard for the two vans. Neighbors at the Eighty-fourth Street hideout had given police the license numbers of the two Symbionese vehicles, and, as soon as the cops spotted them on the morning of May 17, they were staked out.

When Brenda got back with the groceries, she discovered Cinque and Willie busy at work setting up their Browning .30-06 automatic rifle pointing out the front window toward the street. It was one of the only two accurate long-distance weapons S.L.A. possessed. Their modified M-1 carbines and sawed-off shotguns would prove totally unreliable in a long-distance shoot-out.

Freddie Freeman was due to go to work that morning, but when his boss and a friend came to pick him up, he told them all about the S.L.A. number and said that he had a chance to make some "big money" doing them a favor. The unimpressed buddies shrugged their shoulders and split.

Minnie Lewis got her kids off to school and then roused Christine Johnson from a zonked-out sleep. The two had to step over a pile of rifles, Molotov cocktails, and ammunition into the kitchen to make breakfast. Brenda joined them and got upset because Camilla Hall had gone to work making sandwiches. Brenda didn't like Camilla acting as though she were the "woman of the house."

Minnie and Christine were hung over and freaked. They decided they didn't like the way this whole scene was coming together and figured they better get out of it fast. They dropped a couple of handfuls of downers and drank a big bottle of wine. Both stayed passed out for the rest of the morning.

Brenda stayed awake, though, listening to the white girls talk about revolution and watching Willie the Wolfe lying on a bed twirling his big fat .45 around an index finger like some gunslinging character out of a Grade B movie.

About eleven that morning, Cinque handed five hundred dollars to Freddie and told him to go out and buy a car—if he couldn't buy one, steal it! Fred drove away in a green Pontiac LeMans, never to return. The cops grabbed him just a few blocks away, threw him in the local slam, and later revoked his parole.

By 1:00 P.M. the whole neighborhood was aware something big was about to happen. There was plain-clothes heat everywhere. Said Beanie of the 'Ject (a resident of a nearby housing project who was a kind of unofficial "mayor" in these parts), "The word was definitely out that the police were looking for some very important people."

Sam the Hamburger Stand Man could see a small army of cops driving up and down Compton Avenue. "Man, this place was *loaded* with police. . . ."

The word had gotten around to the Fifty-fourth Street neighbors, too, and they crowded in to meet the famous guerrillas. Among the visitors was sixty-three-year-old James Reed, who came by with some fresh collard greens. He took one look at the pile of armaments and left like the wind. Clarence Ross bopped in, and he ended up guzzling beer and wine with the group all afternoon. And then there were Shirley Davis and eighteen-year-old Stephanie Reed. Minnie Lewis's kids would wander back in after school, but all the guns and the strange white people finally spooked them and they made a beeline over to the nearby home of their grandmother, Mary Carr.

When the kids told the pragmatic Ms. Carr about the strange and dangerous goings on at her daughter's house, she quickly made up her mind that things had gotten out of hand. "I'm gonna break this shit up," said she and called the police.

Her call was welcome but not crucial. FBI agents and plain-clothes cops had already surrounded the block where S.L.A. was now arming up for the showdown. All they needed was to know *which* house to attack.

As the police presence became more and more obvious, most of the visitors split. Stephanie Reed, either braver or denser than the rest, stuck around to get into some extensive raps with Cinque.

"When I came in, I saw all those guns on the floor and this black dude with a beard was trying to get things together," she recalled. "He asked me if I had any shells or knives an' I told him no." Things were getting interesting, and Stephanie began to ask a few questions.

"I asked him his name and he said something that sounded like Swahili, something like 'Cinque' . . . then he said, 'We're out to get pigs.' "

The regular visitors to Fifty-fourth Street were now getting high on booze and pills. Although Cin and his buddies were taking little sips of wine and beer, they still appeared quite sober. (Cinque was drinking his favorite beverage, plum wine. He'd settled for Boone's Farm, since the corner store didn't carry his preferred brand, the imported Akadama.)

"I asked him why he wasn't getting high," Stephanie recalled, "and he said, 'We don't get high because we got something to prove today.'

"The women started talking to me," she continued. "One of the women, she was short and stocky and had short blonde hair, tried to get me to join, and the black dude said that 'we need some strong black brothers and sisters to help in the fight.'

"Then I sat in the living room looking around. The black dude said to me, 'Baby, you don't talk much, do you?' I said no, and he kinda laughed. He was looking out the window and then he said to the short, stocky woman, 'It's gettin' hot around here. I think we better split.'

"And the woman said, 'It's hot everywhere.' "

About this point, Brenda Daniels was sent out on another run to the store for more beer and cigarettes. She'd only gotten about a block when plain-clothes cops grabbed her. When she didn't return, Cinque knew things were critical.

Stephanie watched while "they started getting their guns ready. All of them were carrying pistols on their sides, and I saw what looked like a machine gun. The black man started putting it together, putting the handle on the bottom. . . ." Stephanie figured it was time to *split*.

Another neighbor came in to watch these fantastic goings on and talk politics with the busy Cinque. She said that he explained how rich white girls like Patty Hearst could get money from their fathers to finance the revolution. He called Patty "one of his children, like all of the white girls who were fighting with him." He said that all of them knew a gun battle was coming up and they would fight to the death.

"I know I'm going to die," he said, "but we're going to take a lot of motherfucking pigs with us."

Christine Johnson then stumbled out of the bedroom and fell on the kitchen floor. Cinque put her on a couch where she again passed out.

Minnie was still unconscious in the other bedroom. At about 3:30, an outraged Mary Carr burst into the house looking for her daughter. She found Minnie passed out in the darkened bedroom surrounded by a pile of gas masks, guns, and ammunition. She tried to wake Minnie up but couldn't. Ms. Carr then went out to the kitchen and demanded that Cinque and his crew get the hell out of her daughter's house. The revolutionists only grinned. One of the white girls just looked at her, smiling and patting the gun on her hip. The distraught Ms. Carr grabbed up two of her grandchildren and ran out of the house to again call the police.

By 4:00 P.M. the area was surrounded by nearly five hundred armed policemen. In an absolutely unprecedented action, the Los Angeles Police now notified the press, *before* sealing off the area, that there was going to be a dandy gun battle there with the S.L.A.

They obviously wanted a worldwide audience for what they had in mind. Rather than giving out the actual address where the cops already knew Cinque and his comrades were holed up, a police information officer told hundreds of reporters and photographers to assemble at the parking lot a block and a half away, when the two S.L.A. vans were still being staked out. Far enough away to miss the opening shots of the police assault, but close enough to trot right over once it had started and record the extermination of S.L.A. as a grim object lesson for any other "crazies" out there who might be seriously considering fucking with "law 'n' order."

The atmosphere inside the little house was reaching an unbelievable level of tension. There was no way out. They were trapped and they knew it. Minnie Lewis became conscious again and wandered off to the corner store in search of a drink. The cops nabbed her and hauled her off to the station.

This left only six S.L.A. members, Christine Johnson (still passed out), the eight-year-old son of Minnie Lewis, and Clarence Ross inside the house. Ross was drinking and watching TV, too spaced out to comprehend the growing danger.

Over on Fifty-third Street, where the press was assembling, members of the Los Angeles Police SWAT (Special Weapons Assault Teams) division were preparing a mock attack to keep the reporters distracted. The flak-jacketed officers, with their special blue jump-suit uniforms with the nattily visored baseball caps and their superfine sniper rifles and automatic weapons, were laughing to themselves as they crouched down around a mostly burned-out apartment building in which only one of four units was occupied. They knew damn well where the S.L.A. was, but the press had to be kept over here.

One unbelievably audacious television reporter, the very fashionable Christine Lund of KABC, got the cameras properly focused on her trim little figure and sauntered right up to the apartment door. She knocked and waited. What was she about to say? . . . "Oh, hello there! I'm Christine Lund. Are you the S.L.A.?"

The SWAT team stopped laughing long enough to haul her back away from the door and give her a good-natured tongue-lashing. Nothing serious. They went through the motions of glancing into one of the apartment's few unboarded windows and then walked away. They were obviously waiting for something more important to happen.

At exactly 5:52 P.M. they got the signal they'd been waiting for and raced over a block and a half to the little cottage on Fifty-fourth Street, with the press in hot pursuit.

What they heard was the explosion of a tear-gas gun, a gas canister crashing through the front window, and then the rapid crack of semi-automatic weapons. The battle was on.

Exactly how it began and whether or not S.L.A. ever had an adequate chance to surrender before being so publicly annihilated is still being debated by those who believe the police can do no wrong and investigators who have carefully researched just what *did* occur between 5:44 and 7:30 P.M. that May 17.

A Los Angeles *Times* reporter named Robert Kistler wrote in the early editions of his sheet that "one canister of tear gas was fired into the house at 5:50 P.M. and massive volleys of law enforcement gunfire followed immediately.

"Gunfire was returned immediately from the house. . . ."

The official police version claims that at 5:40 P.M. "the squad leader of SWAT Team One deployed his eight men in front and to the east of 1466 East 54th Street. They were armed with two tear gas guns, two 12-gauge shotguns, four AR-180 semi-automatic weapons, one AR-15 semi-automatic weapon, one .243 caliber long rifle and .38 caliber sidearms.

"The squad leader of Team Two deployed his eight men in the rear and to the southeast." Their weapons were about the same as those issued to the first team. After the two groups were in position, at 5:44 P.M., says the report, the leader of the squad in front of the house used a small, battery-powered bullhorn to announce, "Occupants of 1466 East Fifty-fourth Street, this is the Los Angeles Police Department speaking. Come out with your hands up. Comply immediately and you will not be harmed."

The police claim this announcement was rebroadcast loud and clear, and that a few minutes later the eight-year-old son of Minnie Lewis ran out the front door, followed by Clarence Ross. The official report says that a total of eighteen separate surrender announcements were made in this manner in the eight minutes that preceded the gunfire, and then, without further ado, tear gas was fired.

After a second projectile had been lobbed in, "heavy bursts of automatic gunfire came from inside the front and rear of the house." Police claim that they did not fire a single shot until *after* the guerrillas had shot at them first. Some newsmen agree. Others say this is nonsense and question why no attempt was made to negotiate with the rebels over a working telephone police knew was inside the house.

In any case, these arguments would prove academic to the six S.L.A. members inside. They would be dead in a little more than an hour.

By this point, live television cameras were recording the gun battle from about half a block away. (The Last Poets were wrong. The Revolution *will* be televised.)

Millions of Americans would watch the shoot-out as they munched lukewarm TV dinners. Once locked into it, few could pull away, at least not in California, where the timing was perfect. It began just before the regularly scheduled six o'clock news, which it preempted. There was still plenty of daylight to properly illuminate the scene for the fluky new color minicameras, and the whole thing would be over by 7:30 so there would be no conflict with those regularly scheduled make-believe shoot-'em-ups which so amuse and enlighten our bloodthirsty and jaded tastes.

Stephen Weed would watch the gunfight in San Diego not knowing whether Patty Hearst was inside or not. Her parents would be riveted to their own flickering boob tube in Hillsborough, four hundred miles to the north. Nancy Ling Perry's husband, Gilbert, would watch it in San Francisco, finding it hard to believe this was not just one more blood-drenched Hollywood extravaganza.

"I've seen so many cop-and-robber programs that I couldn't relate to the fact that this was real, that my wife was in there," he would say while his set was still cooling.

The Los Angeles SWAT squads, paramilitary units who had never before gotten the chance to use so much weaponry and so many rounds of ammunition on live targets, were overjoyed with this exercise in overkill. Before the battle was over, they would pour over five thousand rounds into the little house and lob in fifty canisters of tear gas—more gas than had ever been used in such a small space before.

Television viewers would watch them run through a perfectly disciplined battle routine in which one marksman would empty a clip from his semiautomatic weapon at the unseen targets within, then step back to reload while his partner moved up and fired off his clip. Vietnam veterans would say that this method was typical of the fire-fight tactics taught by the U.S. Army in Indochina. What many Namvets could not understand was the incredible length of the battle.

"Hell, man, I was over there three years and I never saw that intense a fire fight last longer than fifteen or twenty minutes," said a flabbergasted former Green Beret. "That thing went on for more than an hour!"

Nonsense-blabbing television commentators, who covered the shoot-out with a constant flow of trivial small talk as though it were a minor league baseball game, would call it "the greatest gunfight in the history of the West."

"We've got a small war going," admitted a busy SWAT sniper as he forced a reporter to the ground. Erratic S.L.A. gunfire stitched a weird and uncoordinated pattern across cars and buildings all around them. Amazingly enough, not a single S.L.A. bullet hit anyone.

They would have to send out patrol cars on at least two occasions to bring in more police ammunition for their side of the battle. Reporters saw a car coming back once with so much ammunition packed inside there was barely space for the driver.

SWAT would later charge the City of Los Angeles $1,450 for twelve gun barrels they claimed had been "worn out" in one evening's work.

They would claim that all of this firing had been handled by only three of their eight-man SWAT teams, with a brief assist from five FBI agents. The rest of the five hundred cops called into the area on this amazing "Tactical Alert" were just there to "keep the crowds away."

The official version of the incident would also report that, despite their clear numerical superiority, all these cops versus six guerrillas, "SWAT teams were unable to match the automatic weapons fire coming from within 1466 East 54th Street. If the suspects had shot their way out of the house and through the SWAT line of defense, many residents and police officers in the area would have possibly been killed or injured."

For this reason, the cop in charge of the SWAT teams asked for permission to turn the fire fight into a full-fledged military operation with the use of fragmentation grenades. Permission was supposedly denied, but several reporters wrote that the grenades were used and that those on the scene had to dodge the resulting rain of shrapnel for nearly ten minutes.

At 6:40 P.M., after nearly an hour of pitched battle, SWAT threw two more tear-gas bombs, Federal 555 Riot Canisters, into the house. Such projectiles give off terrific heat.

At 6:41, "the squad leader of Team Two noted black smoke coming out of the window at the rear. . . ." The Team One squad leader also saw the smoke, and he broadcast over his bullhorn, "Come on out. The house is on fire. You will not be harmed."

His announcement was met by the appearance of a dazed and staggering black woman at the front door. The police held fire long enough for Christine Johnson, wounded by both a rifle bullet and buckshot, to get to safety. She was thrown onto the ground and promptly arrested and then charged with harboring fugitives. Later the charge was dropped.

She would be the last person to see Cinque and his doomed guerrilla band alive. As she recalled her terrified departure from the now-burning house:

"I crawled out through the living room," she said. "I passed right by Cinque and he was shooting at the police. Someone shouted, 'Don't open that door! Don't open that door!' But I was so frightened I don't know who was saying it. I still heard shots. . . . I just went on. . . . Then the police grabbed me. . . . They were dragging me." She got one last glimpse of Camilla Hall before she ran out the front door:

"She had two bottles in her hands," said Christine, "and it seems like something white was around the bottles. She was walking around with the bottles, following me. She looked like a zombie or something to me. She was halfway smiling. . . ."

The police took advantage of the momentary halt in firing to bring up four more automatic weapons—two M-16 .223 rifles and two 9mm MP-40 Schmeissers.

At 6:47, the police say, they again broadcast an ultimatum over their bullhorn: "Come out, you will not be harmed. The house is on fire. It's all over. Throw your guns out the windows. You will not be harmed."

The only reply, they say, was "automatic weapons fire" from within the house, which was now fiercely blazing.

By 6:50, the building was "totally engulfed" in flames and the SWAT cops were getting "automatic weapons fire from air vents in the foundation of the house." Some of the S.L.A.ers had crawled through a hole chopped in the floor and were lying flat on their bellies in a twenty-inch-high space between the floor and the ground. The concrete foundation provided a "natural bunker" that protected them from the withering police fire, but overhead the cottage was burning itself to the ground.

Suddenly two S.L.A. members came out of the back of the house. Investigators working for their parents would claim they walked out intending to surrender and that they were unarmed but were met with a merciless police crossfire the moment they showed their faces. The police claimed that Nancy Ling Perry came out firing a revolver and that Camilla Hall was providing cover fire from an automatic pistol.

Whatever the truth of the matter, police bullets immediately killed them both. The myopic Camilla died from a shot right through the center of her forehead. Nancy suffered two gunshot wounds—one severed her spine and the other cut through her right lung.

A third S.L.A. woman, Mizmoon Soltysik, would die from a combination of bullet wounds, smoke inhalation, and burns.

Angela Atwood, whose body was found just inside a crawl-hole opening in the back, was killed by the fire, as was Willie Wolfe. Cinque, who was starting to burn alive, apparently put an end to his misery with a self-inflicted pistol shot through the right temple. The bodies of Willie, Mizmoon, and Cinque were found side by side under the right rear portion of the house. The body of Camilla, curled up next to the skeleton of her favorite Siamese cat, had apparently been pulled in under the left rear part of the building by comrade Angela. Nancy was still outside the house, just beyond the right rear side of the foundation.

The heat of the fire was so intense that bullets in the bandoliers of the women guerrillas continued to explode long after they were dead. Their bodies jumped and writhed from the posthumous explosions.

By 7:00 P.M., almost nothing was left of the building. At 7:01, fire-fighting units that had been standing by since 5:30 were finally allowed to spray in water from a safe distance. The completely leveled ruins of the house continued to smolder until 7:30.

Identification of the blackened corpses would not be completed for another forty-eight hours. The last body removed was that of Camilla Hall. (The little piles of charcoal and bone were in such pathetic shape that at least one family, that of Cinque, was unwilling to believe it was really him. By the time an autopsy surgeon had removed his head and fingers, there was nothing left to recognize.)

Police officials would claim they had "broken the back" of the

S.L.A. in the Fifty-fourth Street auto-da-fé. ("He may have been Cinque yesterday, but he's bar-be-cue today," exulted one SWAT squader on the scene.) The cops would even go on to say they had "wiped out the group entirely," and newscasters would report this assertion to the world. But not everyone would agree, including those who could still count on their fingers. Intelligence reports showed that there had been at least twelve or thirteen active members loose just before the fire fight. Six were dead. That left six or seven comrades still at large, including Patty Hearst and the Harrises. And what about the "fifteen or twenty" support members who had been working with S.L.A. over the past six months? Many of them could now be counted on to seek revenge for their dead comrades —if not under the banner of the seven-headed cobra then as elements of other urban guerrilla organizations.

And what about the thousands of pissed-off Americans who already had grievances against the system and who had come to admire S.L.A. while it was the leading edge of revolution? They had learned some extremely dangerous lessons they would not soon forget.

Some admirers had even taken a hand during the shoot-out itself. Black mobs had twice attacked cops on the periphery of the fire fight, forcing the beleaguered police to call for massive reinforcements. The six dead Symbionese had not started a full-scale revolution as they had planned, but they had left behind the impression they sought so desperately to create—that white revolutionaries could now be counted on to go down fighting rather than to surrender.

A Watts street kid summed it up nicely a few days later:

"They died like revolutionaries are supposed to," he said admiringly. "If you're a revolutionary you don't surrender. They held off more than five hundred pigs."

It would prove easier to praise their courage than their marksmanship.

Not one cop or any member of an uncontrolled crowd of several hundred newsmen and bystanders who were well within gunshot range of the cottage reported even a minor bullet wound. This was hard to understand, downright embarrassing, in fact. Especially after police had proclaimed the group had "superior weaponry" and so much of it that the SWAT teams could not, at first, "match the automatic weapons fire" the guerrillas poured out at them. Why were the Symbionese such bad shots?

The question remained unanswered until July 19, when the official

Los Angeles Police report was issued and some very interesting facts came to light. First of all, the claim that police were completely justified in pouring over five thousand rounds into the cottage and then burning it down because S.L.A. was so lethal and desperate they might shoot their way out was proven an adroit bit of propaganda. The cops had claimed S.L.A. fired "3,771 rounds." But their own report showed that police had included many hundreds, possibly thousands, of bullets that had gone off in the fire. (Witnesses heard these explosions for more than half an hour.) They also did a bit of double counting to include in their grand total not only all the shell casings found inside but 702 slugs that had been fired out of these same shell casings. Only 668 casings could be found that bore firing-pin marks proving they had actually been exploded in a gun rather than set off by the fire. (They also found 475 unexploded rounds that had survived the fire nearly intact.)

Out of the shells that had definitely been ejected from guns, just 63 came from the only two accurate rifles S.L.A. possessed, their .30-06 Browning automatic and their Remington .244 semiautomatic. Fourteen shells had been used in handguns, weapons that are almost useless at a distance. The remaining 494 rifle shells with firing-pin marks had all been expended in the group's four M-1 carbines. A total of 97 shotgun shells with pin marks were found, and these had come out of S.L.A.'s seven 12-gauge sawed-off shotguns.

Sawing off the barrel of a shotgun makes it effective for "scatter-shots" at close range. But a weapon altered in this way is very inaccurate for hitting targets more than a few feet away. The short-barreled, semi-automatic M-1 carbine, a surplus military weapon, is notoriously inaccurate even when it has not been altered. But its conversion into an "automatic weapon" (and all of S.L.A.'s M-1s had been so altered) makes it one of the least accurate rifles imaginable.

In their uninformed efforts to come on like real "baddies" with gangster-type sawed-off shotguns and pitiful little M-1 carbine "machine guns," the Symbionese had done themselves in. Rapid fire is not necessarily accurate fire, as the May 17 fiasco proved. If they just wanted to make a lot of noise, a crate of Chinese firecrackers would have been more effective. It also became apparent that the supersaturation of their cottage with fifty tear-gas shells made it necessary to continually wear gas masks and damned difficult to even *see* their targets, who were combat wise and had plenty of cover. They also had to keep their heads down because of the driving storm of lead whizzing in through broken windows and thin walls. After the six retreated under the floor, they had to shoot from the tiny ventilation holes they found in the concrete foundation, a clumsy job at best. The angle was wrong for accurate sighting, and it was hard even to see the target. Remiro should have taught them better.

The mass media would say little about these military aspects of May 17, but they would expend millions of printed and broadcast words on analysis and personal histories of the six dead comrades.

The most authoritative obituary would not appear until June 7, some three weeks after the Fifty-fourth Street fiasco. The Harrises and Patty Hearst would deliver their eulogy by means of the seventh S.L.A. tape recording. It was left at Los Angeles radical radio station KPFK, and it would be the last message the public would hear between June and the time this book was assembled many months later.

Each of the three took a turn at speaking, and it added up to an extraordinary combination of guilt, remorse, and threatening militancy.

Harris would go to great lengths to deny that he had actually been guilty of the shoplift that had led to the deaths of six friends. He would furiously attack the official story that Cinque had committed suicide:

"Our six comrades were not on a suicide mission," said Teko, who made it clear he was in charge of what remained of S.L.A. "They were attempting to break a battalion-sized encirclement." He claimed the police deliberately burned down the house rather than give the six a chance to surrender. He said of Cinque: "We all know revolutionaries do not kill themselves. Revolutionaries kill the enemy." He promised S.L.A. would continue to fight despite the May 17 tragedy.

Emily Harris said the battle was "not an end, but a beginning. Whether we live or die, the day is close at hand when the people will join together in an army because of the wish to survive on their own terms, and the people will change the course of history through their courage and determination."

Patty Hearst said that their "Malcolm X" group was a "leadership training cell" and not all of S.L.A. She would give individual tributes to each of those who had died and would, for the first time, reveal that it was her love for Willie the Wolfe that had been the key factor in her conversion.

"The pigs think they can deal with a handful of revolutionaries," she said in a voice that alternated between careful intellectual analysis and screaming revolutionary rage. "But they can't defeat the incredible power which the people, once united, represent. It is for this reason," she said, "that we get to see—live and in color—the terrorist tactics of the pigs. The pigs are saying, 'You're next!' I died in that fire on Fifty-fourth Street, but out of the ashes I was reborn. I know now what I have to do. Our comrades did not die in vain. . . ."

19

*'Indeed, Alameda County has never before been confronted
with a case wherein an apparently small band of individuals
described as an army set out to revolutionize the political,
economic and judicial structures by literal overthrow and in so doing
assassinate a prominent educational leader with cyanide bullets
in the back, kidnap the daughter of a leading publicist,
rob a bank of $10,000, calling the act political, and, in fine,
threaten to demolish the very State itself. . . ."*
—Brief by Attorney James Jenner in defense of Remiro and Little

THE SHORT HOUR ALLOWED FOR VISITING JOE REMIRO in the stark and depressing tenth-floor courthouse jail is about up, and I fold my notes and begin to stuff them in my back pocket.

Wrapped inside is a communiqué the two prisoners have put out reacting to the May 17 wipe-out. "The government has claimed this is their victory," writes Joe, "but the objective facts don't support such a theory. The facts are that it took over six months for thousands of specially assigned pigs using millions of dollars to murder six revolutionaries. During the People's Battle and the Pigs' War of May 17, 1974, six true revolutionaries proved their love and dedication to the cause of the poor, oppressed and imprisoned. Now the government claims that the war is over, fully realizing, as we all do, that it's only one battle that is over and that the war has just begun." Little would add a few afterthoughts, including a compliment to "Tania for the skill she displayed in using her submachinegun to free her two comrades at the store. . . ."

Remiro sits there watching the last few minutes of the visit tick off on a wall clock, and he continues to rap about what has happened in L.A. in that same jaunty style he has exhibited throughout his long captivity, smiling from time to time, keeping up his own spirits and trying to act like a winner even though he now expects to spend the rest of his life behind bars.

His energy and optimism are so amazing that the jailers have reached the point where they no longer know how to cope with him. On Easter Day, the two revolutionists spent the afternoon serenading the prison from their isolation cells. For the most part they sang "Here Comes Peter Cottontail" while hopping around their cages like bunnies. When Death Row Jeff sent them public greetings in the "Tiger Cages of Alameda County," they posted a huge sign dubbing their dungeon a "Tiger Cage." When Patty Hearst announced her conversion, they put up a recruiting poster that said "Join the S.L.A." The guards finally got tired of tearing things down and just let them remain.

You can tell that these burly, starchily uniformed deputy sheriffs would just love to beat hell out of the two "soldiers," but close court supervision and the fear of what S.L.A. might do in retaliation have kept Remiro and Little relatively free of the usual prison intimidation.

"They tried to choke us once," Remiro reports, "after the food riots in East Oakland. They were so mad and frustrated. But it never happened again. S.L.A. has managed to keep most of that stuff off of us. Their tactics managed to keep us from being tortured or killed like we might have been."

But now, with the "core" of S.L.A. dead and authorities announcing that the group is permanently out of business, it appears that Joe's "good time" is about up.

"What's going to happen to you now?" I ask.

Joe pauses a moment to think it out.

"Well, it depends on a lot of things," he says. "I know what they want to do. They want to lynch us. Try us and try us until they finally railroad us into a conviction of *something,* and then they're going to throw us off into the prisons and then they'll try to kill us. But it will be hard.

"They finally killed George Jackson, you know, and they got off easy. There are a lot of people they'd like to get, you know, and I guess we're two of 'em. But it's not going to be so easy any more. They're going to lose ten guards for every revolutionary they get in prison, and they're scared. Guards are hard to come by these days."

Remiro considers his grim future in more detail.

"You know, I didn't really do anything, you know. I'm not guilty of what they said I did. I didn't really do anything but look what's been accomplished anyway. They *can't* let us go now, even though we're innocent. We're too dangerous to release, you know. . . . They've made us into something that we never were. Never in our wildest dreams did we think they'd make us into some kind of a mystical symbol. So now they just can't afford to let us go after what they've built us into."

Remiro says that he expects to eventually end up back in the Adjustment Center at San Quentin with the hard-core revolutionists who are the terror of the prison system. He seems pleased that the recent bloody example of his comrades' death has convinced so many black prisoners that young white guerrillas are no longer bullshitting.

"We met some of the finest people in the world in the Adjustment Center," he says. "We'd rather go back in the hole than stay here. We were with our comrades there, man. I've never seen people with such a capacity to live."

He's sure now that he will be welcome in that heavy company. The American underground, including the most deadly and determined of the black groups, has spoken out strongly in favor of the S.L.A.

The loudest and most emphatic response came on May 31, when the Weather Underground blew up the Los Angeles offices of Attorney General Younger in retaliation for the extermination of Cinque and friends. Several communications followed, explaining the bombing and urging unity among armed radicals so guerrillas would not again be allowed to "fight and die alone."

Remiro is even more excited by a May 25 emergency meeting, which unified a number of the underground groups that had not previously worked closely together. He's especially turned on by the praise S.L.A. has finally received from black guerrillas, most notably from Black Liberation Army and the Nationalist Pan-African Organization. It looks like at least a part of the Symbionese dream—bringing black and white fighters together—is coming true.

It was announced that a new "umbrella group" called United People's Liberation Army had been formed, which would coordinate the remaining units of S.L.A. as well as BLA, the Black Guerrilla Family, and the New World Liberation Front. The communiqués were full of praise for everything S.L.A. had been attempting to do.

"It's unreal," says Joe. "They called this emergency war council with representatives from revolutionary organizations throughout the country. What they did was, they gave all the people who were in the house in L.A. the Shao Lin Dragon Award, which is something that was started by George Jackson when Jonathan Jackson was killed, and they gave it to Patty, too, and, like, it was probably the first time, I'm almost positive, it's the first time that any white people had ever received it."

Remiro stops for a moment. He's really carried away by this late-blooming acceptance, but there's an ironic sidelight. For the first time since he began discussing the death of his comrades, there are tears in his eyes and an emotional huskiness in his voice.

"And then there was this one black woman from the BLA," says Joe. "And she says they were contacted by the S.L.A. at one time and that she shunned them because of the color of their skins. And she says right out, you know, that they didn't know if S.L.A. would stay and fight. They didn't know if the whites would turn 'em in. They didn't know how they would react under fire and all of this. And then she starts cryin'. And she says she's sorry and that it will never happen again."

A young guard who has been assigned to keep an especially close eye on Remiro sees that the hour is up and loudly unlocks the door to the visiting room. Joe seems glad for the interruption. He's as close to completely breaking down as I have ever seen him. He starts to get up to leave, and then he remembers something we'd been talking about earlier.

"Look, when you write about me, man, don't make out that I'm some kind of superstar. It just ain't true. I'm no Malcolm X. I'm no George Jackson. I'm not big enough for all that. I don't have enough love in me." The guard takes him back to his cell.

A few days later, I take a dimly lit courthouse elevator up to the seventh floor, where hearings on the question of moving the Remiro-Little trial out of Alameda County and to another part of the state are about to begin before balding old Judge William McGuiness.

Security is fantastically heavy. Everyone entering the courtroom is searched and photographed and questioned. But all of this paranoid bustle is completed outside the double swinging doors; deep within the decorous judicial chamber itself it is quiet, proper, high-ceilinged, dark-paneled, an unlikely place for two cultures to collide. There is a small and drooping California flag beside the bench, a huge and brilliant American banner tacked up on the wall behind the judge's chair, half a dozen lawyers thumbing through the usual stack of interminable briefs. A lovely Eurasian court clerk wears the shortest miniskirt I've seen in years. The audience is comparatively small, mostly a gaggle of Berkeley radicals who cluster together for mutual support.

I take a seat near the window and settle down for a long and dreary afternoon. I've covered a thousand trials and seldom been to one I'd willingly repeat. The defendants have not yet been brought down to the courtroom holding cell, and there is lots of time to sit and think.

I have not yet forgotten the awful vision of that burning ghetto cottage and the barbaric way six people died inside. I'm thinking about Remiro's belief that their death will bring a new and bigger revolution. I've been saying for most of my adult life that a revolution in America is too far away for serious consideration, at least within my lifetime. My own belief in nonviolence has made me search for other ways to change things. Yet what has gone down around me these past few months has made me think again.

The Los Angeles barbecue has deeply disturbed me, and out there in Televisionland there must be thousands who feel as I do. It's not that they seek any kind of specific retribution for those grisly deaths—not that many people really identified with S.L.A. It's the volatile condition of the country in which all of this occurred that has us worried. True revolutions are seldom consciously started by a handful of plotters. They explode like a giant tank of high-octane gasoline that's sprung a leak. S.L.A. and the urban guerrilla movement it represents can only supply the match.

Things are getting bad in America. Something's going to have to give. All the signs are here. Integration is a joke. The races are further apart today than they were ten years ago. The economy is on the verge of self-destruct. "Authority," which once depended on a stable national government, is in full retreat, with the word "Watergate" stamped red and angry on its fleeing ass.

The cities have become jungles. Violent crime has increased 47 percent across the country since 1968 (almost as much as the cost of living). Murders, more than half by handgun, went up 12 percent in the last twenty-four months. America is not isolated any more. In both economics and politics, the world is growing close. There soon will be no more wars that are not world wars, no more recessions or depressions that do not impoverish every nation.

S.L.A. staged the first political kidnapping and one of the first showcase political assassinations in American history. This country's politicians used to boast that such impersonal violence "could not happen here" because "Americans still communicate. There is still a basic fairness, a manly give-and-take in the United States. The rich and poor are not that far apart. We have no rigid class system."

These arguments made sense a decade ago. The situation we're faced with today is vastly different. Things are getting bitter, and more rigid lines are being drawn than ever before. We are rapidly becoming a class society. Trust and communication have broken down. The foreign "terrorist" examples in Europe, the Mideast, and South America, which U.S. radicals once studied with only mild interest, have now become vivid examples of what can be done here as well.

"The possibility must also be faced that the S.L.A.'s exploits and massive media impact may result in emulation by other small bands of domestic revolutionaries," concluded the House Committee on Internal Security in spring, '74.

A spokesman for California's attorney general admitted in early summer that a number of terrorist groups formed in the image of S.L.A. are now gathering.

"There are probably six to eight groups such as the S.L.A., and they represent the dedicated terrorist who believes in the destruction of the present governmental system," said Robert Houghton. "They range anywhere from eight to fifteen members. They are kind of a product of evolution or distillation from the '60s, and they are very well known to each other. Some are Vietnam veterans."

FBI Director Clarence Kelley has predicted that S.L.A.-type capers would encourage others to engage in "kidnappings, skyjackings, riots, and other political crimes."

Frightened California legislators have underlined their conviction that this kind of terrorism is just beginning by drafting laws that would grant special rewards to those who catch political kidnappers, create new agencies to keep a "constant watch" on known radicals, establish a system of informers—one in every neighborhood—and provide super-security for the rich and powerful, including bodyguards and "human shields."

An outraged Attorney General Evelle Younger forecast a great wave of guerrilla violence after the bombing of his Los Angeles office. For once, he was right. A series of bank robberies would begin around California and the nation which would be claimed by BLA and other guerrilla groups. Armory raids would net hundreds of military weapons. A burglary staged in the first week of June, just a few miles from the S.L.A. shoot-out site, would provide "enough guns to supply a combat infantry company" and would force the Army to reveal that it had been hit by a series of similar armory heists dating back to 1968. Hundreds of M-1s, M-16s, and machine guns were taken. The thieves were not exclusively leftists; the extreme right was suspected, too.

Groups like the New World Liberation Front and the Weather Underground would step up their bombings, focusing on large corporations like ITT and Anaconda, which helped to overthrow the Allende government in Chile. American guerrillas would pay more and more attention to the increasingly international nature of big business and would identify with terrorist revolutionaries in Argentina, Mozambique, Santo Domingo, Brazil, Mexico, Uruguay, the Middle East, and Ireland. In early '74 the newspapers would be full of reports on the activities of these foreign "people's armies."

The S.L.A. caper would also dramatically underline the degree to which Americans are now becoming "polarized" for or against the Establishment, with little room in this totally black-and-white stand-off for more carefully considered positions in between.

S.L.A. had obviously pushed all of the emotional buttons at once, all the ancient fears of black violence and the mythologies of miscegenation, the growing suspicion of freaked-out Vietnam vets, the utter horror and dread aroused by militant feminists, the generation chasm between ever more conservative parents and truly rebellious kids. At no time in my own journalistic career of over twenty years had I seen a situation in which so many people took violent and hysterical positions on a subject and were so totally unwilling to talk to someone with an opposing viewpoint.

The word "polarization" even crept into the official report of the L.A. cops on the shoot-out. Said Police Commission President Samuel Williams:

". . . The six deceased seem to have been individuals who were, for the most part, well capable of making positive contributions. But they turned instead, as a matter of tactics, to terror. They were alienated and by personal choice became outlaws. They committed themselves to violence and to provoking an official institutional counter-violence which would and did crush them. They involved all of us in their bizarre fantasy. They initiated a self-corrupting spiral of over-simplification and polarization and violence. But these may have indeed been the very purposes of the Symbionese Liberation Army. . . ."

I'm thinking about all of the frantic rage that S.L.A. kicked up when Remiro and Little in their white prison jumpsuits are led into the courtroom and Judge McGuiness quickly strides up onto the bench. The hearing begins.

Most of the argument for a change of venue comes from Little's lawyer, James Jenner. He offers tons of clippings and complete newspapers to show that prejudicial pretrial publicity has been so heavy in Oakland that a fair hearing is impossible here. He will eventually have his way and the case will be moved to another county.

I take desultory notes, for most of this has been said before and better in previous cases. Toward the end of the afternoon, however, Jenner starts to take issue with the manner in which the prosecutor has introduced a number of newspaper exhibits of his own—the Oakland *Tribune* front pages from April 7 to May 5— to show that ALMOST NOTHING in these newspapers is in any way related to Remiro, Little, or the S.L.A. It is clear that he is ignorant of the politics of the case, for some of the headlines he introduces into evidence are the best possible examples of how very political the matter really is, how much S.L.A. was an outgrowth of current economic and social conditions not only in America but around the world.

"Trials" involving political defendants almost always run into this impasse. It is the job of the prosecutor to try to exclude the very issues that made the accused do the things he's charged with. They don't really want to know "why," just "did he do it?" If he's a draft evader, the prosecutor will not want the court to consider anything except whether or not the man signed certain forms and did or did not show up for induction. He will not want to hear a word about the legality and morality of war. Nothing but the statutory transgressions, chapter and verse, will be allowed.

In the Remiro-Little case, the only issue the prosecution wants discussed is the question of just who fired what bullets into Dr. Marcus Foster. If he possibly can, the D.A. will handle the case as if it has no political content whatsoever.

This practice absolutely enrages Remiro. They are not even speaking the same language. When the D.A. reads off a headline that says "18 Israelis Slain by Guerrillas" and then indicates it has nothing whatever to do with S.L.A., Joe explodes.

"Of COURSE it does," he yells at the prosecutor. "Almost every one of those headlines have *everything* to do with it. You're goddamned right they do."

Judge McGuiness (who reminds me of a benign General Patton up there in front of that huge, day-glo American flag) silences him, and the reading of the headlines continues:

"Calley Sentence Stands," he reads, and I remember that Joe Remiro is here because of what happened to him in Vietnam, because of the massacres he participated in.

"$20 Million in Stolen Art Recovered," the prosecutor notes, referring to an action by Irish terrorists who were emulated by S.L.A.

"Censoring by Prisons Is Limited"—and I remember Joe's deep involvement in the prison movement.

"Subpoena of Nixon Tapes"—and I recall Joe's bitterness when Nixon ignored those years of peace marching.

"Junta Frees Imprisoned in Portugal"—the fate of black rebels in Angola and Mozambique was a continuing concern of S.L.A.

"V.A. Head Johnson Plans to Resign"—Remiro's disillusionment as a veteran turned him toward revolt.

"Corporate Crimes Attacked by Nader"—every Symbionese document overflowed with references to "corporate criminals."

"Shah Hits Oil Prices"—the international oil cartels were prime S.L.A. enemies.

" 'I Hate Americans'—Melina Mercouri"—because of U.S. support for the Greek junta—another S.L.A. cause.

"Bomb Explodes at Teamsters Office"—planted by supporters of the rival Farm Workers Union, for which Joe worked long and hard.

"Prices Soar; Inflation Hits 25-Year High"—the soaring price of food helped spark the S.L.A. food ransom plan.

"14 Firebombs Rip Stores in London"—the Irish terrorists again.

"U.S. Aide Held in Argentina"—by the People's Revolutionary Army, a model S.L.A. drew freely upon.

"UN Warns of World's Problems"—most especially famine, inflation, and an end to the "good life"—and they claim *this* has nothing to do with socialist revolutionaries?

As dozens of these headlines are being read into the record, I begin to stare out the seventh-floor window at the wide expanse of Berkeley and Oakland below. It is a clear day, and I can see the Berkeley Hills and part of the community where Remiro first learned the ABC's of militancy. My eye travels to the fancy apartment house just across Lake Merritt, where I think I see Black Panther Huey Newton standing on his balcony, gazing across the shallow body of water toward this courtroom where his revolutionary successors stand trial. Newton won his own freedom here after a shoot-out with police some four years ago. He spent many months in the very same jail where Remiro and Little now are held.

Off to the west, I can hear the whistle of tugboats and the distant rumble of great cranes loading a dozen freighters for long journeys across the Pacific and into the world. Out there lies the future.

I shift my gaze slightly to the southeast and see the parking lot where Marcus Foster was gunned down on the evening of November 6. A little farther to the south is the strange deserted park that S.L.A.'s assassins ran through on their way to a waiting car parked by the quaint old Civic Auditorium, which lies only a hundred yards below this courtroom.

It is because of the events of that night that Joe Remiro now faces tired old Judge McGuiness.

The prosecution will do its best to narrow the issues down to no more than the murder of Marcus Foster, to a game of cops and robbers, everything reduced to bang-bang-shoot-'em-up simplicity that even the most moronic police reporter can understand.

And the entire trial—and it's bound to be a long and complicated one—will again and again funnel down to a dreary discussion of which statutes were violated and by whom. It will be both tiresome and tragic, because the real issues are vital and will probably be ignored.

A truly political series of acts brought Joe Remiro to this courtroom. And a freaked-out but idealistic young American war veteran who could find no peace in his own country will now be tossed upon the social scrapheap, chewed up in the legal meat grinder and then spoon-fed to a disinterested and somnambulistic public as just one more pablum testimonial to "law 'n' order." It's sad, because so much more is involved here; so much could be learned; the warning is so clear.

The trial which has half begun this day in Oakland is going to be a lot longer than anyone expects. Its ultimate judgment will encompass us all. I think about this as I watch a shadowy mindplay of long-ago events and relentless future possibilities through the double-locked and closely barred courthouse window over Lake Merritt.

I realize that this is going to be more than one man's trial and that it will last more than one man's lifetime.

Before it is done, a lot is going to have to change in this screwed-up country of ours. I wonder who will still be around to judge Joe Remiro's story at its end. I wonder who will be called "innocent" then and who will be "guilty." How great a penalty will the living pay, and how heavy a debt must be passed on to those generations that are not yet even a flicker of unconscious lust in our imagination's wandering eye?

Appendix

DECLARE WAR

THE SYMBIONESE FEDERATION
& THE SYMBIONESE LIBERATION ARMY
DECLARATION OF REVOLUTIONARY WAR
& THE SYMBIONESE PROGRAM

August 21, 1973

The Symbionese Federation and The Symbionese Liberation Army is a united and federated grouping of members of different races and people and socialist political parties of the oppressed people of The Fascist United States of America, who have under black and minority leadership formed and joined The Symbionese Federated Republic and have agreed to struggle together in behalf of all their people and races and political parties' interest in the gaining of **Freedom** and **Self Determination** and **Independence** for all their people and races.

The Symbionese Federation is **not a government,** but rather it is a united and federated formation of members of different races and people and political parties who have agreed to struggle in a **united front** for the independence and self determination of each of their races and people and The Liquidation of the Common Enemy.

And who by this federated formation represent their future and independent pre-governments and nations of their people and races. The Symbionese Federation is **not a party,** but rather it is a Federation, for its members are made up of members of all political parties and organizations and races of all the most oppressed people of this fascist nation, thereby forming unity and the full representation of the interests of all the people.

The Symbionese Liberation Army is an army of the people, and is made up of members of all the people. The S.L.A. has no political power or political person over it that dictates who will fight and die if needed for the freedom of our people and children, but does not risk their life or fight too for our freedom, but rather the S.L.A. is both political and military in that in the S.L.A. the army officer, whether female or male is also the political officer and they both are the daughters and sons of the people and they both fight as well as speak for the freedom of our people and children.

The Symbionese Federation and The Symbionese Liberation Army is made up of the aged, youth and women and men of all races and people. The name Symbionese is taken from the word symbiosis and we define its meaning as a body of dissimilar bodies and organisms living in deep and loving harmony and partnership in the best interest of all within the body.

We of the Symbionese Federation and The S.L.A. define ourselves by this name because it states that we are no longer willing to allow the enemy of all our people and children to murder, oppress and exploit us nor define us by color and thereby maintain division among us, but rather have joined together under black and minority leadership in behalf of all our different races and people to build a better and new world for our children and people's future. We are a United Front and Federated Coalition of members from the Asian, Black, Brown, Indian, White, Women, Grey and Gay Liberation Movements.

Who have all come to see and understand that only if we unite and build our new world and future, will there really be a future for our children and people. We of the People and not the ruling capitalist class, will build a new world and system. Where there is really freedom and a true meaning to justice and equality for all women and men of all races and people, and an end to the murder and oppression, exploitation of all people.

We of the Symbionese Federation and The S.L.A. are the children of all oppressed people, who have decided to redefine ourselves as a Symbionese Race and People. Yet, recognizing the rich cultures of each and enforcing our rights to existence of our many cultures within a united federation of independent and sovereign nations, each of them flourishing and protected by its own laws and codes of self determination.

We are of many colors, but yet of one mind, for we all in history's time on this earth have become part of each other in suffering and in mind, and have agreed that the murder, oppression, and exploitation of our children and people must end now, for we all have seen the murder, oppression and exploitation of our people for too long under the hand of the same enemy and class of people and under the same system.

Knowing this, the Symbionese Federation and The S.L.A. know that our often murderous alienation from each other aids and is one of the fundamental strengths behind the ruling capitalist class's ability to murder and oppress us all. By not allowing them to define us by color, and also recognizing that by refusing ourselves to also internalize this false division definition, knowing that in mind and body we are facing the same enemy and that we are all comrades of one people, the murdered and oppressed, we are now able to become a united people under the Symbionese Federation and make true the words of our codes of unity that **to die a race, and be borne a nation, is to become free.**

Therefore, we of the Symbionese Federation and The S.L.A. **do not** under the rights of human beings submit to the murder, oppression and exploitation of our children and people and do under the rights granted to the people under The Declaration of Independence of The United States, do now by the rights of our children and people and by Force of Arms and with every drop of our blood, *Declare Revolutionary War* against The Fascist Capitalist Class, and all their agents of murder, oppression and exploitaton. We support by Force of Arms the just struggles of all oppressed people for self determination and independence within the United States and The World. And hereby offer to all liberation movements, revolutionary workers groups, and peoples organizations our total aid and support for the struggle for freedom and justice for all people and races. We call upon all revolutionary black and other oppressed people within the Fascist United States to come together and join The Symbionese Federation and fight in the forces of The Symbionese Liberation Army.

"NEW MEANING TO LIFE & LOVE"

THE GOALS OF THE
SYMBIONESE LIBERATION ARMY

1. To unite all oppressed people into a fighting force and to destroy the system of the capitalist state and all its value systems. To create in its place a system and sovereign nations that are in the total interest of all its races and people, based on the true affirmation of life, love, trust, and honesty, freedom and equality that is truly for all.
2. To assure the rights of all people to self determination and the rights to build their own nation and government, with representatives that have shown through their actions to be in the interest of their people. To give the right to all people to select and elect their own representatives and governments by direct vote.
3. To build a people's federated council, who will be a male and female of each People's Council or Sovereign Nation of The Symbionese Federation of Nations, who shall be the representatives of their nations in the forming of trade pacts and unified defense against any external enemy that may attack any of the free nations of the federation and to form other aids to each other's needs.
4. To aid and defend the cultural rights of all the sovereign nations of The Symbionese Federation, and to aid each nation in the building of educational and other institutions to meet and serve this need for its people.
5. To place the control of all the institutions and industries, of each nation into the hands of its people. To aid sovereign nations of the federation to build nations where work contributes concretely to the full interest and needs of its workers and the communal interest of its communities and its people and the mutual interest of all within the federation of nations.
6. To aid and defend the rights of all oppressed people to build nations which do not institute oppression and exploitation, but rather institute the environment of freedom and defend that freedom on all levels and for all of the people, and by any means necessary.
7. To give back to all people their human and constitutional rights, liberty, equality and justice and the right to bear arms in the defense of these rights.
8. To create a system where our aged are cared for with respect, love,

and kindness and aided and encouraged to become assets in their own ways to their nations and to their communal community. That the life that moves around them is not a frightening and murderous one and where life is not a fear, but rather one of love and feeling and of unity.

9. To create a system and laws that will neither force people into nor force them to stay in personal relationships that they do not wish to be in, and to destroy all chains constituted by legal and social laws of the capitalist state which act as a reinforcing system to maintain this form of imprisonment.

10. To create institutions that will aid, reinforce and educate the growth of our comrade women and aid them in making a new true and better role to live in life and in the defining of themselves as a new and free people.

11. To create new forms of life and relationships that bring true meanings of love to people's relationships, and to form communes on the community level and bring the children of the community into being the responsibility of the community, to place our children in the union of real comradeship and in the care and loving interest of the revolutionary community.

12. To destroy the prison system, which the capitalist state has used to imprison the oppressed and exploited, and thereby destroy the love, unity, and hopes of millions of lives and families. And to create in its place a system of comradeship and that of group unity and education on a communal and revolutionary level within the community, to bring home our daughters and sons, and sisters and brothers, fathers and mothers and welcome them home with love and a new revolutionary comradeship of unity.

13. To take control of all state land and that of the capitalist class and to give back the land to the people. To form laws and codes that safeguard that no person can own the land, or sell the land, but rather the nations' people own the land and use it for their needs and interest to live. No one can own or sell the air, the sky, the water, the trees, the birds, the sun, for all of this world belongs to the people of this earth.

14. To take controls of all buildings and apartment buildings of the capitalist class and fascist government and then to totally destroy the rent system of exploitation.

15. To build a federation of nations, who shall formulate programs and unions of actions and interests that will destroy the capitalist value system and its other anti-human institutions and who will be able to do this by meeting all the basic needs of all of the people and their nations. For they will be all able to do this because each nation will

have full control of all of its industries and institutions and does not run them for profit, but in the full interest of all the people of its nation.

16. To destroy all forms and institutions of Racism, Sexism, Ageism, Capitalism, Fascism, Individualism, Possessiveness, Competitiveness and all other such institutions that have made and sustained capitalism and the capitalist class system that has oppressed and exploited all of the people of our history.

By this means and the mutual aid and unity of each nation within The Symbionese Federation, will each nation be able to provide to each person and couple and family free of cost the five basic needs of life, which are food, health care, housing, education and clothing, and in this way allowing people to be able to find and form new values and new systems of relationships and interests based on a new meaning to life and love.

THE WAR COUNCIL

THE UNITED SYMBIONESE WAR COUNCIL
TERMS OF MILITARY/POLITICAL ALLIANCE

Our commitment to the revolutionary struggle for self-determination for all oppressed people and races and the international proletarian revolution is total and fully uncompromisable. Therefore, any relationship the Symbionese War Council has with any group or organization is based on their active military/political commitment to the goal of gaining freedom for all oppressed people and races.

1. Our alliance with any group or organization is based upon their firm decision to fight as well as talk in behalf of the people's interest, and once this commitment is clear then we can come together in order to:

   1) collectively develop a common strategy
   2) work together to develop tactical co-ordination
   3) Assist each other in developing the abilities and talents of all the members of the Symbionese War Council and to analyze the strengths and weaknesses of the leadership in order to constantly better all aspects of the ability and actions of the War Council, and its individual leadership from other organizations.

2. Command positions of The War Council are subject to the approval of all members of the council, based upon the military/political thinking and ability of the presented officer to work with others in the interest of freedom for all people and races.

3. Command positions in The War Council are not appointed by one who knows, one's sex, one's color or by the group or organization one belongs to, but only by one's Courage, Determination, Intelligence, Aggressive Initiative and Capability as a leader and one's Military/Political thinking.

4. All members of The War Council are expected and fully are responsible for the military/political leadership of The S.L.A., they must fight and speak for the people and this must be understood clearly by all members.

5. No member of The War Council can elect or select himself or herself to a position such as the head of a government or people's council; the War Council is totally an alliance **of war against the common enemy.**

The people themselves shall have and hold the **only right** to select and elect their governments and government heads of state.

6. It is **not** the policy of The War Council to rip off leadership or membership from other organizations, but rather it is the policy of The War Council to aid and support the development and education of leadership to fulfill truly its responsibility to the people, and to allow the collective intelligence, leadership and resourcefullness of the leadership from different organizations and groups to flourish together and grow together; thereby forming an area where the collective interests and needs as well as weaknesses and strengths of each can benefit each **in the common struggle to liquidate the common enemy.**

7. A successful military force is a necessity for actualizing political goals and must therefore be held as a priority; therefore, the true assistance in the supplying of military equipment, materials, finances, and personnel is of the upmost importance, once these forces have fully committed themselves to open and total warfare against the common enemy and members of The War Council must understand this clearly.

8. Leadership of any group of organization which is truly committed and in agreement with the goals of The S.L.A. and the terms of military/ political alliance may be presented to The War Council; however, the presented officer's membership is not confirmed until it is verified that prior to presentation for membership a combat action has been taken part in by that group or organization within the past 12 months.

9. Once The War Council collectively agrees to an action or plan of strategy then that action shall be understood as an action of The S.L.A., and not of any single group or organization. Just as the fingers cannot call themselves a fist, and the fist cannot call itself the fingers. From time to time the membership on The War Council may disagree upon a particular action or strategy. When in disagreement, that particular membership need not participate in The S.L.A. action, but membership on The War Council is maintained only as long as all commitments made to the collective Symbionese War Council are continued to be fully adhered to. It is the disagreeing group or organization's responsibility to, on its own, prove out their ideas in order to change or modify its own or The collective War Council's direction.

10. It is the policy of The War Council not to involve itself in the internal political affairs of disagreements that may result within different organizations or groups. However, The War Council recognizes and accepts membership to the Council of any military/political unit, cell or organization that qualifies and shall recognize them as true representatives of that particular organization or group. It is the collective policy of The War Council that the failure of the elected leadership to fulfill her or his revolutionary responsibility as far as the War

Council is concerned shall be totally the responsibility of the elected leader and not that of The War Council.

11. Organizations or groups that wish to serve in combat units must select two persons, one female and one male (if possible), who have full responsibility and authority to act and represent their group or organization and who will hold a command position in the unified command of The United Symbionese War Council.

All members of The Symbionese War Council must clearly understand that our commitment is total and our goal is the total freedom of the people and children and the destroying totally of the common enemy. Therefore, it is held that any restraining of supplies or other war materials etc. for political reasons or reactionary reasons or political chess games with the enemy, by any officer or other person in the War Council that by its actions endangers the lives of the women and men of The Symbionese Liberation Army shall be held as a full and total violation of this alliance pact and compromising with the enemy and the freedom and life of the people and children and therefore is punishable by death.

TO THOSE WHO WOULD BEAR
THE HOPES AND FUTURE OF THE PEOPLE,
LET THE VOICE OF THEIR GUNS
EXPRESS THE WORDS OF FREEDOM.

Gen. Field Marshal
CIN
S.L.A.

WILLING TO DIE

TACTICAL SUPPORT UNITS

Each cell of The S.L.A. **tactical support units** is composed of elements of other organizations and groups and individuals. Under the strategy of The S.L.A. it is totally impossible to follow the egotistic aspirations of many leaders of political organizations, since they continue to organize new organizations every time one falls apart, when they fail to understand that the people always organize to fight the enemy. When leaders fail to start the fight, then the people fall from that organization.

To continue in this manner is totally reactionary, egotistic, opportunist and anti-revolutionary, since to do so only allows for the continued grouping and regrouping of the same revolutionary people for the fight that never comes and with the only purpose of organizing.

This is totally anti-revolutionary for within the true purpose of revolution there is only **two deep purposes: to destroy the enemy and free the people.** This in itself means the need for an army of the people that fights the enemy.

In order to organize, one must organize in support of something, one does not organize in support of having or belonging to or just to organize, but rather one must have a purpose to organize around, and since in revolution it is the purpose to organize to fight the enemy and to support those who fight on the front lines, it is then clear that the people organize to fight and destroy the enemy. They do not organize to fight the enemy and then when it comes time to fight, claim that to fight the enemy will endanger the organization for this would show them to be lovers of positions and the organization and not true revolutionaries who love the people and children.

Since you, as members of the people, have organized to fight the enemy, for the reason that you are and do love the people, then it is clear to you where your true responsibility is, and that it is to join and support those who are in the front lines fighting the enemy of us all, regardless of what color, group or organization they belong to, for the people are just this, they are not organization or color or group, they are the oppressed, exploited and the murdered, they are those we love and for whom we, if needed, are willing to die. They are our children.

Therefore, it is now for you as lovers of the people to select in what area you are able and willing to fight in or give support to, either in

[319]

the combat units or support units of The S.L.A. The choice is yours alone: either to be and show yourselves as lovers of the people and our children and true to the word revolutionary or as egotistic opportunists and lovers of a group and organization and enemies of the people.

7 AIMS

Umoja - La Unidad - Unity - To strive for and maintain unity in our household, our nation and in The Symbionese Federation.

Kujichagulia - La Libre Determinacion - Self Determination - To define ourselves, name ourselves, speak for ourselves and govern ourselves.

Ujima - Trabajo Colectivo y Responsibilidad - Collective Work and Responsibility - To build and maintain our nation and the federation together by making our brothers' and sisters' and the Federation's problems our problems and solving them together.

Ujamaa - Produccion Cooperativa - Cooperative Production - To build and maintain our own economy from our skills, and labor and resources and to insure ourselves and other nations that we all profit equally from our labor.

Nia - Proposito - Purpose - To make as our collective vocation the development and liberation of our nation, and all oppressed people, in order to restore our people and all oppressed people to their traditional greatness and humanity.

Kuumba - Creativo - Creativity - To do all we can, as best we can, in order to free our nation and defend the federation and constantly make it and the earth that we all share more beautiful and beneficial.

Imani - Fe - Faith - To believe in our unity, our leaders, our teachers, our people, and in the righteousness and victory of our struggle and the struggle of all oppressed and exploited people.

MEANING OF
THE COBRA SYMBOL

The emblem of the Symbionese Liberation Army is 170,000 years old, and it is one of the first symbols used by people to signify God and life. The two bottom heads on each side of the Cobra represent the four principles of life: the sun, the moon, the earth, and the water. The three center heads represent God and the universe, and are called the God head. The number seven as embracing all the universal forces of God and life can be traced to the Egyptian temples and their seven pillars, to the seven candles of the pre-Zionist, North African religions, to the Buddhist and Hindu religions, and to the North and South American Indian religions. This is because the seven principles explain the inter-relationships of life, of the family and the state, of the human anatomy and the universe. And because the basic principle behind any kind of union and series of relationships must be equally accessible to all concerned, we see why the seven heads of the cobra have but one body. The thoughts and purpose in each of the seven heads of the cobra penetrate its common body and soul, and from this we see how the source of the cobra's survival lies not in any individual head, but rather in the relationship and unity of all the heads to each other.

The Symbionese Liberation Army has selected the Seven-Headed Cobra as our emblem because we realize that an army is a mass that needs unity in order to become a fighting force, and we know that true unity among people must be based upon a concern that is universal. It is a revolutionary unity of all people against a common oppressor enemy of the people. This unity of seven heads in one body defines the essence of co-operation and socialism in the great undertaking of revolutionary war. Through the puritan capitalist ethics of competition, individualism, fascism, racism, sexism, and imperialism the enemy is attacking us. This enemy functions by means of attacking one race or group among us in an attempt to force us into submission and division and isolation from each other. From these attacks, we have learned that our common enemy will not stop until we come together to stop him, for he lives off the murder and oppression of our divided and therefore defenseless people.

We have chosen the Seven-Headed Cobra as the emblem of the S.L.A. because our forces are from every walk of life, from every religion, and of every race, and by our unity does our strength and our common goal for freedom from the chains of capitalism make true the meaning of our seven principles of unity. Our military and political strength arises from the masses of all our people, for when the people are at one in their inmost body, they shatter even the hardest of iron or of bronze, and when the people understand each other in their inmost heart, their words are sweet and strong.

The seven memberships of our federation are men and women who are black, brown, yellow, red, white, young and old. Each of these members joins together and speaks and fights for the best interests of all within the body, just as one head of the cobra can be attacked without the others rising to strike with venom in self-defense to destroy the attacker. Each head of the cobra stands in organic need of all the others in order to maintain its survival.

From this example of the necessity of unity in order to survive, the S.L.A. will build and fight for the socialist unity of all oppressed peoples. A cry from any one of us will echo in the body of our common ear, and we will attack out of instinct, and in self-defense, for our survival. And with the venom of our seven heads we will destroy the fascist insect which preys upon the life of the people; and with the minds of our seven heads, and the spirit of our one body and soul, we will secure a future for our children.

CODES OF WAR OF THE UNITED SYMBIONESE LIBERATION ARMY

PENALTY BY DEATH

ALL CHARGES THAT FACE A DEATH PENALTY SHALL BE PRESENTED TO A JURY TRIAL MADE UP OF THE MEMBERS OF THE GUERRILLA FORCES. THE JURY SHALL BE SELECTED BY THE CHARGED AND THE JUDGE CONDUCTING THE TRIAL SHALL BE SELECTED BY THE CHARGED ALSO. THE CHARGED SHALL SELECT HIS OR HER DEFENSE, AND THE TRIAL JUDGE SHALL SELECT THE PROSECUTOR. THE JURY SHALL NUMBER AT LEAST ¾ths OF THE REMAINING MEMBERS OF THE CELLS, AND THE VERDICT MUST BE UNANIMOUS.

1. THE SURRENDER TO THE ENEMY.

2. THE KILLING OF A COMRADE OR DISOBEYING ORDERS THAT RESULT IN THE DEATH OF A COMRADE.

3. THE DESERTING OF A COMRADE ON THE FIELD OF WAR.

   a. LEAVING A TEAM POSITION, THEREBY NOT COVERING A COMRADE.

   b. LEAVING A WOUNDED COMRADE.

4. THE INFORMING TO THE ENEMY OR SPYING AGAINST THE PEOPLE OR GUERRILLAS.

5. LEAVING A CELL UNIT OR BASE CAMP WITHOUT ORDERS.

Any comrade may leave the guerrilla forces if she or he feels that they no longer feel the courage or faith in the people and the struggle that we wage. A comrade, however, must follow the CODES OF WAR in doing this: that is, he or she must inform the commanding guerrilla of their wish to go from the guerrilla force. Thereupon, the guerrilla in command will release them in a safe area. The ex-combatant may only leave with his or her personal side-arm. REMEMBER, this is the ONLY way a comrade may leave the S.L.A., any other way is deserting, punishable by death.

6. ALL PAID OR UNPAID INFORMANTS OPERATING WITHIN THE COMMUNITY AGAINST THE PEOPLE AND THE GUERRILLA FORCES ARE SENTENCED WITHOUT TRIAL TO IMMEDIATE DEATH.

PENALTY BY DISCIPLINARY ACTION

DISCIPLINARY ACTION SHOULD BE PRIMARILY TO AID THE COLLECTIVE GROWTH OF THE CELL, SO THAT THROUGH POSITIVE ACTION THE MISTAKE IS UNDER-STOOD. ALL CHARGES THAT FACE DISCIPLINARY ACTION SHALL BE UNDER THE FULL CONTROL OF THE GUER-RILLA IN COMMAND, AND SHE OR HE SHALL WEIGH ALL EVIDENCE AND SHALL DECIDE THE VERDICT, AND IF NEEDED, DIRECT THE DISCIPLINARY ACTION TO BE TAKEN BY THE CHARGED COMRADE NECESSARY TO DIRECT HIM OR HER. EXAMPLES OF DISCIPLINARY ACTION ARE: THE CLEANING AND MAINTENANCE OF ALL CELL ARMS, AMMUNITION AND EXPLOSIVES FOR ONE WEEK, THE UP-KEEP OF OUTHOUSES, THE FULL SUSPENSION OF WINE OR CIGARETTES, AND EXTRA DUTIES SUCH AS AD-DITIONAL WATCHES, PRACTICE AND STUDY PERIODS, CORRESPONDENCE, FILING, TYPING, WASHING, CLEAN-ING, COOKING, AND PHYSICAL EXERCISES.

1. LACK OF RESPONSIBILITY AND DETERMINED DE-CISIVENESS IN FOLLOWING ORDERS.

2. NON-VIGILANCE OR THE LEAVING OF AN ASSIGNED POST WITHOUT ORDERS.

3. LACK OF RESPONSIBILITY IN MAINTAINING EQUIP-MENT OR PROFICIENCY IN ALL GUERRILLA SKILLS, ESPECIALLY SHOOTING.

4. THE USE OF ANY UNMEDICALLY PRESCRIBED DRUG:

THIS RULE RELATES TO THE USE OF SUCH DRUGS AS HEROIN, SPEED, PEYOTE, MESCALINE, REDS, PEP PILLS, WHITES, YELLOW JACKETS, BENNIES, DEXIES, GOOF BALLS, LSD, AND ANY OTHER KIND OF HALLUCINATORY DRUGS. HOWEVER, PERMISSION IS GRANTED FOR THE USE OF ONLY TWO TYPES OF RELAXING DRUGS: THESE ARE MARIJUANA, AND/OR BEER AND WINE AND OTHER AL-

COHOL. THIS PERMISSION IS ONLY GRANTED WHEN AP-PROVED BY THE GUERRILLA IN COMMAND, AND WITH VERY RESTRAINING USE ONLY. NO OFFICER MAY GRANT THE USE OF ANY OF THESE SAID DRUGS TO THE FULL NUMBER OF FORCES UNDER HIS OR HER COMMAND. IF THIS PERMISSION IS GRANTED, ONLY HALF THE FORCE WILL BE ALLOWED TO TAKE PART, WHILE THE OTHER HALF WILL STAND GUARD DUTY.

THE PAST HAS SHOWN ONCE TRUE REVOLUTIONARIES HAVE SERIOUSLY UNDERTAKEN REVOLUTIONARY ARMS STRUGGLE, MARIJUANA AND ALCOHOL ARE NOT USED FOR RECREATIONAL PURPOSES OR TO DILUTE OR BLUR THE CONSCIOUSNESS OF REALITY, BUT VERY SMALL AMOUNTS FOR MEDICINAL PURPOSES TO CALM NERVES UNDER TIMES OF TENSION, NOT TO DISTORT REALITY.

5. THE FAILURE TO SEVER ALL PAST CONTACTS OR FAILING TO DESROY ALL EVIDENCE OF IDENTIFICATION OR ASSOCIATION.

PENALTY BY DISCIPLINARY ACTION

6. KILLING OF AN UNARMED ENEMY: IN THIS INSTANCE THE ENEMY REFERS TO MEMBERS OF USA RANK AND FILE ONLY AND NOT TO ANY MEMBERS OF THE CIA, FBI, OR OTHER SPECIAL AGENTS OR ANY CITY, POLITICAL POLICE STATE AGENTS. MEMBERS OF THE USA MILITARY RANK AND FILE ARE TO BE ACCORDED THIS DISTINCTION BE-CAUSE WE RECOGNIZE THAT MANY OF THEM HAVE BEEN FORCED INTO MEMBERSHIP EITHER DIRECTLY, THROUGH THE DRAFT, OR INDIRECTLY DUE TO ECONOMIC PRES-SURES.

7. TORTURES OR SEXUAL ASSAULT ON EITHER A COM-RADE OR PEOPLE OR THE ENEMY.

8. CRIMINAL ACTS AGAINST THE POOR COMRADES OR GUERRILLA FORCES.

9. MALICIOUS CURSING OF ANY KIND OF DISRESPECT TO THOSE IN COMMAND, A COMRADE, OR THE PEOPLE.

10. DECEIVING OR LYING TO FELLOW COMRADES OR THE PEOPLE. IF ANY OF THESE ACTS ARE COMMITTED ON A CONTINUOUS BASIS, THE CHARGED COMRADE SHALL BECOME A PRISONER OF THE CELL AND SHALL REMAIN IN THIS PRISONER STATUS UNTIL SUCH TIME AS SHE OR

HE IS ABLE TO PROVE THEIR RENEWED COMMITMENT TO REVOLUTIONARY DISCIPLINE AND REVOLUTIONARY PRINCIPLES OR THE CHARGED MAY REQUEST TO BE DIS-HONORABLY DISCHARGED.

CONDUCT OF GUERRILLA FORCES TOWARDS THE ENEMY SOLDIERS AND PRISONERS

1. PRISONERS OF WAR SHALL BE HELD UNDER THE INTERNATIONAL CODES OF WAR, THEY SHALL BE PROVIDED WITH ADEQUATE FOOD, MEDICAL AID, AND EXERCISES.

2. ALL USA MILITARY RANK AND FILE FORCES SHALL BE ALLOWED TO SURRENDER UPON OUR CONDITIONS OF SURRENDER, AND THEREUPON THEY SHALL BE CAREFULLY SEARCHED AND INTERROGATED. ALL PRISONERS ARE TO RECEIVE INSTRUCTION ON THE GOALS OF THE SYMBIONESE LIBERATION ARMY, THEN RELEASED IN A SAFE AREA.

3. ALL WEAPONS, MEDICAL AND FOOD SUPPLIES, MAPS, MILITARY EQUIPMENT AND MONEY ARE TO BE CONFISCATED AND TURNED IN TO THE GUERRILLA IN CHARGE.

4. UNDER NO CONDITIONS SHALL ANY RANK AND FILE ENEMY SOLDIER BE RELIEVED OF HIS OR HER PERSONAL PROPERTY.

CONDUCT OF GUERRILLA FORCES TOWARDS THE PEOPLE

ALL GUERRILLA FORCES SHALL CONDUCT THEMSELVES IN A MANNER OF RESPECT TOWARD THE PEOPLE, AND SHALL, WHEN ABLE AND SAFE TO DO SO, PROVIDE FOOD AND OTHER AID TO THE PEOPLE. THEY SHALL, WHEN POSSIBLE, INFORM THE PEOPLE OF THE GOALS OF THE UNITED SYMBIONESE FEDERATION AND ENCOURAGE OTHER WOMEN AND MEN TO JOIN OUR FORCES AND TO SERVE THE PEOPLE AND FIGHT FOR FREEDOM.

ALL COMRADES HAVE ONE MAIN RESPONSIBILITY, THAT IS TO STRUGGLE AND WIN AND STAND TOGETHER, SO NO COMRADE STANDS ALONE. ALL MUST LOOK OUT FOR EACH OTHER, ALL MUST AID THE OTHER BLACK, BROWN, RED, YELLOW, WHITE, MAN OR WOMAN, ALL OR NONE.

THIS DOCUMENT MAY CHANGE FROM TIME TO TIME, SO OFFICERS ARE REQUESTED TO FOLLOW THE CHANGES WITH DISCIPLINE.

TO THOSE WHO WOULD BEAR THE HOPES AND FUTURE OF THE PEOPLE, LET THE VOICE OF THEIR GUNS EXPRESS THE WORD OF FREEDOM.

Gen. Field Marshal
S.L.A.
CIN

Index

Donald David DeFreeze (alias Cinque Mtume, Donald DeFrez, John DeFrield, David Kenneth Robinson, Steven Robinson, and Donald David Thompson). Enough names and accusations for ten men.

BANK ROBBERY

Patricia Michelle Soltysik

FBI No.: 313,208 L6   Date Photographs Taken Unknown
Aliases: Mizmoon Monique Soltysik, "Mizmoon," "Pat," "Zoya"
Age: 23, born May 17, 1950, Santa Barbara, California (not supported by birth records)
Height: 5'3" to 5'4"   **Eyes:** Brown
Weight: 116 pounds   **Complexion:** Medium
Build: Small   **Race:** White
Hair: Dark brown   **Nationality:** American
Occupations: Janitor, school bus driver, restaurant hostess
Social Security No. Used: 568-76-1137

Camilla Christine Hall

FBI No.: 313-207 L9   Date Photographs Taken Unknown
Age: 29, born March 24, 1945, Minnesota (not supported by birth records)
Height: 5'6"   **Eyes:** Blue
Weight: 125 pounds   **Race:** White
Build: Medium   **Nationality:** American
Hair: Blonde
Occupations: Gardener, house to house salesman, social worker
Remarks: Usual attire reportedly levis and boots
Social Security No. Used: 470-50-2876

Nancy Ling Perry

FBI No.: 313,206 L1   Date Photograph Taken Unknown
Aliases: Nancy Cecile Devoto, Lynn Ledworth, Nancy Gail Ling, Nancy Gail Perry, "Fahizah"
Age: 26, born September 19, 1947, Oakland, California (not supported by birth records)
Height: 5'
Weight: 95 to 105 pounds
Build: Small
Hair: Reddish brown
Eyes: Hazel
Occupations: Card dealer, clerk, laboratory technician, vendor
Remarks: Reportedly a vegetarian, likes camping, jazz music, suffers from claustrophobia; hair may be worn shoulder length

THE ABOVE INDIVIDUALS ACCOMPANIED BY DONALD DAVID DE FREEZE, FBI WANTED FLYER 473, ALLEGEDLY ROBBED A SAN FRANCISCO BANK ON APRIL 15, 1974, USING AUTOMATIC WEAPONS. TWO INDIVIDUALS WERE KNOWN TO HAVE BEEN SERIOUSLY WOUNDED DURING SHOOTING AT THE BANK. ALL SHOULD BE CONSIDERED ARMED AND EXTREMELY DANGEROUS.

Federal warrants were issued on April 15, 1974, at San Francisco, California, charging the above individuals with bank robbery (Title 18, U. S. Code, Sections 2113a and 2113d).

IF YOU HAVE ANY INFORMATION CONCERNING THESE PERSONS, PLEASE NOTIFY ME OR CONTACT YOUR LOCAL FBI OFFICE. TELEPHONE NUMBERS AND ADDRESSES OF ALL FBI OFFICES LISTED ON BACK.

C. m. Kelley
DIRECTOR
FEDERAL BUREAU OF INVESTIGATION
UNITED STATES DEPARTMENT OF JUSTICE
WASHINGTON, D. C. 20535
TELEPHONE, NATIONAL 8-7117

Entered NCIC
Wanted Flyer 474
April 18, 1974

Really wanted was translated by television commentators into "the greatest gunfight in the history of the West."

S.L.A. poster, Ho Chi Minh Park, Berkeley, June 2, 1974.

A *memento mori* of the S.L.A. food program.

VIVA TANIA

I Have Chosen to Stay and FIGHT ··

The only way to support the SLA is to make revolution.

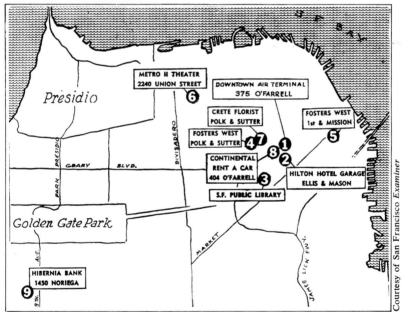

(Top left) On Patty Hearst's conversation and stick-up bravado: "It was bodacious," said Remiro. "Absolutely bodacious," said Little. "That's a prison word that means just too much!" *(Top right)* Flyer produced by the Weather Underground, June, 1974. *(Bottom)* Map showing the activities of S.L.A. in central San Francisco.

Weather Underground poster, June 2, 1974.

Those sad & joyous eyes that
  blazed at bank guards across
  rifle barrels, those lips
that sang equality for the children,
  prison walls in rubble, hungry
  being fed, earth & the people
renewed returned lovers to each
  other again:
              those same eyes are mouldy
  by now; the first bugs
              have tasted those charred
  & blistered lips.

YET EVEN NOW A VAST INVISIBLE
ARMY IS SPRINGING FORTH IN
10 THOUSAND PLACES AT ONCE, AS
GRASS AFTER RAIN, WOMEN MEN
OF ALL RACES, TO STRIKE AGAINST
THE CARRIERS OF THE PLAGUE!

  Camelia   Angela   Fahiza
William   Mizmoon   Cinque,
  warrior flesh in clotted blood &
  fractured bone, lie quiet now rotting in
  our mother's dark & fruitful womb & know
YOUR TRUTH BLASTS
    SUBMACHINEGUNNING ON

Another S.L.A. poster in Ho Chi Minh Park, June 2, 1974.

SLA
MEMORIAL

WE MUST QUIT THESE PATHS

IN LONELY OUTRAGE

OF QUIET DESPERATION

SUN ★ JUNE 2 ★ 12 noon

HO CHI MINH PARK

DERBY & HILLEGASS

by Friends of Angela Atwood

S.L.A. Memorial poster—"In lonely outrage . . ."

"I died in that fire on Fifty-fourth Street, but out of the ashes I was reborn. I know now what I have to do. . . ."

Joe Remiro in his prison garb.